D0331868

Cooking
a commonsense guide

MURDOCH
BOOKS

CONTENTS

Commonsense—an introduction 6
Kitchen management 8
Cookery terms 10
Basic kitchen equipment 12

Meat sense 14
Meat identification charts 18

Chicken sense 24
Chicken identification chart 28

Seafood sense 30
Seafood identification chart 36

Vegetable sense 38
Vegetable identification chart 40
Herb identification chart 42

Pasta and rice sense 44
Pasta and rice identification chart 46

Freezing chart 48

Measurements made easy 50

Breakfast and Brunch 52

Soups 66

Meat 88

Chicken 124

Cooking

a commonsense guide

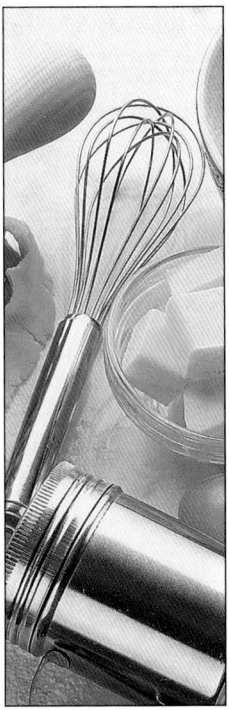

Seafood	140
Vegetarian	160
Pasta and Rice	174
Vegetables and Salads	190
Savoury Pastries	216
Bread and Buns	234
Cakes and Biscuits	244
Desserts	298
Sweet Treats	336
Jams and Pickles	344
Basic recipes	356
Index	372

COOKERY RATINGS

A simple and, generally, quick recipe. Perfect for beginners.	A dish that requires a little more care and time.	A special dish that requires a greater investment of time, care and patience.

COMMONSENSE

Cooking is not difficult. To be a great chef you need flair and imagination. But to produce delicious foolproof everyday meals all you need is a little commonsense.

Good cooking begins with sensible shopping, correct storage of ingredients, handling food safely and enthusiasm for the task at hand.

The first decision you will make is 'what to cook?'. To a certain extent this question should be answered by what is in season. Make friends with your greengrocer, butcher and fishmonger and don't be afraid to ask 'what's good today?' Ideally, shop for fresh fruit and vegetables regularly, if not daily. This prevents waste and ensures that you are using the freshest possible produce. Of course this is not always possible, so if you need to shop less frequently, try to plan your meals to make the best use of your fresh ingredients. Produce which is in season is better value and quality. Don't try to make asparagus hollandaise for eight dinner guests if there are no good-quality fresh asparagus available. Choose another recipe.

The golden commonsense rule of cooking is *always read the recipe before you start*. Don't rush in at step 1 and work your way through blind, only to discover in step 4 that you need a food processor which you don't have. Even more serious, don't start working through a recipe for a dinner party that starts in 2 hours, only to get to the end and discover your fabulous centrepiece needs to be chilled overnight.

Read through the recipe and get together all the ingredients and equipment required. Preheat the oven and prepare the cooking dish. Prepare as much as you can beforehand, so you are not caught out during cooking. If you are making a stew, or a slow-cooking dish, you can probably get away with leaving some ingredients to cook by themselves while you prepare others as you go along. However, don't try this if you are making a stir-fry! There is nothing more panic-inducing than having a sizzling wok, burning onions and a pile of ingredients that need chopping. So, always anticipate what you are going to have to do next.

If the recipe states to use a large bowl, do so, even if at first you're only mixing two ingredients. Later on you might need to add a large quantity of other ingredients.

We employ some basic commonsense rules in our recipes... If the recipe doesn't state to 'cover' the pan or dish, then it is to be cooked uncovered. We assume basic preparation of ingredients, such as washing and trimming, and peeling of vegetables such as potatoes and onions—the recipe will, however, state if these are to be left unpeeled. With well-known vegetables such as leeks, we assume that the reader knows to use the white part of the leek only. But with less familiar ingredients such as lemon grass, we will state 'white part only' where necessary.

KITCHEN MANAGEMENT

A good cook keeps a good kitchen. This means efficient shopping, and knowing what you have (and should have) in your storecupboard and fridge. You may be shopping every few days for fresh produce, but there are certain ingredients that should have a permanent home in your kitchen.

SHOPPING

Like most other aspects of preparing food, shopping is not difficult—in fact, many of us do it fairly successfully every day. However, there is a such a thing as efficient shopping, and much of it relies on commonsense.

Check what needs topping up in your storecupboard (see opposite) and put those into your trolley first. Avoid cans that have dents in them. Meats, dairy products and other refrigerated items should be kept well chilled, so choose them last, just before you head to the checkout. A handy tip is to choose items which are stored towards the back of the refrigerator cabinet or underneath the top layer (these are sometimes close to lights and not cold enough). Don't choose refrigerator items which have swollen packaging. Vacuum packaging should not be loose. Read use-by dates (this applies to everything, not just refrigerated goods) and buy products as far from the date as possible (you might find these have been stacked at the back of the cabinet).

Frozen food should be obviously frozen, with no large ice crystals and without the food being frozen into clumps (this shows that the food has partially thawed and been refrozen). In hot weather, carry an insulated container in the car to transport shopping home.

YOUR STORECUPBOARD

Although it is best to shop regularly for meat, seafood and seasonal vegetables, there are certain products that you will want to keep permanently in your storecupboard, to provide the backbone of your daily cooking. As a general rule, you should try to have in your pantry:

Baking powder
Beans, canned and dried
Breadcrumbs, dry
Capers
Cocoa powder
Coconut milk
Cornflour
Couscous
Dried fruits, such as raisins, currants, apricots
Flour (plain and self-raising)

Gelatine
Honey
Mustards
Noodles
Nuts
Oils (olive; sesame; vegetable)
Olives
Pasta
Polenta
Rice, long-grain, short-grain and arborio
Soy sauce
Stocks
Sugars
Tabasco
Tomatoes, canned
Tomato paste
Vinegars, white wine, red wine, brown and balsamic
Worcestershire sauce
Yeast

These are best stored in a cool, dark dry pantry. Most will keep for at least 3, if not 6, months.

It is best to buy whole spices and grind them yourself, as needed—they stay fresher than the jars. Make sure bottles of oil are kept out of direct light, as they can become rancid; however, if you keep them in the fridge the oil will thicken and appear cloudy—it will return to normal once it has reached room temperature again. Most bottles of sauces and condiments should be refrigerated once opened: check the label.

Keep potatoes and onions in a cool, dark place—though not without adequate ventilation. Tomatoes, like most fruit, are best kept at room temperature, unless the weather is very hot or they are very ripe.

YOUR FRIDGE

Your fridge is somewhere where important hygiene rules come into play. When you get home with your shopping, unwrap meat or chicken and place on a plate large enough to prevent drips falling on to other food. Cover loosely with foil or plastic wrap.

Bacteria in food is killed by cooking, but take care not to put cooked food back into the fridge touching raw food, which could contaminate it. For example, never let raw meat drip onto cooked dishes. The same goes for when you are preparing food: if you chop raw meat, don't then use the same, unwashed chopping board and knife to prepare salad, or slice the cooked meat.

Store vegetables unwashed (unless they are dried thoroughly, the moisture contributes to deterioration) in the crisper compartment of the fridge.

Many recipes will instruct you to cook something, then 'cool and refrigerate'. When you are doing this, cool the food as quickly as possible before refrigerating. Transfer it from the cooking pan to a wide bowl and stir frequently to release the heat. It is not necessary for the food to be completely cold before it is refrigerated, just cooled. Don't put hot food in the fridge or freezer or it will raise the temperature inside, putting other foods at risk of deterioration.

The remaining contents of half-used cans should be transferred to a bowl or plastic container and refrigerated. Use within 2–3 days or discard.

Thaw frozen food in the fridge, not at room temperature and never in a sink full of water. If you haven't removed food from the freezer in enough time, thaw in the microwave, or have something else.

Never refreeze thawed food. (Of course, you can thaw something, cook it and then freeze again—for instance frozen chicken that you might casserole and then freeze.)

Clean out your fridge, freezer and storecupboard regularly and remember—if you ever have any doubts about the freshness of a product, throw it out.

COOKERY TERMS

This is a commonsense cookbook, so you will find every step fully explained in the recipe. But if there are any terms which aren't familiar you should find them here.

AL DENTE Italian phrase meaning 'to the tooth'. Refers to pasta and sometimes vegetables. Means slightly underdone, so still with some 'bite'.

BAIN-MARIE Also called a 'water bath'. Usually a baking dish half-filled with water so delicate food is protected from direct heat. Often used for custards.

BAKE BLIND To bake an empty pastry case before the filling is added. Ensures the pastry is cooked through and not soggy. Usually lined with baking paper and baking beads or rice or beans so it keeps its shape.

BASTE To spoon or brush cooking juices or other fat over food during cooking.

BOIL To cook liquid, or food in liquid, at 100°C. Large bubbles will break on the surface.

BOUQUET GARNI A small bunch of herbs used to flavour stocks, soups and stews. Removed before serving.

BROWN To fry food (usually meat) quickly so the outside is cooked and has changed colour.

CREAM To beat butter or butter and sugar together until light and creamy.

CUBE To chop food into even cubes. Usually bite-sized and for use in soups or stews so the size is not overly important.

DICE To chop food into very small even cubes.

DRAIN To remove liquid from food (usually with a colander or sieve). The food is kept and the liquid discarded unless specified.

EN CROUTE Cooked entirely encased in pastry. Usually refers to meat.

ESCALOPE Very thin slice of meat, such as veal or chicken.

FILLET To cut meat from the bones.

FLAMBE To pour liqueur over food (usually in the pan, over heat) and set fire to it.

FOLD To mix one ingredient into another very gently (usually flour or egg whites) with a metal spoon or plastic spatula. The idea is to combine the mixture without losing the air. To fold properly, cut through the centre of the mixture, then run the edge of the spoon or spatula around the outer edge of the bowl, turning the bowl as you go.

GLAZE A substance (often warmed jam or beaten egg) brushed over food to give it shine and colour.

GREASE To lightly coat a tin or dish with oil or melted butter to prevent food sticking.

INFUSE To flavour a liquid by heating it with aromatic ingredients (often spices) and leaving to let the flavour develop.

JULIENNE To cut into uniform thin matchsticks for quick cooking. Often used for stir-fries or in French cuisine.

KNEAD To stretch and fold dough to make it firm and smooth. This stretches the gluten in the flour and gives elasticity. Used for bread making but not for pastry making (over-handling will make pastry tough).

MARINATE To tenderize and flavour food (usually meat) by leaving it in an acidulated seasoned liquid (a marinade).

PARBOIL To partially cook in boiling water before some other form of cooking. Most commonly used for roast potatoes which are parboiled before being added to the roasting meat.

PINCH A small amount of something—as much as can be held between your thumb and forefinger.

POACH To cook food immersed in a gently simmering liquid.

PUNCH DOWN THE DOUGH A term used in bread making. A yeast dough which is left to rise is then punched with one firm blow of the fist, to remove the air from it.

PUREE Food blended or processed to a pulp.

REDUCE To boil or simmer liquid in an uncovered pan so that the liquid evaporates and the mixture becomes thicker and more concentrated in flavour. Most soups and stews are reduced—this should usually be done at a simmer so the flavour of the dish is not impaired by long hard boiling.

ROUX The basic mixture of many sauces—fat (usually melted butter) and flour. Used to thicken. Liquid is added to make a sauce.

RUB IN To mix together flour and butter with your fingertips, usually for pastry. It will resemble fine breadcrumbs.

SCORE To ensure even cooking. Make incisions with a knife (usually into fish or meat) that do not cut all the way through.

SIFT To shake dry ingredients (usually flour) through a sieve to aerate and remove lumps.

SIMMER To cook liquid, or food in liquid, over low heat, below boiling point. The surface of the liquid will be moving with a few small bubbles.

SKIM To remove fat or scum that comes to the surface of a liquid.

SOFT PEAKS A term used when egg whites are whipped. The peak will fold over on itself when the beater is lifted.

STIFF PEAKS A term used when egg whites are whipped. The peak will hold its shape when the beater is lifted.

STIR-FRY To quickly fry (usually in a wok) over high heat while stirring.

STRAIN To remove solids from a liquid by pouring through a sieve. The solids are discarded, unless specified.

WHISK To beat rapidly with a wire whisk, to incorporate air and add volume.

ZEST The coloured skin of citrus fruits. Avoid the bitter white pith below.

BASIC KITCHEN EQUIPMENT

A good cook needs good tools. Buy the best you can afford and look after them—they'll last you for years.

KNIVES Quality knives are expensive but it is worth saving up for stainless steel or carbon steel knives. To keep your knives sharp, use a steel and stone and make sure you cut on a chopping board.

WHISK A wire whisk is essential for beating egg whites—nothing else can incorporate as much air.

LARGE METAL SPOON Ideal for folding mixtures together without losing volume, and skimming froth from stocks.

WOODEN SPOON Perfect for long stirring jobs, since their handles don't get hot. Best for use with non-stick pans.

SPATULA Flexible rubber spatulas are ideal for folding in, and for getting every bit of cake mix out of the bowl.

TONGS Use tongs to turn frying food or pick vegetables out of boiling water.

PEELER Peels vegetable skins and the tip removes 'eyes'. Shaves Parmesan.

LADLE For safely spooning hot soups and stews from a pan.

ROLLING PIN Rolls pastry and pizza dough; beats veal, chicken or steak to flatten fillets; and crushes biscuits.

SAUCEPANS Stainless steel is the best material, even better if it has a heavy copper base. Most recipes state a 'heavy-based pan' as this distributes heat more evenly. A very large saucepan or stock pot is needed to cook pasta and stock.

FRYING PAN A non-stick deep frying pan will reduce the amount of oil needed and can be used for stir-frying if you don't have a wok. An ovenproof pan with a metal handle can go straight from stove top to oven or grill for browning. Otherwise, cover the handle with foil.

BAKING DISH You'll need a baking dish for roasting meat and vegetables. Buy one with a rack so the fat can drip down into the pan. Make sure it's heavy enough to put on top of the stove without warping. When stirring gravy, use a plastic or a wooden spoon to prevent scratching.

MIXING BOWLS The best all-purpose mixing bowls also double as pudding basins. Use them to make cakes, beat cream, and a hundred other kitchen tasks. As long as they have no metal trim, china or ceramic mixing bowls are ideal for cooking or heating food in a microwave.

CASSEROLE DISH Make sure your casserole dish has a tight-fitting lid and is a generous size. You can use ceramic dishes for oven only, but a good flameproof dish, as shown, can go straight from oven to stove top if you need to reduce a sauce over heat. Pyrex casserole dishes are also available.

COLANDER Ideal for draining pasta, vegtables or anything else cooked in liquid (except small items, such as rice, which may need a strainer). Also ideal for washing salad leaves or placing on top of a saucepan to steam vegetables.

MEAT SENSE

From a great Sunday roast to a quick steak sandwich, meat is versatile and easy to prepare. While not such a staple of our daily menu these days, meat still plays an important role in providing essential proteins and iron in the diet.

BUYING AND STORING

Correct handling and preparation of meat is crucial, both for safety reasons and for good eating. When buying, look for meat that has a clear, fresh appearance: meat with a greyish tinge has been poorly handled and stored and must be avoided. An unpleasant odour and slimy surface are other indicators that the product is unacceptable. Offal such as kidneys and liver that have a strong smell of ammonia should be rejected.

Meat should be kept refrigerated, so buy it last on your shopping trip and bring it straight home. Unwrap the meat and put it on a plate, then loosely wrap it with foil or greaseproof paper and place in the refrigerator. Be sure to use within a couple of days.

Meat also freezes very successfully if you need to store it for longer. Remove the original wrapping and seal the meat in a freezer bag, first expelling as much air as possible. Double bag the meat if there is any danger of the bag tearing, as meat exposed to air will suffer from freezer burn. Clearly label the bag, including the date. Most cuts of meat can be frozen for up to 6 months.

There is a huge variety of meat available. The main types are beef, veal, lamb and pork. Within these types there are myriad cuts, and each cut has its most suitable cooking method. See page 18 for our chart of cuts and their suggested cooking methods. Buy the appropriate cut for the cooking process you will be using. Each cut has distinctive qualities that can be used to advantage in a specific instance. Don't buy a cut that is more expensive than you need—a cheaper one may well give a better result in your particular recipe.

Different types of meat and cooking methods require different preparation. A general first step in meat preparation is to remove the meat from the refrigerator a little while before cooking, to allow it to cool to room temperature. This ensures the meat will cook evenly and quickly, which is particularly important when using a quick cooking method such as pan-frying a steak.

Sometimes the recipe will instruct you to cut away any visible fat and sinew, particularly when stewing. However, sometimes some fat present on the meat can be desirable, for instance when you are cooking a roast: the fat will melt and baste the meat as it cooks, contributing to the tenderness and flavour.

PAN-FRYS, GRILLS AND BARBECUES

Steaks and chops are the most suitable cuts for these cooking methods. Preparation is minimal, just trim away fat as required and perhaps marinate, depending on the recipe.

Marinating before cooking will tenderize the meat as well as add flavour. Always marinate meat in a glass or ceramic dish, covered and refrigerated until needed—a metallic dish will react with any acid in the marinade and give a metallic flavour.

Some recipes may say to flatten steaks before cooking, which makes the meat more tender. To do this, place the meat between two layers of plastic wrap and pound evenly with a meat mallet or rolling pin. Thin steaks, such as veal escalopes, should be nicked along the edges to prevent them curling during cooking.

Cooking times will depend on the thickness of the meat and your taste.

Pan-frying: To fry steak (not thin escalopes), heat a little oil or butter in a heavy-based frying pan over high heat, add the meat and cook for 2–3 minutes on each side. If you like your meat rare, you would remove it from the pan now. Otherwise, reduce the heat to medium and continue cooking for up to 10 minutes each side for well-done meat.

Test for doneness by pressing the centre of the meat with blunt tongs, rather than piercing (this will let the juices escape).

Turn meat once only during cooking and leave the pan uncovered. Too low a heat, turning too often, or covering the pan will make the meat tough.

Always drain marinated meat thoroughly before pan-frying or it will create steam and not fry efficiently.

Grilling: Drain marinated meat thoroughly before grilling to reduce steam and ensure a tender result. If your grill pan is lined with foil, puncture a few holes to allow fat to drain away. Ideally, put meat on a cold, lightly-oiled grill and cook under high heat to seal, turning once. Then lower the grill tray and continue cooking if you prefer your meat more well done.

Barbecuing: Give the barbecue plenty of time to heat up so the meat is cooking over glowing coals, not over flames.

When you are barbecuing kebabs, oiled metal skewers are ideal because it is easier to remove the cooked meat from them. If threading meat onto bamboo skewers, first soak the skewers in water for 30 minutes to prevent the ends burning during cooking. Marinades add flavour and tenderness to barbecued meat.

RARE OR WELL-DONE?

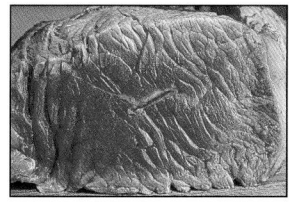

Rare: Soft to touch, red centre with a thin cooked edge.

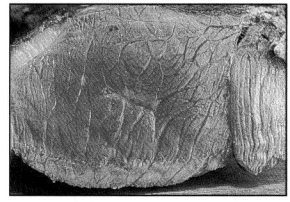

Medium rare: Springy to touch, moist, pale-red centre.

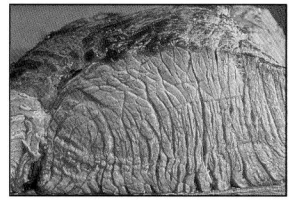

Medium: Firm to touch, pink centre and brown edge.

Well done: Very firm to touch, brown and evenly cooked.

STEWS AND SOUPS

Less expensive cuts of meat come into their own when you are stewing, as the long slow cooking time allows the connective tissue in the meat to break down and become tender. Cooking the same type of meat quickly by pan-frying or grilling would render it tough and inedible, but, by the same token, if you casserole best fillet steak it will dry out and become tough.

Meat for stewing is usually cut into cubes (though not always—for Irish stew the lamb neck chops are left whole and on the bone). Cut the meat into even pieces, usually bite-sized or as instructed in the recipe, so that they all cook at the same rate.

Next, the recipe may say to toss the meat in seasoned flour. This helps to thicken the pan juices, creating a sauce in the finished dish. The cleanest and easiest way to do this is to put plain flour in a plastic bag, season it well with salt and pepper and then add the meat. Hold the bag tightly closed and gently toss the meat. Remove the meat from the bag, shaking off the excess flour.

Put the meat and flour in a bag and toss well.

The meat will usually now be browned in batches. Make sure that you follow the instruction 'in batches', even though it will take a little longer. If you put all the meat in the pan at once, it will be overcrowed, the heat will be reduced and the meat will stew in its own juices rather than brown.

Brown the meat in small batches so it doesn't stew in its own juices.

The recipe will now probably instruct you to add the other ingredients, usually including stock or other liquid, and then leave the pan either on the stove top or in the oven to cook. If you are cooking on the stove top you will be instructed to 'simmer'. Long-cooking dishes such as stews and soups are always cooked at a lazy simmer—long boiling of the ingredients would impair their flavour. If the recipe instructs you to cover the pan, don't forget to do so. If you don't cover the pan, the liquid will evaporate into steam as it cooks and your dish will become much thicker and 'reduced'. There are times when you will want to deliberately reduce a stew, casserole or soup, by removing the lid at the end of cooking time, increasing the heat slightly and letting some of the liquid boil off so the sauce becomes thicker and the flavours stronger.

Stews and soups are often best cooked a day in advance and left in the fridge overnight to let the flavours develop, before being gently reheated to serve. An added bonus is that any excess fat will come to the surface and solidify, so that you can just spoon it off the top.

Most stews and soups also freeze successfully (although there are some ingredients, such as cream, which are best added when you are reheating). Spoon into a plastic bag, seal and label. Most will keep for 6 months.

Spoon the stew or soup into a bag to freeze.

MINCE

Beef, lamb, chicken, pork and veal (the last two usually as a combination) are all available minced. Mince, (known as ground meat in the USA), is suitable for all manner of fillings, or to be shaped into meatloaves, burgers, meatballs or kebabs.
Beef mince now comes in different grades such as lean, extra lean, premium or hamburger—choose the fat content and price that suits you.
If you are very concerned

Chop lean meat into mince with a sharp knife.

about fat on your meat, the best way to guarantee virtually fat-free mince is to buy lean meat and then mince it yourself at home, either with a sharp knife or in a food processor. Don't overwork the meat or it will end up as mush.

If you use a processor, don't overwork the mince.

ROASTS

Roasted meat, such as a leg of lamb or rolled roast, is usually a large piece, so to help keep the shape neat, you may want to tie it with kitchen string before cooking.

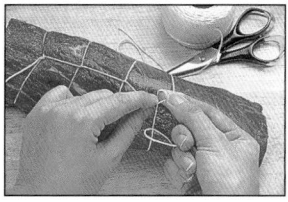

Tie meat with string so it keeps a neat shape.

Depending on the recipe, the meat is sometimes browned on top of the stove first, then transferred to the oven. Obviously, you will need a large pan to do this.

Sometimes meat is browned before roasting in the oven.

Cooking times will vary considerably depending on the cut and size of the meat, whether or not it is boned or stuffed, and your own personal taste. The most important thing is to weigh your meat properly before cooking. The following is a rough guide to cooking times in a moderate 180°C (350°F/Gas 4) oven. For rare meat: 15–20 minutes per 500 g (1 lb); for medium: 20–25 minutes per 500 g (1 lb); for well done: 25–30 minutes per 500 g (1 lb). Large joints of pork might need an extra 30 minutes if very thick. The pinch test is a simple way to test your meat. When you think it is ready, pinch the meat in a lean section. If it springs back easily, it's rare; it it's less resilient, it's medium; and if it's firm, the meat is well done.
When the meat is cooked, set it on a board or large plate and leave it to rest for about 10 minutes before carving. This lets the juices be reabsorbed and ensures moist, tender meat. If you need to cover it, do so very loosely with foil so the steam can escape.
Carve the meat evenly across the grain using a knife with a straight, rather than serrrated, edge. Use the full length of the blade, rather than a sawing motion.

Carve roast meat across the grain to minimize chewiness.

BEEF CUTS

There are many different cuts of beef and often their names can vary from country to country. For quick pan-frying, choose the best lean fillets you can afford. For casseroles, the more economical cuts will produce a tender flavoursome meal.

1. Whole Rump
Oven roast.

2. Fillet
Oven roast or barbecue.

3. Fillet Steak
Pan-fry, stir-fry, grill or barbecue.

4. Silverside Steak
Oven roast, pot roast or casserole.

5. Rump Steak
Pan-fry, stir-fry, grill or barbecue.

6. Diced Chuck Steak (stewing steak)
Pot roast or casserole.

7. Shin (gravy beef)
Casserole.

8. Silverside Roast
Oven roast, pot roast or casserole.

9. Chuck
Pot roast or casserole

10. Oyster Blade
Pan-fry, grill or barbecue.

11. Shin (with bone)
Casserole.

12. Topside Steak
Pan-fry or stir-fry.

13. Topside
Oven roast or pot roast.

14. Blade (with bone)
Casserole or barbecue.

15. Blade Steak
Pan-fry, stir-fry, casserole or barbecue.

16. Whole Bolar Blade
Oven roast or pot roast.

17. T-bone
Pan-fry, grill or barbecue.

18. Sirloin Steak (porterhouse, with bone)
Pan-fry, stir-fry, grill or barbecue.

19. Sirloin Steak (new york cut, without bone)
Pan-fry, stir-fry, grill or barbecue.

20. Rib Eye Steak (scotch fillet)
Pan-fry, stir-fry, grill or barbecue.

21. Rolled Roast (of ribs)
Oven roast.

22. Round Steak
Pan-fry or stir-fry.

23. Skirt
Oven roast, pot roast or casserole.

24. Rib-eye Fillet (delmonico)
Oven roast or barbecue.

25. Rib Steak
Pan-fry, grill or barbecue.

26. Standing Rib Roast
Oven roast.

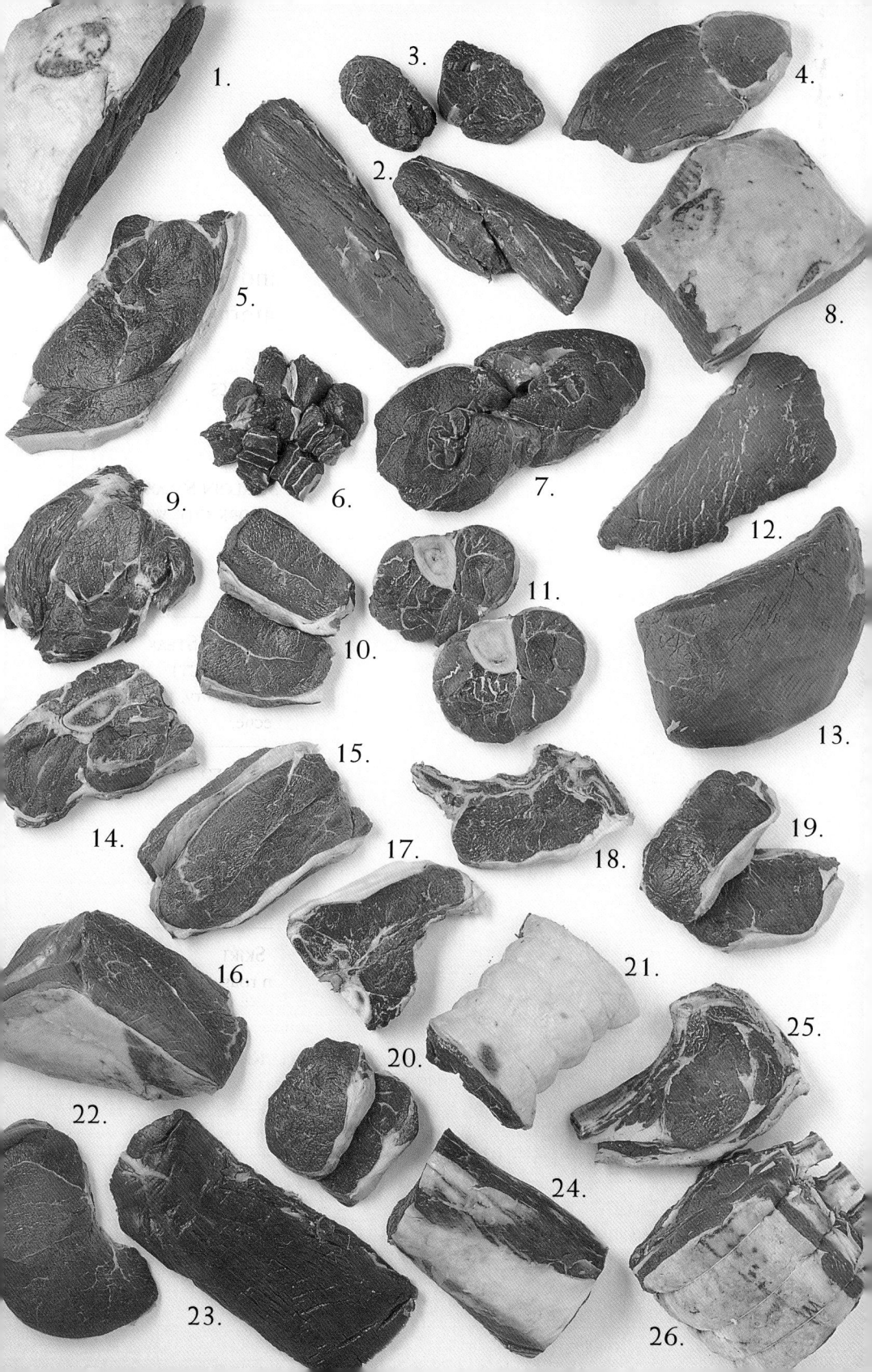
1.
2.
3.
4.
5.
6.
7.
8.
9.
10.
11.
12.
13.
14.
15.
16.
17.
18.
19.
20.
21.
22.
23.
24.
25.
26.

VEAL AND LAMB CUTS

Here are the most popular cuts of veal and lamb and their recommended cooking methods.

1. Veal Schnitzel
Pan-fry.

2. Veal Osso Buco (knuckle slices)
Casserole.

3. Veal Leg Steak
Grill or barbecue.

4. Veal Knutt
Oven roast.

5. Veal Rump Roast
Oven roast.

6. Veal Rump Steak
Pan-fry, stir-fry, grill or barbecue.

7. Veal Shank
Pot roast or casserole.

8. Veal Neck (boned and rolled)
Oven roast or pot roast.

9. Rack of Veal
Oven roast or pot roast.

10. Veal Loin Cutlet
Pan-fry, grill or barbecue.

11. Veal Loin Roast (boned and rolled)
Pot roast.

12. Veal Shoulder
Oven roast, pot roast or casserole.

13. Veal Loin Chops
Pan-fry, grill or barbecue.

14. Veal Forequarter Chops
Pan-fry, grill or barbecue.

15. Mid-Loin Lamb Chops
Pan-fry, grill or barbecue.

16. Rolled Lamb Shoulder
Oven roast or pot roast.

17. Lamb Forequarter Chops
Pan-fry, grill, barbecue or casserole.

18. Lamb Shanks
Oven roast, pot roast or casserole.

19. Lamb Leg Chops
Grill or barbecue.

20. Eye of Lamb Loin
Pan-fry, stir-fry, grill, barbecue or oven roast.

21. Lamb Loin (boned and rolled)
Oven roast or pot roast.

22. Lamb Neck Chops
Pan-fry, grill, barbecue or casserole.

23. Lamb Cutlets
Pan-fry, grill or barbecue.

24. Lamb Fillet
Pan-fry, stir-fry, grill or barbecue.

25. Lamb Chump Chops
Pan-fry, grill, barbecue or pot roast.

26. Rack of Lamb
Oven roast.

27. Leg of Lamb
Oven roast or pot roast. Available with bone in or removed for easy carving.

1.
2.
3.
4.
5.
6.
7.
8.
9.
10.
11.
12.
13.
14.
15.
16.
17.
18.
19.
20.
21.
22.
23.
24.
25.
26.
27.

PORK CUTS

Pork really is one of our most adaptable and easy-to-use meats, from a Sunday roast with apple sauce and crackling, to chops, steaks and even a crispy bacon sandwich. Today's cuts of pork are leaner than ever before—don't ever overcook pork or it will lose its delicious juicy texture. Here are the most popular cuts and cooking methods.

1. Rolled Loin
Oven roast.

2. Foreloin Neck
Oven roast.

3. Foreloin Steak
Pan-fry, grill or barbecue.

4. Spare Ribs
Grill, barbecue or oven roast.

5. Loin Steaks
Pan-fry, grill or barbecue.

6. Forequarter Chops
Pan-fry, grill, barbecue or oven roast.

7. Rolled Shoulder (hand of pork)
Oven roast.

8. American-style Ribs
Grill, barbecue or oven roast

9. Loin Medallion Steak
Pan-fry, grill, barbecue or oven roast.

10. Loin Cutlet
Pan-fry, grill or barbecue.

11. Rack of Pork
Oven roast.

12. Pork Rump
Barbecue or oven roast

13. Mid-Loin Butterfly Steak
Pan-fry, grill or barbecue.

14. Loin Chop (trimmed)
Pan-fry, grill or barbecue.

15. Loin Chop
Pan-fry, grill or barbecue.

16. Fillet
Pan-fry, grill or oven roast.

17. Rump Steak
Pan-fry, grill or barbecue.

18. Leg Schnitzels
Pan-fry, grill or oven roast.

19. Leg Strips (pork strips)
Pan-fry or stir-fry.

20. Loin Roast
Oven roast.

21. Leg Steak
Pan-fry, grill or barbecue.

22. Silverside
Barbecue or oven roast.

23. Topside
Barbecue or oven roast.

24. Leg
Oven roast.

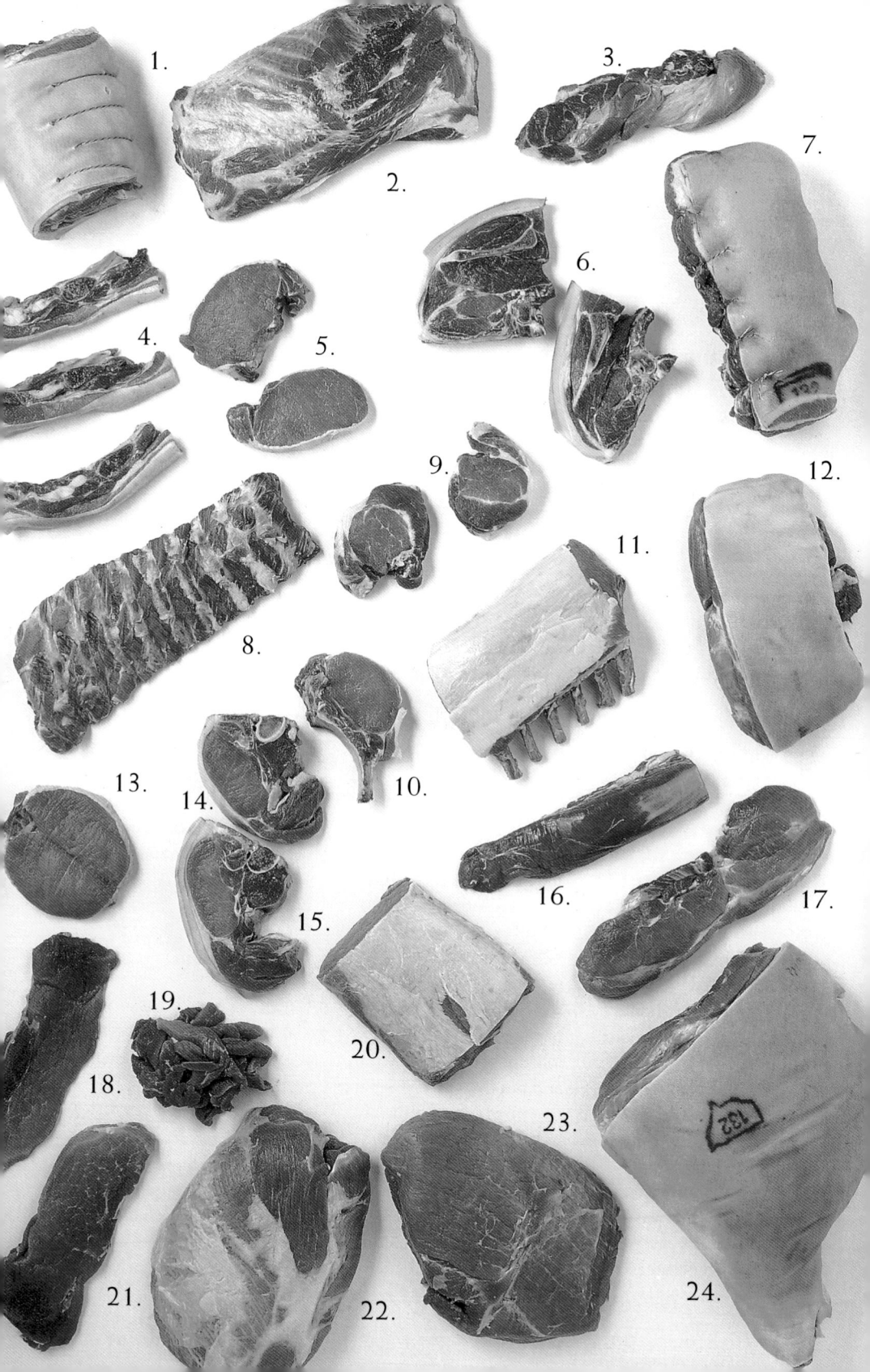
1.
2.
3.
4.
5.
6.
7.
8.
9.
10.
11.
12.
13.
14.
15.
16.
17.
18.
19.
20.
21.
22.
23.
24.

CHICKEN SENSE

Chicken is a versatile and affordable food that is eaten all over the world. It is a complete protein, with minerals such as potassium and phosphorous, as well as some B vitamins and, without its skin, it is relatively low in fat.

BUYING CHICKEN

Free-range and corn-fed chickens are now widely available and have a better flavour and texture than intensively farmed chickens. Free-range chickens can be identified by a label stating that they have been reared humanely. Corn-fed chickens have a yellowy skin and flesh, but are not necessarily free-range. You will, of course, pay more for a free-range bird, but it will have better flavour. Whole chickens are sold by a number that relates to their weight, for example, a no.15 chicken will weigh 1.5 kg (3 lb) and should feed 4 people. Larger birds will feed 4–6.

Breasts can be bought on the bone or as 'fillets' (bone removed)—both are available as single or double, joined breasts. In our recipes, when we ask for '1 chicken breast' we mean one single breast. Breasts will have a small tenderloin underneath. Thighs have darker, more succulent meat than breasts, work well in curries and stews and for kebabs and satays. Thigh cutlets have both skin and a thigh bone, thigh fillets have no skin or bone, and thighs have some backbone and an 'oyster'.

STORING

Make chicken the last item to be bought and have it out of the fridge for the shortest possible time. Frozen chicken must be solid and tightly wrapped. Fresh chicken should be taken out of its packaging, covered loosely with plastic wrap and put on a plate to catch any drips. Keep it in the fridge, and not where it can drip onto other food. Cook it within 2 days. Chicken can be frozen for up to 3 months, sealed in a freezer bag with the air expelled (make sure you write the date on a label). Defrost chicken carefully as bacteria, such as salmonella, can be activated if it gets too warm. Defrost in the fridge, not at room temperature. Chicken pieces can be defrosted in the microwave (arrange the thickest portions to the outside of the plate). Don't defrost whole birds in the microwave—they defrost unevenly and some parts may start to cook. Use thawed chicken within 12 hours and never refreeze. Cooked chicken can be kept in the fridge for up to 3 days.

Put the thickest part of the chicken to the outside.

JOINTING A CHICKEN

Cutting a whole chicken into pieces is called 'jointing'. The flavour of a dish will often be better if, rather than buying pieces, you cut up a whole bird. Large birds can be cut into four, six, eight or ten pieces. Use a pair of

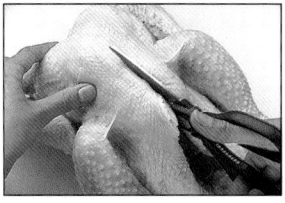

Cut down the length of the backbone on either side.

kitchen scissors to cut through the length of the breastbone, then turn the chicken over and cut down either side of the backbone to remove it in one piece. Cut the bird into four pieces following the natural contours. For

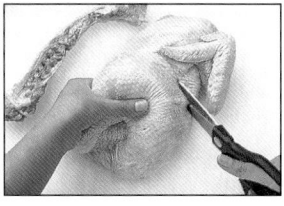

Cut the chicken into pieces following the natural contours.

eight pieces, cut each breast in half, so one piece has the wing attached—you can remove the wings by bending them outwards and snipping around the joint if you want. Cut through the leg joint to separate the drumstick from the thigh (leg pieces with the drumstick still attached to the thigh are called 'marylands').

A chicken can be cut into four, six, eight or 10 pieces.

BONING A CHICKEN

For special occasions, sometimes a chicken will be boned and then stuffed and rolled, and then usually served cold. To bone a chicken, use a small sharp knife to cut through the skin on the centre back. Separate the flesh from the bone down one side to the breast, being careful not to pierce the skin. Follow closely along the bones with the knife, gradually easing meat from the thigh, drumstick and wing. Cut through the thigh bone and cut off the wing tip. Repeat on the other side, then lift the rib cage away, leaving the flesh in one piece. Scrape all the meat from the drumsticks and wings. Turn the wing and drumstick flesh inside the chicken and lay the bird out flat, skin-side-down.

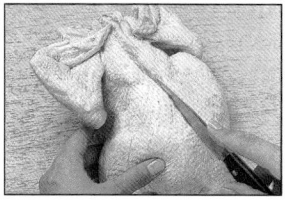

Cut through the skin on the centre back.

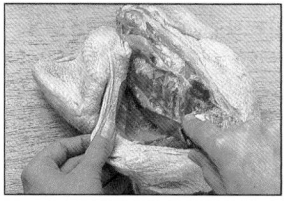

Separate the flesh from the bone down one side.

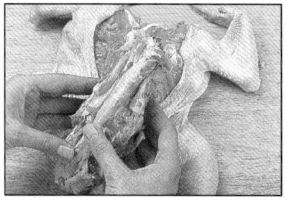

Repeat on the other side and lift away the rib cage.

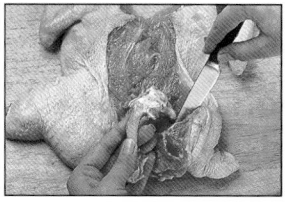

Scrape all the meat from the drumsticks and wings.

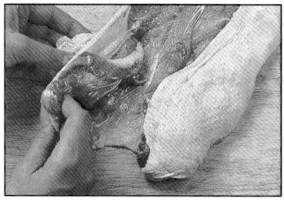

Turn the drumstick and wing flesh inside the chicken.

GRILLING AND PAN-FRYING

Chicken breasts are the whitest and leanest portions of meat on the chicken. While thighs and drumsticks, with their darker, more succulent meat, are more suitable for stews and curries, breasts can be grilled, fried, poached and roasted. Be careful not to overcook, however, as they dry out. To grill chicken, preheat the grill and put the chicken pieces, skin-side-down, on a cold, oiled grill pan. Cook them about 10 cm (4 inches) from the heat for 15–20 minutes, then turn and cook until the juices run clear when tested with a skewer. Brush with marinade during cooking to prevent drying out. If you aren't using a marinade, brush with butter or oil.

Pan-frying is the best cooking method for small tender pieces such as breast fillets. Heat oil or butter in a heavy-based pan over high heat, pat the chicken dry with paper towels and cook for 2–3 minutes on each side to brown and seal in the juices, turning with tongs. Reduce the heat and cook until the juices run clear. Never overcrowd the pan. Always fry the chicken in a single layer and if you don't have a pan big enough, use two small pans or cook the chicken in batches.

Cook in one layer without overcrowding the pan.

POACHING

Poaching is an easy and healthy way to cook chicken. The chicken is gently simmered in water, stock or wine, sometimes with vegetables and herbs added for flavour. The cooking liquid must never boil or the flavour will be impaired. This method is suitable for chicken breasts, but also for cooking whole large birds. After cooking, the liquid can be strained and used to make a sauce to serve with the chicken, or it can be saved for stock. Because of the low fat content, poaching is ideal for dieters—especially if the skin is removed first.

Simmer the chicken gently, without boiling the liquid.

STEWS AND CASSEROLES

The long slow cooking process is best for tougher cuts of meat, and it will make even a 'tough old bird' meltingly tender. The chicken should be gently simmered, never boiled, in the cooking liquid. Boiling will only make the flesh tough. Brown pieces or whole birds in a large pan in butter or oil, then transfer to a casserole with vegetables and cooking liquids such as stock and wine. As with other long-cooked dishes, chicken stews benefit from being left in the fridge overnight for the flavours to develop and reheated gently to serve. This also means you can scoop off any fat which solidifies on the surface.

ROASTS

To prepare a chicken for roasting, first make sure that there is nothing inside the cavity (the giblets and neck are sometimes stored in there in a plastic bag, which could lead to disaster).

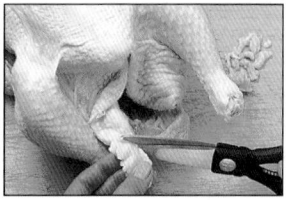

Trim off any excess fat with a pair of kitchen scissors.

Trim off any excess fat with a pair of kitchen scissors and then rinse and dry the skin and the cavity with a paper towel.
Stuffing a whole chicken before roasting adds flavour and plumps up the bird. Do not stuff a bird more than 3 hours before cooking. If you are using warm stuffing, cook the bird immediately. A stuffed bird will take a little longer to cook.
Once you have stuffed the chicken you can truss it so it keeps its shape during cooking. You can simply tuck the wings behind the body and tie the legs together with some kitchen string or you can truss the bird thoroughly. Tie the legs together, wrapping the string under the parson's nose first. After the legs, take the string towards the neck of the bird, passing it down between the legs and the body. Turn the bird over and cross the string over in the centre, underneath the wings. Wrap the string around the wings to keep them flat. Tie the string into a knot or bow to secure the chicken wings in place. Trim off the ends of the string and the chicken is ready.
Cook at moderately hot 200°C (400°F/Gas 6) for 40–45 minutes per kilo. Test by inserting a skewer into the thickest part of the thigh—if the juices run clear, it is cooked. If the juices are pink, put the bird back in the oven for 10 minutes before retesting. Chicken must always be thoroughly cooked—pink meat is unappealing and unsafe.

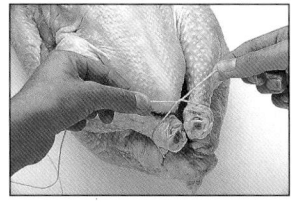

Tie the drumsticks together, closing the body cavity.

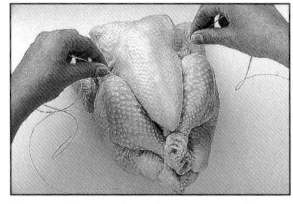

Pass the string between the legs and body of the bird.

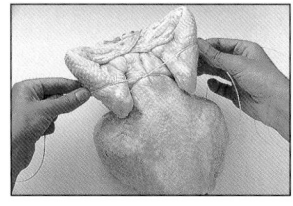

Turn over and cross the string over in the centre.

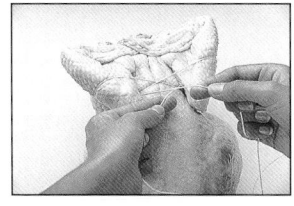

Tie into a knot or bow to secure the wings in place.

CARVING

Leave the roast chicken to 'rest', loosely covered with foil for 10 minutes before carving to allow the juices to settle. Some people advise leaving the chicken upside-down while it is resting, so the juices run into the breast.

Use a two-pronged fork to hold the chicken.

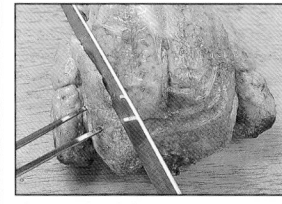

Cut around the leg, separating the bone at the joint.

Cut the leg into thigh and drumstick.

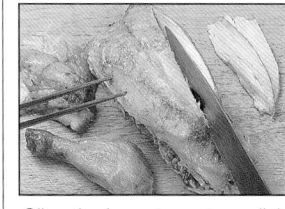

Slice the breast meat parallel to the rib cage.

CHICKEN CUTS

There are many different cuts of chicken available and which one you use will depend on how you are intending to cook it. You might prefer lean chicken breast fillets (which have had the bone removed) when quickly pan-frying or stir-frying, but when you are casseroling, you would probably prefer to use a cut of chicken which still contains the bone and will cook more slowly and add more flavour to the dish. Without its skin, chicken is now well-known as a healthy 'white meat' alternative to beef and lamb. Free-range chicken has more flavour than intensively reared.

1. Whole Chicken
Oven roast, pot roast or barbecue.

2. Boned Whole Chicken
Ask your butcher to bone the chicken for you. Oven roast, pot roast, barbecue

3. Breast on the Bone
Oven roast, pot roast or casserole.

4. Drumsticks
Pan-fry, grill, oven roast, pot roast, casserole or barbecue.

5. Chicken Marylands (leg and thigh pieces)
Oven roast, casserole or barbecue.

6. Double (Joint) Breast Fillet (two skinless fillets)
Pan-fry, stir-fry, grill or barbecue.

7. Chicken Thighs (with bone)
Oven roast, grill, casserole or barbecue.

8. Chicken Thigh Fillets (without bone)
Pan-fry, grill, casserole or barbecue.

9. Chicken Tenderloins (small strips removed from the underside of the breast)
Pan-fry, stir-fry, grill or barbecue.

10. Breast Fillet (with skin)
Pan-fry, stir-fry, grill, oven roast or barbecue.

11. Wings
Grill, oven roast or barbecue.

12. Chicken Mince
Pan-fry.

13. Chicken Livers
Pan-fry or stir-fry.

14. Breast Fillet (without skin)
Pan-fry, stir-fry, grill, oven roast or barbecue.

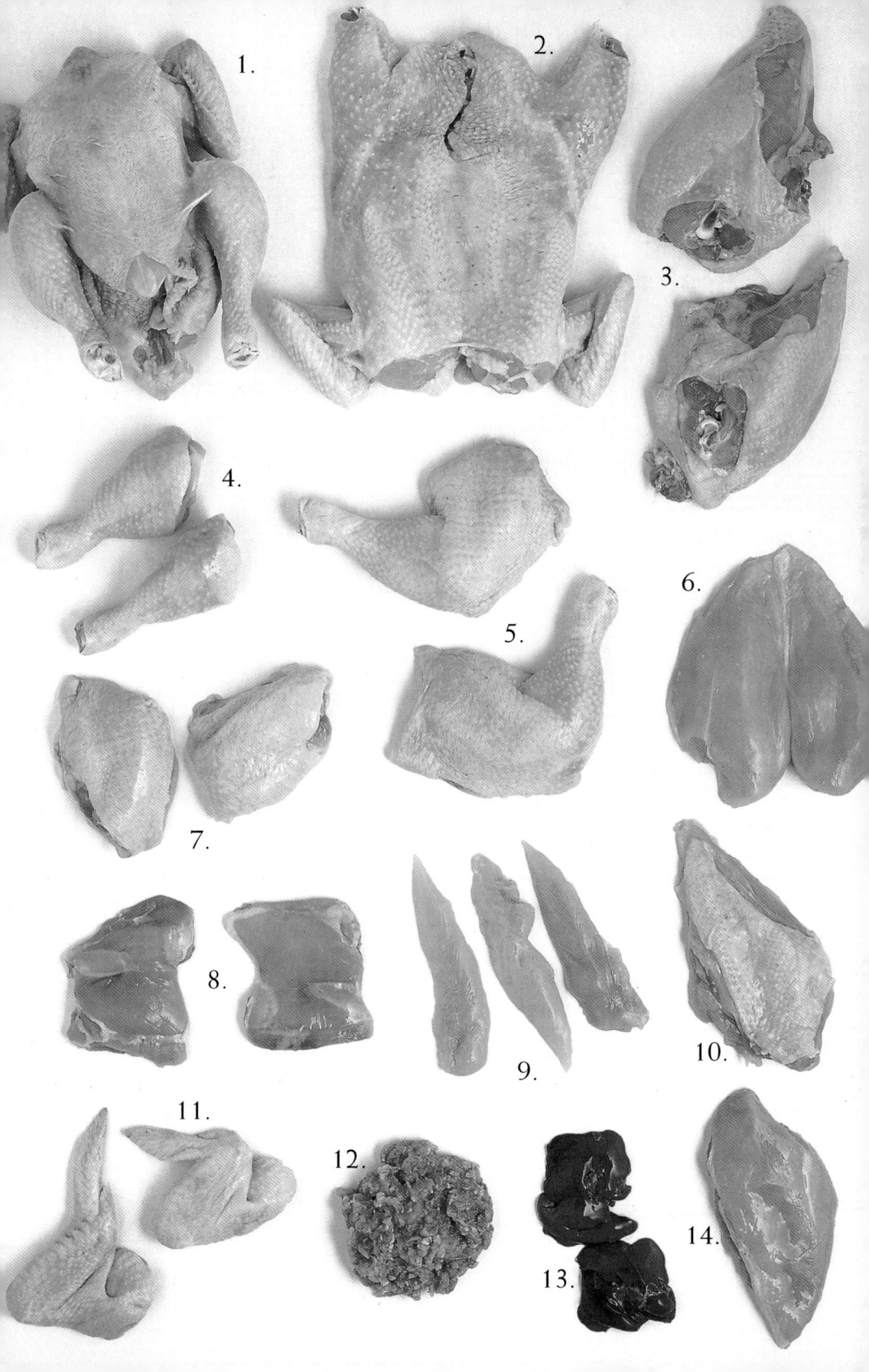
1.
2.
3.
4.
5.
6.
7.
8.
9.
10.
11.
12.
13.
14.

FISH AND SEAFOOD SENSE

Delicious, nutritious, generally quick cooking and easy to prepare, seafood is arguably one of nature's perfect foods. One drawback is that it is highly perishable and care must be taken when shopping for, storing and preparing seafood.

BUYING

Ideally, seafood should be the last thing you buy on your shopping trip, to ensure the shortest time possible out of refrigeration. Your fishmonger should wrap the seafood in a plastic bag to keep in the moisture and then several insulating layers of paper. While you pretty much have to take your fishmonger's word for the freshness of his wares, there are some general signs to look for. Fresh fish should have bulging and clear eyes, not sunken and cloudy. The skin should be plump and moist. Fish fillets should be plump, moist and evenly coloured. There should be no dry edges. Shellfish such as lobsters and crabs are generally best bought live, though they are also available already cooked or frozen. If you are buying them live, they should be fairly active. If you are buying them cooked, make sure the shell is intact and the there is no discoloration around the joints.

Fresh, raw prawns (also known as green prawns) should be plump and firm (not mushy), and without black spots. Cooked prawns should have a firm head and shell, and no black discoloration.

Generally, all seafood should have a pleasant, characteristically fresh, fishy smell. Avoid anything that looks or smells at all unappealing.

STORING

Seafood has a very short storage life and is best used within a day of purchase. Place fish on a plate, to prevent dripping onto other foods, cover with plastic wrap or foil and store in the fridge. Seafood can actually give an undesirable smell to other foods—another reason not to store it for too long. Seafood can be frozen, if absolutely necessary. It is a great way to store fish you have caught yourself, as you can be assured of the freshness. If freezing bought fish, check with the fishmonger whether it has already been frozen and thawed—if it has been, don't ever re-freeze it (this applies to all food to be frozen, not just seafood).

Fish: Fish can be frozen whole, but must be cleaned first, and rinsed to remove any traces of blood (pat dry with paper towels). If a whole fish is going to be filleted, then do so before freezing. Put the fish into a freezer bag and extract as much air as possible. Seal firmly and clearly label with the date. To make separation easier when you come to use frozen fillets, place a sheet of freezer wrap between them. Freeze non-oily fish for up to 4 months and oily fish for up to 3 months.

Shellfish: Lobsters, crabs, prawns and other crayfish can be frozen raw or cooked, and don't need to be cleaned first. Wrap larger shellfish in plastic wrap or foil, then in a freezer bag, extracting as much air as possible. Take care that any sharp parts of the shell don't pierce the bag. Freeze for up to 2 months.

Squid and Octopus: Clean and cut into pieces for cooking. Freeze raw, in a freezer bag with as much air extracted as possible. Freeze for up to 4 months.

Molluscs: Mussels, oysters, scallops, pipis and clams should be cooked and the meat frozen, without the shell, in a freezer bag with as much air extracted as possible. Freeze for up to 3 months.

THAWING

There is no need to thaw small or thin fillets of fish, just cook a little longer than the given time. If the fillet is to have further preparation, such as coating with crumbs or batter, just thaw enough to make it easy to handle. Alternatively, fish can be crumbed before freezing—the coating sticks better this way and there is no need to defrost. Other seafood should be thawed in the fridge, never at room temperature, and never in a sink full of water. Cook any seafood as soon as it has thawed.

PREPARING

Fish: While any good fishmonger will scale and clean your fish on request, it is worth knowing how to do this yourself.

Soak the fish in cold water for a few minutes to make it easier to scale. Then scale the fish by holding it firmly by the tail; and using a fish scaler or knife to scrape the the scales from the skin, working from the tail towards the head against the 'lie' of the scales. This is a messy job, so work outdoors if possible, or on the draining board. It is also a smelly job so be careful not to leave any stray scales lying around when you have finished. Rinse the fish regularly under running water to remove the loosened scales.

Scrape against the direction of the scales with a fish scaler.

To gut a fish, slit the belly from the gills back towards the tail, but not as far as the tail (roughly two-thirds of the way along). Take care not to cut too far into the fish. Pull out the insides and rinse the fish under running water, inside and out. The other method of gutting is through the gills; this is done when you want to preserve the shape of the fish (when poaching whole, for instance). To do this, hook your fingers through the gills and remove them. Reach in and pull the guts out through the opening. Once the fish has been gutted, it can be filleted, if required. To fillet a fish, make a cut across the body, just behind the gills. Only cut halfway through

Remove the gut and rinse the fish under cold water.

the fish. Using this cut as a starting point, slice horizontally along the body, as close to the backbone as possible, and down to the tail,

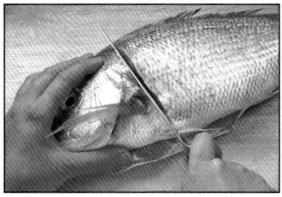

Cut across the body, just behind the gills.

Slice horizontally along the body. Keep close to the bone.

separating the flesh from the bone. The fillet should lift off. Repeat with the other side and lift away the fillet. If you want to skin the fillet, hold it by the tail end, skin-side-down. Dip your fingers in salt to help you grip. Cut away from you, between the flesh and the skin. Push down as you go, to stay close to the skin.

If the fish is to be cooked whole, it is a good idea to bone it first. After gutting through the stomach, extend the cut as far as the tail, on one side of the backbone. Open the fish out and run the knife between the flesh and the bones (which will be fairly close to the cut surface), from the head to the tail. Repeat with the other side. Using scissors, snip the backbone at the tail and the head, then pull the whole bone structure out with your fingers.

When cooking a whole large fish, it is advisable to score the flesh to ensure even cooking. Make three or four diagonal slashes in the fattest part of the fish, on either side.

There are many different ways to cook fish, as many as there are to cook meat or poultry. The one common factor is that fish should be cooked until it is just done, because overcooking causes the flesh to dry out and become very unappetising. The flesh of fish is naturally tender, and therefore does not require the long cooking time that some cuts of meat do. The fact that fish cooks quickly is both a blessing and a headache to the cook, as it can cause some anxiety as to the correct cooking time. Always follow the time given in the recipe, however, remember that size and thickness, particularly of fillets, can vary and will determine the cooking time. If you are unsure, check the fish a little before the given time. This does take practice and an eye for the required result, but the most common way to check is to 'flake' the flesh gently with a fork or point of a knife. It should be opaque, separate into characteristic flakes and come away from the bone,

Gently 'flake' the flesh with a fork to see if the fish is cooked.

where appropriate. While it is best to check the thickest part of the flesh, try to be gentle, so that you do not spoil the appearance of the piece.

Careful cooking also applies to other seafood, not just fish. Overcooking of shellfish, such as clams and mussels, can render them rubbery and inedible.

While seafood is a major ingredient in many grand, glamorous and complicated dishes, simple treatment is usually the best. A squeeze of lemon, a dab of butter, or a sprinkling of herbs. Just remember to always try to enhance the flavour, rather than mask it, to truly appreciate seafood.

Lobster: As lobsters are best bought live, it is necessary to kill them before preparing. The most humane way to do this is to put the lobster in the freezer for an hour first—this will stun it. Then with a large, heavy knife, cut through the centre of the back of the head. Plunge the knife right through to the cutting board, then through the rest of the head. To cut the lobster in half, cut lengthways along the body and tail, using firm pressure.

Cut through the centre of the back of the head with a knife.

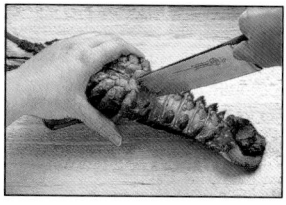

Cut the lobster in half, cutting lengthways along the body.

Grasp the body and tail and twist to separate.

Remove the meat from the shell for easy serving.

Cut a cooked lobster in half the same way, or it may be a little easier to turn it over and cut lengthways along the underside. To extract cooked meat from the legs and claws, first remove by twisting them, close to the body. Break the legs in half and insert a skewer into the cavity to push out the meat. Claws can be cracked with a hammer, or a special cracker.

To extract the cooked tail meat to cut into medallions, grasp the body and tail firmly in each hand and twist to separate. Cut through the underside of the tail with scissors, and pull away the soft undershell. Ease the meat from the tail, in one piece. Cut the meat into slices about 1 cm (1/2 inch) thick.

Crabs: Like lobsters, crabs are best bought live. They should also be put in the freezer for an hour before cooking.

To extract the meat from a cooked crab, take the body and lift the tail flap (apron) from the underside. The body of the crab is in two sections: the central part, where the legs are attached, and the shell. Tuck your thumb in under the tail flap, where the central section and the shell meet, and ease open to separate the two halves. Scoop the meat from the

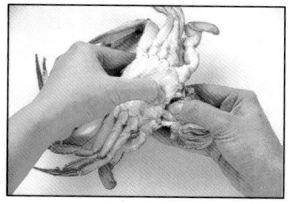

Remove the tail flap, or apron, from the underside of the crab.

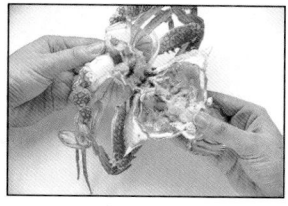

Ease the central section away from the shell.

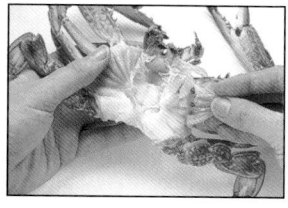

Remove the gills from the central section of the crab.

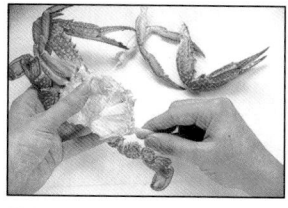

Remove the claws and legs and pull out the meat.

shell. Take the central section and remove the gills. Then remove the legs and claws by twisting them away from the body.

A skewer may be needed to remove the meat in the body.

Crackers, or the back of a knife, crack open the claws.

Cut the body section in half, and then, using a pick or skewer, extract all the meat you can find (this is a fiddly job). Crack the claws open and break the legs apart with your fingers. Pull out the meat with a skewer.

Prawns: To peel prawns, whether raw or cooked, grasp the head and the body close to the joint,

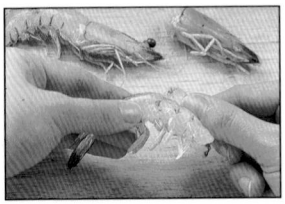

Twist the head off before removing the shell and legs.

and twist in opposite directions. The head can either be thrown away or used to make delicious stocks or soups. Remove the legs from the underside of the prawn and then use your thumbs to prise the shell from the flesh. If the recipe says to leave the tail intact, only work down as far as the last section before the tail, otherwise, also remove the tail. Pull away the shell and legs and discard. To devein the prawn, cut a shallow slit along the

Cut a slit along the 'back' and pull out the intestinal tract.

'back' and pull out the intestinal tract. Both raw and cooked prawns can be deveined.

Mussels: To prepare black mussels for cooking, discard those without tightly closed shells (or shells that do not close when tapped on the work surface)—this means they are already dead and could lead to food poisoning. Scrub the shells with a stiff brush, and tear away the beards (small hairy strands) from the shell. Discard any mussels that

Scrub the mussel shell and tear away the beard.

do not open during the cooking process, as this also indicates that something may be awry. However, green-lipped mussels (which are larger than the black variety) will be open when you buy them and don't close when tapped.

Octopus: To prepare the octopus, first cut into sections: the head and the tentacles. Clean the head by turning it inside out to push out the insides. The 'beak' is found at the centre of the tentacles and is removed by squeezing

Turn the head of the octopus inside out to clean it.

Squeeze the 'beak' out of the centre of the tentacles.

on either side while pushing from behind. If the octopus is very small and you want to serve it whole, clean the head by cutting a slit in the back of it and pulling out the insides. Remove the beak as before.

Oysters: Fresh, opened oysters need to be consumed within a day. To keep fresh oysters for longer than this, buy closed ones and open them yourself when you are ready to serve them. However, be careful: oyster shells can have very sharp edges. First, scrub the outside of the oyster shell under cold runnning water. Then wrap the oyster, rounded-side-down, in a thick cloth and hold it in the palm of your hand. Insert an oyster knife into the pointed end of the oyster at the hinge, to about 3 cm, and work the knife into the shell, twisting the knife to separate the shells. Slide the knife between the oyster and the top shell, cutting through the hinge muscle and removing the top shell. Similarly, cut between the oyster and the bottom shell to release the oyster. Rinse the shells and wipe the oyster clean with a damp cloth to remove any grit or sand before returning the oyster to the shell.

Squid (calamari): To prepare squid, grasp the body pouch in one hand and, with the other, reach in and pull out the whole lower section, which includes the head and tentacles. Feel the pouch to find the transparent quill and pull it out. Throw this away. Loosen the skin by sliding a finger between it and the flesh, then pull firmly away. Trim the flaps and skin them also. If you wish to use the tentacles, cut them from the head and remove the beak as you would for octopus.

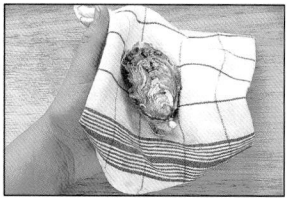

Wrap oyster shells in a thick cloth when handling them.

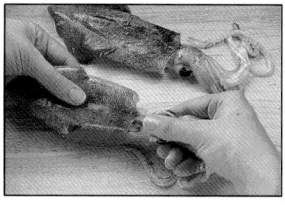

Remove the whole of the lower section of the squid.

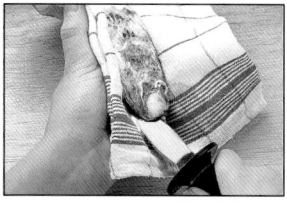

Hold the oyster in a cloth and work the knife into the shell.

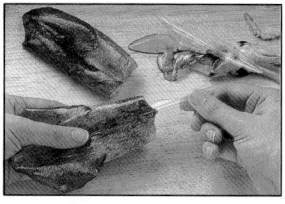

Pull the transparent quill out of the body pouch.

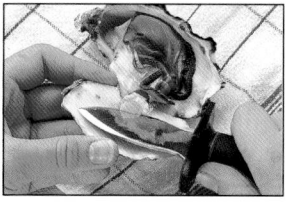

Slide the knife between the oyster and the shell.

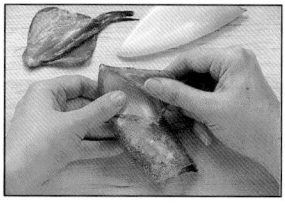

Loosen the skin by sliding a finger between it and the flesh.

Release the oyster from the shell and remove any grit.

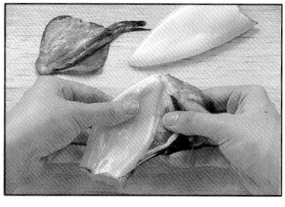

Remove the skin from the squid before cooking.

FISH AND SEAFOOD

Fish and seafood can throw many people into confusion. Here are the most common types of fish and seafood, with a quick guide to the most successful ways to cook them.

1. Snapper
Pan-fry, grill, barbecue, oven roast, poach or steam.

2. Rainbow Trout
Pan-fry, grill, barbecue or oven roast.

3. John Dory
Pan-fry, grill, barbecue, oven roast, poach or steam.

4. Flounder
Pan-fry, grill, barbecue, oven roast, poach or steam.

5. Smoked Trout
Already cooked. Use in salads and dips.

6. Bream
Pan-fry, grill, barbecue, oven roast, poach or steam.

7. Sardines
Pan-fry, grill or barbecue.

8. Squid
Pan-fry, stir-fry, grill, barbecue or casserole.

9. Whitebait
Pan-fry, deep-fry or bake.

10. Firm White Fish Fillet (ling fillets and swordfish steak)
Pan-fry, stir-fry, grill, barbecue, oven roast, poach or steam.

11. Salmon Cutlet
Pan-fry, grill, barbecue, oven roast, casserole, steam or poach.

12. Tuna Steak
Pan-fry, stir-fry, grill, barbecue, oven roast, casserole or steam.

13. Calamari (whole, tube and rings)
Pan-fry, stir-fry, barbecue or deep-fry.

14. Skate
Pan-fry or grill.

15. Octopus
Pan-fry, stir-fry, grill or barbecue.

16. Scallops
Pan-fry, stir-fry, grill, barbecue, oven roast or steam.

17. Raw Prawns
Pan-fry, stir-fry, grill, barbecue or casserole.

18. Cooked Prawns
Already cooked. Use in salads, cold dishes, or add to dishes at the end of the cooking time.

19. Lobster
Pan-fry, stir-fry, grill, barbecue or oven roast.

20. Blue Swimmer Crabs (cooked and uncooked)
Stir-fry, barbecue, oven roast, pot roast or casserole.

21. Oysters
Grill or barbecue.

22. Clams (vongole)
Pan-fry, grill or casserole.

23. Mussels (black and New Zealand green-lipped)
Pan-fry, grill, barbecue, oven roast, casserole or poach.

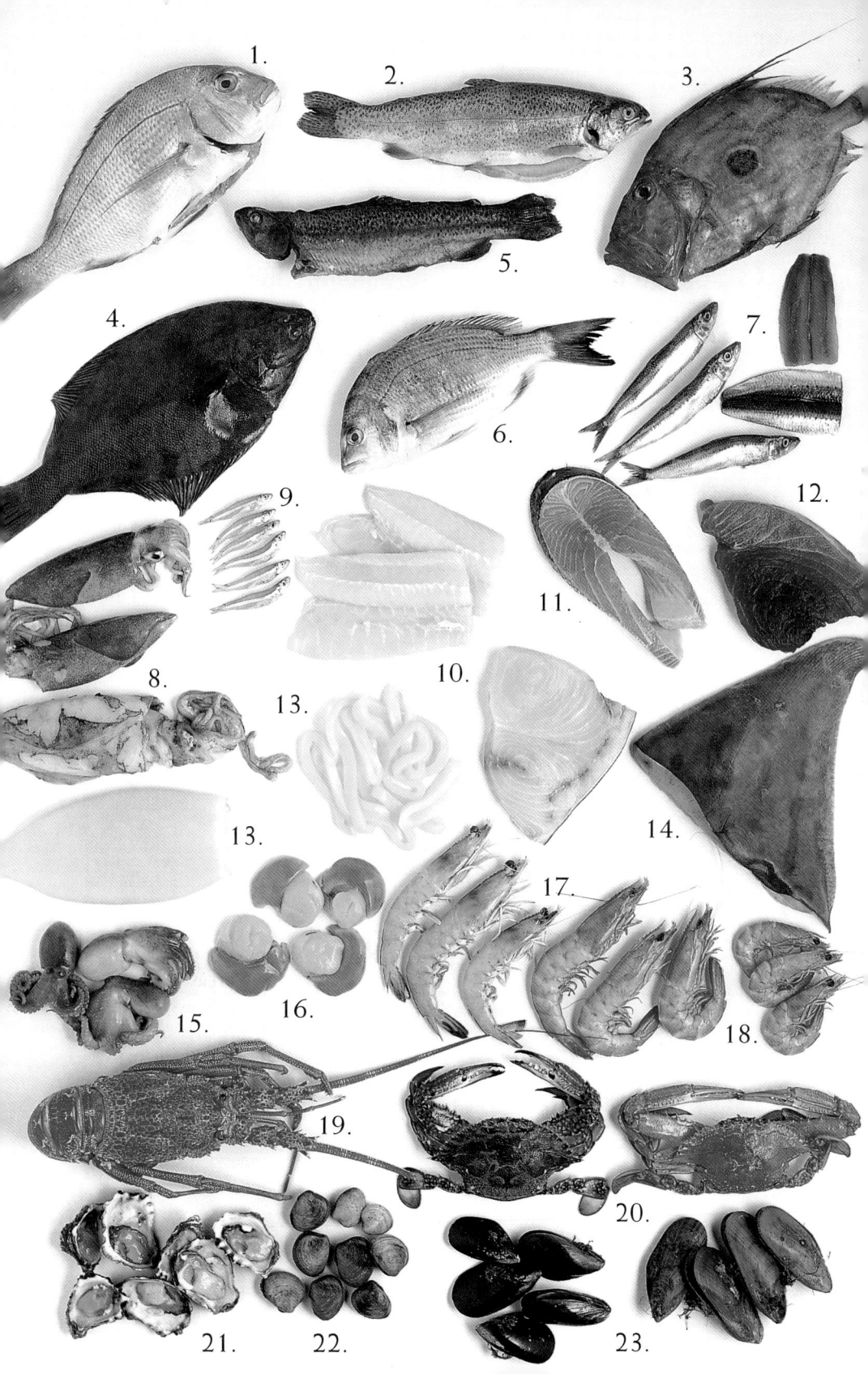
1.
2.
3.
4.
5.
6.
7.
8.
9.
10.
11.
12.
13.
13.
14.
15.
16.
17.
18.
19.
20.
21.
22.
23.

VEGETABLE SENSE

The variety of fresh vegetables available to us today is quite wonderful. Quick and easy to cook, packed with vitamins and fibre, we can revel in the colour, crunch and flavour of fresh vegetables and treat them with the respect they deserve.

ASPARAGUS

To remove the sometimes tough and woody end of the asparagus, bend the stem end of each spear. It will snap where it begins to get tough. Blanch to use in salads or, if very tender, use raw. Blanching makes vegetables such as asparagus and snow peas tender without cooking them, and preserves the bright colour. To do this, place the vegetables in a pan and cover with boiling water (it's easier to tie asparagus together into a bunch). Leave for 30–60 seconds, depending on the size. Drain, then plunge into iced water. Drain again and pat dry.

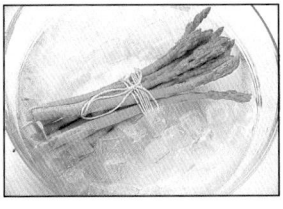

The iced water prevents the vegetables cooking further.

BEANS

Trim both ends of the bean ('top and tail') and remove the fibrous string that runs down each side, if necessary. Steam, boil or microwave until tender.

BEETROOT

Raw beetroot will stain, so take care. Trim the stalks to 2 cm (1 inch) above the bulb, leaving the skin intact. Boil whole until tender, then cool and slip off the skins. Also good raw, peeled and grated.

BROCCOLI

Cut into florets (make them fairly small if stir-frying) and steam, boil or microwave until tender.

BRUSSELS SPROUTS

Remove any tough or yellow outer leaves and score a cross in the base so the sprout cooks all the way through. Steam, boil or microwave until tender.

CABBAGE

Remove any tough outer leaves and chop or shred the inner leaves. Serve raw and shredded in coleslaw, or steam, microwave or stir-fry very briefly.

CAPSICUM

Cut into quarters and remove the seeds and white membrane. Serve raw or stir-fry, or leave whole and stuff. Removing the skin from capsicums by grilling or roasting makes the flavour of the flesh even sweeter. Cut the capsicums into large,

Grill the capsicum until the skin is black and blistered.

Cool in a plastic bag to make the skin peel away easily.

flattish pieces, removing the seeds and membrane. Place, skin-side-up, under a hot grill until the skin is black and blistered. Put in a plastic bag or under a tea towel to cool—this steams and loosens the skin, which can be peeled away.

CARROTS
Scrub the skin or peel if you like. Serve raw or steam, boil, microwave, roast or stir-fry.

CAULIFLOWER
Cut into florets. Steam, boil, microwave or stir-fry.

CELERY
Trim the stalks, removing the leaves and thick root end. Good raw, stir-fried or in soups or stews.

CORN
Remove the outside husk and silk. Boil or microwave, but take care not to overcook or the corn will become tough. Also good roasted, either in foil, or in the husk: peel back the husk and remove the silk, then pull the husk back into place to cover the kernels and roast.

EGGPLANT
The flesh from large eggplants can contain bitter juices—this is why the recipe will tell you to chop the flesh, put in a colander and sprinkle generously with salt to draw out the juice. Leave for 20 minutes, then rinse and pat dry. Fry, stir-fry or cook in curries or stews.

MUSHROOMS
Don't wash mushrooms before cooking or they will become soggy. Wipe clean with paper towels or peel, if necessary.

PARSNIPS
Peel and cut off the stalk end. Steam, microwave, roast or boil, as for potatoes.

PEAS
Remove from the pod and boil or steam until tender.

POTATOES
Peel or scrub the skin, removing any 'eyes'. Use floury or waxy variety if stated in the recipe.

PUMPKIN
Peel and remove the seeds and membrane, then steam, boil or microwave. If you are roasting pumpkin, you don't need to peel it first—the peel is easier to remove after.

SNOW PEAS
Top and tail, then stir-fry or serve raw or blanched.

SWEET POTATO
Peel and then steam, microwave, boil or roast. Mash just like potatoes. Also good roasted in the skin, after which the soft flesh can be scooped out.

TOMATO
Serve raw in salads, or fry, grill, or roast. Recipes will occasionally ask for tomatoes to be peeled, particularly in sauces where the peel can add an unpleasant texture. To do this, score a cross in the base of each tomato. Put in a heatproof bowl and cover with boiling water. Leave for about 1 minute (the ripeness of the tomato will determine how easily the skin comes

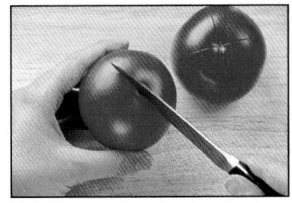

Score a cross in the base of the tomato with a knife.

The skin will easily peel away from the cross.

Cut the tomato in half and scoop out the seeds.

away), then transfer to a bowl of cold water. Peel the skin away from the cross. To remove the seeds, cut in half horizontally and scoop them out with a teaspoon.

ZUCCHINI
Trim the ends and chop. Steam, stir-fry or cook in curries or stews.

VEGETABLES

There is now a huge range of fresh vegetables available all year round. Names may vary from country to country so, if you are unsure, check the photograph opposite.

1. Lettuce
2. Bok Choy (pak choy/Chinese cabbage)
3. Chinese Broccoli (gai larn)
4. Chillis
5. Capsicums (peppers)
6. Globe Artichoke
7. Button Mushrooms
8. White, Brown and Red Onions
9. Sugar Snap Peas
10. Peas in the pod
11. Snow Peas (mange-tout)
12. Cauliflower
13. Tomato
14. Cherry Tomato
15. Garlic
16. Bulb Spring Onion
17. Spring Onion (green onion)
18. Shallot
19. Eggplant (aubergine)
20. Broccoli
21. Fennel
22. Green Beans (string beans)
23. Leek
24. Zucchini (courgette)
25. Brussels Sprouts
26. Squash
27. Avocado
28. Belgian Endive (witlof)
29. Parsnip
30. Turnip
31. Lebanese Cucumber
32. Celery
33. Cucumber (ridged cucumber)
34. Carrot
35. Asparagus
36. Ginger
37. Jerusalem Artichoke
38. Sweet Potato
39. Beetroot
40. English Spinach
41. Silverbeet (chard)
42. Corn
43. Pumpkin
44. Swede (rutabaga)
45. Potato
46. Cabbage

1.
2.
3.
4.
5.
6.
7.
8.
9.
10.
11.
12.
13.
14.
15.
16.
17.
18.
19.
20.
21.
22.
23.
24.
25.
26.
27.
28.
29.
30.
31.
32.
33.
34.
35.
36.
37.
38.
39.
40.
41.
42.
43.
44.
45.
46.

HERBS

Fresh herbs give delicate flavour and colour to dishes. They all have their favourite partners in the food world and listed below are some of the most popular pairings.

1. Curly Leaf Parsley
Pasta, mornays, egg dishes and salads.

2. Flat-leaf Parsley (continental parsley)
Mediterranean cooking—tabbouleh, fish, chicken and vegetables.

3. Rosemary
Meat (especially lamb), potatoes, breads and tomato-based sauces.

4. Tarragon
French cooking—fish, poultry and sauces such as hollandaise and bearnaise.

5. Sorrel
Soups, marinades and omelettes.

6. Bay Leaf
Used in bouquet garni for stews, soups, chicken dishes, sweet syrups and poaching liquids.

7. Lemon Thyme
Best with fish and chicken dishes.

8. Thyme
Soups, stews, tomato-based sauces, veal, lamb and roast poultry.

9. Garlic Chives
Asian cuisine—rice paper rolls, noodles and soups.

10. Chives
Used with eggs, potatoes and creamy soups.

11. Dill
Best with salmon, potatoes and pickled cucumbers.

12. Chervil
French cuisine—salads, omelettes, butter sauces, poached chicken and fish.

13. Peppermint
Used in tea, sweet dishes, cordials and liqueurs.

14. Spearmint
Mint jelly, African and Middle Eastern food.

15. Holy Basil (kaprow)
Asian curries, stir-fries and soups.

16. Coriander
Roots, stems and leaves all used in Asian cooking, salads, curries and salsas.

17. Marjoram
Used in omelettes, stuffings, soups and stews.

18. Oregano
Used in Mediterranean cooking—tomato-based sauces, cheese and beans.

19. Lemon Grass
Asian soups, curries and salads.

20. Rocket
Salads, pasta, soups, pesto.

21. Purple Basil
Use as basil.

22. Basil
Tomatoes, pesto, fish, chicken and rice.

23. Lemon Basil
Asian salads, soup, curries.

24. Sage
Pumpkin, game, pork.

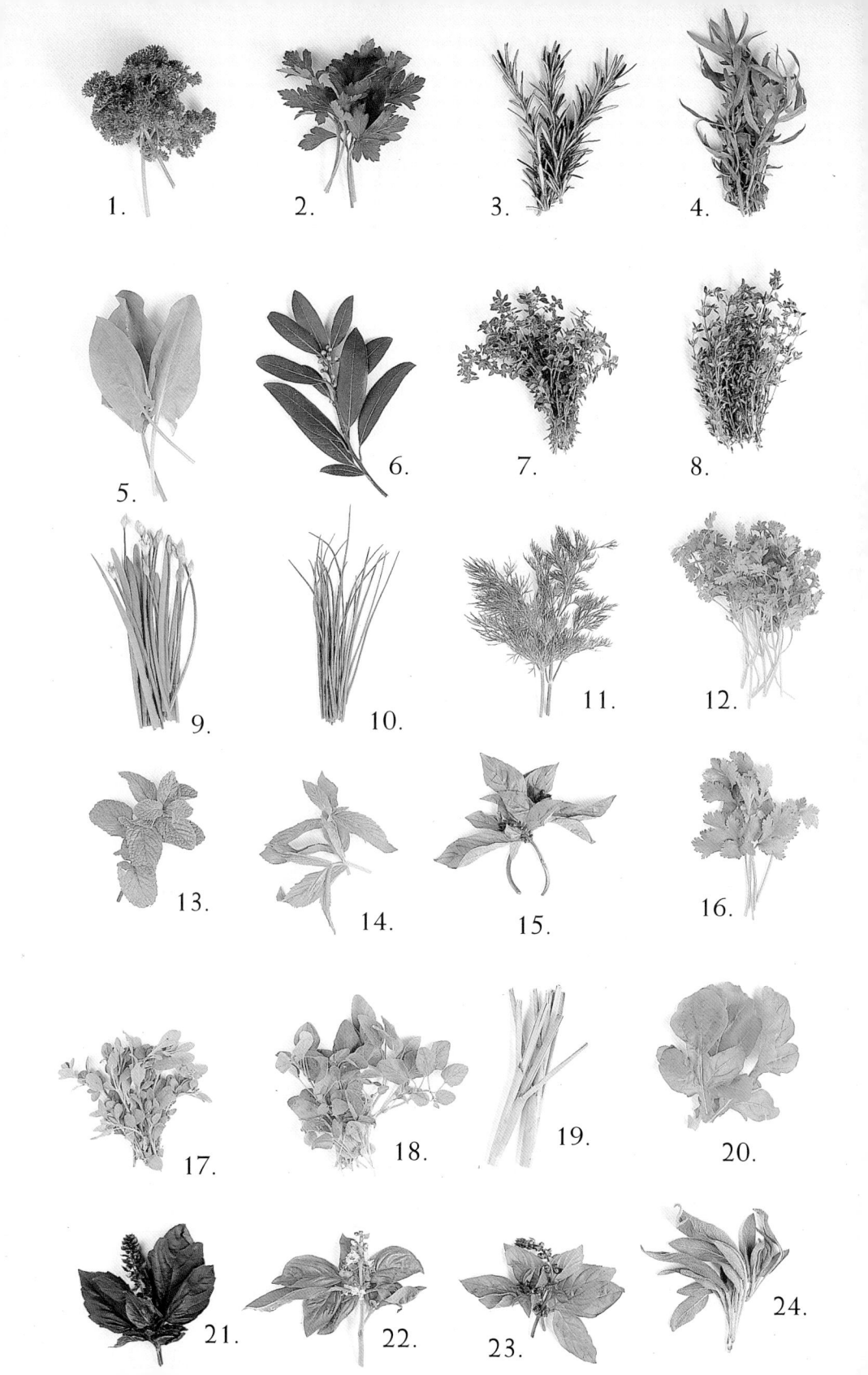
1.
2.
3.
4.
5.
6.
7.
8.
9.
10.
11.
12.
13.
14.
15.
16.
17.
18.
19.
20.
21.
22.
23.
24.

PASTA AND RICE SENSE

For two such simple foods, it is amazing how many varied opinions there are on how to cook pasta and rice. Here are our commonsense thoughts on the subject.

PASTA VARIETIES

There are a huge number of pasta varieties and shapes and each is traditionally partnered with a specific type of sauce. Smooth pastas are typically served with smooth oily sauces, while ridged or shaped pastas are perfect for holding chunky sauces (see the identification chart overleaf). You can buy pasta dried or fresh and dried pasta made in Italy is considered to be the best. It is made from semolina flour (which is made from durum wheat), a hard flour that is high in gluten. Always check that your pasta packet says 'made with durum wheat'.

COOKING PASTA

To cook perfect pasta, you will need a very large pan. Allow at least 2 litres of water for every 250 g (8 oz) pasta—this allows the pasta plenty of room to move and expand and prevents it clumping together. Bring the water to a rapid boil (cover the pan to make it come to the boil faster), then add the pasta and leave the pan uncovered.

Some people like to add a little oil to the water to prevent the pasta sticking together, but if the pan is big enough the pasta won't stick. Add salt if you like, but topped with a flavoursome sauce the pasta shouldn't need extra seasoning. Give the pasta a quick stir, then bring it back to the boil. Once it is boiling you can start timing. Use the time given on the packet as a guide, but the only way to really know if pasta is ready is to taste it. Lift a small piece from the pan, cool it slightly, then bite. The pasta should be just tender, with no raw taste, but certainly not soft and gluggy. This is known as 'al dente' and is the correct way to serve pasta. Fresh pasta cooks much more quickly than dried—in some cases it takes only a couple of minutes. Ravioli, tortellini and gnocchi will float as soon as they are cooked: test a piece, then drain immediately.

Once drained, return to the hot pan and toss with sauce. If the pasta has to sit for a couple of minutes, some people toss it with a little olive oil to prevent it clumping: this is fine depending on what sort of sauce you are then using, as the oil will prevent the sauce coating the pasta thoroughly. It is best just to make sure that your sauce is ready (it can be cooked and then reheated) when the pasta is cooked.

RICE VARIETIES

There are many different types of rice. Some are named for their origins but most are distinguished by the size of their grains: long, medium or short. Longer grains contain less starch and remain separate during cooking. Short grains contain more starch and become gluey when cooked so that they stick together. Glutinous rice has very high amounts of starch. Brown rice still has the husks which have been removed from white rice (this is what makes it higher in fibre and a healthy alternative to white rice). Wild rice is technically not a rice at all, but the grain of a water grass. It was originally grown by the Native Americans and harvested by hand. Although it is now also farmed by machine, it is expensive in comparison to other rices. It is now available mixed with brown rice and sold as a wild rice blend which is more economical.
Brown rice takes much longer to cook than white because it takes time for the the water to break through the bran layer.
In some recipes, such as risottos, rice is fried in oil or butter before adding any liquid. The oil then impregnates the outer layer of the rice and keeps the grains separate. The rice used for risotto is arborio rice, which swells when liquid is added and produces a creamy sauce. Even after cooking, arborio should retain a slight 'bite' in the centre. Always use the type specified in the recipe—don't try risotto with long-grain rice, or a pudding with arborio rice.

HOW MUCH WATER?

Rice absorbs water when cooking and almost trebles in bulk as a result. Many new cooks will have experienced welding a portion of rice to the base of a pan by letting it boil dry. We would love to have a fail-safe rule for preventing this but unfortunately there can be no strict water to rice ratio: the greater the quantity of rice, the less water is needed proportionately. As a very general rule, long-grain rice will absorb about three times its bulk in water, while short-grain will take far more.

COOKING RICE

With over half the population of the world eating rice two or three times a day, it is not surprising that there are many arguments over how it should be cooked. Some say you must never lift the lid, while others cook their rice uncovered. One widely accepted hint is to always use a big pan. This allows the rice to expand and lie as shallow as possible, stopping the lower levels being crushed, cooking faster and becoming soggy. A rice cooker will produce perfect rice every time. If you don't have one, try the following methods:
Absorption: Put the rice in a large pan. For every 200 g (6½ oz) rice add 315 ml (10 fl oz) water. Bring to the boil, cover tightly with a lid and reduce the heat to very low. Cook for 10 minutes. Remove from the heat and leave, covered, for 10 minutes. When you take off the lid the surface of the rice should be dotted with steam holes. Fluff up with a fork.

When it is fully cooked, the rice will be dotted with holes.

Fast boiling: Bring a pan of water to a fast boil. Add the rice and cook uncovered for 12 minutes. Stir occasionally (brown rice will take 40 minutes).

PASTA AND RICE

Certain pastas are best used for smooth or chunky sauces depending on their own smoothness and shape. Rice varieties, too, are suited to certain dishes, as shown below.

1. Spaghetti
Smooth long strands. Serve with pesto, creamy, tomato and meat sauces.

2. Fettucine (fresh and dried)
Smooth, long flat strands. Serve with pesto, creamy and tomato-based sauces.

3. Lasagne
Smooth, flat sheets. Layer with meat, seafood or vegetable sauce and bake.

4. Canneloni
Smooth or ridged tubes. Stuff with meat, seafood or vegetable sauce; bake.

5. Farfalle
Smooth 'bows'. Good with all sauces and in salads.

6. Penne
Smooth or ridged quills (rigate). Good with chunky sauces or in salads.

7. Fusilli
Smooth spirals. Good with all sauces or in salads.

8. Macaroni
Smooth, short tubes. Good with creamy sauces, in soups, salads and bakes.

9. Risoni
Small, smooth grains like rice. Used in soups.

10. Fresh Gnocchi
Ridged potato dumplings. Good with creamy, cheese or tomato-based sauces.

11. Fresh Tortellini
Smooth stuffed crescents. Serve with a sauce to match filling, or in soups.

12. Fresh Ravioli
Smooth stuffed 'pillows'. Serve with a sauce to match the filling.

13. White short-grain
Sushi and paella.

14. White long-grain
Chinese cooking.

15. Basmati
Indian cooking, biryani and pilaf.

16. Jasmine
Served with Thai dishes and curries.

17. Arborio
Risotto.

18. Brown short-grain
Soups and patties.

19. Brown long-grain
Salads, vegetarian loaves and as an accompaniment.

20. Wild Rice
Salads and as an accompaniment.

21. Black Glutinous
Asian sweet dishes.

22. White Glutinous
Asain sweet dishes and sticky rice.

23. Couscous
Used in African cooking, salads and tagines.

24. Polenta
Used in Italian cooking, as a soft accompaniment or pressed into a cake.

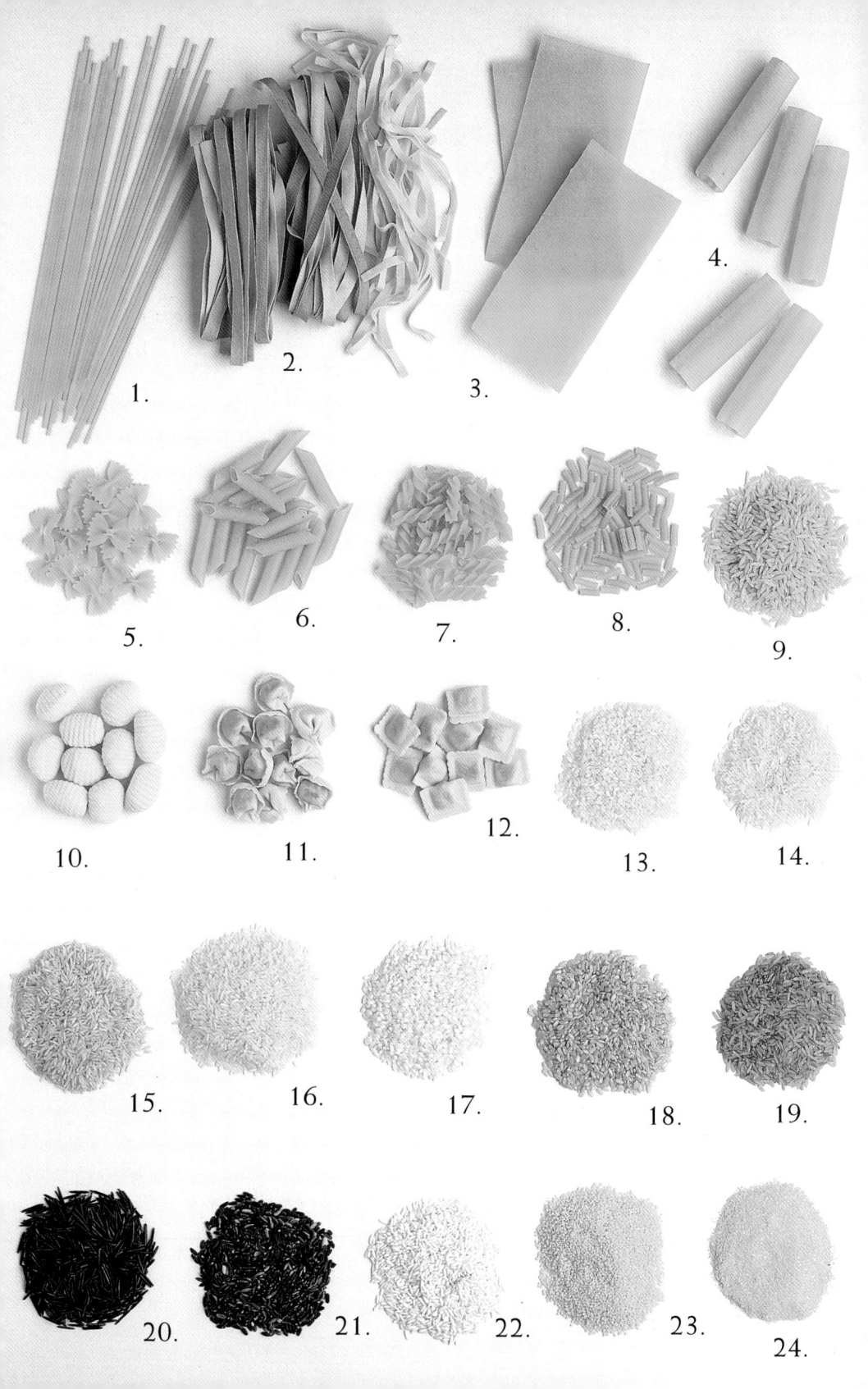
1.
2.
3.
4.
5.
6.
7.
8.
9.
10.
11.
12.
13.
14.
15.
16.
17.
18.
19.
20.
21.
22.
23.
24.

FREEZING CHART

Freezing means you can prepare food in bulk, cooking larger portions when you have the time and making the most of foods that are in season. Your freezer should be at -18°C and, if you don't have a frost-free model, it should be defrosted every 6–12 months, depending on how much you use it (more frost will build up if it is opened often). If you have a large freezer, don't let it become a black hole where things disappear, only to be discovered years later and thrown away. Keep a notebook next to the freezer to record dishes and dates frozen and make sure you use them within the recommended period of time (opposite).

Once something has been frozen and thawed, never refreeze it, or you run the risk of multiplying bacteria and food poisoning. Containers suitable for freezing are plastic containers with airtight lids and aluminium foil containers with lids. Plastic clip-lock bags are also very convenient. Remove the air from the packaging before sealing—a vacuum pump is good for this. Freeze soups and stews by lining a bowl with a plastic bag, pouring the soup or stew into the bag and sealing. Freeze, then remove the bag from the bowl. Waxed or baking paper is great for separating layers or items such as crepes, fish fillets and chops, so that you can defrost one at a time, rather than the whole batch.

There are some foods that simply can't be frozen. Hard-boiled eggs will go rubbery; fried and crumbed meats will go soggy; whole egg in their shells will break the shell as they expand; vegetables with a high water content will spoil; sour cream and yoghurt separate; meringue weeps; custards, mayonnaise and dishes containing gelatine can't be frozen; herbs and spices lose their flavour after about 2 weeks.

Don't forget to label everything with a permanent marker or self-adhesive labels—it's no good knowing how long something can be stored if you don't know the date that you froze it.

Peeled fruit that discolours easily, such as apples and pears, can be dipped in a lemon juice solution (3 tablespoons lemon juice to 2 cups water) before freezing. Berries can be frozen uncovered on a tray until firm, then transferred to an airtight container for further freezing. You can also layer fruit that is to be used as pie filling with sugar (only fruit that doesn't discolour is suitable for this method of freezing).

1–2 MONTHS

Bread (sliced)
Milk
Soups
Stews
Sausages
Pancakes, pikelets and waffles
Shellfish (raw and cooked)
Scones (unbaked)
Cakes (unbaked)
Biscuits (unbaked)
Sandwiches (2 weeks to a month, depending on the filling)

2–3 MONTHS

Cream
Cottage cheese
Cakes
Scones
Ice cream
Bread (unbaked)
Pastry (baked and unbaked)
Offal and bacon
Oily fish (sardines, trout, mullet)
Filled pies (unbaked)
Minced meats (except beef)
Poultry giblets
Leftover dishes

3–4 MONTHS

Ham
Lamb
Cheddar cheese, grated
Butter (salted)
White-fleshed fish
Fruit cake (unbaked)

4–6 MONTHS

Minced beef
Veal
Game
Pork
Butter (unsalted)

6–8 MONTHS

Bread (unsliced)
Biscuits
Pizza
Filled pies

8–12 MONTHS

Beef
Poultry
Fruit
Vegetables
Fruit cake

MEASUREMENTS

The recipes in this book were developed using a tablespoon measure of 20 ml. In some other countries the tablespoon is 15 ml. For most recipes this difference will not be noticeable but, for recipes using baking powder, gelatine, bicarbonate of soda, small amounts of flour and cornflour, we suggest that, if you are using the smaller tablespoon, you add an extra teaspoon for each tablespoon.

Weighing scales will obviously give you more accurate measurements, but many people find it very convenient to use cup measurements. You can buy special measuring cups in the supermarket or use an ordinary household cup: first you need to check it holds 250 ml (8 fl oz) by filling it with water and measuring the water (pour it into a measuring jug or even an empty yoghurt carton). This cup can then be used for both liquid and dry cup measurements.

OVEN TEMPERATURES

DESCRIPTION	°C	°F	GAS MARK
Very slow	120	250	1/2
	140	275	1
Slow	150	300	2
Warm	160	315	2–3
	170	325	3
Moderate	180	350	4
Moderately hot	190	375	5
	200	400	6
Hot	210	415	6–7
	220	425	7
Very hot	230	450	8
	240	475	9

LIQUID CUP MEASURES

1/4 cup	60 ml	2 fluid oz
1/3 cup	80 ml	2 1/2 fluid oz
1/2 cup	125 ml	4 fluid oz
3/4 cup	180 ml	6 fluid oz
1 cup	250 ml	8 fluid oz

SPOON MEASURES

1/4 teaspoon	1.25 ml
1/2 teaspoon	2.5 ml
1 teaspoon	5 ml
1 tablespoon	20 ml

WEIGHT

10 g	1/4 oz
30 g	1 oz
60 g	2 oz
90 g	3 oz
125 g	4 oz
150 g	5 oz
185 g	6 oz
220 g	7 oz
250 g	8 oz
275 g	9 oz
300 g	10 oz
330 g	11 oz
375 g	12 oz
400 g	13 oz
425 g	14 oz
475 g	15 oz
500 g	1 lb
600 g	1 1/4 lb
650 g	1 lb 5 oz
750 g	1 1/2 lb
1 kg	2 lb

LENGTH

5 mm	1/4 inch
1 cm	1/2 inch
2 cm	3/4 inch
2.5 cm	1 inch
5 cm	2 inches
6 cm	2 1/2 inches
8 cm	3 inches
10 cm	4 inches
12 cm	5 inches
15 cm	6 inches
18 cm	7 inches
20 cm	8 inches
23 cm	9 inches
25 cm	10 inches
28 cm	11 inches
30 cm	12 inches
46 cm	18 inches
50 cm	20 inches
61 cm	24 inches
77 cm	30 inches

CUP CONVERSIONS

1 cup plain/self-raising flour	125 g (4 oz)
1 cup grated Parmesan cheese	100 g (3 1/2 oz)
1 cup grated Cheddar cheese	125 g (4 oz)
1 cup breadcrumbs (fresh)	80 g (2 3/4 oz)
1 cup breadcrumbs (dry)	100 g (3 1/2 oz)
1 cup dried chickpeas	220 g (7 oz)
1 cup grated chocolate	125 g (4 oz)
1 cup choc bits	175 g (6 oz)
1 cup rice, uncooked	200 g (6 1/2 oz)
1 cup rice, cooked	185 g (6 oz)
1 cup sugar, caster/granulated	250 g (8 oz)
1 cup icing sugar	125 g (4 oz)
1 cup fresh basil/coriander/mint leaves, firmly packed	30 g (1 oz)
1 cup chopped fresh basil/coriander/mint leaves, firmly packed	60 g (2 oz)

ALTERNATIVE INGREDIENT NAMES

bicarbonate of soda	—	baking soda
capsicum	—	red or green (bell) pepper
chickpeas	—	garbanzo beans
choc bits	—	chocolate chips
chocolate melts	—	chocolate buttons
cornflour	—	cornstarch
fresh coriander	—	cilantro
cream	—	single cream
dark chocolate	—	plain/bittersweet chocolate
eggplant	—	aubergine
fruit mince	—	mincemeat
golden syrup	—	light corn syrup
hazelnut	—	filbert
icing sugar	—	confectioners' sugar
Madeira cake	—	pound cake
plain flour	—	all-purpose flour
prawns	—	shrimp
Rice Bubbles	—	Rice Krispies
sambal oelek	—	chilli paste
snow pea	—	mange tout
spring onion	—	scallion
thick cream	—	double/heavy cream
tomato paste (US/Aus.)	—	tomato purée (UK)
zucchini	—	courgette

BREAKFAST AND BRUNCH

Breakfast is the most important meal of the day, so make it a little bit special. Instead of packet cereals and burnt toast, whip up something worthwhile in the morning. Eggs can be incredibly simple (but deliciously nutritious) and making your own muesli is as easy as it is satisfying.

SCRAMBLED EGGS

To make scrambled eggs for 2 people, beat 4 eggs and 1/4 cup (60 ml/2 fl oz) milk or cream lightly with a whisk or fork. Melt 15 g (1/2 oz) butter in a heavy-based pan over very low heat and pour in the egg. Stir constantly with a wooden spoon, lifting the mixture from the bottom of the pan so that it cooks evenly. The eggs are ready when they are just set but are still creamy—remove from the heat and serve immediately as they will continue to cook and harden. Serve on toast or English muffins. Or top with a spoonful of caviar or some strips of smoked salmon. Alternatively, stir in a couple of tablespoons of chopped fresh chives or parsley or grated cheese during cooking.

BOILED EGGS

Fill a pan three-quarters full with cold water. Add the egg gently—it is less likely to crack if it is at room temperature, rather than straight from the fridge. If it does crack and the white starts to seep out, add a tablespoon of vinegar or salt to the water. Place over medium heat and slowly bring to the boil. Do not start timing until the water comes to the boil. Reduce the heat and simmer for 3 minutes for soft-boiled eggs and 10 minutes for hard-boiled. Remove the egg from the water with a slotted spoon.

FRIED EGGS

Heat 20 g (3/4 oz) butter or 1 tablespoon oil in a frying pan until sizzling, or use the hot fat from frying bacon. Gently break up to 4 eggs into the pan (break in a cup first and slide into the pan). For eggs 'sunny-side up', cook until the white has set and the yolk is still runny. If you want, turn the eggs over with a spatula when the white is set, but lift them out of the pan after a few seconds so the yolk is just sealed on the outside, not hard all the way through. If you prefer your eggs set, turn them over when the white is set, and cook until the egg is cooked through. Remove from the pan with the spatula.

EGGS are ideal breakfast food—quick and easy to prepare but packed full of nutrition.

POACHED EGGS

Fill a frying pan three-quarters full with cold water and add a couple of tablespoons of white vinegar (this stops the egg white spreading in the water). Bring to a gentle boil. Gently break an egg into the water (or into a cup and then slide into the water). Reduce the heat so that the water is barely simmering. Cook for 1–2 minutes, or until just set. Remove from the water with a slotted spoon, draining well.

NOTE: Use the freshest eggs you can find for poaching—the white will hold together better.

VARIATION: Eggs Benedict is a popular brunch dish. Serve poached eggs on toasted English muffins with a couple of slices of ham. Top with hollandaise sauce (see page 146). For Eggs Florentine, use cooked chopped spinach in place of the ham.

OMELETTE

Preparation: 5 minutes
Cooking: 2 minutes
Serves 1–2

3 eggs
30 g (1 oz) butter

1 Put the eggs in a bowl with 2 tablespoons water and some salt and pepper. Whisk together well.
2 Heat the butter in a small non-stick frying pan over high heat. When the butter is foaming, reduce the heat and add the egg mixture all at once. Swirl with a fork several times.
3 Cook until the eggs are almost set, tilting the pan and lifting the edge of the omelette occasionally to allow the uncooked egg to flow underneath.
4 Using an egg slice, fold the omelette in half in the pan. Flip it over onto a warm serving plate and serve immediately.

VARIATION: Sprinkle the omelette with shredded ham, bacon, fried mushrooms or freshly grated Gruyère cheese before folding.

An OMELETTE with fresh herbs makes a lovely light brunch.

HERB OMELETTE

Preparation: 10 minutes
Cooking: 5 minutes
Serves 2

4 eggs
2 tablespoons chopped fresh parsley
2 tablespoons chopped fresh chives
30 g (1 oz) butter
1/3 cup (40 g/1 1/4 oz) grated Cheddar

1 Break the eggs into a large bowl and whisk with a fork. Add 2 tablespoons of water and the parsley and chives. Season well.
2 Heat the butter in a small non-stick frying pan over high heat. When the butter is foaming, reduce the heat and add the omelette mixture all at once. Swirl with a fork several times.
3 While the mixture is cooking, tilt the pan and lift the edge of the omelette occasionally to allow the uncooked egg to flow underneath. When the mixture is half cooked, sprinkle with the grated cheese, then leave to cook a little more (the base should be golden brown and the inside nearly set). Using an egg slice, fold the omelette in half in the pan. Flip it over onto a warm serving plate and serve immediately.

For a weekend brunch a PANCAKE STACK is hard to beat.

PANCAKE STACK

Preparation: 5 minutes + 20 minutes resting
Cooking: 20 minutes
Serves 4

1 1/2 cups (185 g/6 oz) self-raising flour
1 teaspoon baking powder
2 tablespoons caster sugar
2 eggs, lightly beaten
1 cup (250 ml/8 fl oz) milk
60 g (2 oz) butter, melted
100 g (3 1/2 oz) butter
maple syrup, to serve

1 Sift the flour, baking powder, sugar and a pinch of salt into a bowl and make a well in the centre. Mix the eggs, milk and melted butter in a jug and pour into the well all at once, whisking to form a smooth batter. Cover the bowl with plastic wrap and set the batter aside to rest for 20 minutes. You could also mix the batter in a food processor.
2 Heat a frying pan and brush lightly with melted butter or oil. Pour 1/4 cup (60 ml/2 fl oz) batter into the pan and swirl gently to make a pancake about 10 cm (4 inches) in diameter. Cook over low heat for 1 minute, or until the underside is golden.
3 Turn the pancake over with a spatula and cook the other side very quickly, about 10 seconds. Transfer to a plate and keep warm while cooking the remaining batter. Whip the butter with a wooden spoon or electric beaters. Serve the pancakes stacked, warm or cold, with whipped butter and maple syrup.

VARIATION: For blueberry pancakes, add 1 cup (155 g/5 oz) of blueberries to the batter.

SWISS MUESLI

Preparation: 10 minutes
Cooking: Nil
Serves 2

1 apple, cored
1/2 cup (125 g/4 oz) thick plain yoghurt
2 tablespoons chopped almonds or hazelnuts
1 cup (100 g/3 1/2 oz) rolled oats

1 Grate the apple, including the skin. Mix well with the yoghurt, nuts and oats. Serve immediately. Delicious with fresh or canned fruit.

TOASTED MUESLI

Preparation: 20 minutes
Cooking: 50 minutes
Serves 10–12

3 cups (300 g/10 oz) rolled oats
1/3 cup (30 g/1 oz) desiccated coconut
1/3 cup (30 g/1 oz) wheat germ
2 tablespoons sunflower seeds
2 tablespoons sesame seeds
1/3 cup (50 g/1 3/4 oz) chopped almonds
50 g (1 3/4 oz) butter
2 tablespoons oil
3 tablespoons honey
1/3 cup (60 g/2 oz) chopped dried apricots
1/3 cup (30 g/1 oz) chopped dried apples
1/2 cup (60 g/2 oz) sultanas

1 Preheat the oven to moderate 180°C (350°F/Gas 4). Mix the oats, coconut, wheat germ, seeds and almonds in a baking dish.
2 Put the butter, oil and honey in a pan and stir over low heat until melted and warmed through.
3 Pour into the baking dish and stir to coat the dry ingredients. Bake for 45 minutes, stirring well every 10 minutes.
4 Leave until cold, then stir in the fruit. Keep in an airtight container for up to 4 weeks.

SWISS MUESLI.

TOASTED MUESLI.

Home-made MUESLI and TOASTED GRAPEFRUIT make a wholesome and delicious breakfast.

MUESLI

Preparation: 15 minutes
Cooking: Nil
Serves 8

2 cups (200 g/6 1/2 oz) rolled oats
2 tablespoons wheat germ
1/4 cup (20 g/3/4 oz) bran
1/2 cup (90 g/3 oz) dried apricots, chopped
1/2 cup (35 g/1 1/4 oz) dried apple, chopped
1/3 cup (40 g/1 1/4 oz) sultanas
1/2 cup (60 g/2 oz) slivered almonds

1 Combine all the ingredients in a bowl and mix well. Serve with milk. Keep in an airtight container for up to 4 weeks. Muesli is delicious served with fresh fruit, thick yoghurt and a drizzle of honey.

VARIATIONS: For a lighter muesli, use puffed corn or puffed rice instead of rolled oats. Also, experiment with your choice of nuts: try replacing the almonds with brazil nuts, hazelnuts or pecans. You can buy a packet of dried fruit salad and chop the fruit to use instead of the apricot, apple and sultanas.

TOASTED GRAPEFRUIT

Preparation: 2 minutes
Cooking: 2 minutes
Serves 2

1 grapefruit
2 tablespoons sugar

1 Cut the grapefruit in half. Place cut-side-up on a baking tray and sprinkle a tablespoon of sugar over each half. Grill under moderate heat until the sugar melts and bubbles.

HOME-MADE YOGHURT

Preparation: 20 minutes + 12 hours standing/chilling
Cooking: 5 minutes
Makes about 600 ml (20 fl oz)

2 cups (500 ml/16 fl oz) milk
2 1/2 tablespoons milk powder
2 tablespoons plain yoghurt

1 Combine 2 tablespoons of the milk with the milk powder to form a smooth paste. Add the remaining milk, whisking to ensure the mixture is free of lumps. Transfer to a medium pan and heat almost to boiling point.
2 Pour the mixture into a large casserole dish and cool until it is lukewarm. Blend 3 tablespoons of the lukewarm milk with the plain yoghurt, then gently stir it back into the remaining lukewarm milk. Cover with the lid of the casserole dish or foil.
3 Wrap the dish in thick towels or a blanket. Leave undisturbed in a warm place for 6–8 hours, or until thickened. Chill for at least 4 hours before using. Do not keep the yoghurt for more than 1 week—it becomes very acidic if it is stored for too long.

HINT: For a firmer consistency, wrap the yoghurt in a piece of muslin and hang over a bowl in the fridge overnight. Keep 1/4 cup (60 g/2 oz) of your yoghurt in a sealed jar in the refrigerator and use this as the starter for your next batch of yoghurt. Use within 3–4 days or the yoghurt will become acidic. Fruits and nuts can be added to the yoghurt just before serving.

BANANA SMOOTHIE

Preparation: 5 minutes
Cooking: Nil
Serves 2

2 bananas
1/4 cup (60 g/2 oz) plain yoghurt
1 tablespoon honey
2 tablespoons wheat germ
2 cups (500 ml/16 fl oz) milk
ground nutmeg, to taste

1 Put the bananas in a blender or food processor. Add the yoghurt, honey, wheat germ, milk and nutmeg.
2 Process or blend until smooth. Taste before serving and add more honey if you like.

VARIATION: Use other fresh fruit or drained canned fruit—berries are delicious. Fruit-flavoured yoghurt will add more flavour to your smoothie. Soy milk is a delicious, healthy alternative.

BREAKFAST SHAKE

Preparation: 10 minutes
Cooking: Nil
Serves 2

150 g (5 oz) fruit (mango, strawberries, blueberries, banana, passionfruit, peach)
1 cup (250 ml/8 fl oz) milk
2 teaspoons wheat germ
1 tablespoon honey
1/4 cup (60 g/2 oz) vanilla yoghurt
1 egg, optional
1 tablespoon malt powder

1 Put all the ingredients in a blender and blend for 30 seconds to 1 minute, or until well combined. Pour into chilled glasses and serve.

Clockwise from top: BREAKFAST SHAKE, HOME-MADE YOGHURT and a BANANA SMOOTHIE.

Dip the bread in eggy milk and fry, for FRENCH TOAST.

FRENCH TOAST

Preparation: 10 minutes
Cooking: 10 minutes
Serves 2

2 eggs
1 cup (250 ml/8 fl oz) milk
1/2 teaspoon vanilla essence
40 g (1 1/4 oz) butter
4 thick slices of day-old bread, halved diagonally
cinnamon and sugar, to serve

1 Break the eggs into a wide, shallow dish and add the milk and vanilla essence. Whisk well.
2 Melt half the butter in a frying pan. When the butter begins to foam, quickly dip both sides of the bread into the egg mixture, letting the excess run off, then fry in the butter for 1–2 minutes, or until the underside is golden. Turn the bread and cook the other side.
3 Transfer the cooked French toast to a warm plate and cover with foil. Add more butter to the pan as necessary and cook the remaining bread. Serve sprinkled with cinnamon and sugar. Also good with maple syrup, or lemon juice and sugar.

HASH BROWNS

Preparation: 10 minutes
Cooking: 20 minutes
Serves 4

2 large potatoes, halved
oil, for shallow-frying

1 Add the potato to a pan of boiling water. Return to the boil, then boil for 10 minutes, or until the potato is just tender when pierced with a knife.

Serve HASH BROWNS on their own, or with bacon and egg.

2 Drain the potatoes, and leave until cool enough to handle. Grate the potato and place in a bowl. Season with salt and pepper, and mix through.
3 Shape the grated potato roughly into patties about 10 cm (4 inches) round. The starchiness of the potato will hold the patties together.
4 Pour enough oil into a frying pan to cover the base. Heat up the oil and cook the patties over medium heat for 2–3 minutes on each side, or until golden and crispy. Drain on paper towels.

Worcestershire sauce adds tang to LAMB'S FRY AND BACON.

LAMB'S FRY AND BACON

Preparation: 20 minutes
Cooking: 15 minutes
Serves 4

500 g (1 lb) lamb's liver ('lamb's fry')
plain flour, to dust
30 g (1 oz) butter
1 tablespoon oil
2 onions, sliced
4 rashers bacon, chopped
1 1/2 cups (375 ml/ 12 fl oz) chicken stock
1 teaspoon Worcestershire sauce

1 Peel off and discard the outer membrane from the lamb's fry. Cut the lamb's fry into 1 cm (1/2 inch) slices. Put some of the flour in a shallow bowl and season with salt and pepper. Dust the lamb's fry with the seasoned flour and shake off the excess flour, reserving 2 tablespoons.
2 Heat the butter and oil in a frying pan and cook the onion over medium heat for 3 minutes, or until golden. Remove the onion from the pan and set aside.
3 Add the bacon to the pan and cook over medium heat until brown. Remove from the pan and set aside.
4 Add the lamb's fry to the pan and cook over high heat for 1 minute on each side, or until lightly browned. Return the onion to the pan. Blend the chicken stock, Worcestershire sauce and reserved flour in a jug. Pour into the pan and stir until the mixture boils and thickens. Reduce the heat to low and simmer for 3 minutes, or until the lamb's fry is tender. Stir in the cooked bacon. Serve immediately with toast.

NOTE: Lamb's fry should be pink in the centre when cooked. Do not be tempted to overcook it or it will become tough.

The dried fruits in the COMPOTE are simmered until plump.

DRIED FRUIT COMPOTE

Preparation: 10 minutes
Cooking: 15 minutes
Serves 4

400 g (13 oz) dried fruit salad (dried peaches, prunes, pears, apricots, apple and nectarines)
1 3/4 cups (440 ml/ 14 fl oz) orange juice
1 tablespoon soft brown sugar
1–2 star anise
1 vanilla bean, halved lengthways
yoghurt or crème fraîche, to serve

1 Put the dried fruit salad in a pan. Add the orange juice, sugar, star anise and vanilla bean.
2 Bring slowly to the boil, then reduce the heat, cover and leave to simmer, stirring occasionally, for 15 minutes, or until the fruit is plump and juicy.
3 Discard the star anise and vanilla bean. Serve the fruit drizzled with the cooking syrup and topped with the yoghurt or crème fraîche.

VARIATION: Try flavouring with a cinnamon stick and 2 cloves instead of the star anise and vanilla bean.

CITRUS SUMMER SALAD

Preparation: 15 minutes
Cooking: 5 minutes
Serves 4–6

3 ruby grapefruits
3 large oranges
1 tablespoon caster sugar
1 cinnamon stick
3 tablespoons whole mint leaves

1 Peel and remove the pith from the grapefruit and oranges. Carefully cut out the segments and mix together in a bowl.
2 Put the sugar, cinnamon stick and mint in a small pan with 3 tablespoons water and stir over low heat until the sugar has dissolved.
3 Remove the cinnamon stick and mint, and drizzle the syrup over the fruit. If you are serving this for a special occasion, garnish with fresh mint leaves.

VARIATION: Another good combination for a citrus fruit salad is mandarines, tangelos and pomelos when they are in season.
STORAGE: This salad can be kept in the refrigerator for up to 2 days and the flavour will actually improve as it develops.

Use ruby grapefruit for a colourful CITRUS SUMMER SALAD.

PORRIDGE can be served with sugar and plain yoghurt.

PORRIDGE

Preparation: 5 minutes
Cooking: 10 minutes
Serves 2

1 cup (100 g/3 1/2 oz) rolled oats
1/2 cup (125 ml/4 fl oz) milk
soft brown sugar, plain yoghurt, cream or extra milk, to serve

1 Mix the oats with 1 1/2 cups (375 ml/12 fl oz) cold water in a small heavy-based pan. Stir in the milk and bring to the boil.
2 Cook the oats for about 7 minutes, stirring constantly until thick and creamy. Serve immediately with soft brown sugar, yoghurt, cream or extra milk.

VARIATIONS: Stir 1/4 cup (30 g/1 oz) of sultanas into the mixture for the last 3 minutes of cooking. Serve the porridge with stewed apple or dried fruit compote (see opposite).
For a quick stove-top porridge, replace the rolled oats with 1-minute oats (these have been precooked). Cook for 1 minute, stirring constantly until thick.

OAT AND DATE MUFFINS

Preparation: 15 minutes
Cooking: 20 minutes
Makes 12

1 cup (125 g/4 oz) self-raising flour
1 cup (150 g/5 oz) wholemeal self-raising flour
1/2 teaspoon bicarbonate of soda
1 cup (100 g/3 1/2 oz) quick rolled oats
1/4 cup (45 g/1 1/2 oz) soft brown sugar
1 cup (185 g/6 oz) chopped pitted dates
1 egg, lightly beaten
2 tablespoons vegetable oil
1/4 cup (90 g/3 oz) golden syrup
1 1/4 cups (315 ml/ 10 fl oz) milk

1 Preheat the oven to moderately hot 200°C (400°F/Gas 6). Lightly grease twelve 1/2-cup (125 ml/4 fl oz) muffin holes. Sift the flour and bicarbonate of soda into a bowl and add the husks.
2 Stir in the rolled oats, brown sugar and dates. Make a well in the centre.
3 Combine the egg, oil, golden syrup and milk in a jug. Pour the liquid all at once into the dry ingredients and stir until just combined. Do not overmix—the dough should be lumpy.
4 Fill the muffin holes three-quarters full and bake for 20 minutes, or until well risen and golden brown. Cool in the tin for 5 minutes before transferring to a wire rack.

WHOLEMEAL MUFFINS

Preparation: 20 minutes
Cooking: 20 minutes
Makes 12

2 1/2 cups (375 g/12 oz) wholemeal self-raising flour
1/3 cup (75 g/2 1/2 oz) raw sugar
2 eggs, lightly beaten
75 g (2 1/2 oz) butter, melted
1 1/4 cups (315 ml/ 10 fl oz) buttermilk

1 Preheat the oven to hot 210°C (415°F/Gas 6–7). Lightly grease twelve 1/2-cup (125 ml/4 fl oz) muffin holes. Sift the flour into a large bowl, return the husks and stir in the sugar. Make a well.
2 Stir the combined egg, butter and buttermilk into the well. Don't overmix—the dough will be lumpy.
3 Spoon into the tin and bake for 15–20 minutes, or until golden brown. Transfer to a rack to cool.

CORNMEAL BREADS

Preparation: 15 minutes
Cooking: 25 minutes
Makes 12

2 cups (250 g/8 oz) plain flour
1 teaspoon salt
3 teaspooons baking powder
1 cup (150 g/5 oz) fine cornmeal
1 cup (125 g/4 oz) grated Cheddar
2 eggs, lightly beaten
90 g (3 oz) butter, melted
1 cup (250 ml/8 fl oz) milk

1 Preheat the oven to hot 210°C (415°F/Gas 6–7). Lightly grease twelve 1/2-cup (125 ml/4 fl oz) muffin holes. Sift the flour, salt and baking powder into a large bowl. Stir in the cornmeal and cheese and make a well.
2 Pour the combined egg, butter and milk into the well. Stir to just combine. Don't overmix—the dough should be lumpy.
3 Spoon into the tin and bake for 20–25 minutes, or until golden brown. Cool on a wire rack.

From the top: CORNMEAL BREADS; WHOLEMEAL MUFFINS; OAT AND DATE MUFFINS.

SOUPS

There are few more simple or delicious ways to prepare a meal than to throw some fresh seasonal ingredients into a saucepan with a handful of herbs and a cupful or two of stock or wine, and then leave it all to simmer lazily until the aroma becomes irresistible. There are no difficult techniques for making soups so they are an enjoyable part of every cook's repertoire.

SPRING VEGETABLE SOUP

Preparation: 30 minutes + overnight soaking
Cooking: 1 1/4 hours
Serves 8

- 1/2 cup (100 g/3 1/2 oz) pinto beans (see Note)
- 2 teaspoons olive oil
- 2 onions, finely chopped
- 2 cloves garlic, finely chopped
- 10 cups (2.5 litres) vegetable stock
- 2 celery sticks, finely chopped
- 2 carrots
- 2 potatoes
- 150 g (5 oz) green beans
- 2 zucchini
- 100 g (3 1/2 oz) shelled peas (see Hint)
- 2 tablespoons chopped fresh parsley

1 Soak the pinto beans in plenty of cold water overnight, then drain.
2 Heat the oil in a large pan, add the onion and cook over low heat until soft and translucent. Add the garlic and cook for 1 minute. Add the pinto beans, stock and celery and bring to the boil. Reduce the heat to low and simmer, covered, for 45 minutes, or until the beans are almost cooked.
3 Finely chop the carrots, potatoes, green beans and zucchini and add to the pan. Simmer gently for 15 minutes, or until the vegetables are almost cooked but still a little firm. Stir in the peas and simmer for a further 10 minutes. Season well and stir through the chopped parsley.

NOTE: If you can't find pinto beans, use borlotti beans or the smaller haricot beans.
HINT: If fresh peas aren't available, use frozen peas; add them to the soup during the last 5 minutes of cooking.

Always season soups (and also stews) at the end of the cooking time. As the liquid reduces, the flavours become stronger and you won't need as much salt. If you find you have overseasoned, simmer a slice of bread in the soup for 5 minutes: you will find it soaks up the excess salt.

SPRING VEGETABLE SOUP makes a hearty main meal when served with fresh bread.

If you don't have macaroni, use any small pasta variety for MINESTRONE.

MINESTRONE

Preparation: 30 minutes + overnight soaking
Cooking: 2¾ hours
Serves 6–8

- 1 1/4 cups (250 g/8 oz) dried borlotti beans
- 2 tablespoons oil
- 2 onions, chopped
- 2 cloves garlic, crushed
- 1/2 cup (80 g/2 3/4 oz) chopped bacon pieces
- 400 g (13 oz) can peeled chopped Italian tomatoes
- 1/4 cup (15 g/1/2 oz) chopped fresh parsley
- 9 cups (2.25 litres) beef or vegetable stock
- 1 carrot, chopped
- 1 swede, diced
- 2 potatoes, diced
- 1/4 cup (60 g/2 oz) tomato paste
- 2 zucchini, sliced
- 1/2 cup (90 g/3 oz) peas
- 1/2 cup (90 g/3 oz) small macaroni
- Parmesan and pesto (see page 180), to serve

1 Soak the borlotti beans in water overnight and drain. Add to a pan of boiling water, simmer for 15 minutes, or until tender, and drain. Heat the oil in a large heavy-based pan and cook the onion, garlic and bacon pieces, stirring, until the onion is soft and the bacon golden.
2 Add the tomato, parsley, borlotti beans and stock. Simmer, covered, over low heat for 2 hours. Add the carrot, swede, potato and tomato paste, cover and simmer for 15–20 minutes.
3 When you are nearly ready to serve, add the zucchini, peas and pasta. Cover and simmer for 10–15 minutes, or until the vegetables and macaroni are tender. Season to taste and serve topped with grated Parmesan cheese and a little pesto.

HINT: The macaroni can become soggy if left to sit around in the soup before serving. If you prefer, it can be cooked separately in boiling water and added to the soup just before serving. If you're short on time, use canned beans (drained well).

CHICKEN NOODLE SOUP

Preparation: 15 minutes + 1 hour refrigeration
Cooking: 1 hour 20 minutes
Serves 4–6

1.25 kg (2½ lb) chicken wings
2 celery sticks, chopped
1 carrot, chopped
1 onion, chopped
1 bay leaf
1 sprig fresh thyme
4 fresh parsley stalks
45 g (1½ oz) dried fine egg noodles, lightly crushed
250 g (8 oz) chicken breast fillets, diced
2 tablespoons chopped fresh parsley
chopped chives, to serve

1 To make the chicken stock, rinse the chicken wings and place in a large pan with the celery, carrot, onion, bay leaf, thyme, parsley stalks, 1 teaspoon salt and 8 cups (2 litres) of water. Bring to the boil slowly, skimming the surface as required to remove any froth. Simmer, covered, for 1 hour. Cool slightly, then strain the liquid, discarding the chicken and vegetables.
2 Leave the stock until cold, then cover and refrigerate for at least 1 hour, or until fat forms on the surface and can be spooned off.
3 Transfer the stock to a large pan and bring to the boil. Add the noodles, return to the boil and simmer for 8 minutes, or until tender. Add the chicken and parsley and simmer for a further 4–5 minutes, or until the chicken is cooked. Serve topped with the chives.

Lightly crush the noodles for CHICKEN NOODLE SOUP so they are in manageable lengths.

CHICKEN AND VEGETABLE SOUP

Preparation: 1 hour + cooling
Cooking: 1½ hours
Serves 6

1.5 kg (3 lb) chicken
2 carrots, roughly chopped
2 celery sticks, roughly chopped
1 onion, quartered
4 sprigs fresh parsley
2 bay leaves
2 teaspoons salt
4 black peppercorns
50 g (1¾ oz) butter
2 tablespoons plain flour
2 potatoes, chopped
250 g (8 oz) butternut pumpkin, cut into bite-sized pieces
2 carrots, extra, cut into matchsticks
1 leek, cut into matchsticks
3 celery sticks, extra, cut into matchsticks
100 g (3¼ oz) green beans, chopped
200 g (6½ oz) broccoli, cut into small florets
100 g (3¼ oz) sugar snap peas, trimmed
50 g (1¾ oz) English spinach, shredded
½ cup (125 ml/4 fl oz) cream
¼ cup (15 g/½ oz) chopped fresh parsley

1 Place the chicken in a large pan with the carrot, celery, onion, parsley, bay leaves, salt and peppercorns. Add 3 litres of water. Bring to the boil, then reduce the heat and simmer for 1 hour, skimming the surface as required. Allow to cool for at least 30 minutes. Remove the chicken and leave until cool enough to handle. Strain and reserve the liquid.
2 Remove the chicken skin and shred the chicken meat.
3 Heat the butter in a large pan over medium heat and, when foaming, add the flour. Cook,

Making chicken stock beforehand gives this CHICKEN AND VEGETABLE SOUP great flavour.

stirring, for 1 minute. Remove from the heat and gradually stir in the reserved liquid. Return to the heat and bring to the boil, stirring constantly. Add the potato, pumpkin and extra carrot, and simmer for 7 minutes. Add the leek, extra celery and beans, and simmer for 5 minutes. Finally, add the broccoli and sugar snap peas and cook for 3 minutes.

4 Just before serving, add the chicken meat, spinach, cream and parsley. Reheat gently and keep stirring until the spinach has wilted. Season with plenty of salt and freshly ground black pepper and serve immediately.

HINT: Do not overcook the vegetables—they should be tender but not soggy.

NOTE: The chicken stock (up to the end of Step 1) can be made a day in advance and kept, covered, in the refrigerator. This can, in fact, be beneficial—before reheating the stock, spoon off the fat which will have formed on the surface.

Serve FRENCH ONION SOUP with toasted cheese croûtes.

FRENCH ONION SOUP

Preparation: 15 minutes
Cooking: 1½ hours
Serves 6

60 g (2 oz) butter
6 onions (about 1 kg), sliced into thin rings
1 teaspoon sugar
¼ cup (30 g/1 oz) plain flour
9 cups (2.25 litres) beef stock
1 stick French bread, sliced
½ cup (65 g/2¼ oz) grated Gruyère cheese

1 Heat the butter in a large pan, add the onion and cook slowly over low heat for about 20 minutes, or until very tender and a deep golden brown (don't try to rush this stage).

2 Add the sugar and flour and cook, stirring, for 1–2 minutes, or until just starting to turn golden. Remove from the heat.

3 Stir in the stock gradually, return to the heat and stir until the soup boils and thickens. Reduce the heat and simmer, partially covered, over low heat for 1 hour. Season to taste.

4 Toast the bread on both sides until golden. Top with cheese and grill to melt. Serve the cheese croûtes on top of the soup.

A CHOWDER is a traditional thick soup containing potatoes.

SMOKED HADDOCK CHOWDER

Preparation: 20 minutes
Cooking: 35 minutes
Serves 4

500 g (1 lb) smoked haddock
1 potato, diced
1 celery stick, diced
1 onion, finely chopped
50 g (1 3/4 oz) butter
1 rasher bacon, rind removed, diced
2 tablespoons plain flour
1/2 teaspoon mustard powder
1/2 teaspoon Worcestershire sauce
1 cup (250 ml/8 fl oz) milk
1/2 cup (15 g/1/2 oz) chopped fresh parsley
1/4 cup (60 ml/2 fl oz) cream

1 To make the fish stock, put the fish in a frying pan, cover with water and bring to the boil. Reduce the heat and simmer for 8 minutes, or until the fish flakes easily when tested with a knife. Drain the fish, reserving the stock. Remove any bones and skin and flake the fish.
2 Put the potato, celery and onion in a pan and add enough of the fish stock to cover the vegetables (add water if necessary). Bring to the boil, reduce the heat and simmer for 8 minutes, or until the vegetables are all tender.
3 Melt the butter in a large pan, and cook the bacon, stirring, for 3 minutes. Stir in the flour, mustard and Worcestershire sauce. Cook for 1 minute, then remove from the heat and gradually pour in the milk, stirring continuously until smooth. Return to the heat and stir for 5 minutes, or until the mixture comes to the boil and thickens. Stir in the vegetables in their stock, then add the parsley and fish. Simmer the chowder over low heat for 5 minutes, or until heated through. Check the seasoning (smoked haddock can be quite salty so you may not need to add any more) and stir in the cream.

VARIATION: To make clam chowder, simply use 500 g (1 lb) fresh clams instead of the smoked haddock. Cook as for the smoked haddock chowder, but discard any clams which do not open when cooked. Alternatively, you can use 500 g (1 lb) drained canned clams.

Ask your butcher to chop the oxtails for OXTAIL SOUP.

OXTAIL SOUP

Preparation: 35 minutes + 2 hours refrigeration
Cooking: 2½ hours
Serves 4

2 oxtails, chopped (your butcher will do this)
2 tablespoons oil
3 onions, chopped
4 cloves garlic, chopped
1 tablespoon plain flour
4 cups (1 litre) beef stock
2 bay leaves, torn in half
2 tablespoons tomato paste
2 teaspoons Worcestershire sauce
4 potatoes, chopped
2 parsnips, chopped
2 carrots, chopped
3 tomatoes, chopped
2 tablespoons chopped fresh parsley

1 Cut the excess fat from the oxtail. Heat the oil in a heavy-based pan and brown the oxtail in batches. Return all the meat to the pan. Add the onion and garlic and cook until just softened. Add the flour and cook, stirring, for 1 minute. Mix in half the stock and bring to the boil, stirring. Remove from the heat and refrigerate for 2 hours, or until the fat can be spooned from the surface.
2 Add the remaining stock, 1 litre of water, the bay leaves, tomato paste, Worcestershire sauce and salt and pepper. Bring to the boil, reduce the heat to low and simmer, covered, for 2 hours, stirring occasionally.
3 Add the potato, parsnip and carrot and simmer for 10 minutes, or until tender. Remove the bay leaves before serving. Serve with the chopped tomato and parsley as a garnish.

Fresh ripe tomatoes will give the best flavour to CREAM OF TOMATO SOUP.

CREAM OF TOMATO SOUP

Preparation: 25 minutes
Cooking: 30 minutes
Serves 4

- 1.25 kg (2 1/2 lb) ripe tomatoes
- 1 tablespoon oil
- 1 onion, chopped
- 1 1/2 cups (375 ml/ 12 fl oz) chicken stock
- 2 tablespoons tomato paste
- 1 teaspoon sugar
- 1 cup (250 ml/8 fl oz) cream

1 To peel the tomatoes, score a cross in the base of each tomato with a sharp knife. Put the tomatoes in a bowl, cover with boiling water and leave for 1 minute. Transfer them to a bowl of cold water and peel away the skin from the cross. Cut the tomatoes in half around their equators and scoop out the seeds with a teaspoon. Roughly chop the flesh.

2 Heat the oil in a large pan and cook the onion over moderate heat for 3 minutes, or until soft. Add the tomato and cook, stirring occasionally, for 5 minutes, or until very soft. Stir in the stock, bring to the boil, reduce the heat and simmer for 10 minutes.

3 Cool slightly, then transfer to a food processor or blender. Process in batches until smooth, then return to the pan. Add the tomato paste and sugar and bring to the boil, stirring. Reduce the heat and stir in the cream. Season and serve with a swirl of cream and a little chopped parsley.

VARIATION: If good fresh tomatoes are not available, use tinned. Cook the onion and garlic as above, then add 3 undrained 400 g (13 oz) cans of tomatoes to the pan with 2 cups (500 ml/16 fl oz) stock, 1 tablespoon tomato paste and 2 teaspoons soft brown sugar. Partially cover the pan and simmer for 20 minutes. Purée before adding the cream.
NOTE: Shop-bought stock can be very salty—if you are using it for soups you may prefer to use half stock, half water.

PEA AND HAM SOUP

Preparation: 20 minutes + 4–8 hours soaking
Cooking: 2½ hours
Serves 4–6

2 cups (440 g/14 oz) green split peas
750 g (1½ lb) ham bones
1 celery stick, including leaves, chopped
1 carrot, chopped
1 onion, chopped
3 leeks, sliced
1 potato, chopped

1 Place the split peas in a large bowl, cover with water and leave to soak for 4–8 hours. Drain.
2 Put the ham bones, split peas, celery, carrot and onion in a large pan with 2.5 litres of water. Bring to the boil, then reduce the heat and simmer, covered, for 2 hours, or until the split peas are very soft.
3 Add the leek and potato and cook for 30 minutes, or until the vegetables are tender and the ham is falling off the bone.
4 Remove the ham bones from the soup; cut off all the meat and finely chop.
5 Transfer the soup to a bowl to cool, then push it through a large wire sieve. Return the soup to the pan, stir in the chopped ham and reheat the soup to serve.

NOTE: For a chunkier soup, don't push the mixture through a sieve. Alternatively, mash lightly with a potato masher.
HINT: This is a great recipe for using up your ham bones at Christmas. Some ham can be quite salty—soaking the bone in cold water overnight will draw out a lot of the saltiness. Always taste at the end of cooking before adding extra salt.

Soak the split peas before making PEA AND HAM SOUP.

WON TON SOUP

Preparation: 45 minutes + 30 minutes soaking
Cooking: 20 minutes
Serves 4

4 dried Chinese mushrooms
4 spring onions, very finely sliced, to garnish
125 g (4 oz) pork and veal mince
60 g (2 oz) raw prawn meat, finely chopped
3 teaspoons soy sauce
1 teaspoon sesame oil
1 spring onion, chopped
2 teaspoons grated fresh ginger
1 tablespoon finely chopped water chestnuts
24 won ton wrappers
5 cups (1.25 litres) chicken stock

1 Place the mushrooms in a small bowl, cover with boiling water and leave to soak for 30 minutes. Meanwhile, to prepare the garnish, put the very fine strips of spring onion in a bowl of icy cold water (this makes the strips curl elegantly).

Garnish your WON TON SOUP with curled strips of spring onion.

2 Drain the mushrooms well, using your hands to squeeze out the excess liquid. Remove the stems and chop the caps finely. Mix together the mushrooms, mince, prawn meat, soy sauce, sesame oil, chopped spring onion, ginger, water chestnuts and a little salt.
3 Working with one won ton wrapper at a time (cover the other wrappers with a damp tea towel), place a level teaspoon of the filling in the centre of each wrapper. Moisten the edges of the wrapper with a little water and bring the sides up to form a pouch. As you fill the won tons set them aside on a plate dusted with flour.
4 Cook the won tons in batches in a large pan of rapidly boiling water for 4–5 minutes, then drain. Bring the stock to the boil in another pan. Put the won tons in small bowls, garnish with the curls of spring onion and pour in the hot stock.

NOTE: Won ton wrappers are available from Asian food stores and can be frozen very successfully.

For a special occasion serve PUMPKIN SOUP in a hollowed pumpkin shell.

PUMPKIN SOUP

Preparation: 25 minutes
Cooking: 40 minutes
Serves 4

1 kg (2 lb) pumpkin
60 g (2 oz) butter
1 onion, chopped
4 cups (1 litre) chicken stock
3/4 cup (185 ml/6 fl oz) cream

1 Peel the pumpkin and chop into chunks. Heat the butter in a large pan, add the onion and cook gently for 15 minutes, or until soft.
2 Add the pumpkin and stock and simmer, covered, for 20 minutes, or until the pumpkin is tender. Allow to cool a little, then process in batches in a food processor or blender until smooth. Return the soup to the pan.
3 Stir in the cream and stir over low heat to heat through. Season with salt and pepper to taste. If you like, swirl in a little more cream to serve.

HINT: If you have time, bake your pumpkin and onion, then transfer to a pan, stir in the stock and cream and heat through.

CREAM OF CHICKEN SOUP is simple but enduringly popular.

CREAM OF CHICKEN SOUP

Preparation: 15 minutes
Cooking: 20 minutes
Serves 4

60 g (2 oz) butter
1/3 cup (40 g/1 1/4 oz) plain flour
2 cups (500 ml/16 fl oz) chicken stock
1 cup (250 ml/8 fl oz) milk
1 chicken breast fillet, finely chopped
1 cup (250 ml/8 fl oz) cream
1 celery stick, chopped
fresh parsley, to serve

1 Melt the butter in a large pan, add the flour and stir over low heat for 2 minutes, or until lightly golden. Remove from the heat and add the stock gradually, stirring until smooth. Return to the heat and stir until it comes to the boil and thickens.
2 Add the milk, chicken, cream and celery. Simmer for 5 minutes, or until the chicken is tender. Season and sprinkle with parsley.

VICHYSSOISE

Preparation: 20 minutes
Cooking: 25 minutes
Serves 4

60 g (2 oz) butter
2 leeks, chopped
2 large potatoes, chopped
3 cups (750 ml/24 fl oz) chicken stock
1 cup (250 ml/8 fl oz) milk
sour cream and chives, to serve

1 Heat the butter in a large pan and cook the leek for 5 minutes, or until soft.
2 Add the potato and stock and simmer for 15–20 minutes, or until

VICHYSSOISE can be served warm or chilled.

the potato is tender. Stir in the milk and season with salt and pepper.
3 Let the soup cool a little, then blend in a food processor or blender, in batches, until smooth. Vichyssoise is traditionally served well chilled but if you prefer to serve it hot, return to the pan and reheat gently without boiling. Whether hot or chilled, spoon sour cream on top and sprinkle with chives to serve.

NOTE: Vichyssoise is a classic chilled cream soup which was created at the Ritz-Carlton, New York.

CREAM OF BROCCOLI SOUP

Preparation: 15 minutes
Cooking: 25 minutes
Serves 4

750 g (1 1/2 lb) broccoli
3 cups (750 ml/24 fl oz) chicken stock
pinch of ground nutmeg
1 cup (250 ml/8 fl oz) cream

1 Cut the broccoli stems and florets into chunks. Place in a large pan with 1 cup (250 ml/8 fl oz) of stock, cover and bring to the boil. Reduce the heat to low, cover and simmer for 10 minutes, or until tender, stirring often.
2 Let the soup cool a little, then blend in batches in a food processor or blender. Return to the pan with the remaining stock. Add the nutmeg and cream and stir over moderate heat until heated through. Before serving, season to taste with salt and freshly ground black pepper.

HINT: If you prefer a chunkier soup, in step 2 transfer a batch of the mixture to a food processor or blender and process until finely chopped. Add a little of the remaining stock and blend to a purée. Return to a pan. Transfer the remaining broccoli and stock to the processor in batches and process until finely chopped. Return all the soup to the pan, add the nutmeg and cream and heat through.
VARIATION: Make creamy cauliflower soup in exactly the same way, simply substituting cauliflower for broccoli.

CREAM OF BROCCOLI SOUP has a fine colour and flavour.

VEGETABLE SOUP

Preparation: 25 minutes + overnight soaking
Cooking: 1 hour
Serves 6

1 cup (220 g/7 oz) dried soup mix
2 tablespoons oil
1 large onion, chopped
1 green capsicum, chopped
2 zucchini, sliced
2 celery sticks, sliced
125 g (4 oz) button mushrooms, sliced
2 carrots, sliced
1 large potato, chopped
500 g (1 lb) pumpkin, peeled and chopped
8 cups (2 litres) vegetable stock

1 Soak the soup mix in water overnight, then drain. Heat the oil in a large heavy-based pan and cook the onion over medium heat for 5 minutes, or until soft. Add the capsicum, zucchini, celery and mushrooms and cook for about 5 minutes.
2 Stir in the carrot, potato and pumpkin. Pour in the stock and add the soup mix. Bring to the boil, then reduce the heat.
3 Partially cover the soup with a loose-fitting lid and simmer for 45 minutes, or until the vegetables and soup mix are very soft. If you prefer a thinner soup add a little water. Season with salt and pepper before serving.

STORING: Vegetable soup will keep for 2 days in the fridge or can be frozen for 1 month.
NOTE: Soup mix is a mixture of dried barley, lentils and split peas and can be bought in packets at the supermarket.

Use the freshest seasonal produce for VEGETABLE SOUP.

SEAFOOD LAKSA

Preparation time: 45 minutes
Cooking: 45 minutes
Serves 6

1 kg (2 lb) raw prawns
1/2 cup (125 ml/4 fl oz) oil
2–6 red chillies, seeded
1 onion, roughly chopped
3 cloves garlic, halved
2 cm (3/4 inch) piece of ginger or galangal, quartered
1 teaspoon ground turmeric
1 tablespoon ground coriander
3 stalks lemon grass, white part only, chopped
1–2 teaspoons shrimp paste
2 1/2 cups (600 ml/ 20 fl oz) coconut cream
2 teaspoons grated palm sugar
4 kaffir lime leaves
200 g (6 1/2 oz) packet fish balls
190 g (6 1/2 oz) packet fried bean curd pieces

LAKSA, a coconut cream-based soup, originated in Singapore.

250 g (8 oz) fresh thin egg noodles
250 g (8 oz) bean sprouts
chopped fresh mint and coriander leaves, to serve

1 To make the prawn stock, peel and devein the prawns, keeping the shells, heads and tails. Heat 2 tablespoons of the oil in a large, heavy-based pan and add the prawn trimmings. Stir until bright orange, then add 1 litre of water. Bring to the boil, reduce the heat and simmer for 15 minutes. Strain through a fine sieve, discarding the shells. Clean the pan.
2 Put the chillies, onion, garlic, ginger (or galangal), turmeric, coriander, lemon grass and 3 tablespoons of the prawn stock in a food processor and process until finely chopped.
3 Heat the remaining oil in the clean pan and add the chilli mixture and shrimp paste. Stir over medium heat for 3 minutes, or until fragrant. Pour in the remaining stock and simmer for 10 minutes. Add the coconut cream, palm sugar, lime leaves and 2 teaspoons of salt. Simmer for 5 minutes.
4 Add the prawns and simmer for 2 minutes, or until just pink. Remove and set aside. Add the fish balls and bean curd and simmer gently until just heated through.
5 Bring a pan of water to the boil and cook the noodles for 2 minutes. Drain and divide among bowls. Top with the bean sprouts and prawns and pour the soup over the top. Sprinkle with the chopped mint and coriander leaves to serve.

VARIATIONS: For chicken laksa, replace the seafood with 1 kg (2 lb) chicken thigh fillets, thinly sliced. Use chicken stock instead of prawn stock. Laksa can also be made with fresh or dried rice noodles. Shredded cucumber can be added with the bean sprouts and, for a really fiery finish, garnish with red chilli.

HOT BEEF BORSCHT

Preparation: 30 minutes
Cooking: 2¾ hours
Serves 4

500 g (1 lb) shin of beef, cut into large pieces
500 g (1 lb) beetroot
1 onion, finely chopped
1 carrot, cut into short strips
1 parsnip, cut into short strips
1 cup (60 g/2 oz) finely shredded cabbage

1 Put the meat in a large heavy-based pan with 4 cups (1 litre) water and bring slowly to the boil. Reduce the heat, cover and simmer for 1 hour, skimming the surface as required, to remove any froth or scum.
2 Cut away the stems from the beetroot, leaving about 2 cm (1 inch) of the stem above the bulb, and place in a large heavy-based pan with 4 cups (1 litre) water. Bring slowly to the boil, reduce the heat and simmer for 40 minutes, or until tender when pierced with a skewer or sharp knife. Drain, reserving 1 cup (250 ml/8 fl oz) of the liquid. Leave the beetroot to cool, then peel and grate—wear plastic or rubber gloves to prevent staining your hands.
3 Use tongs to remove the meat from the stock. Let the meat cool, then pull from the bones and cut into small cubes. Skim any fat from the stock. Return the meat to the stock and add the onion, carrot, parsnip and grated beetroot. Add the beetroot liquid, bring to the boil, reduce the heat, cover and simmer for 45 minutes. Add more beetroot liquid if you prefer a thinner soup.
4 Add the cabbage, stir and simmer for a further 15 minutes. Add salt and pepper and serve hot. Borscht is delicious with sour cream and chives.

STORAGE TIME: Hot beef borscht can be kept covered and refrigerated for up to 4 days or frozen for up to 1 month.
NOTE: Borscht is a very hearty main meal soup, a traditional favourite in the bitter cold of the Eastern European winters. It is best served as a main meal with rye or black bread.

Serve BORSCHT topped with a dollop of sour cream.

TOM KHA GAI is a traditional Thai soup of chicken in coconut milk.

TOM KHA GAI

Preparation: 20 minutes
Cooking: 20 minutes
Serves 4

5 cm (2 inch) piece fresh galangal or 5 slices dried (see Note)
6 kaffir lime leaves
1 stem lemon grass, white part only, quartered
1–2 teaspoons finely chopped red chillies
2 cups (500 ml/16 fl oz) coconut milk
2 cups (500 ml/16 fl oz) chicken stock
3 chicken breast fillets, cut into thin strips
1/4 cup (60 ml/2 fl oz) lime juice
2 tablespoons fish sauce
1 teaspoon soft brown sugar
1/4 cup (15 g/1/2 oz) fresh coriander leaves

1 Peel the galangal and cut it into thin slices. Mix the galangal, kaffir lime leaves, lemon grass and chilli with the coconut milk and stock in a large pan. Bring to the boil, reduce the heat and simmer for 10 minutes, stirring occasionally.

2 Add the chicken strips and simmer for 8 minutes. Mix in the lime juice, fish sauce and sugar. Serve with the coriander leaves and garnish with a few coriander sprigs.

NOTE: If you can't find fresh galangal, use 5 large slices of dried galangal instead. Soak in 1 cup (250 ml/8 fl oz) of boiling water for 10 minutes. Drain the galangal and cut into thin slices. Proceed with the recipe as above.

CONSOMME is a clear light soup, of beef or chicken.

BEEF CONSOMME

Preparation: 30 minutes + overnight refrigeration
Cooking: 5 hours
Serves 4–6

1 kg (2 lb) gravy beef, cut into small pieces
500 g (1 lb) beef bones with marrow, cut into small pieces (ask your butcher to do this)
1 leek, finely sliced
2 onions, quartered
2 carrots, chopped
2 sticks celery, chopped
6 black peppercorns
6 whole cloves
3 sprigs fresh thyme
3 sprigs fresh parsley
3 bay leaves
1 egg shell, crumbled
1 egg white, lightly beaten
2 tablespoons chopped fresh parsley

1 Preheat the oven to moderate 180°C (350°F/Gas 4). Put the gravy beef and bones in a single layer in a baking dish. Bake for 45 minutes, or until just lightly browned, turning once.

2 Put the meat, bones, vegetables, peppercorns, cloves, herbs, bay leaves and 1 teaspoon of salt in a large pan. Add 3 litres of water and slowly bring to the boil. Reduce the heat to low, cover and simmer for 4 hours. Set aside to cool slightly. Remove the beef bones and discard. Ladle the liquid through a muslin-lined sieve into a bowl—if you don't have any muslin, line the sieve with a clean dry chux cloth. Discard the remaining meat and vegetables.

3 Cover the liquid and refrigerate for several hours, or overnight. You will then be able to spoon off the fat from the top. Return to a clean pan with the egg shell and the lightly beaten egg white.

4 Slowly heat the stock to simmering and simmer for 10 minutes. A frothy scum will form on the surface. Remove from the heat and leave for 10 minutes. Skim the surface and ladle the stock through a muslin-lined sieve. Reheat, season if needed, and serve with the chopped parsley.

NOTE: The egg shells are added to clarify the soup.

MULLIGATAWNY

Preparation: 20 minutes
Cooking: 1¼ hours
Serves 6

30 g (1 oz) butter
375 g (12 oz) chicken thighs, skin removed
1 large onion, finely chopped
1 green apple, peeled, cored and finely chopped
1 tablespoon curry paste
2 tablespoons plain flour
3 cups (750 ml/24 fl oz) chicken stock
3 tablespoons basmati rice
1 tablespoon chutney
1 tablespoon lemon juice
3 tablespoons cream

1 Heat the butter in a large heavy-based pan and brown the chicken for 5 minutes. Remove the chicken from the pan. Add the onion, apple and curry paste to the pan. Cook for 5 minutes, or until the onion is soft. Stir in the flour and cook for 2 minutes, then remove from the heat and stir in half the stock until smooth. Return to the heat and stir until the soup boils and thickens.
2 Return the chicken to the pan with the remaining stock. Stir until boiling, then reduce the heat, cover and simmer for 1 hour. Add the rice for the last 15 minutes of cooking (make sure it is tender by the time you finish cooking).
3 Remove the chicken with tongs, bone and dice the meat finely and return to the pan. Add the chutney, lemon juice, cream and seasoning. For a thinner soup, add up to a cup of water.

NOTE: You could use chicken thigh fillets (which have no bones).

MULLIGATAWNY is a curry-flavoured soup of Anglo-Indian origin.

CHICKEN AND CORN CHOWDER

Preparation: 15 minutes
Cooking: 30 minutes
Serves 4

20 g (3/4 oz) butter
5 spring onions, finely chopped
2 rashers bacon, diced
1 celery stick, finely chopped
450 g (14 oz) potatoes, diced
2 cups (500 ml/16 fl oz) chicken stock
2 cups (350 g/11 oz) cooked diced chicken meat (or from a small barbecued chicken)
1 1/2 cups (375 ml/12 fl oz) milk
420 g (14 oz) can creamed corn

CHICKEN AND CORN CHOWDER.

1 Melt the butter in a large pan. Cook the spring onion, bacon and celery over medium heat for 3 minutes, or until cooked but not browned. Add the potato and cook for 2 minutes. Add the chicken stock. Cook for 20 minutes, or until the potato is tender.
2 Add the diced chicken, milk and creamed corn and heat through. Season to taste with black pepper before serving.

Purée the ASPARAGUS SOUP, then add the tender tips.

CREAM OF ASPARAGUS SOUP

Preparation: 20 minutes
Cooking: 55 minutes
Serves 4

1 kg (2 lb) asparagus
30 g (1 oz) butter
1 onion, finely chopped
4 cups (1 litre) chicken stock
1/4 cup (7 g/1/4 oz) fresh basil leaves, chopped
1 teaspoon celery salt
1 cup (250 ml/8 fl oz) cream

1 Break off the woody ends from the asparagus by holding each end of the asparagus and bending firmly. The asparagus will snap naturally where the woodiness ends. Cut off the asparagus tips and blanch (see page 38) in boiling water for 1–2 minutes, then refresh in cold water (so they stop cooking and keep their bright colour) and set aside. Chop the remaining asparagus spears into large pieces.
2 Melt the butter in a large pan and cook the onion for 3–4 minutes over low heat, or until soft and golden. Add the asparagus spears and cook for 2 minutes, stirring continuously.
3 Add the stock, basil and celery salt. Bring to the boil, reduce the heat and simmer gently, covered, for 30 minutes.
4 Check that the asparagus is well cooked and soft. If not, simmer for a further 10 minutes. Allow to cool slightly.
5 Process in batches in a food processor or blender until smooth. Sieve into a clean pan. Return to the heat, pour in the cream and gently reheat. Season with salt and white pepper, stir in the asparagus tips and serve immediately.

Use large field mushrooms for a chunky MUSHROOM SOUP.

CREAM OF MUSHROOM SOUP

Preparation: 30 minutes
Cooking: 15 minutes
Serves 4

500 g (1 lb) large field mushrooms
50 g (1 3/4 oz) butter
4 spring onions, finely chopped
3 cloves garlic, chopped
1 teaspoon chopped fresh lemon thyme
2 teaspoons plain flour
4 cups (1 litre) chicken or vegetable stock
1 cup (250 ml/8 fl oz) cream
fresh chives and thyme, to garnish

1 Thinly slice the mushroom caps, discarding the stalks. Melt the butter in a heavy-based pan and cook the spring onion, garlic and lemon thyme, stirring, for 1 minute, or until the garlic is golden. Add the mushrooms and 1/2 teaspoon each of salt and white pepper. Cook for 3–4 minutes, or until the mushrooms start to soften. Add the flour and cook, stirring, for 1 minute.
2 Remove from the heat and add the stock, stirring continuously until smooth. Return to the heat and bring to the boil, stirring. Reduce the heat and simmer gently for 2 minutes, stirring occasionally.
3 Stir the cream into the soup, then reheat gently, stirring. Season with salt and pepper and garnish with the chives and thyme to serve.

MEAT

Many of the most well-known recipes in the world are for meat. Succulent, tender and bursting with flavour, these are dishes that should inspire enthusiasm in every cook.

ROAST BEEF AND YORKSHIRE PUDDINGS

Preparation: 15 minutes + 30 minutes standing
Cooking: 2 hours
Serves 6

2.5 kg (5 lb) roasting beef (rib eye roast, rump, or Scotch fillet)
2 cloves garlic, crushed
2 teaspoons plain flour
2 tablespoons red wine
1 1/4 cups (315 ml/ 10 fl oz) beef stock

Yorkshire puddings
2 cups (250 g/8 oz) plain flour
pinch of salt
4 eggs
400 ml (13 fl oz) milk

1 Preheat the oven to very hot 240°C (475°F/ Gas 9). Rub the outside of the roasting beef with the garlic and some freshly cracked black pepper. Place on a rack in a baking dish and roast for 15 minutes.
2 Meanwhile, to make the Yorkshire puddings, sift the flour and salt into a bowl and make a well in the centre. Add the eggs and begin to whisk them. Gradually pour in the milk as you draw in the flour, whisking to a smooth batter. Pour into a jug, cover and leave for about 30 minutes.
3 Reduce the heat to moderate 180°C (350°F/ Gas 4), and roast the meat: 1 hour for rare beef and 1 1/2 hours for well done. Cover the meat loosely with foil and leave in a warm place for 15 minutes before carving. Increase the oven to hot 220°C (425°F/Gas 7).
4 Pour off all but a tablespoon of the pan juices into a jug. Pour 1 teaspoon of pan juice into each hole of a 12-hole, deep patty pan. (If there aren't enough pan juices, use oil or melted lard.) Heat in the oven for 2–3 minutes, or until lightly smoking. Pour in the pudding batter to three-quarters fill each hole, and bake for 5 minutes. Reduce the oven to moderately hot 200°C (400°F/Gas 6) and bake for 10 minutes, or until the puddings are risen, crisp and golden. While the puddings are baking, make the gravy.
5 Put the baking dish with the 1 tablespoon of pan juices on the stove over low heat. Add the flour and stir well to scrape all the bits from the bottom of the tin. Cook over medium heat, stirring, until the flour is well browned. Combine the wine and stock, and gradually stir into the flour mixture. Cook, stirring, until the gravy boils and thickens. Simmer for 3 minutes, then season to taste and serve with the sliced beef and Yorkshire puddings.

BEEF WELLINGTON

Preparation: 25 minutes
Cooking: 1 hour 35 minutes
Serves 6

1.2 kg (2 lb 7 oz) piece beef fillet or rib eye
1 tablespoon oil
125 g (4 oz) pâté
60 g (2 oz) button mushrooms, sliced
375 g (12 oz) block puff pastry, thawed
1 egg, lightly beaten
1 sheet ready-rolled puff pastry, thawed

1 Preheat the oven to hot 210°C (415°F/Gas 6–7). Trim the meat of any excess fat and sinew. Fold the thinner part of the tail end under and tie the meat securely with kitchen string at intervals.
2 Rub the meat with freshly ground black pepper. Heat the oil in a large frying pan. Add the meat and cook over high heat, browning well all over. Remove from the heat and leave to cool. Remove the string.
3 Spread the pâté over the top and sides of the beef. Cover with the mushrooms, pressing them onto the pâté. Roll the block pastry out on a lightly floured surface to make a rectangle large enough to completely enclose the beef.
4 Place the beef on the pastry, brush the edges with egg, and fold over to enclose the meat completely, brushing the edges of the pastry with the egg to seal and folding in the ends.
5 Put on a greased baking tray with the seam underneath. Cut leaf shapes from the sheet of pastry and use to decorate the Wellington, sticking with the egg. Brush the top of the pastry with the beaten egg. Cut a few slits in the top to allow the steam to escape. Brush the top and sides with egg and cook for 45 minutes for rare, 1 hour for medium or 1½ hours for well done. Leave in a warm place for 10 minutes before cutting into slices to serve.

NOTE: Cover the beef Wellington loosely with foil if the pastry begins to brown too much.

BEEF WELLINGTON is also known as Boeuf en croûte.

The STROGANOFF was named after a nineteenth century Russian diplomat, Count Paul Stroganoff.

BEEF STROGANOFF

Preparation: 25 minutes
Cooking: 30 minutes
Serves 6

- 1 kg (2 lb) piece rump steak
- 1/3 cup (40 g/1 1/4 oz) plain flour
- 1/4 teaspoon black pepper
- 3 tablespoons oil
- 1 large onion, chopped
- 500 g (1 lb) baby mushrooms
- 1 tablespoon ground sweet paprika
- 1 tablespoon tomato paste
- 2 teaspoons French mustard
- 1/2 cup (125 ml/4 fl oz) dry white wine
- 1/4 cup (60 ml/2 fl oz) chicken stock
- 3/4 cup (185 g/6 oz) sour cream
- 1 tablespoon finely chopped fresh parsley

1 Trim the meat of excess fat and sinew, and slice across the grain evenly into thin strips. Mix the flour and pepper in a plastic bag, add the meat and shake to coat. Shake off the excess seasoned flour.
2 Heat 2 tablespoons of the oil in a heavy-based pan. Brown the meat quickly in small batches over medium-high heat. Drain on paper towels.
3 Heat the remaining oil in the pan. Add the onion and cook over medium heat for 3 minutes, or until soft. Add the mushrooms and cook stirring, for 5 minutes.
4 Add the paprika, tomato paste, mustard, wine, stock and meat to the pan, and bring to the boil. Reduce the heat and simmer for 5 minutes, stirring occasionally. Add the sour cream and stir until just heated through—do not boil or the sour cream may split and look curdled. Sprinkle with the parsley just before serving. Serve with rice.

TRADITIONAL CORNED BEEF AND VEGETABLES

Preparation: 25 minutes + 1 hour soaking
Cooking: 2 hours
Serves 4

- 1.2 kg (2 lb 7 oz) corned silverside (beef)
- 10 whole cloves
- 1 onion
- 8 black peppercorns
- 2 bay leaves
- 2 tablespoons soft brown sugar
- 4 carrots
- 4 potatoes
- 1/4 large cabbage

Parsley sauce

- 40 g (1 1/4 oz) butter
- 2 tablespoons plain flour
- 2 cups (500 ml/16 fl oz) milk
- 2 tablespoons chopped fresh parsley

CORNED BEEF AND VEGETABLES is a great family meal.

1 Soak the beef in cold water for 1 hour, changing the water 3 times. Remove the beef from the water and pat dry. Using a sharp knife, cut a diamond pattern into the white layer of fat. Press the cloves into the flesh of the onion.

2 Place the beef in a large heavy-based pan. Add enough water to just cover the beef, and add the clove-studded onion, peppercorns, bay leaves and brown sugar. Cover and bring the water to a gentle simmer. Cook for about 1 1/2 hours, spooning the cooking liquid over the top of the meat occasionally. Do not allow the water to boil or the meat will become tough. While the beef is cooking, make the parsley sauce.

3 To make the parsley sauce, melt the butter in a pan over medium heat. When the butter is foaming, stir in the flour and cook, stirring, for 1 minute. Remove from the heat and add the milk, stirring constantly until the sauce is smooth. Return the pan to the heat and cook, stirring constantly, until the sauce boils and thickens. Boil for 1 minute further. Season well with salt and black pepper. Cover the surface of the sauce with baking paper to prevent a skin forming. Set aside.

4 When the meat is cooked and tender, remove it from the pan, wrap in foil and set aside for 15 minutes while cooking the vegetables. Halve the carrots and potatoes and add to the pan that the beef was cooked in. Simmer for 10 minutes, then add the wedge of cabbage and cook for about 4 minutes. Test all the vegetables with a sharp knife—when they are tender, remove them from the pan and set aside. Reserve about ½ cup (125 ml/4 fl oz) of the cooking liquid to add to the sauce.

5 To serve, remove the paper from the sauce, stir in the reserved cooking liquid and parsley, and stir over low heat until the sauce is heated through. Slice the meat and arrange on a serving platter. Slice the cabbage and arrange the vegetables around the meat. Spoon a little parsley sauce over the beef and serve the remaining sauce in a jug.

BEEF BOURGUIGNON

Preparation: 10 minutes
Cooking: 2 hours
Serves 6

1 kg (2 lb) topside or round steak, cubed
plain flour, seasoned with salt and black pepper
2 tablespoons oil
3 rashers bacon, rind removed, chopped
12 pickling onions
1 cup (250 ml/8 fl oz) red wine
2 cups (500 ml/16 fl oz) beef stock
1 teaspoon dried thyme
200 g (6½ oz) button mushrooms
2 bay leaves

1 Toss the meat in the seasoned flour to coat, shaking off the excess.

2 Heat the oil in a large pan and cook the bacon over medium heat. Remove from the pan, then add the meat and brown well in batches. Remove and set aside. Add the onions to the pan and cook until golden.

3 Return the bacon and meat to the pan with the remaining ingredients. Bring to the boil, reduce the heat and simmer, covered, for 1½ hours, stirring occasionally, until the meat is very tender.

STORAGE: Can be refrigerated in an airtight container for up to 3 days.

BEEF BOURGUIGNON means 'beef in the style of Burgundy' (a region of France).

Flambé the brandy sauce for the PEPPER STEAK, then add cream.

PEPPER STEAK

Preparation: 15 minutes + standing
Cooking: 15 minutes
Serves 4

4 pieces rib eye steak
1 clove garlic, halved
1 tablespoon oil
2 tablespoons black peppercorns
1 tablespoon white peppercorns (optional)
50 g (1 3/4 oz) butter
3 tablespoons brandy
1/2 cup (125 ml/4 fl oz) cream

1 Trim the meat of fat and sinew. Rub both sides of the steak with the cut edge of the garlic and then brush lightly with the oil. Coarsely crush the peppercorns and press in a thin layer all over the steaks. Leave for at least 30 minutes for the steak to absorb the flavours.
2 Heat the butter in a heavy-based frying pan and add the steaks. For rare steaks, cook the steaks for 3 minutes on each side. For medium steaks, lower the heat and cook for a further 2–3 minutes on each side. For well done, cook for a further 4–6 minutes on each side.
3 Remove the pan from the heat. Add the brandy, ignite using a long match or taper, then shake the pan until the flame subsides. Transfer the steaks to serving plates. Cover and keep warm. Add the cream to the pan, stirring to mix in the pan juices. Return to the heat and stir for 1–2 minutes to warm through. Pour over the steaks and serve.

NOTE: Use fillet or sirloin if preferred. Instead of brandy and cream, add 1 tablespoon lemon juice to the pan juices. Reheat until foaming, stirring to incorporate the pan juices. Pour over the steaks.

STEAK DIANE

Preparation: 20 minutes
Cooking: 20 minutes
Serves 4

4 fillet steaks (about 150 g/5 oz each)
2 cloves garlic, crushed
50 g (1 3/4 oz) butter
4 spring onions, finely chopped
2 teaspoons Dijon mustard
2 tablespoons Worcestershire sauce
1 tablespoon brandy
1/3 cup (80 ml/2 3/4 fl oz) cream
2 tablespoons finely chopped fresh parsley

1 Trim the fat and sinew from the steaks. Lay each steak between 2 sheets of plastic wrap and flatten it with a meat mallet or rolling pin until it is about 1.5 cm (1/2 inch) thick.
2 Spread the garlic over both sides of the steak and grind some black pepper over the top.
3 Heat half the butter in a frying pan and add the steaks. For rare steaks, cook over high heat for 3 minutes on each side. For medium steaks, lower the heat and cook for a further 1 minute on each side, and for well-done steaks cook for a further 3–4 minutes on each side. Remove the meat from the pan, cover loosely with foil and keep warm.
4 Heat the remaining butter in the pan, add the spring onion and cook for 1 minute. Add the mustard, Worcestershire sauce and brandy. Stir well to mix in all the bits from the base of the pan.
5 Stir in the cream and boil for 3–4 minutes, or until the sauce has reduced and thickened slightly. Stir in the parsley. Return the steaks to the pan so that they just heat through. Serve the steaks immediately with the sauce.

HINT: Sometimes it is good to have a little fat on your steak: if you enjoy your steak well done, a marbling of fat will make it less likely to dry out and become tough during cooking. To test if your meat is cooked to your liking, press the centre of the steak with cooking tongs. Rare steak will be springy to the touch, medium a little firmer, and well-done steak very firm. Don't pierce the steak with a skewer or knife—the juices will escape and the meat may dry out.

Use lean trimmed fillet steak for STEAK DIANE.

FILET MIGNON

Preparation: 5 minutes
Cooking: 15 minutes
Serves 4

4 pieces fillet steak (each about 4 cm/1 1/2 inches thick)
4 small rashers bacon, rind removed
30 g (1 oz) butter
2 teaspoons oil

1 Trim the meat of excess fat and sinew. Put the steaks between two sheets of plastic wrap and flatten with a meat mallet to 1.5 cm (1/2 inch) thick. Wrap a rasher of bacon around each steak and secure with a toothpick.
2 Heat the butter and oil in a heavy-based frying pan and add the steaks. For rare steaks, cook for 3 minutes on each side. For medium steaks, reduce the heat to medium-high and cook for a futher 2–3 minutes each side. Cook for a further 4–6 minutes each side for well done. Remove the toothpicks before serving.

FILET MIGNON is simple and relies on the best-quality meat.

STEAK SANDWICH

Preparation: 20 minutes
Cooking: 10 minutes
Serves 2

2 fillet steaks
30 g (1 oz) butter
1 small onion, cut into rings
4 slices thick toasting bread
2 lettuce leaves
1 small tomato, sliced
barbecue sauce

1 Trim any fat and sinew from the steaks. Put the steaks between two sheets of plastic wrap and flatten with a meat mallet or rolling pin, until about 5 mm (1/4 inch) thick. Nick the edges of the steak to prevent the meat curling as it cooks.
2 Melt the butter in a frying pan and fry the onion rings until soft and lightly golden.
3 Push the onion to one side of the pan. Add the steaks and cook for 1–2 minutes on each side. Keep warm.
4 Toast the bread and put some lettuce and tomato on two of the slices. Top with the steak, onions and barbecue sauce and remaining bread. Serve immediately.

A STEAK SANDWICH makes a quick and easy dish.

MEAT LOAF

Preparation: 20 minutes
Cooking: 1½ hours
Serves 6

- 1 kg (2 lb) lean minced beef
- 1 cup (100 g/3½ oz) dry breadcrumbs
- 1 onion, grated
- 2 teaspoons mixed dried herbs
- 1 egg
- 1 cup (250 ml/8 fl oz) tomato purée
- 2 tablespoons tomato sauce

1 Preheat the oven to moderate 180°C (350°F/Gas 4). Place the minced beef, breadcrumbs, onion, herbs, egg, tomato purée and some salt and pepper in a large bowl and mix together with your hands.
2 Shape the mixture into a firm loaf. Place in a greased baking dish and bake for 1 hour.
3 Carefully tip away any excess fat from the bottom of the baking dish. Spread the tomato sauce over the top of the meat loaf and bake for a further 30 minutes.

Spread the sauce over the MEAT LOAF and bake for 30 minutes.

BOMBAY CURRY

Preparation: 20 minutes
Cooking: 1–1¾ hours
Serves 4–6

- 1 tablespoon ghee or oil
- 1 kg (2 lb) beef or lamb, cubed
- 2 onions, chopped
- 2 cloves garlic, crushed
- 2 green chillies, chopped
- 1 tablespoon grated fresh ginger
- 1½ teaspoons turmeric
- 1 teaspoon ground cumin
- 1 tablespoon ground coriander
- ½–1 teaspoon chilli powder
- 1 teaspoon salt
- 400 g (13 oz) can crushed tomatoes
- 1 cup (250 ml/8 fl oz) coconut milk

1 Heat the ghee or oil in a large pan and brown the meat in small batches. Remove from the pan. Cook the onion, stirring, until it is just soft. Add the garlic, chilli, ginger, turmeric, cumin, coriander and chilli powder. Stir until just heated through.
2 Return the meat to the pan and stir until well coated with the spices.
3 Stir in the salt and tomatoes. Simmer, covered, for 1–1½ hours, or until the meat is tender.
4 Stir in the coconut milk and simmer, uncovered, for another 5 minutes, or until the sauce has thickened slightly.

NOTE: Fresh coriander leaves or raw, unsalted cashew nuts (available from health food stores and most supermarkets) make a good garnish for this dish.

BOMBAY CURRY.

BEEF IN BLACK BEAN SAUCE

Preparation: 15 minutes + 1 hour marinating
Cooking: 10 minutes
Serves 4

- 750 g (1½ lb) rump steak
- 2 cloves garlic, crushed
- 2 teaspoons grated fresh ginger
- 2 tablespoons dry sherry
- 1 tablespoon soy sauce
- 3 tablespoons peanut oil
- 2 onions, cut into wedges
- 1 large green capsicum, cut into strips
- 230 g (7½ oz) can sliced bamboo shoots, drained
- 2 tablespoons canned black beans, rinsed, chopped
- 1 tablespoon cornflour

1 Trim the meat of any fat and sinew and slice across the grain into long, thin strips. Combine the garlic, ginger, sherry and soy sauce in a non-metallic bowl. Add the meat, stirring to coat. Cover and refrigerate for at least an hour, turning occasionally. Drain the meat, reserving the marinade.

BEEF IN BLACK BEAN SAUCE is a classic, but easy, Chinese dish. Serve with rice.

2 Heat 1 tablespoon of the oil in a wok or heavy-based frying pan, swirling gently to coat the base and side. Cook the meat quickly in small batches over high heat until browned but not cooked through. Remove from the wok and drain on paper towels. Heat the remaining oil in the wok, swirling gently to coat the base and side. Add the onion and capsicum, and stir-fry over high heat for 3 minutes, or until the onion is soft. Add the bamboo shoots and black beans; cook for 1 minute.
3 Mix the cornflour and remaining marinade with 2 tablespoons water until smooth. Add to the wok with the meat and stir-fry over high heat until the meat is cooked through and the sauce has thickened. Serve immediately with rice.

STORAGE: Store the leftover black beans in an airtight jar in the refrigerator for up to 2 weeks.

RISSOLES WITH GRAVY

Preparation: 25 minutes
Cooking: 10 minutes
Serves 4

500 g (1 lb) beef mince
1 onion, finely chopped
2 tablespoons tomato sauce
1 teaspoon dried mixed herbs
1 egg, lightly beaten
1 cup (80 g/2¾ oz) fresh breadcrumbs
oil, for shallow-frying

Gravy
2 tablespoons plain flour
2 cups (500 ml/16 fl oz) chicken stock
1 tablespoon tomato paste
2 tablespoons chopped fresh parsley (optional)

1 Place the mince, onion, tomato sauce, herbs, egg and breadcrumbs in a bowl. Mix together well with your hands. Divide into eight portions and shape into patties.
2 Heat the oil in a large heavy-based pan and cook the rissoles four at a time. Cook over high heat for 1 minute on each side, turning once. Reduce the heat to medium and cook for 2 minutes on each side, or until cooked through. Drain on paper towels and keep warm.
3 To make the gravy, blend the flour with the chicken stock and tomato paste in a small jug until the mixture is smooth. Add to the pan juices and stir over medium heat for 3 minutes, or until the gravy boils and thickens. Strain, then stir in the chopped parsley. Serve with the rissoles.

Children love RISSOLES WITH GRAVY.

BEEF POT ROAST

Preparation: 20 minutes
Cooking: 2½ hours
Serves 6

2 kg (4 lb) piece of topside
1 tablespoon oil
60 g (2 oz) butter
6 baby onions
4 carrots, cut into chunks
3 parsnips, cut into chunks
1 cup (250 ml/8 fl oz) beef stock
bouquet garni
1 tablespoon plain flour

1 Remove the excess fat and sinew from the meat. Heat the oil and 40 g (1¼ oz) of the butter in a large heavy-based pan. Brown the meat all over, then remove from the pan.
2 Add the vegetables to the pan and cook over medium heat until golden brown, stirring

The vegetables are cooked with the meat, so BEEF POT ROAST is a complete one-pot meal.

occasionally. Remove from the pan.

3 Return the meat to the pan and add the beef stock and bouquet garni. Heat until simmering, cover with a tight-fitting lid and simmer for 2–2¼ hours, turning once or twice during cooking. Be sure to simmer gently and not boil, otherwise you will find the meat shrinks and toughens. Return the vegetables to the pan for the last 30 minutes of cooking.

4 Remove and discard the bouquet garni. Transfer the meat and vegetables to a serving plate, cover and keep warm. Combine the remaining butter with the flour to form a smooth paste (this is called a *beurre manié* and is used for thickening). Stir into the pan juices. Bring to the boil, whisking until the mixture thickens slightly. Serve with the meat.

VARIATION: Silverside and bolar blade can also be used for pot roast.

HAMBURGER WITH THE WORKS

Preparation: 20 minutes
Cooking: 20 minutes
Serves 4

500 g (1 lb) lean beef mince
1 onion, finely chopped
1 egg, lightly beaten
1/3 cup (25 g/3/4 oz) fresh breadcrumbs
2 tablespoons tomato sauce
1 teaspoon steak seasoning
40 g (1 1/4 oz) butter
2 onions, extra, cut in thin rings
oil, for cooking
4 slices Cheddar, halved
4 eggs, extra
4 slices rindless bacon, halved
4 large hamburger buns
shredded lettuce
1 large tomato, sliced
4 large beetroot slices
4 pineapple rings
tomato sauce, to serve

1 Place the beef mince, onion, egg, breadcrumbs, tomato sauce, steak seasoning and some salt and pepper in a large bowl. Use your hands to mix well. Divide into four portions and shape into round patties—the flatter the patties, the quicker they will cook.
2 Heat 30 g (1 oz) butter in a frying pan and cook the onion rings over medium heat until brown. Remove and keep warm.
3 Heat a frying pan or barbecue grill or flatplate and brush lightly with oil. Cook the patties for 3–4 minutes each side, or until cooked through. Place a cheese slice on each patty.
4 Heat the remaining butter in another frying pan and fry the eggs and the bacon separately. Halve and toast the buns and top each one with lettuce, tomato, beetroot and pineapple. Add a meat patty and finish with the onion, egg, bacon and tomato sauce.

Pile everything on, for your HAMBURGER WITH THE WORKS.

CHILLI CON CARNE is a traditional Mexican dish, meaning 'chilli with meat'.

CHILLI CON CARNE

Preparation: 10 minutes
Cooking: 50 minutes
Serves 4

1 tablespoon olive oil
1 onion, chopped
3 cloves garlic, crushed
1 celery stick, sliced
500 g (1 lb) lean beef mince
2 teaspoons chilli powder
pinch of cayenne pepper
1 tablespoon chopped fresh oregano
400 g (13 oz) can crushed tomatoes
2 tablespoons tomato paste
1 teaspoon soft brown sugar
1 tablespoon cider vinegar or red wine vinegar
420 g (13 oz) can red kidney beans, rinsed

1 Heat the oil in a large, heavy-based pan. Add the onion, garlic and celery and stir over medium heat for 5 minutes, or until softened.
2 Add the mince and cook over high heat for 5 minutes, or until well browned. Add the chilli powder, cayenne and oregano. Stir well and cook over medium heat for 5 minutes.
3 Mix in the tomatoes, tomato paste and 1/2 cup (125 ml/4 fl oz) of water. Leave the chilli to simmer for 30 minutes, stirring occasionally.
4 Add the sugar, vinegar and beans, and season with salt and freshly ground black pepper. Heat through for 5 minutes before serving.

NOTE: Chilli is most commonly served with rice, but why not try it with corn chips and a topping of sour cream?

THAI BEEF SALAD

Preparation: 35 minutes
Cooking: 10 minutes
Serves 4

3 cloves garlic, finely chopped
4 coriander roots, finely chopped
1/2 teaspoon freshly ground black pepper
1/4 cup (60 ml/2 fl oz) oil
400 g (13 oz) piece rump or sirloin steak
1 small soft-leaved lettuce
200 g (6 1/2 oz) cherry tomatoes, halved
1 Lebanese cucumber, cut into chunks
4 spring onions, chopped
1/2 cup (15 g/1/2 oz) fresh coriander leaves

Dressing
2 tablespoons fish sauce
2 tablespoons lime juice
1 tablespoon soy sauce
2 teaspoons chopped fresh red chilli
2 teaspoons soft brown sugar

1 Combine the garlic, coriander roots, pepper and 2 tablespoons of the oil. If you have a mortar and pestle, use it to finely grind the mixture. Alternatively, blend the mixture well in a food processor or spice blender. Spread evenly over the steak.

The beef should be rare and succulent in a THAI BEEF SALAD.

2 Heat the remaining oil in a heavy-based frying pan or wok over high heat. Add the steak to the pan and cook for about 4 minutes on each side, turning once only during the cooking time. Remove the steak from the pan and allow to cool.
3 To make the dressing, combine the fish sauce, lime juice, soy sauce, chilli and brown sugar in a small bowl, stirring until the sugar has dissolved.
4 Cut the cooled steak into thin strips across the grain. Arrange the lettuce on a plate and arrange the tomatoes on top, with the cucumber, spring onion and strips of steak. Drizzle with the dressing and scatter the coriander leaves over the top. Serve immediately.

HINT: Be careful that you don't overcook the steak—it should be pink and, therefore, succulent and tender.
NOTE: Ground herbs and spices are used extensively for flavouring in Asian cookery. Small amounts can be done with a mortar and pestle or a clean coffee grinder. For larger quantities, use a blender or food processor. To help clean the bowl after grinding spices, run some stale bread or rice through the processor.

BEEF NACHOS

Preparation: 30 minutes
Cooking: 25 minutes
Serves 4

oil, for cooking
400 g (13 oz) lean beef mince
1 onion, chopped
1–2 teaspoons chopped fresh chilli
1 tablespoon ground cumin
3 teaspoons ground coriander
1/4 cup (60 g/2 oz) tomato paste
1/2 cup (125 g/4 oz) bottled tomato pasta sauce or salsa
1/2 cup (115 g/4 oz) refried beans or 425 g (14 oz) can red kidney beans, drained and rinsed
corn chips, grated Cheddar cheese and sour cream, for serving
chilli powder, to sprinkle

Guacamole
1 ripe avocado
1 small onion, finely chopped
1 tomato, finely chopped
2 tablespoons chopped fresh coriander
2–3 tablespoons sour cream
3–4 teaspoons lemon juice
Tabasco, to taste

For a Mexican theme, serve BEEF NACHOS.

1 Heat a little oil in a frying pan and brown the beef mince in batches, stirring and breaking up any lumps with a fork or wooden spoon. Transfer to a bowl and set aside.
2 Add a little more oil to the pan and stir in the onion, chilli, cumin and coriander. Cook over medium heat for 2–3 minutes. Return the mince to the pan and stir in the tomato paste, pasta sauce and beans. Simmer for 5–10 minutes.
3 To make the guacamole, peel the avocado and mash the flesh in a bowl. Add the onion, tomato, coriander, sour cream and lemon juice. Mix well with a fork. Add some salt, freshly ground black pepper and Tabasco.
4 Spoon the mince into a large ovenproof dish. Arrange the corn chips around the mixture and sprinkle with the cheese. Place under a preheated grill or in a moderate 180°C (350°F/Gas 4) oven for about 5–10 minutes, or until the cheese has melted. Top with the guacamole, a spoonful of sour cream and a dash of chilli powder.

NOTE: Traditionally, nachos were made using shredded cooked beef rather than mince.

LAMB SHANKS are an excellent cut for long slow cooking in a casserole.

MINTY LAMB SHANKS

Preparation: 20 minutes
Cooking: 2¼ hours
Serves 6

2 tablespoons olive oil
6 lamb shanks
1 red onion, chopped
2 cloves garlic, crushed
1 sprig fresh thyme
2 bay leaves
¾ cup (35 g/1¼ oz) chopped fresh mint
425 g (14 oz) can crushed tomatoes
2 cups (500 ml/16 fl oz) vegetable stock
3 tablespoons white wine

1 Preheat the oven to moderately hot 200°C (400°F/Gas 6). Heat a tablespoon of oil in a flameproof baking dish on the stove top. Brown the shanks in batches then remove from the heat and return them all to the dish in a single layer, close together. Season with salt and pepper and bake for 20 minutes. Turn over, reduce the heat to 180°C (350°F/Gas 4) and bake for a further 20 minutes.
2 Heat the remaining oil in a heavy-based frying pan. Add the onion and garlic and fry for 5–8 minutes, or until soft. Stir in the thyme, bay leaves and ½ cup (25 g/¾ oz) of the mint leaves. Scatter the onion and herbs over the meat, return to the oven and bake for 15 minutes.
3 Combine the tomato, stock and wine and pour over the meat. Cover the dish tightly with foil or a lid and bake for a further 1¼ hours. Garnish with the remaining mint and serve with pasta. The flavour of the dish actually improves if it is made a day or two in advance and refrigerated.

SHEPHERD'S PIE

Preparation: 30 minutes
Cooking: 1 hour
Serves 6

750 g (1 1/2 lb) lean cooked roast lamb
25 g (3/4 oz) butter
2 onions, chopped
3 tablespoons plain flour
1/2 teaspoon mustard powder
1 1/2 cups (375 ml/12 fl oz) chicken stock
2 tablespoons Worcestershire sauce

Potato topping
1/2 cup (125 ml/4 fl oz) hot milk
30 g (1 oz) butter
4 large potatoes, cooked and mashed

SHEPHERD'S PIE is always made with cooked lamb.

1 Grease a 2 litre casserole dish and preheat the oven to hot 210°C (415°F/Gas 6–7). Trim the meat of any fat and cut it into small cubes. Melt the butter in a large pan. Add the onion and cook until golden.
2 Sprinkle the flour and mustard into the pan and stir for 1 minute. Remove from the heat, gradually add the stock and stir until smooth. Return to the heat, bring to the boil, then reduce the heat and simmer for 3 minutes.
3 Add the meat and Worcestershire sauce to the pan and stir. Season with salt and pepper. Remove from the heat and spoon the mixture into the casserole dish.
4 To make the potato topping, mix the milk, butter and salt and pepper, to taste, into the mashed potato. Spread evenly over the meat and rough up the surface with a fork. Bake for 40–45 minutes, or until the topping is lightly golden and the pie is completely heated through.

NOTE: To make a really creamy mash, push the potato through a sieve with the back of a spoon, before mixing in the milk and butter.

Shepherd's pie is so called because it is always made with lamb. Cottage pie is made with beef mince, which is cooked with the onion and other vegetables to make the pie filling. It too has a mashed potato topping.

ROASTED RACK OF LAMB

Preparation: 15 minutes
Cooking: 45 minutes
Serves 4

2 six-cutlet racks of lamb
1 tablespoon olive oil

1 Preheat the oven to moderate 180°C (350°F/Gas 4). Trim the meat of excess fat and sinew, brush with the oil and season with freshly ground black pepper. Wrap the ends of the bones in foil to prevent them burning.
2 Place the meat, with the bones upright and interlocking, in a baking dish. Bake for 40 minutes. When cooked, transfer to a plate, cover with foil and set aside for 5 minutes before carving. Cut the racks into portions of three cutlets to serve.

MINTED RACK OF LAMB

Preparation: 15 minutes
Cooking: 45 minutes
Serves 4

4 four-cutlet racks of lamb
1 cup (300 g/10 oz) mint jelly
2 tablespoons white wine
1/4 cup (15 g/1/2 oz) chopped fresh chives

1 Preheat the oven to moderately hot 200°C (400°F/Gas 6). Trim any excess fat from the racks of lamb, leaving a thin layer of fat, and clean any meat or sinew from the bones with a small sharp knife. Cover the bones with foil. Place on a rack in a baking dish.
2 Mix the mint jelly and white wine together in a small pan over high heat. Cook for about 4 minutes, or until the mixture is reduced and thickened. Cool slightly, then add the chives.
3 Brush the racks of lamb with the glaze. Roast for 35 minutes for rare or 40 minutes for medium rare, brushing with the glaze every 10 minutes. Remove the foil from the lamb and leave for 5 minutes before serving.

VARIATIONS: For a mustard-crusted rack of lamb, spread the lamb with wholegrain mustard. Alternatively, mix 2 cups (160 g/5 1/2 oz) fresh breadcrumbs with a lightly beaten egg and chopped mixed herbs, press onto the lamb and bake for 40 minutes. Cover with foil if the crumbs are overbrowning.

RACKS OF LAMB are particularly good with a mint glaze.

Fry CRUMBED LAMB CUTLETS a few at a time to get a good crunchy finish.

CRUMBED LAMB CUTLETS

Preparation: 30 minutes + 30 minutes chilling
Cooking: 30 minutes
Serves 4

12 lamb cutlets
1/4 cup (30 g/1 oz) plain flour
2 eggs
1 1/2 cups (150 g/5 oz) dry breadcrumbs
oil, for shallow-frying

1 Trim the cutlets of excess fat and sinew. Season the flour with salt and pepper on a sheet of greaseproof paper. Toss the cutlets lightly in the seasoned flour and then shake off any excess.
2 Break the eggs into a shallow bowl and beat lightly with a fork. Dip each cutlet into the egg, drain off the excess, and then quickly coat with the breadcrumbs. Using your fingers, press the crumbs lightly onto the cutlets, then shake off any excess.
3 Place the cutlets in a single layer on a paper-lined tray. Cover and refrigerate for 30 minutes. Heat the oil in a frying pan and add the cutlets a few at a time. Cook over medium heat for about 3 minutes on each side, or until golden and tender. Do not have the oil too hot or the crumbs will burn before the meat is cooked through. Drain on paper towels and serve immediately.

Serve ROAST LEG OF LAMB with roast vegetables and mint sauce.

ROAST LEG OF LAMB WITH MINT SAUCE

Preparation: 20 minutes
Cooking: 1¾ hours
Serves 6

2 kg (4 lb) leg of lamb
2 cloves garlic, cut into thin slivers
2 tablespoons fresh rosemary sprigs
2 teaspoons oil

Mint sauce
3 tablespoons caster sugar
½ cup (10 g/¼ oz) fresh mint leaves
¾ cup (185 ml/6 fl oz) malt vinegar

1 Preheat the oven to moderate 180°C (350°F/Gas 4). Using a small sharp knife, cut small slits all over the lamb. Push the garlic and rosemary into the slits.
2 Brush the lamb with the oil and sprinkle with salt and black pepper. Place on a rack in a baking dish. Add ½ cup (125 ml/4 fl oz) water to the dish.
3 Roast for about 1½ hours for medium, or 1¾ hours for well done, basting often with the pan juices. Keep warm and leave for 10–15 minutes before serving.
4 To make the mint sauce, sprinkle 1 tablespoon of the caster sugar over the mint leaves on a chopping board. Chop the mint finely. Place in a bowl and add the remaining caster sugar. Cover with 3 tablespoons boiling water and stir until the sugar has dissolved. Stir in the vinegar. Serve with the roast lamb.

LANCASHIRE HOTPOT

Preparation: 20 minutes
Cooking: 2¼ hours
Serves 8

8 forequarter lamb chops, cut 2.5 cm (1 inch) thick
4 lamb kidneys, cut in quarters, cores removed
¼ cup (30 g/1 oz) plain flour
50 g (1¾ oz) butter
4 potatoes, thinly sliced
2 large onions, sliced
2 celery sticks, chopped
1 large carrot, chopped
1¾ cups (440 ml/14 fl oz) chicken or beef stock
200 g (6½ oz) button mushrooms, sliced
2 teaspoons chopped fresh thyme
1 tablespoon Worcestershire sauce

1 Preheat the oven to warm 160°C (315°F/Gas 2–3). Brush a large casserole dish with melted butter or oil. Trim the meat of excess fat and sinew, and toss the chops and kidneys in the flour, shaking off the excess.
2 Heat the butter in a large frying pan and quickly brown the chops, in batches, on both sides. Remove the chops from the pan and brown the kidneys. Layer half the potato slices in the base of the dish and place the chops and kidneys on top of them.
3 Add the onion, celery and carrot to the pan and cook until the carrot begins to brown. Layer on top of the chops and kidneys. Sprinkle the remaining flour over the base of the pan and cook, stirring, until brown. Remove from the heat, pour in a little stock and stir until smooth. Add the rest of the stock gradually, return to the heat and stir until the mixture boils and thickens.
4 Add the mushrooms, thyme and Worcestershire sauce and season to taste with salt and black pepper. Reduce the heat and leave to simmer for 10 minutes. Pour into the casserole dish.
5 Layer the remaining potato over the top of the casserole, to cover the meat and vegetables. Bake, covered, for 1¼ hours. Uncover and cook for a further 30 minutes, or until the potatoes are brown.

Use lamb chops and kidneys in a LANCASHIRE HOTPOT.

IRISH STEW

Preparation: 20 minutes
Cooking: 2½ hours
Serves 4

1 kg (2 lb) lamb neck chops
3 tablespoons plain flour
4 onions, sliced
8 potatoes (about 2 kg/ 4 lb), quartered
¼ cup (15 g/½ oz) chopped fresh parsley

1 Preheat the oven to warm 160°C (315°F/ Gas 2–3). Trim the lamb chops of fat and sinew and toss in the flour. Shake off the excess flour.
2 Place the chops in a 2 litre ovenproof dish with the onion and 2 cups (500 ml/16 fl oz) water. Bake, covered, for 1½ hours.
3 Add the potato and bake, covered, for 1 hour, or until the meat and potato are tender. Stir in the parsley just before serving.

NOTE: Traditionally Irish stew was made using mutton, which is no longer such a popular meat. We've modernized our version to use lamb.

IRISH STEW is a simple but satisfying meal.

ROAST PORK AND APPLE SAUCE

Preparation: 30 minutes
Cooking: 3¼ hours
Serves 6–8

4 kg (8 lb) leg of pork
oil and salt

Apple sauce
6 green apples
2 tablespoons caster sugar
2 cloves
1 cinnamon stick
1–2 teaspoons lemon juice

Gravy
1 tablespoon brandy
2 tablespoons plain flour
1½ cups (375 ml/ 12 fl oz) chicken stock
½ cup (125 ml/4 fl oz) unsweetened apple juice

1 Preheat the oven to very hot 250°C (500°F/ Gas 10). Score the rind of the pork with a sharp knife at 2 cm (¾ inch) intervals. Rub in some oil and plenty of salt to make crisp crackling.
2 Place the pork, rind-side-up, on a rack in a large baking dish. Add a little water to the dish—this will help prevent the meat drying out. Roast for 30 minutes, or until the rind turns golden and

For really crispy crackling, ROAST PORK is best served soon after cooking.

begins to crackle and bubble. Reduce the heat to moderate 180°C (350°F/Gas 4). Roast for 2 hours 40 minutes (20 minutes per 500 g/ 1 lb). The juices should run clear when the pork is pierced with a fork. Do not cover the pork or the crackling will soften. Leave in a warm place for 10 minutes.

3 To make the apple sauce, peel, core and chop the apples and place in a small pan with the sugar, cloves, cinnamon and ½ cup (125 ml/4 fl oz) water. Cover and simmer over low heat for 10 minutes, or until the apple is soft. Remove the cloves and cinnamon and mash the apples. Stir in the lemon juice, to taste.

4 To make the gravy, drain off all except 2 tablespoons of the pan juices from the baking dish. Place on top of the stove over moderate heat, add the brandy and stir quickly to scrape up the bits from the bottom of the pan. Cook for 1 minute. Remove from the heat, stir in the flour and mix well. Return the pan to the heat and cook for 2 minutes, stirring. Gradually add the stock and apple juice and cook, stirring, until the gravy boils and thickens. Season to taste with salt and pepper. Slice the pork and serve with the crackling, gravy and apple sauce.

NOTE: Any leftover pork can be kept refrigerated, covered, for up to 3 days.

Choose one of the marinades below for your ribs.

PORK RIBS

Preparation: 30 minutes + marinating
Cooking: 20 minutes
Serves 6

1 kg (2 lb) American-style ribs

Plum sauce marinade

1/2 cup (160 g/5 1/2 oz) plum sauce
2 tablespoons soy sauce
2 tablespoons honey
2 teaspoons grated fresh ginger
2 cloves garlic, crushed

Barbecue marinade

1 cup (250 ml/8 fl oz) tomato sauce
1/2 teaspoon onion powder
1/2 teaspoon garlic powder
2 tablespoons vinegar
2 tablespoons soft brown sugar
2 tablespoons Worcestershire sauce

Ginger marinade

2 tablespoons grated fresh ginger
1/2 teaspoon ground pepper
1 teaspoon sesame oil
1 tablespoon lemon juice
1 small onion, grated

Chilli marinade

1/2 cup (125 ml/4 fl oz) tomato purée
2 tablespoons honey
2 tablespoons chilli sauce, or to taste
1 tablespoon hoisin sauce
2 cloves garlic, crushed

1 Cut the ribs into smaller portions and trim off any fat. Place the ribs in a single layer in a shallow glass or ceramic dish.
2 Choose one of the marinades and mix together the ingredients. Pour the marinade over the meat, turning to coat well. Cover with plastic wrap and refrigerate for at least 2 hours and no longer than 8 hours, turning occasionally.
3 Preheat a barbecue flatplate or grill and brush it lightly with oil. Drain any excess marinade from the ribs, then cook them over moderate heat for 20 minutes, or until tender, turning occasionally.

VARIATION: Pork spareribs can be used instead of American-style ribs for this recipe. Remove the rind from the ribs and trim of fat. Depending on the size, you may need to cut them in half. Marinate and cook as above.

Deep-fry the pork then finish off in the wok for SWEET AND SOUR PORK.

SWEET AND SOUR PORK

Preparation: 35 minutes + 30 minutes marinating
Cooking: 40 minutes
Serves 6

2 teaspoons sugar
1/4 cup (60 ml/2 fl oz) soy sauce
1 tablespoon dry sherry
1 egg yolk
1 kg (2 lb) lean pork, cut into cubes
1 cup (125 g/4 oz) cornflour
oil, for deep-frying
1 onion, sliced
1 red capsicum, chopped
1 green capsicum, chopped
440 g (14 oz) can pineapple pieces, drained, juice reserved
1/4 cup (60 ml/2 fl oz) tomato sauce
1/4 cup (60 ml/2 fl oz) white vinegar
1 tablespoon cornflour, extra

1 Mix together the sugar, soy sauce, sherry and egg yolk. Pour over the pork and refrigerate, covered, for 30 minutes.
2 Drain the pork, reserving the marinade, and pat dry with paper towels. Toss the pork in the cornflour and shake off any excess. Heat the oil in a large heavy-based pan until a cube of bread browns in 15 seconds. Deep-fry the pork, in batches, until crisp and golden brown. Drain on paper towels.
3 Heat a little oil in a wok and cook the onion for 3 minutes, or until golden brown. Add the capsicum and cook for 2 minutes.
4 Mix together the pineapple juice, tomato sauce, vinegar and the reserved marinade, and add to the wok. Dissolve the extra cornflour in 1 cup (250 ml/8 fl oz) of water, add to the wok and stir until the mixture boils and thickens.
5 Add the pork and pineapple and cook until heated through.

ORANGE-GLAZED HAM is a perfect festive party meal.

ORANGE-GLAZED HAM

Preparation: 45 minutes
Cooking: 3 hours 40 minutes
Serves 20

7 kg (14 lb) cooked ham leg
1 large orange
6 whole cloves
3/4 cup (140 g/4 1/2 oz) soft brown sugar
1 tablespoon French mustard
1/2 cup (175 g/6 oz) honey
2 teaspoons soy sauce
2 tablespoons Grand Marnier
whole cloves, extra

Mustard cream
2 tablespoons French mustard
1/2 cup (125 g/4 oz) sour cream
1/2 cup (125 ml/4 fl oz) cream

1 Preheat the oven to moderate 180°C (350°F/Gas 4). Remove the rind from the ham by running a thumb around the edge, under the rind. Begin pulling at the widest edge. When the rind has been removed to within 6 cm (2 1/2 inches) of the shank end, cut through the rind around the shank. Using a sharp knife, remove some of the excess fat from the ham (but leave enough to give a good crispy skin).
2 Peel the orange, cut the white pith off the rind and cut the rind into long, thin strips. Squeeze about 1/2 cup (125 ml/4 fl oz) of juice from the orange.
3 Put the ham on a rack in a deep baking dish. Add 2 cups (500 ml/16 fl oz) water to the dish with the orange rind and cloves. Cover securely with foil and cook for 2 hours.
4 Remove from the oven. Increase the heat to hot 210°C (415°F/Gas 6–7). Drain the meat and reserve 1 cup (250 ml/8 fl oz) of the pan juices. Using a sharp knife, score the fat with cuts into a diamond pattern.
5 Mix together the sugar, mustard, honey, soy sauce and Grand Marnier. Brush some glaze over the ham. Return to the oven and cook, uncovered, for 30 minutes, glazing every 10 minutes.
6 Remove the ham from the oven. Press one of the extra cloves into each diamond. Roast, uncovered, for 1 hour, brushing with the glaze every 10 minutes.
7 Meanwhile, to make the mustard cream, mix together the mustard, sour cream and cream. Cover and leave for 1 hour.
8 Place the reserved pan

juices and 1/2 cup (125 ml/4 fl oz) of the brown sugar glaze in a small pan. Stir in the reserved orange juice. Stir over low heat until the mixture boils, then boil, without stirring, for 3 minutes. Leave the ham for 10 minutes before slicing. Serve hot or cold, with the orange glaze and mustard cream.

NOTE: The ham can be refrigerated, covered with a damp cloth, for about 10 days. Change the cloth regularly.

Use cider and apples for PORK WITH NORMANDY SAUCE.

PORK WITH NORMANDY SAUCE

Preparation: 25 minutes
Cooking: 45 minutes
Serves 4

40 g (1 1/4 oz) butter
12 French shallots
2 cloves garlic, chopped
4 thick pork chops
1 1/2 cups (375 ml/ 12 fl oz) apple cider
1 tablespoon white wine vinegar
3 teaspoons French mustard
1 green apple, cored and cut into 8 slices
2 teaspoons soft brown sugar
3 tablespoons cream
2 teaspoons cornflour

1 Heat half the butter in a large heavy-based frying pan. Add the shallots and garlic, and cook for 3–4 minutes, or until soft. Remove and set aside. Trim the chops of any excess fat and add to the pan. Brown over high heat for 2–3 minutes, turning once.
2 Reduce the heat and return the shallots and garlic to the pan. Pour in the combined cider, vinegar and mustard. Cover and simmer for about 20 minutes, or until the pork chops are tender. (The cooking time will depend on the thickness of the pork chops.)
3 Meanwhile, heat the remaining butter in a small frying pan. Add the apple slices and brown sugar. Cook, turning occasionally, for 3 minutes, or until the apple has lightly browned and softened. Remove and set aside.
4 Remove the pork chops from the pan, cover with foil and keep warm. Combine the cream and cornflour, then add to the cider mixture. Whisk quickly for 5–10 minutes, or until the sauce has come to the boil and thickened slightly. Add the apple and pork chops, and heat through for 5 minutes. Garnish with a few fresh thyme sprigs.

The dish is lined with thin rashers of bacon that will cover the PORK AND VEAL TERRINE.

PORK AND VEAL TERRINE

Preparation: 20 minutes + overnight refrigeration
Cooking: 1 hour 20 minutes
Serves 6

8–10 thin rashers bacon
1 tablespoon olive oil
1 onion, chopped
2 cloves garlic, crushed
1 kg (2 lb) pork and veal mince
1 cup (80 g/2¾ oz) fresh breadcrumbs
1 egg
3 tablespoons brandy
3 teaspoons chopped fresh thyme
¼ cup (15 g/½ oz) chopped fresh parsley

1 Preheat the oven to moderate 180°C (350°F/Gas 4). Lightly grease a 1.5 litre terrine dish or tin. Line with the rashers of bacon, leaving them hanging over the sides of the dish.
2 Heat the oil in a frying pan and fry the onion and garlic for 2–3 minutes, or until the onion is soft.
3 Mix together the fried onion, mince, breadcrumbs, egg, brandy, thyme and parsley in a large bowl. Use your hands to mix it thoroughly. Season with salt and pepper. To taste that there is enough seasoning in the terrine, fry a spoonful of the mixture. Taste and adjust the seasoning accordingly.
4 Spoon the mixture into the dish, pressing it in firmly. Fold the bacon over the top of the terrine to enclose the mixture,

cover with foil and place the terrine in a deep baking tray. Pour enough cold water into the baking tray to come halfway up the side of the terrine (this makes a *bain marie*).
5 Bake for 1–1 1/4 hours, or until the juice runs clear when pierced with a skewer. Remove from the *bain marie* and pour off the excess juice. Cover with foil and place heavy tins directly on top of the terrine to press it down. Refrigerate overnight.

WIENER SCHNITZEL

Preparation: 15 minutes + 30 minutes refrigeration
Cooking: 10 minutes
Serves 4

4 thin veal steaks
plain flour, for coating
1 egg, lightly beaten
1 cup (100 g/3 1/2 oz) dry breadcrumbs
1/4 cup (60 ml/2 fl oz) oil
30 g (1 oz) butter
1 lemon, sliced
2 tablespoons capers
2 gherkins, sliced

1 Trim the meat of any fat and sinew. Place between sheets of plastic wrap and flatten with a meat mallet to 5 mm (1/4 inch) thick. Nick the edges to prevent them from curling up when the steaks are cooked. Pat dry with paper towels.
2 Season the flour with salt and pepper. Coat the veal with the seasoned flour, shaking off the excess (the least messy way to do this is to put the flour in a plastic bag, add the meat and shake well). Dip into the egg, then coat with the breadcrumbs. Place on a foil-lined tray. Cover and refrigerate for at least 30 minutes to firm up the breadcrumb coating.
3 Heat the oil and butter in a large heavy-based pan and cook the veal over medium heat for 3–4 minutes. Turn over and cook for 2–3 minutes, or until golden. Serve at once with lemon, capers and gherkins.

WIENER SCHNITZEL.

NOTE: The schnitzels can be coated with breadcrumbs several hours in advance. Keep them covered and refrigerated until ready to fry.
VARIATION: Prepare chicken schnitzel in the same way. Use chicken breast fillets and flatten with a meat mallet before cooking.

VEAL PARMIGIANA

Preparation: 30 minutes + 30 minutes refrigeration
Cooking: 30 minutes
Serves 4

4 thin veal steaks
1 cup (100 g/3 1/2 oz) dry breadcrumbs
1/2 teaspoon dried basil
3/4 cup (75 g/2 1/2 oz) finely grated Parmesan
plain flour, for coating
1 egg, lightly beaten
1 tablespoon milk
oil, for shallow-frying
1 cup (250 g/8 oz) tomato pasta sauce
100 g (3 1/2 oz) mozzarella, thinly sliced

1 Trim the meat of any fat and sinew. Place between sheets of plastic wrap and flatten with a meat mallet to 5 mm (1/4 inch) thick. Nick the edges to prevent the meat curling.
2 Combine the breadcrumbs, basil and 1/4 cup (30 g/1 oz) of the Parmesan on a sheet of greaseproof paper.
3 Coat the veal in flour, shaking off the excess. Working with one at a time, dip the steaks in the combined egg and milk, then coat with the breadcrumbs. Lightly shake off the excess. Refrigerate on a paper-lined tray for 30 minutes to firm the coating.
4 Preheat the oven to moderate 180°C (350°F/Gas 4). Heat 2 cm (1 inch) oil in a frying pan and brown the veal steaks over medium heat for 2 minutes on each side, in batches if necessary, until crisp and golden brown. Drain on paper towels.
5 Spread half the pasta sauce in a shallow ovenproof dish. Arrange the veal steaks on top in a single layer and spoon in the remaining sauce. Top with the remaining Parmesan and the mozzarella and bake for 20 minutes, or until the cheese is melted and golden brown.

PARMIGIANA can also be made with chicken and even eggplant.

OSSO BUCO WITH GREMOLATA

Preparation: 40 minutes
Cooking: 2 hours 20 minutes
Serves 4

Gremolata
1 tablespoon finely shredded lemon rind
1–2 cloves garlic, finely chopped
1/4 cup (15 g/1/2 oz) finely chopped fresh parsley

plain flour, for coating
4 veal shank pieces, each 5 cm (2 inches) thick
2 tablespoons olive oil

OSSO BUCO is a traditional Italian dish, made from veal shanks.

2 large onions, sliced
6 Roma tomatoes, finely chopped
2 tablespoons tomato paste
1 1/2 cups (375 ml/ 12 fl oz) white wine
1 tablespoon cornflour
2–3 cloves garlic, crushed
1 cup (60 g/2 oz) finely chopped fresh parsley

1 To make the gremolata, mix together the lemon rind, garlic and parsley and set aside.
2 Season the flour with salt and pepper and use to coat the veal pieces, shaking off any excess. Heat half the oil in a heavy-based pan large enough to fit the meat in a single layer. When the oil is hot, brown the veal well on both sides. Remove and set aside.
3 Heat the remaining oil in the pan and cook the onion for 2–3 minutes, or until soft but not brown. Add the meat in a single layer so that it fits snugly in the pan. Season with salt and pepper.
4 Mix together the tomatoes, tomato paste and wine and pour the mixture over the meat. Bring to the boil, then reduce the heat, cover and simmer for 1 1/2 hours.
5 Remove 1 cup (250 ml/ 8 fl oz) of the cooking liquid and allow to cool a little. Place the cornflour in a small bowl and whisk in the liquid, then stir in the garlic and chopped parsley and add the mixture to the dish. Simmer, uncovered, for about 30 minutes, or until the meat is very tender and the sauce has thickened. Sprinkle with the gremolata just before serving.

Use a boned loin of veal for VEAL WITH PEPPERCORN SAUCE.

VEAL WITH PEPPERCORN SAUCE

Preparation: 20 minutes
Cooking: 1 hour 10 minutes
Serves 6–8

1.5 kg (3 lb) loin of veal, boned
2 tablespoons Dijon mustard
1 tablespoon oil
15 g (1/2 oz) butter
1/2 cup (125 ml/4 fl oz) dry white wine
bouquet garni
1 tablespoon canned green peppercorns
2 tablespoons brandy
3 tablespoons cream

1 Place the veal, fat-side-down, on a flat surface. Spread with 1 tablespoon of the mustard and sprinkle with freshly ground black pepper.
2 Roll up the veal neatly and tie securely at regular intervals with kitchen string. Spread with the remaining mustard.
3 Preheat the oven to moderate 180°C (350°F/Gas 4). Heat the oil and butter in a large frying pan. Add the veal and cook quickly, turning to brown all sides.
4 Put the veal in a baking dish. Add the wine and bouquet garni. Cover the dish with foil and bake for 45 minutes, or until tender, basting frequently. Transfer to a serving plate, remove the string, cover and keep warm.
5 Strain the cooking liquid into a small pan, discarding the bouquet garni. Skim off any excess fat. Bring to the boil, reduce the heat and simmer for 5–10 minutes, or until reduced and slightly thickened. Crush the green peppercorns and stir in with the brandy and cream. Heat the sauce through, but do not boil. Season to taste with salt. Slice the veal thinly and serve with the peppercorn sauce.

VEAL SCALOPPINI

Preparation: 5 minutes
Cooking: 5 minutes
Serves 4

plain flour, for coating
8 thin veal steaks
1/4 cup (60 ml/2 fl oz) olive oil
60 g (2 oz) butter
2 tablespoons lemon juice
2 tablespoons finely chopped fresh parsley
lemon slices, to garnish

1 Season the flour with salt and pepper and coat the veal steaks with the flour, shaking off the excess. (The least messy way to do this is to put the flour in a plastic bag, add the meat and shake well.) Heat the oil and half the butter in a large frying pan. Add the meat to the pan, in batches if necessary (if you overcrowd the pan the meat will stew rather than frying). Cook over high heat until lightly browned on one side, then turn over and brown the other side. The veal steaks should take only 1 minute on each side—cooking longer will toughen the meat. Remove from the pan.
2 Reduce the heat and add the lemon juice, parsley and remaining butter to the pan, stirring well. Add the veal steaks, turning them in the sauce.
3 Serve the veal steaks with the sauce. Garnish with lemon slices.

NOTE: If you can't buy really thin veal steaks, put your steaks between two sheets of plastic wrap and beat with a rolling pin or meat mallet until about 5mm (1/4 inch) thick. Nick the edges to prevent them curling.

Add lemon juice and parsley to the buttery pan juices, for VEAL SCALOPPINI.

CHICKEN AND OTHER POULTRY

Chicken is just perfect for today's cooking—it's quick to prepare for the after-work cook, but also good value for a family. Everyone has a favourite chicken dish, whether it's a creamy curry or a crisp-skinned roast. Once reserved for special occasions, chicken is now a versatile meat to be enjoyed every day.

ROAST CHICKEN WITH BREADCRUMB STUFFING

Preparation: 40 minutes
Cooking: 1 1/2 hours
Serves 6

3 rashers bacon, rind removed, finely chopped
6 slices wholegrain bread, crusts removed
3 spring onions, chopped
2 tablespoons chopped pecans
2 teaspoons currants
1/4 cup (15 g/1/2 oz) finely chopped fresh parsley
1 egg, lightly beaten
1/4 cup (60 ml/2 fl oz) milk
1.4 kg (2 lb 13 oz) chicken
40 g (1 1/4 oz) butter, melted
1 tablespoon oil
1 1/2 cups (375 ml/ 12 fl oz) chicken stock
1 tablespoon plain flour

1 Preheat the oven to moderate 180°C (350°F/ Gas 4). To make the stuffing, cook the bacon in a dry frying pan over high heat for 5 minutes, or until crisp. Cut the bread into 1 cm (1/2 inch) cubes and place in a large mixing bowl. Add the bacon, spring onion, pecans, currants, parsley and combined egg and milk. Season with salt and pepper and mix well.
2 Remove the giblets and any large amounts of fat from the cavity of the chicken. Rinse and pat the chicken dry, inside and out, with paper towels. Spoon the stuffing into the cavity and close with a skewer or toothpick. Tuck the wings under the chicken and tie the legs securely with string.
3 Place the chicken on a rack in a deep baking dish. Brush with the combined butter and oil. Pour any of the remaining butter and oil mixture into the baking dish with half the stock. Roast the chicken for 1–1 1/4 hours, or until brown and tender, basting occasionally with the pan juices. Transfer the chicken to a large serving dish. Cover loosely with foil and leave in a warm place for 5 minutes before carving (some people turn their chicken breast-side-down while it 'rests'—this is so

Order a free-range bird from your butcher for the best flavoured ROAST CHICKEN.

that the juices run into the breast, making the meat more moist and tender).

4 Discard all but a tablespoon of the pan juices from the baking dish. Transfer the baking dish to the stove top. Add the flour to the pan juices and blend to a smooth paste. Stir constantly over low heat for 5 minutes, or until the mixture browns. Gradually add the remaining stock and stir until the mixture boils and thickens. (Add a little extra stock or water if the gravy is too thick.) Season with salt and pepper, and strain into a jug. Serve the hot gravy with the chicken and stuffing.

VARIATION: Use white wine instead of some of the stock in the gravy.

Serve the ROAST TURKEY with stuffing and gravy made from the pan juices.

ROAST TURKEY WITH CASHEW STUFFING

Preparation: 45 minutes
Cooking: 2¼ hours
Serves 6–8

3 kg (6 lb) turkey
60 g (2 oz) butter
1 onion, chopped
2 cups (370 g/12 oz) cooked brown rice
1 cup (185 g/6 oz) chopped dried apricots
½ cup (90 g/3 oz) unsalted cashews
¼ cup (15 g/½ oz) chopped fresh parsley
2 tablespoons chopped fresh mint
1 tablespoon lemon juice
2 tablespoons oil
2 cups (500 ml/16 fl oz) chicken stock
2 tablespoons plain flour

1 Remove the neck and giblets from inside the turkey. Rinse the turkey well and pat dry inside and out with paper towels.
2 Preheat the oven to moderate 180°C (350°F/Gas 4). Heat the butter in a pan, add the onion and cook, stirring, until golden. Allow to cool, then mix thoroughly with the rice, apricots, cashews, parsley, mint and lemon juice. Season with salt and pepper.
3 Spoon the stuffing loosely into the turkey cavity. Tuck the wings underneath and close the cavity with a skewer or toothpick. Tie the legs together. Place on a rack in a deep baking dish. Brush with the oil. Pour any of the remaining oil into the baking dish with ½ cup (125 ml/4 fl oz) of the stock. Roast for 2 hours, basting with the pan juices. Cover the breast and legs with foil after 1 hour if the turkey is overbrowning. Cover and leave for 15 minutes.
4 To make the gravy, drain off all but 2 tablespoons of the pan juices from the dish. Place the dish over low heat, add the flour and stir well. Stir over medium heat until well browned. Gradually add the

remaining stock, stirring until the gravy boils and thickens. Serve with the turkey and stuffing.

ROAST DUCK WITH ORANGE SAUCE

Preparation: 40 minutes
Cooking: 2 hours 20 minutes
Serves 4

2 kg (4 lb) duck
2 chicken wings
1/2 cup (125 ml/4 fl oz) white wine
1 onion, chopped
1 small carrot, sliced
1 tomato, chopped
bouquet garni
1 tablespoon orange zest
1/3 cup (80 ml/2 3/4 fl oz) orange juice
2 tablespoons Cointreau
1 teaspoon cornflour

1 To make stock, place the duck neck in a pan. Chop the chicken wings roughly and add to the pan with the wine. Simmer over medium heat for 5 minutes, or until the liquid has reduced by half. Add the onion, carrot, tomato, bouquet garni and 2 cups (500 ml/16 fl oz) water. Bring to the boil and simmer gently for 40 minutes. Strain and set aside 1 cup (250 ml/8 fl oz) of the stock.
2 Preheat the oven to moderate 180°C (350°F/Gas 4). Place the duck in a large pan, cover with boiling water, then drain. Dry with paper towels. Using a fine skewer, prick all over the outside of the duck, piercing only the skin, not the flesh. Place the duck breast-side-down in a baking dish and roast for 50 minutes.
3 Drain off the fat from the dish, turn the duck over and add the stock. Roast for 40 minutes, or until the breast is golden brown. Pour off and reserve the stock. Remove the duck from the pan and leave in a warm place.
4 Place the stock in a pan, skimming off any fat that you can see on top. Add the orange zest, orange juice and Cointreau. Bring to the boil, then reduce the heat and simmer gently for 5 minutes. Blend the cornflour into a smooth paste with 2 teaspoons water and stir into the sauce until it boils and thickens. Serve with the roast duck.

ROAST DUCK WITH ORANGE SAUCE.

CHICKEN SATAY

Preparation: 40 minutes + 30 minutes marinating
Cooking: 20 minutes
Serves 4

500 g (1 lb) chicken thigh fillets
2 tablespoons honey
1/2 cup (125 ml/4 fl oz) soy sauce
2 teaspoons sesame oil
1/4 cup (60 ml/2 fl oz) oil
1 tablespoon soft brown sugar
cucumber slices and chopped roasted peanuts, to garnish

Peanut sauce
1/2 cup (125 g/4 oz) crunchy peanut butter
1 cup (250 ml/8 fl oz) coconut milk
1–2 tablespoons sweet chilli sauce
1 tablespoon soy sauce
2 teaspoons lemon juice

1 Soak 20 wooden skewers in cold water for 30 minutes. Cut the chicken into flattish thick strips about 6 cm (2 inches) long and 2 cm (1 inch) wide. Thread a strip of chicken onto each skewer, flattening it on the skewer.

You can also make beef, lamb or seafood SATAY.

2 Mix together the honey, soy sauce and sesame oil and spread over the chicken. Cover and refrigerate for 30 minutes.
3 Put all the peanut sauce ingredients in a heavy-based pan with 1/2 cup (125 ml/4 fl oz) water. Stir over low heat, until the mixture boils. Remove from the heat. The sauce will thicken on standing.
4 Heat a grill, char-grill pan or barbecue flatplate until very hot and brush with 1 tablespoon oil. Cook the chicken for 2–3 minutes on each side, sprinkling with brown sugar and the remaining oil. Top with the peanut sauce and garnish with cucumber and peanuts. Serve the remaining peanut sauce for dipping.

TANDOORI CHICKEN

Preparation: 25 minutes + 4 1/2 hours marinating
Cooking: 45 minutes
Serves 4

6 chicken thighs
1/3 cup (80 ml/2 3/4 fl oz) lemon juice
1/2 small onion, chopped
4 cloves garlic
1 tablespoon grated fresh ginger
3 teaspoons ground coriander

Learn to make your own spice paste and tandoori mix, for TANDOORI CHICKEN.

1 tablespoon ground cumin
1 teaspoon salt
1/4 teaspoon paprika
pinch of chilli powder
1 cup (250 g/8 oz) yoghurt
red food colouring

1 Remove the skin from the chicken thighs and brush the flesh with 3 tablespoons of the lemon juice. Cover and refrigerate for 30 minutes.
2 Put the onion, garlic, ginger, coriander, cumin, salt and the remaining lemon juice in a food processor or spice grinder and process to make a smooth paste.
3 Combine the spice paste with the paprika, chilli powder and yoghurt and mix together until smooth. Add enough food colouring to turn the mixture deep red.
4 Place the chicken pieces in a large shallow dish, and spread liberally with the tandoori mixture. Cover with plastic wrap and refrigerate for at least 4 hours (leave overnight for the best flavour).
5 Preheat the oven to moderate 180°C (350°F/Gas 4). Place the chicken pieces on a wire rack over a large baking dish. Bake for 45 minutes, or until tender and cooked through. Serve with rice.

CHICKEN CORDON BLEU

Preparation: 15 minutes + 30 minutes refrigeration
Cooking: 10 minutes
Serves 4

- 4 chicken breast fillets
- 4 thick slices Swiss cheese
- 4 slices double-smoked ham
- plain flour, for coating
- 1 egg, lightly beaten
- 1/2 cup (50 g/1 3/4 oz) dry breadcrumbs
- 1/2 cup (125 ml/4 fl oz) oil

1 Slice through the middle of each chicken fillet without cutting right through. Open out flat and season well.
2 Place a slice of Swiss cheese and ham on one half of each fillet and fold the other half over.
3 Season the flour well and use to coat the chicken fillets, shaking off the excess. Dip into the egg, then coat with the breadcrumbs. Place on a foil-lined tray. Cover and refrigerate for 30 minutes.
4 Heat the oil in a frying pan and cook the chicken over medium heat for 5 minutes on each side, or until golden and cooked through. Serve immediately.

Cut into CHICKEN CORDON BLEU to reveal ham and cheese.

CHICKEN CHASSEUR

Preparation: 20 minutes
Cooking: 1 1/2 hours
Serves 4

- 1 kg (2 lb) chicken thigh fillets
- 2 tablespoons oil
- 1 clove garlic, crushed
- 1 large onion, sliced
- 100 g (3 1/2 oz) button mushrooms, sliced
- 1 teaspoon fresh thyme
- 400 g (13 oz) can chopped tomatoes
- 3 tablespoons chicken stock
- 3 tablespoons white wine
- 1 tablespoon tomato paste

CHICKEN CHASSEUR means 'hunter's chicken' in French.

1 Preheat the oven to moderate 180°C (350°F/ Gas 4). Trim the chicken of any fat. Heat the oil in a heavy-based frying pan and brown the chicken in batches over medium heat. Drain on paper towels, then transfer to a casserole dish.
2 Add the garlic, onion and mushrooms to the pan and cook over medium heat for 5 minutes, or until soft. Add to the chicken with the thyme and tomatoes.
3 Combine the stock, wine and tomato paste and pour over the chicken. Cover and bake for 1 1/4 hours, or until the chicken is tender. Serve with rice, pasta, or crusty French bread to mop up the juices.

CHICKEN KIEV

Preparation: 35 minutes + 2 hours refrigeration
Cooking: 20 minutes
Serves 6

125 g (4 oz) butter, softened
1 clove garlic, crushed
2 tablespoons chopped fresh parsley
2 teaspoons lemon juice
2 teaspoons grated lemon rind
6 small chicken breasts, tenderloins removed
1/2 cup (60 g/2 oz) plain flour
4 cups (400 g/13 oz) dry breadcrumbs
2 eggs, beaten
3 tablespoons milk
oil, for frying
lemon wedges, to serve

1 Mix together the butter, garlic, parsley, lemon juice and rind. Spoon onto a sheet of foil and shape into a rectangle about 5 x 8 cm (2 x 3 inches). Roll up the foil and chill until firm.
2 Place each piece of chicken between 2 sheets of plastic wrap and use a meat mallet or rolling pin to gently flatten to about 5 mm (1/4 inch) thick.
3 Cut the chilled butter into 6 pieces. Place a piece in the centre of each chicken slice, fold in the edges and roll up to completely enclose. Fasten with toothpicks and chill until firm.
4 Place the flour and breadcrumbs on separate plates or greaseproof paper. Toss the chicken in the flour, dip in the combined egg and milk, then coat with the breadcrumbs. Chill on a paper-lined tray in the fridge for 1 hour, then toss in the egg and breadcrumbs again. Half fill a heavy-based frying pan with oil and cook the chicken, in batches, for 5 minutes on each side, or until golden and cooked through. Drain on paper towels, remove the toothpicks and serve with the lemon wedges.

Roll the chicken breast around garlic butter for CHICKEN KIEV.

Serve COQ AU VIN with hunks of crusty French bread to mop up the sauce.

COQ AU VIN

Preparation: 20 minutes
Cooking: 1 hour
Serves 6

2 sprigs fresh thyme
4 sprigs fresh parsley
2 bay leaves
plain flour, for coating
2 kg (4 lb) chicken pieces
3 tablespoons oil
4 rashers bacon, sliced
12 pickling onions
2 cloves garlic, crushed
2 tablespoons brandy
1 1/2 cups (375 ml/ 12 fl oz) red wine
1 1/2 cups (375 ml/ 12 fl oz) chicken stock
1/4 cup (60 g/2 oz) tomato paste
250 g (8 oz) button mushrooms
fresh herbs, for serving

1 To make a bouquet garni, tie together the thyme, parsley and bay leaves with string, or tie them between two short lengths of celery.
2 Season the flour with salt and pepper. Toss the chicken in the flour to coat well, shaking off any excess. Heat 2 tablespoons of the oil in a heavy-based pan and brown the chicken in batches over medium heat. Remove all the chicken from the pan and drain on paper towels.
3 Heat the remaining oil in the pan. Add the bacon, onions and garlic and cook, stirring, until the onions are browned. Add the chicken, brandy, wine, stock, bouquet garni and tomato paste. Bring to the boil, then reduce the heat and simmer, covered, for 40 minutes.
4 Stir in the mushrooms and simmer, uncovered, for 10 minutes, or until the chicken is tender and the sauce has thickened. Remove the bouquet garni, sprinkle with fresh herbs and serve with crusty French bread.

Chill the CHICKEN LIVER PATE until it is firm before serving.

CHICKEN LIVER PATE

Preparation: 10 minutes + overnight refrigeration
Cooking: 10 minutes
Serves 4

1 onion, finely chopped
100 g (3 1/2 oz) butter, melted
1 clove garlic, crushed
1 tablespoon chopped fresh thyme
500 g (1 lb) chicken livers, cleaned
2 teaspoons green peppercorns in brine, roughly chopped
1 tablespoon brandy
6 tablespoons ghee (see Note)

1 Fry the onion in 2 tablespoons butter until soft. Add the garlic and thyme and cook for 1 minute. Add the livers and cook for 5 minutes, or until firm and cooked.
2 Transfer to a food processor and add the remaining butter. Blend until smooth, then season. Add the peppercorns and brandy and blend briefly.
3 Spoon into ramekins and cover the surface with plastic wrap. Refrigerate overnight to firm. Cover the pâté with ghee.

NOTE: Ghee is a form of clarified butter which cooks at high temperatures without burning. You can buy it as 'ghee' or you can clarify your own butter at home. Ghee is commonly used for cooking curries, and it is worth knowing how to make your own. To make 100 g (3 1/2 oz) clarified butter, cut 180 g (6 oz) butter into cubes. Heat in a small pan set in a larger pan of hot water, over low heat. Melt the butter without stirring. Skim the foam from the top. Remove from the heat, cool slightly and pour off the clear yellow liquid, being careful to leave the milky sediment behind in the pan. Refrigerate the clarified butter in an airtight container.

THAI GREEN CHICKEN CURRY

Preparation: 25 minutes
Cooking: 35 minutes
Serves 4

- 2 cups (500 ml/16 fl oz) coconut milk
- 2 tablespoons oil
- 1 onion, chopped
- 2 tablespoons green curry paste
- 500 g (1 lb) chicken thigh fillets, cut into strips
- 4 kaffir lime leaves
- 100 g (3 1/2 oz) snake beans, chopped
- 2 tablespoons fish sauce
- 2 tablespoons lime juice
- 1 teaspoon finely grated lime rind
- 3 teaspoons grated palm sugar or soft brown sugar
- fresh coriander leaves, to garnish

Garnish THAI GREEN CHICKEN CURRY with fresh coriander.

1 In a pan, bring the coconut milk to the boil and cook over high heat for about 10 minutes, or until small bubbles of oil begin to crack the surface of the coconut milk.
2 Heat the oil in a wok or a heavy-based pan. Add the onion and curry paste and cook over high heat for about 1 minute, or until the curry paste is fragrant. Add the chicken and stir-fry for 5 minutes, or until the chicken is almost cooked.
3 Add the coconut milk, kaffir lime leaves, snake beans and 3 tablespoons water to the wok. Bring to the boil, stirring occasionally. Reduce the heat and simmer for 10 minutes, or until the chicken is tender.
4 Stir in the fish sauce, lime juice, rind and sugar. Garnish with the coriander leaves and serve with steamed rice.

NOTE: The 'cracking' of the coconut milk is a traditional technique used in Thai cookery. It separates the oils in the coconut milk, making it more glossy.
Thai green curry paste is made using green chillies. Thai red curry paste is made from red chillies, which is why it is hotter. You can use this recipe to make a Thai red chicken curry.

SWEET CHILLI CHICKEN WINGS

Preparation: 30 minutes + overnight marinating
Cooking: 1 hour
Serves 10

2 kg (4 lb) chicken wings
2 cloves garlic, crushed
1/4 teaspoon salt
1 teaspoon ground black pepper
1 tablespoon oil
1/4 cup (60 ml/2 fl oz) sweet chilli sauce
2 tablespoons honey
1 tablespoon white vinegar
1/4 cup (60 ml/2 fl oz) soy sauce
2 teaspoons grated ginger
1 tablespoon soft brown sugar

1 Trim the chicken of excess fat and sinew. Cut each wing into three sections, discarding the tips (you can freeze them and use for making stock).
2 Mix together the remaining ingredients in a large bowl. Add the chicken pieces and stir until coated. Cover and refrigerate overnight (or for several hours).
3 Preheat the oven to moderate 180°C (350°F/Gas 4). Drain the chicken pieces and reserve the marinade. Place the chicken pieces on a roasting rack over a baking tray or in a deep baking dish. Bake for 1 hour, or until the chicken is crisp and cooked through. Brush the pieces with the reserved marinade several times during cooking. Serve hot.

SWEET CHILLI CHICKEN WINGS are ideal party food.

STORAGE: The chicken can be cooked up to 2 days in advance and stored, covered, in the fridge. Reheat in a moderate 180°C (350°F/Gas 4) oven for 10–15 minutes.
VARIATION: For devilled chicken wings to serve four people, mix together 1 teaspoon Dijon mustard, 1 clove crushed garlic, 2 tablespoons hoisin sauce, 1 tablespoon Worcestershire sauce, 2 tablespoons tomato sauce, 1 tablespoon lemon juice and a few drops of Tabasco in a large bowl. Season 12 chicken wings and add to the bowl. Toss and cover with plastic wrap. Refrigerate for 2 hours or overnight. Preheat the oven to moderately hot 200°C (400°F/Gas 6). Arrange the wings on a wire rack above a baking tray or in a deep baking dish and bake for 30–40 minutes, or until browned and cooked through. Eat hot or as cold picnic food.

COUNTRY RABBIT IN RED WINE

Preparation: 45 minutes
Cooking: 1½ hours
Serves 4

1.25 kg (2½ lb) rabbit
½ cup (125 ml/4 fl oz) olive oil
2 cloves garlic, crushed
1 sprig of fresh rosemary, finely chopped
1 cup (250 ml/8 fl oz) red wine
½ cup (125 ml/4 fl oz) chicken stock
4 tomatoes, peeled and chopped

1 Cut the forelegs from the rabbit by cutting through the connective tissue joining the body. Cut across the back of the rabbit just above the legs, then cut the legs in half. Cut the body (saddle) of the rabbit into 2 pieces, then cut the ribcage and backbone into 4 pieces, to form 8 portions.
2 Heat the oil in a heavy-based pan and brown the rabbit, in batches, over medium heat. Add the garlic and rosemary and cook for 1 minute.
3 Add the wine and stock, and season with salt and freshly ground black pepper. Cover and simmer gently for 30 minutes. Add the tomato and cook, covered, for 45 minutes over low heat, or until the rabbit is tender. Serve with crusty Italian bread.

COUNTRY RABBIT IN RED WINE.

SOUTHERN FRIED CHICKEN

Preparation: 15 minutes + 2 hours marinating
Cooking: 30 minutes
Serves 4

1 kg (2 lb) chicken pieces
2 cups (500 ml/16 fl oz) buttermilk
oil, for deep-frying
1½ cups (185 g/6 oz) plain flour

1 Place the chicken in a bowl and pour in the buttermilk. Mix well. Cover and refrigerate for 2 hours, turning occasionally.
2 Half fill a large, deep pan with oil and heat to 180°C (350°F), or until a cube of bread browns in 15 seconds. Place the flour in a shallow dish and season with salt and pepper. Remove the chicken from the buttermilk, shake off any excess, dip it into the flour and coat well.
3 Lower the chicken into the oil, in small batches, and deep-fry for 12 minutes on each side, making sure that the oil is not too hot or the chicken will brown on the outside before it is cooked through. Drain the chicken well on paper towels before serving.

SOUTHERN FRIED CHICKEN.

CHICKEN NUGGETS WITH DIPPING SAUCE.

NOTE: For southern fried chicken, use chicken pieces that are all a similar size, or some will cook faster than others.

CHICKEN NUGGETS WITH DIPPING SAUCE

Preparation: 30 minutes + 30 minutes refrigeration
Cooking: 30 minutes
Serves 6

4 chicken breast fillets
1/2 cup (60 g/2 oz) plain flour
1 tablespoon chicken seasoning
2 eggs
1 1/2 cups (150 g/5 oz) dry breadcrumbs
oil, for frying

Dipping sauce
1 cup (250 ml/8 fl oz) pineapple juice
1/4 cup (60 ml/2 fl oz) white wine vinegar
2 teaspoons soy sauce
2 tablespoons soft brown sugar
2 tablespoons tomato sauce
1 tablespoon cornflour

1 Cut the chicken fillets into strips about 2 cm (3/4 inch) wide. Mix the flour and seasoning in a plastic bag and add the chicken. Toss until the chicken is evenly coated with flour. Remove and shake off the excess.
2 Beat the eggs lightly in a shallow bowl, and put the breadcrumbs in a shallow bowl. Working with a few strips at a time, dip the chicken in the egg, then coat with the breadcrumbs. Refrigerate for at least 30 minutes.
3 Heat 3 cm (1 1/4 inches) of the oil in a large frying pan to moderately hot, or until a cube of bread browns in 15 seconds. Fry the nuggets in batches for 3–5 minutes, or until golden brown. Drain on paper towels.
4 To make the dipping sauce, mix the juice, vinegar, soy sauce, sugar and tomato sauce in a small pan. Stir over low heat until dissolved. Mix the cornflour to a paste with 1 tablespoon water. Add to the pan and stir until the mixture boils and thickens. Simmer for 2 minutes. Cool and serve with the chicken.

Serve CHICKEN AND ALMONDS with steamed rice.

TERIYAKI CHICKEN.

CHICKEN AND ALMONDS

Preparation: 30 minutes
Cooking: 20 minutes
Serves 4

1 tablespoon soy sauce
1 tablespooon cornflour
300 g (10 oz) chicken breast fillets, sliced diagonally across
oil, for cooking
2 cm (3/4 inch) piece fresh ginger, finely grated
1 onion, roughly chopped
1 celery stick, thinly sliced diagonally
50 g (1 3/4 oz) green beans, sliced in half
1/4 cup (60 g/2 oz) canned bamboo shoots, drained
1/4 cup (60 ml/2 fl oz) chicken stock
2 tablespoons Chinese rice wine or medium sherry
1 teaspoon sesame oil
2 teaspoons cornflour, extra
125 g (4 oz) blanched almonds, roasted

1 Mix together the soy sauce and cornflour in a small bowl. Pour over the chicken and leave for about 5 minutes.
2 Heat 2 tablespoons of the oil in a wok or heavy-based pan until it is extremely hot. Stir-fry the

APRICOT CHICKEN is a quick and simple family dish.

chicken over high heat for 2 minutes, then remove from the wok.

3 If there is very little oil in the wok, add an extra tablespoon, reheat the wok and stir-fry the ginger, onion and celery for 4 minutes. Add the beans and bamboo shoots, and cook for 1 minute. Add the stock, rice wine, sesame oil and 2 tablespoons of water, cover and steam for 30 seconds.

4 Mix the extra cornflour with 1 tablespoon water, stir into the sauce and stir until it comes to the boil and thickens. Return the chicken to the wok and add the almonds. Toss until heated through.

TERIYAKI CHICKEN

Preparation: 15 minutes
Cooking: 45 minutes
Serves 6

1/2 cup (125 ml/4 fl oz) Japanese soy sauce
2 tablespoons mirin
1 tablespoon sugar
2 tablespoons oil
12 chicken drumsticks

1 Place the soy sauce, mirin and sugar in a small pan and stir over low heat until the sugar dissolves. Bring to the boil, then reduce the heat and simmer for 2 minutes.

2 Heat the oil in a large heavy-based frying pan, add the chicken drumsticks in batches and cook over high heat until browned all over.

3 Return all the chicken to the pan, add the sauce, cover and cook for 30 minutes, or until the chicken is tender. Serve with rice.

APRICOT CHICKEN

Preparation: 30 minutes
Cooking: 55 minutes
Serves 4

6 chicken thigh cutlets, skin removed
40 g (1 1/4 oz) packet French onion soup mix
425 ml (14 fl oz) can apricot nectar
425 g (14 oz) can apricot halves, drained

1 Preheat the oven to moderate 180°C (350°F/Gas 4). Place the chicken in an ovenproof dish. Mix the onion soup mix with the apricot nectar and pour over the chicken.

2 Bake, covered, for 50 minutes, add the apricot pieces and bake for a further 5 minutes. Serve with creamy mashed potato or rice to soak up the juices.

Ginger
Nutmeg

SEAFOOD

Many people find the thought of cooking seafood a little daunting. They see it as difficult and unpredictable. Few cookery myths are more undeserved than this one. Fish is really very easy to cook, and if you have a good fishmonger you won't have to do much preparation either.

FISHERMAN'S PIE

Preparation: 40 minutes
Cooking: 1 hour
Serves 4

800 g (1 lb 10 oz) firm white fish fillets
1 1/2 cups (375 ml/ 12 fl oz) milk
1 onion, roughly chopped
2 cloves
50 g (1 3/4 oz) butter
2 tablespoons plain flour
pinch of ground nutmeg
2 tablespoons chopped fresh parsley
1 cup (155 g/5 oz) peas
750 g (1 1/2 lb) potatoes, quartered
2 tablespoons hot milk
1/4 cup (30 g/1 oz) grated Cheddar

1 Place the fish fillets in a frying pan and cover with the milk. Add the onion and cloves, and bring to the boil. Reduce the heat and simmer for about 5 minutes, or until the fish is cooked—the flesh should be opaque and flake easily with a fork.
2 Preheat the oven to moderate 180°C (350°F/ Gas 4). Remove the fish from the pan, reserving the milk and onion mixture. Discard the cloves. Allow the fish to cool then remove any skin and bones and flake into bite-sized pieces.
3 Heat half of the butter in a pan, stir in the flour and cook, stirring, for 1 minute. Remove from the heat, add the reserved milk mixture and stir until smooth. Return to the heat and cook, stirring, until the sauce comes to the boil and thickens. Cook for 1 minute. Remove from the heat, allow to cool slightly, then add the nutmeg, parsley and peas. Season well with salt and freshly ground black pepper, and gently fold in the fish. Spoon into a 1.25 litre ovenproof dish.
4 Cook the potatoes in boiling water until tender. Drain and add the hot milk and remaining butter. Mash until very smooth. Add the cheese. If the mash is very stiff you may need to add a little more milk—the mash should be fairly firm.
5 Spoon the mashed potato into a piping bag and pipe it over the filling; or alternatively, spoon it over the top of the filling and rough it up with a fork. Bake for about 30 minutes, or until heated through.

THAI FISH CAKES

Preparation: 30 minutes
Cooking: 10 minutes
Serves 4–6

450 g (14 oz) firm white boneless fish fillets
1/4 cup (45 g/1 1/2 oz) rice flour or cornflour
1 tablespoon fish sauce
1 egg, beaten
1/2 cup (25 g/3/4 oz) chopped fresh coriander
3 teaspoons Thai red curry paste
1–2 small red chillies, finely chopped
100 g (3 1/2 oz) green beans, very finely sliced
2 spring onions, chopped
1/2 cup (125 ml/4 fl oz) oil
sweet chilli sauce, to serve

1 Work the fish in a food processor for 20 seconds, or until smooth. Add the rice flour, fish sauce, egg, coriander, curry paste and chilli. Mix for 10 seconds. Transfer to a bowl and mix in the beans and spring onion. Using wet hands, make into patties.
2 Heat the oil in a heavy-based frying pan until a cube of bread browns in 15 seconds. Cook four fish cakes at a time until golden brown on both sides. Serve with sweet chilli sauce.

FISH AND CHIPS

Preparation: 25 minutes
Cooking: 25 minutes
Serves 4

Beer batter
1 1/2 cups (375 ml/12 fl oz) beer
1 1/4 cups (155 g/5 oz) plain flour

4 potatoes
oil, for deep-frying
4 firm white fish fillets
cornflour, to coat
lemon wedges, to serve

1 To make the batter, gradually whisk the beer into the flour to make a smooth batter.

Use red curry paste for THAI FISH CAKES.

2 Peel the potatoes and cut into chips 1 cm (3/4 inch) thick. Soak for 10 minutes in cold water. Drain and pat dry.
3 Fill a large, deep heavy-based pan two-thirds full with oil and heat until a cube of bread browns in 30 seconds. Cook the chips in batches for 4–5 minutes, or until pale golden. Remove with tongs or a slotted spoon and drain on paper towels.
4 Just before serving, reheat the oil until a cube of bread browns in 15 seconds. Re-cook the chips in batches until crisp and golden. Drain and keep hot.
5 Dry the fish on paper towels. Lightly dust with cornflour and dip into the batter. Deep-fry in batches for 5–7 minutes, or until cooked through. Drain on paper towels and serve with lemon wedges.

FISH AND CHIPS (top) with SMOKED TROUT PATE.

SMOKED TROUT PATE

Preparation: 10 minutes
Cooking: Nil
Serves 4–6

250 g (8 oz) smoked trout, skinned, boned
125 g (4 oz) butter, softened
125 g (4 oz) cream cheese, softened
1 tablespoon lemon juice
1 teaspoon horseradish cream
1/4 cup (15 g/1/2 oz) chopped fresh parsley
1/4 cup (15 g/1/2 oz) finely chopped chives
toasted brown bread, to serve

1 Place the trout, butter and cream cheese in a food processor. Process for 20 seconds, or until the mixture is smooth.
2 Add the lemon juice, horseradish, parsley and chives, and process for 10 seconds. Season with salt and freshly ground black pepper and more lemon juice, if desired.
3 Transfer to a small serving dish. Serve with the hot toasted brown bread and maybe lemon wedges on the side.

STORAGE: Best eaten on the same day, but can be kept for up to 4 days in the fridge.
VARIATION: Try smoked haddock or mackerel.

TROUT WITH ALMONDS

Preparation: 25 minutes
Cooking: 20 minutes
Serves 2

2 rainbow trout, cleaned
flour, to coat
60 g (2 oz) butter
1/4 cup (25 g/3/4 oz) flaked almonds
2 tablespoons lemon juice
1 tablespoon finely chopped fresh parsley

1 Wash the trout and pat dry with paper towels. Open the trout out, skin-side-up. Using a rolling pin, run along the backbone starting from the tail, pressing gently down. Turn the trout over and cut through the backbone at each end of the fish with a pair of scissors. Lever the backbone out. Check for any remaining bones, and trim the fins with scissors.
2 Coat the fish with the flour. Heat half the butter in a large frying pan and add the fish. Cook for 7 minutes on each side, or until golden brown and cooked through. Remove and place on heated plates. Cover with foil.
3 Heat the remaining butter, add the flaked almonds and stir until the almonds are light golden brown. Add the lemon juice, parsley and some salt and pepper. Stir until the sauce is heated through. Pour over the trout and serve.

NOTE: The trout can be boned several hours ahead and refrigerated.

You could ask your fishmonger to bone the TROUT for you.

BAKED SNAPPER WITH GARLIC AND TOMATOES

Preparation: 25 minutes
Cooking: 30–40 minutes
Serves 4–6

1 kg (2 lb) whole snapper, scaled and cleaned
1 lemon, sliced
1 small onion, thickly sliced
1 clove garlic
sprig of fresh thyme
1 tablespoon olive oil
extra thyme leaves and lemon slices, to garnish

Sauce
2 tablespoons olive oil
1 clove garlic, crushed
1 small onion, chopped
1 teaspoon sugar
3 anchovies, mashed
1/2 cup (125 ml/4 fl oz) white wine
440 g (14 oz) can tomatoes, chopped, juice reserved
1/3 cup (80 ml/2 3/4 fl oz) lemon juice
sprig of fresh thyme

1 Preheat the oven to moderately hot 200°C (400°F/Gas 6). Remove any loose scales from the fish, trim the tail to a V shape and remove the fins. Wipe out the gut area with damp paper towels. Place the lemon slices, onion, garlic and

BAKED SNAPPER WITH GARLIC AND TOMATOES.

thyme into the gutted cavity. Score the thickest part of the fish with two diagonal slashes. Turn the fish over and slash the other side. Rub the outside of the fish with the olive oil. Place in a baking dish.

2 To make the sauce, heat the oil in a pan, add the garlic and onion, and cook, stirring, until the onion is golden. Stir in the sugar, anchovies, wine, tomato and juice, lemon juice and fresh thyme. Simmer until the sauce has reduced by one third and has thickened slightly.

3 Pour the sauce over the fish. Bake for 20 minutes, or until the fish flakes easily. Serve on a heated platter, garnished with thyme leaves and lemon.

HINT: This dish can be served either hot or cold. Many people don't think of serving fish cold, but it is delicious. It is important to serve it at room temperature, not chilled. Cook as above, cover and set aside until it cools. To remove the bone neatly when serving, cut through the centre of the fish on one side and gently push the flesh away to either side, so the bone is exposed. Lift the tail and remove the bone.

POACHED SALMON WITH HOLLANDAISE SAUCE

Preparation: 20 minutes
Cooking: 10 minutes
Serves 4

1 cup (250 ml/8 fl oz) white wine
2 cups (500 ml/16 fl oz) fish stock
1 tablespoon lemon juice
1 large slice of onion
4 Atlantic salmon cutlets, 2.5 cm (1 inch) thick
fresh dill, to garnish

Hollandaise sauce
3 egg yolks
125 g (4 oz) butter, melted and hot
1/2 teaspoon grated lemon rind
1 tablespoon lemon juice

1 Place the wine, stock, lemon juice and onion in a shallow pan. Bring to the boil, then reduce the heat to simmer.
2 Place the salmon cutlets in a single layer in the simmering stock. Poach the fish gently for about 7 minutes, or until it is just cooked, turning once.
3 Remove the fish from the pan and drain on paper towels. Cover the fish with foil to keep it warm.
4 To make the hollandaise sauce, put the egg yolks in a food processor and process for 10 seconds. With the motor running pour the hot and bubbling butter in a slow stream onto the egg yolks. Discard the white butter residue that will be left at the bottom of the pan. Add the grated lemon rind and juice, and process for another 30 seconds, or until the sauce thickens.
5 Arrange the fish on serving dishes. Serve with the hollandaise sauce and garnish with the fresh dill.

NOTE: The hollandaise sauce is best served immediately. If necessary it can be stored in an airtight container in the fridge for up to 2 days. Reheat in a heatproof bowl over a pan of gently simmering water.
VARIATION: Ocean trout cutlets can be used instead of salmon. Or you may prefer to use a large salmon fillet or whole salmon, including the head. If using a whole salmon it is best to skin the fish after poaching. If serving whole salmon cold, leave it in the stock until it is cooled. Remove the skin when cool.

Poach the SALMON in a mixture of wine, stock and lemon juice.

Use floury potatoes that mash well for SALMON PATTIES.

SALMON PATTIES

Preparation: 1 hour
Cooking: 25 minutes
Serves 4

650 g (1 lb 5 oz) floury potatoes, chopped
425 g (14 oz) can red salmon, drained
2 spring onions, finely chopped
1/4 cup (15 g/1/2 oz) chopped fresh parsley
2 teaspoons grated lemon rind
1 egg
5 slices bread, crusts removed
40 g (1 1/4 oz) butter
1/4 cup (60 ml/2 fl oz) olive oil
lemon wedges, to serve

1 Cook the potato in boiling water until very tender. Drain well and mash until smooth.
2 Place the salmon in a large bowl and break up the flesh with a fork, removing any bones and skin. Add the spring onion, parsley, lemon rind, egg and mashed potato. Season with salt and pepper and stir well. Shape into rough patties, using about a third of a cup for each patty.
3 Chop the bread in a food processor until it forms fine crumbs. Gently roll the patties in the breadcrumbs and neaten the shape. Press the breadcrumbs firmly onto the patties with your fingertips to coat well.
4 Heat the butter and oil in a large frying pan. When the butter is foaming, add the patties and cook each side for 3–5 minutes, or until golden and browned. Drain on paper towels. Serve with lemon wedges.

VARIATION: Use canned tuna in brine, drained, instead of the salmon.
NOTE: Suitable floury potatoes (those good for mashing) are Idaho, Sebago, King Edward and Coliban. Or you could even try using mashed sweet potato.

TUNA MORNAY

Preparation: 40 minutes
Cooking: 35 minutes
Serves 4

1 1/2 cups (375 ml/ 12 fl oz) milk
1 bay leaf
1 slice of onion
5 whole black peppercorns
60 g (2 oz) butter
1 onion, finely chopped
1 celery stick, finely chopped
1/4 cup (30 g/1 oz) plain flour
425 g (14 oz) can tuna in brine, drained, flaked, brine reserved
1/4 teaspoon ground nutmeg
1/3 cup (80 ml/2 3/4 fl oz) cream
1/4 cup (15 g/1/2 oz) finely chopped fresh parsley
1 cup (125 g/4 oz) grated Cheddar
1/2 cup (40 g/1 1/4 oz) fresh breadcrumbs
paprika, to taste

1 Heat the milk, bay leaf, onion slice and peppercorns in a small pan. Bring to the boil, then remove from the heat, cover and leave to infuse for 15 minutes. Strain and reserve the milk.

Brown the topping of the TUNA MORNAY under the grill.

2 Preheat the oven to moderate 180°C (350°F/ Gas 4). Heat the butter in a pan and add the onion and celery. Cook, stirring, for 5 minutes, or until the onion is soft. Add the flour and stir for 1 minute, or until the mixture is bubbly. Remove from the heat and gradually stir in the combined reserved milk and tuna brine. Stir until smooth. Return to the heat and stir until the mixture almost boils. Reduce the heat to low and simmer for 5 minutes, or until thickened.
3 Add the nutmeg, cream, parsley and half of the cheese. Stir for 2 minutes, or until the cheese is melted. Remove from the heat, add the flaked tuna and season with salt and freshly ground black pepper. Stir to combine.
4 Spoon the mixture into a 3-cup (750 ml/24 fl oz) greased ovenproof dish. Sprinkle the top with the combined breadcrumbs, paprika and remaining cheese. Bake for 15 minutes, then place the dish under a hot grill for 2 minutes to brown the breadcrumb topping.

NOTE: Tuna mornay can be used as a filling for pancakes or pastry cases.
VARIATION: Use canned salmon instead of tuna.

SEAFOOD CREPES

Preparation: 50 minutes + 30 minutes standing
Cooking: 30 minutes
Serves 8

1 cup (125 g/4 oz) plain flour
1 egg, plus 1 egg yolk
1 cup (250 ml/8 fl oz) milk
20 g (3/4 oz) butter, melted
1 tablespoon poppy seeds, optional

Seafood filling
1 cup (250 ml/8 fl oz) white wine
1/2 cup (125 ml/4 fl oz) fish stock or water
200 g (6 1/2 oz) small scallops
400 g (13 oz) raw prawns, peeled, deveined and halved
200 g (6 1/2 oz) boneless white fish fillets
60 g (2 oz) butter
3 spring onions, chopped
2 bacon rashers, chopped
1/4 cup (30 g/1 oz) plain flour
3/4 cup (185 ml/6 fl oz) cream
1 teaspoon lemon juice
1/4 cup (15 g/1/2 oz) chopped fresh parsley
2 tablespoons chopped fresh chives

We've added poppy seeds to our SEAFOOD CREPES.

1 Mix together the flour, egg, egg yolk and half the milk. Add the remaining milk, butter, and poppy seeds if you are using, and mix until smooth. Cover and leave for 30 minutes. Transfer to a jug.

2 Heat a crepe pan and brush lightly with melted butter. Add enough batter to thinly cover the base, pouring the excess back into the jug. Cook for 30 seconds, turn over and cook until lightly browned. Remove and cover while cooking the remaining crepes.

3 To make the filling, heat the wine and stock in a pan until simmering. Add the seafood and cook for 4 minutes. Drain, reserving the liquid. Flake the fish. Melt the butter in a pan, add the spring onion and bacon, and stir for 2–3 minutes, or until cooked. Add the flour, stir for 1 minute and remove from the heat. Add 1 cup (250 ml/8 fl oz) of the reserved stock mixture, return to the heat and stir for 2 minutes, or until it boils and thickens. Stir in the cream, lemon juice, parsley, chives and some pepper. Add the seafood and heat gently for 2–3 minutes, taking care not to overcook.

4 Place 2 tablespoons of the filling over a quarter of each crepe. Fold in quarters to serve.

GARLIC PRAWNS

Preparation: 20 minutes
Cooking: 5 minutes
Serves 4

1 cup (250 ml/8 fl oz) oil
60 g (2 oz) butter, cut into 4 cubes
8 garlic cloves
20 raw king prawns, peeled and deveined, tails left intact
2 tablespoons chopped fresh parsley
French bread, for serving

1 Heat the oil, butter and garlic in a pan. When bubbling, add all the prawns and cook until they turn pink.

2 Preheat the oven to hot 210°C (415°F/Gas 6–7). Heat four heatproof serving dishes in the oven until quite hot. Remove the dishes from the oven and place 5 prawns in each dish. Spoon some oil into each dish. Sprinkle with the parsley and serve with French bread.

VARIATION: Give your garlic prawns a little extra bite by adding 2 small red sliced chillies to the garlic butter, when you add the garlic in step 1. Remove the seeds from the chillies first (unless you like them extra hot).

NOTE: Garlic prawns can also be cooked on the barbecue. Divide the oil among four flameproof dishes. Add a cube of butter to each dish and heat the barbecue. Crush 2 cloves of garlic into each dish. Heat the dishes on a barbecue flatplate until the butter is very hot and bubbling. Add 5 prawns to each dish and cook for 3–4 minutes, or until the prawns are pink and cooked through. Sprinkle with the chopped parsley and serve with French bread.

Add a little extra bite to GARLIC PRAWNS with sliced red chillies.

SPAGHETTI MARINARA

Preparation: 50 minutes
Cooking: 30 minutes
Serves 4

olive oil, for cooking
1 onion, chopped
2 cloves garlic, crushed
1/2 cup (125 ml/4 fl oz) red wine
2 tablespoons tomato paste
425 g (14 oz) can chopped tomatoes
1 cup (250 ml/8 fl oz) bottled tomato pasta sauce
1 tablespoon chopped fresh basil
1 tablespoon chopped fresh oregano
12 mussels, scrubbed, beards removed
30 g (1 oz) butter
125 g (4 oz) small calamari tubes, sliced
125 g (4 oz) boneless white fish fillets, cubed
200 g (6 1/2 oz) raw prawns, shelled and deveined, leaving tails intact
500 g (1 lb) spaghetti

SPAGHETTI MARINARA.

1 Heat a little of the oil in a large pan and cook the onion and garlic over low heat for 2–3 minutes. Increase the heat to moderate and add the wine, tomato paste, tomato and pasta sauce. Simmer for 5–10 minutes, stirring occasionally, until the sauce reduces and thickens slightly. Stir in the herbs and season to taste with salt and pepper. Keep warm.

2 Heat 1/2 cup (125 ml/4 fl oz) water in a pan. Add the mussels (discarding any which are already open and don't close when tapped), cover and steam for 3–5 minutes, or until the mussels have opened (discard any mussels which haven't opened after 5 minutes). Remove and set aside. Stir the remaining liquid into the tomato sauce.

3 Heat the butter in a pan and fry the calamari, fish and prawns, in batches, for 1–2 minutes, or until cooked. Add the seafood to the warm tomato sauce and stir gently.

4 Cook the spaghetti in a large pan of rapidly boiling salted water until just tender, then drain. Toss the sauce through the spaghetti and serve.

VARIATION: Use 500 g (1 lb) marinara mix instead of the seafood.

OYSTERS MORNAY

Preparation: 15 minutes
Cooking: 10 minutes
Serves 4

30 g (1 oz) butter
1 tablespoon plain flour
2/3 cup (170 ml/ 5 1/2 fl oz) hot milk
pinch of cayenne pepper
1 tablespoon cream
24 fresh oysters in shells
rock salt
1/3 cup (40 g/1 1/4 oz) grated Cheddar
paprika, to sprinkle

1 Melt the butter in a small pan. Stir in the flour and cook for 2 minutes. Remove from the heat and gradually stir in the hot milk. Stir over medium heat until the mixture boils and thickens. Season with salt, pepper and the cayenne pepper.
2 Simmer the sauce very gently for 2 minutes, stirring occasionally. Stir in the cream. Remove from the heat and lay baking paper directly on the surface to prevent a skin forming.
3 Drain the juice from the oysters and add the juice to the sauce. Arrange the oysters in shells on a bed of rock salt on a baking or grill tray. Top the oysters with a teaspoon of the hot sauce and sprinkle with the cheese. Place under a hot grill for 2–3 minutes, or until lightly browned. Sprinkle with the paprika.

OYSTERS MORNAY.

VARIATIONS:
For Oysters Rockefeller, arrange 24 fresh oysters in half shells on rock salt. Cover and refrigerate. Melt 60 g (2 oz) butter in a pan and cook 2 finely chopped rashers of bacon over medium heat until browned. Add 8 finely chopped English spinach leaves, 2 tablespoons each of chopped parsley and spring onion, 1/3 cup (30 g/1 oz) dry breadcrumbs and a drop of Tabasco. Cook for 5 minutes, or until the spinach wilts. Spoon a little over each oyster and grill for 2–3 minutes, or until lightly browned.

For Oysters Kilpatrick, Place 24 oysters in half shells on a grill tray. Heat 30 g (1 oz) butter in a small pan. Add 2 tablespoons Worcestershire sauce and simmer for 2 minutes. Spoon half a teaspoon of the sauce onto each oyster. Sprinkle with 3 finely chopped rashers of bacon and some ground black pepper. Grill for 3–4 minutes, or until the bacon is crisp. Serve immediately on a bed of rock salt.

Use scallops in their shells for COQUILLES SAINT JACQUES.

COQUILLES SAINT JACQUES

Preparation: 20 minutes
Cooking: 15 minutes
Serves 4

12 scallops on shells
1 cup (250 ml/8 fl oz) white wine
1 bay leaf
4 peppercorns
1 onion, chopped
30 g (1 oz) butter
1 1/2 tablespoons flour
3/4 cup (185 ml/6 fl oz) milk
1/2 cup (60 g/2 oz) grated Cheddar
2 tablespoons dry breadcrumbs

1 Remove the black vein from the side of each scallop with scissors.
2 Place the wine, bay leaf, peppercorns and onion in a small pan. Bring to the boil, then reduce the heat and simmer until the liquid has reduced by three quarters. Strain the liquid and set aside.
3 Melt the butter in a small pan. Add the flour and cook for 1 minute. Remove the pan from the heat and gradually stir in the milk and the strained liquid, stirring until smooth. Return to medium heat and stir until the mixture boils and thickens. Season with salt and pepper and stir in half of the cheese.
4 Spoon over the scallops in their shells. Sprinkle with the combined breadcrumbs and remaining cheese, and grill until crisp and golden brown.

PRAWN COCKTAIL

Preparation: 20 minutes
Cooking: Nil
Serves 4

Cocktail sauce
1 cup (250 g/8 oz) whole egg mayonnaise
2 tablespoons tomato sauce
2 tablespoons thick cream
dash of Tabasco sauce
1 teaspoon lemon juice
1 teaspoon Worcestershire sauce
24 cooked prawns, peeled and deveined, tails left intact
lettuce, lemon wedges and buttered brown bread, to serve

1 Mix together all the sauce ingredients in a large bowl.
2 Keep six or eight prawns on one side to garnish. Remove the tails from the remaining prawns and mix gently with the sauce.
3 Arrange the lettuce in serving bowls and spoon the prawns over the top. Decorate with the reserved prawns and serve with the lemon wedges and slices of brown bread.

PRAWN COCKTAIL (top) and PRAWN CUTLETS.

PRAWN CUTLETS WITH TARTARE SAUCE

Preparation: 40 minutes
Cooking: 10 minutes
Serves 4–6

24 raw king prawns, peeled, tails intact
4 eggs
2 tablespoons soy sauce
cornflour, to coat
dry breadcrumbs
oil, for deep-frying
lemon wedges, to serve

Tartare sauce
1 cup (250 g/8 oz) mayonnaise
1 tablespoon grated onion
1 tablespoon capers, chopped
1 tablespoon gherkins, finely chopped
1 tablespoon lemon juice
1 tablespoon finely chopped fresh parsley
dash of Tabasco sauce

1 Butterfly the prawns by slitting them open down the back. Devein and flatten with your hand.
2 Beat the eggs and soy sauce in a small bowl. Dip the prawns in the cornflour, then in the egg

mixture and finally in the breadcrumbs. Refrigerate for 10 minutes to firm up.
3 Heat the oil in a deep pan until a cube of bread dropped into the oil browns in 15 seconds. Deep-fry the prawns in batches until lightly golden and then drain on paper towels.
4 To make the tartare sauce, mix together all the ingredients. Serve the prawns with the tartare sauce and lemon wedges.

MOULES MARINIERE

Preparation: 15 minutes
Cooking: 40 minutes
Serves 4

1 kg (2 lb) mussels, scrubbed, beards removed
1 onion, chopped
1 celery stick, chopped
1 cup (250 ml/8 fl oz) white wine
1 1/2 cups (375 ml/ 12 fl oz) fish stock
4 sprigs of fresh parsley
1 sprig of fresh thyme
1 bay leaf
50 g (1 3/4 oz) butter
2 cloves garlic, crushed
2 onions, extra, chopped
1 teaspoon plain flour
fresh dill sprigs, to serve

1 Rinse the mussels several times under cold running water and discard any which are already open and don't close when tapped (it's a good idea to buy a few extra mussels in case any need to be thrown away).
2 Put the mussels, onion, celery and wine in a large pan and bring rapidly to the boil. Cover and cook, shaking the pan frequently, for 3 minutes. After 3 minutes, start removing mussels as they open. Pull apart the shells and discard the empty half. Set aside the half shells with the mussels attached, cover and keep warm. After 5 minutes discard any mussels which haven't opened.
3 Strain and reserve the remaining liquid and discard the vegetables.
4 Heat the fish stock, parsley, thyme and bay leaf in a pan. Bring to the boil, then reduce the heat, cover and simmer for 10 minutes. Strain and remove the herbs.
5 Heat the butter in a large pan. Add the garlic and extra onion, and cook gently for 5 minutes, or until the onion is soft but not browned. Stir in the flour and cook, stirring, for 1 minute. Remove from the heat and slowly stir in the reserved mussel liquid and hot fish stock. Stir until smooth, return to the heat and stir until the sauce boils and thickens. Reduce the heat and leave to simmer for 10 minutes.
6 Place the mussels in four soup bowls. Ladle the liquid over the top and garnish with dill sprigs. Serve with crusty bread.

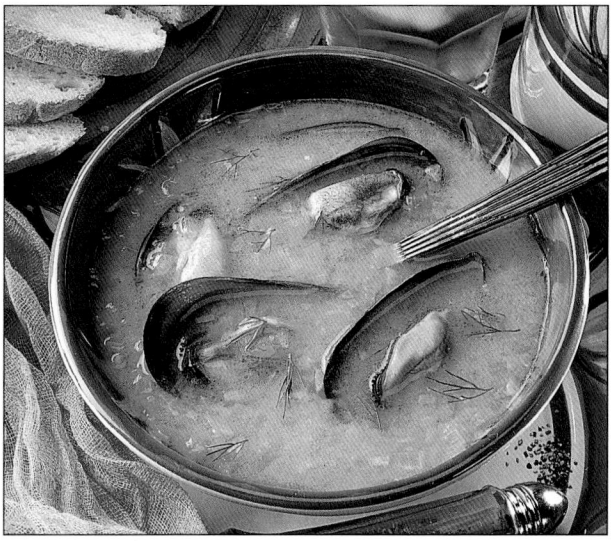

Mussels and wine combine in MOULES MARINIERE.

MUSSELS WITH TOMATO AND WINE

Preparation: 20 minutes
Cooking: 30 minutes
Serves 6

1.5 kg (3 lb) mussels
1 1/2 cups (375 ml/ 12 fl oz) white wine
1 tablespoon olive oil
1 onion, chopped
3 cloves garlic, chopped
425 g (14 oz) canned tomatoes, chopped
1 tablespoon tomato paste
1/3 cup (10 g/1/4 oz) chopped fresh parsley

1 Scrub the mussels under cold running water and remove their beards. Discard any which are already open and don't close when tapped. Place the mussels and wine in a large pan. Cover and simmer over medium heat for 3–5 minutes. After 3 minutes, start removing mussels as they open. After 5 minutes discard any which haven't opened. Keep the wine.
2 Heat the oil in a frying pan and cook the onion and garlic for 3 minutes, or until the onion is soft. Stir in the tomatoes, tomato paste and reserved wine. Bring to the boil, then reduce the heat and simmer for 15–20 minutes, or until the sauce has reduced and thickened slightly. Season to taste.
3 Add the mussels and parsley to the pan. Toss through the tomato sauce.

Always buy a few extra MUSSELS in case some don't open.

LOBSTER THERMIDOR

Preparation: 25 minutes
Cooking: 15 minutes
Serves 2

1 cooked lobster
80 g (2 3/4 oz) butter
4 spring onions, finely chopped
2 tablespoons plain flour
1 teaspoon English mustard
2 tablespoons white wine or sherry
1 cup (250 ml/8 fl oz) milk
1/4 cup (60 ml/2 fl oz) cream
1 tablespoon chopped fresh parsley
1/2 cup (60 g/2 oz) grated Parmesan

1 Using a sharp knife, cut the lobster in half lengthways. Lift the meat from the tail and body. Crack the legs and prise the meat from them. Remove the intestinal vein and soft body matter and discard. Cut the meat into bite-sized pieces, cover and refrigerate. Wash the shell halves, drain and dry.
2 Heat 60 g (2 oz) of the butter in a frying pan and cook the spring onion for 2 minutes, or until soft. Add the flour and mustard, and cook for 1 minute. Remove from the heat and gradually stir

in the wine and milk. Return to the heat and cook, stirring, until the mixture boils and thickens. Simmer for 1 minute. Stir in the cream, parsley and lobster meat, and season with salt and freshly ground black pepper. Heat gently.

3 Spoon the mixture into the lobster shells, sprinkle with the cheese and dot with the remaining butter. Place under a preheated grill for 2 minutes, or until lightly browned.

LOBSTER MORNAY

Preparation: 25 minutes
Cooking: 15 minutes
Serves 2

1 cooked lobster
1 1/4 cups (315 ml/ 10 fl oz) milk
1 slice onion
1 bay leaf
6 black peppercorns
30 g (1 oz) butter
2 tablespoons plain flour
pinch of nutmeg
2 tablespoons cream
1/2 cup (60 g/2 oz) grated Cheddar

1 Using a sharp knife, cut the lobster in half lengthways. Lift the meat from the tail and body. Crack the legs and prise the meat from them. Remove the intestinal vein and soft body matter and discard. Cut the meat into bite-sized pieces, cover and refrigerate. Wash the shell halves, drain and dry.

2 Heat the milk, onion, bay leaf and peppercorns in a small pan. Bring to the boil then remove from the heat, cover and leave for 15 minutes. Strain.

3 Melt the butter in a large pan, add the flour and stir for 1 minute. Remove from the heat and gradually add the infused milk. Stir until smooth. Cook, stirring over medium heat, until the mixture boils and thickens. Season with salt, white pepper and nutmeg. Stir in the cream.

4 Fold the lobster meat through the sauce. Divide the mixture between the shells and sprinkle the top with the cheese. Place under a preheated grill for 2 minutes, or until the cheese has melted.

LOBSTER THERMIDOR (top) and LOBSTER MORNAY.

Crumb and deep-fry the CALAMARI WITH CHILLI PLUM SAUCE.

CALAMARI WITH CHILLI PLUM SAUCE

Preparation: 30 minutes
Cooking: 20 minutes
Serves 4

500 g (1 lb) calamari tubes, rinsed
3 tablespoons plain flour
2 eggs, lightly beaten
3 cups (240 g/7½ oz) fresh or dry white breadcrumbs
oil, for deep-frying

Chilli plum sauce
1 teaspoon oil
1 clove garlic, crushed
1 cup (315 g/10 oz) dark plum jam
⅓ cup (80 ml/2¾ fl oz) white vinegar
1–2 tablespoons bottled chopped chilli or sweet chilli sauce

1 Dry the calamari with paper towels. Remove any spine and skin. Cut the calamari into rings.
2 Season the flour well and use to coat the calamari rings. Then dip in the beaten egg, drain off the excess and toss in the breadcrumbs, patting them lightly onto the rings and shaking off the excess. Refrigerate for 10 minutes. Heat the oil in a large heavy-based pan to 180°C (350°F), or until a bread cube browns in 15 seconds.
3 Fry the calamari in batches until crisp and golden; drain well. Use a slotted spoon to remove the crumbs from the oil between batches.
4 To make the sauce, heat the oil in a small pan. Add the garlic and cook until it is just starting to colour. Add the jam, vinegar and chilli. Stir over medium heat until well blended. Thin with a little warm water if necessary. Serve with the calamari rings.

Cook CHAR-GRILLED BABY OCTOPUS under a grill or on a barbecue hotplate.

CHAR-GRILLED BABY OCTOPUS

Preparation: 20 minutes + 2 hours marinating
Cooking: 5 minutes
Serves 4

500 g (1 lb) baby octopus
1/2 cup (125 ml/4 fl oz) olive oil
2 tablespoons lemon juice
2 tablespoons finely chopped fresh coriander
2 tablespoons sweet chilli sauce

1 Using a sharp knife, cut the head from the octopus and remove the gut from inside. Push the beak up and out of the lower section and discard. Wash the octopus thoroughly and dry on paper towels.
2 Place the olive oil, lemon juice, coriander and sweet chilli sauce in a bowl with some salt and freshly ground black pepper, and whisk well. Add the octopus and stir well. Cover and refrigerate for 2 hours or overnight, stirring occasionally. Drain the octopus, reserving the marinade for brushing.
3 Heat the grill or a barbecue plate until very hot and brush it with oil to prevent the octopus sticking. Cook the octopus for 3–5 minutes, turning frequently until it is just tender. Brush with the marinade during cooking. Serve immediately, perhaps garnished with a few fresh coriander leaves.

STORAGE: Cover and refrigerate the cooked octopus for up to 2 days.
HINT: Octopus will toughen if overcooked.

corymbosum

VEGETARIAN

Today many of us live on a virtually meat-free diet without even considering ourselves vegetarian. As more and more people turn to a vegetarian lifestyle, or even just try to cut down the amount of red meat they eat, it is important to have a few delicious and reliable recipes tucked up your sleeve. Vegetarian food is usually good value and easy to cook, so if you have vegetarian friends don't just serve them up another baked potato.

NUT ROAST

Preparation: 30 minutes
Cooking: 1 hour
Serves 6

2 tablespoons olive oil
1 large onion, diced
2 cloves garlic, crushed
300 g (10 oz) field mushrooms, finely chopped
200 g (6 1/2 oz) raw cashews
200 g (6 1/2 oz) brazil nuts
1 cup (125 g/4 oz) grated Cheddar
1/4 cup (25 g/3/4 oz) freshly grated Parmesan
1 egg, lightly beaten
2 tablespoons chopped fresh chives
1 cup (80 g/2 3/4 oz) fresh wholemeal breadcrumbs

Tomato sauce
30 ml (1 fl oz) olive oil
1 onion, finely chopped
1 clove garlic, crushed
400 g (13 oz) can tomatoes, chopped
1 tablespoon tomato paste
1 teaspoon caster sugar

1 Grease a 14 x 21 cm (5 1/2 x 8 1/2 inch) loaf tin and line the base with baking paper. Heat the oil in a frying pan and add the onion, garlic and mushrooms. Fry until soft, then allow to cool.
2 Process the nuts in a food processor until finely chopped, but do not overprocess. Preheat the oven to moderate 180°C (350°F/Gas 4).
3 Mix together the nuts, mushroom mixture, cheese, egg, chives and breadcrumbs. Press firmly into the loaf tin and bake for 45 minutes, or until firm. Leave in the tin for 5 minutes, then turn out.
4 To make the sauce, heat the oil in a pan and add the onion and garlic. Fry for 5 minutes, or until soft but not brown. Add the chopped tomatoes, tomato paste, sugar and 1/3 cup (80 ml/2 3/4 fl oz) water. Simmer for 3–5 minutes, or until the sauce has slightly thickened. Season to taste with salt and pepper. Serve the tomato sauce with the sliced nut roast.

FELAFEL

Preparation: 1 hour + 4 hours soaking + resting
Cooking: 25 minutes
Serves 6

2 cups (440 g/14 oz) chickpeas
1 small onion, chopped
2 cloves garlic, crushed
2 tablespoons chopped fresh parsley
1 tablespoon chopped fresh coriander
2 teaspoons ground cumin
1/2 teaspoon baking powder
oil, for deep-frying

Hummus
425 g (14 oz) can chickpeas
2–3 tablespoons lemon juice
2 tablespoons olive oil
2 cloves garlic, crushed
3 tablespoons tahini

Tomato salsa
2 tomatoes, peeled and finely chopped
1/4 Lebanese cucumber, finely chopped
1/2 green capsicum, finely chopped
2 tablespoons chopped fresh parsley
1 teaspoon sugar
2 teaspoons chilli sauce
grated rind and juice of 1 lemon

Serve FELAFEL with hummus and a tomato salsa.

1 Soak the chickpeas in 3 cups (750 ml/24 fl oz) water for at least 4 hours. Drain and mix in a food processor for 30 seconds, or until finely ground.
2 Add the onion, garlic, parsley, coriander, cumin, baking powder and 1 tablespoon water, and process for 10 seconds, or until the mixture forms a rough paste. Cover and set aside for 30 minutes.
3 To make the hummus, place the drained chick peas, lemon juice, oil and garlic in a food processor. Season and process for 20–30 seconds, or until smooth. Add the tahini and process for a further 10 seconds.
4 To make the tomato salsa, mix together all the ingredients and season with plenty of freshly ground black pepper.
5 Shape heaped tablespoons of the felafel mixture into balls. Squeeze out the excess moisture. Heat the oil in a deep, heavy-based pan, until a cube of bread browns in 15 seconds. Lower the felafel into the oil in batches of five. Cook for 3–4 minutes each batch. When well browned, remove with a large slotted spoon. Drain on paper towels and serve hot or cold with Lebanese bread, hummus and tomato salsa.

CHILLI BEANS.

THAI VEGETABLE CURRY.

CHILLI BEANS

Preparation: 20 minutes
Cooking: 25 minutes
Serves 4

- 1 tablespoon oil
- 2 cloves garlic, crushed
- 2 small fresh red chillies, finely chopped
- 1 onion, finely chopped
- 1 green capsicum, diced
- 440 g (14 oz) can red kidney beans, rinsed
- 440 g (14 oz) can crushed tomatoes
- 1/2 cup (125 g/4 oz) tomato pasta sauce
- 1 teaspoon soft brown sugar

1 Heat the oil in a heavy-based pan and cook the garlic, chilli and onion for 3 minutes, or until the onion is golden.

2 Add the remaining ingredients, bring to the boil, then reduce the heat to simmer for 15 minutes, or until thickened.

THAI VEGETABLE CURRY

Preparation: 25 minutes
Cooking: 30 minutes
Serves 4

- 2 tablespoons Thai red curry paste
- 2 cups (500 ml/16 fl oz) coconut milk
- 4 kaffir lime leaves
- 1 onion, finely chopped
- 2 potatoes, chopped
- 200 g (6 1/2 oz) pumpkin, chopped
- 1 red capsicum, chopped
- 3 zucchini, chopped
- 90 g (3 oz) baby corn
- 150 g (5 oz) beans, chopped
- 2 tablespoons lime juice
- 2 tablespoons fish sauce
- 2 tablespoons chopped fresh coriander
- 1 tablespoon soft brown sugar

1 Mix the curry paste, coconut milk and 1/2 cup (125 ml/4 fl oz) water in a large pan. Bring to the boil, stirring occasionally.
2 Add the lime leaves and onion and boil for 3 minutes. Add the potato and pumpkin and cook for 15 minutes, or until tender. Add the capsicum, zucchini, corn and beans and cook for 10 minutes, or until tender.
3 Add the lime juice, fish sauce, coriander and sugar, and cook for 2 minutes. Serve with rice.

VEGETABLE LASAGNE

Preparation: 40 minutes + 20 minutes standing
Cooking: 2¼ hours
Serves 6

2 large eggplants
½ cup (125 ml/4 fl oz) olive oil
2 onions, chopped
3 cloves garlic, crushed
1 carrot, diced
1 celery stick, diced
100 g (3½ oz) button mushrooms, sliced
1 red capsicum, chopped
810 g (1 lb 10 oz) can crushed tomatoes
2 tablespoons tomato paste
1 cup (250 ml/8 fl oz) red wine
1 tablespoon balsamic vinegar
1 tablespoon soft brown sugar
¼ cup (15 g/½ oz) chopped fresh basil
250 g (8 oz) dried lasagne sheets
350 g (11 oz) English spinach, chopped
½ cup (50 g/1¾ oz) grated Parmesan
½ cup (60 g/2 oz) grated Cheddar

Bechamel sauce

60 g (2 oz) butter
3 tablespoons plain flour
2 cups (500 ml/16 fl oz) milk
300 g (10 oz) ricotta

Leave VEGETABLE LASAGNE for 10 minutes before cutting.

1 Slice the eggplants lengthways. Sprinkle generously with salt and leave for 20 minutes. (This draws out the bitterness. It is easiest to stand the eggplant in a colander.) Rinse well and pat dry. Brush lightly with half the olive oil. Grill under moderate heat until golden brown, then drain on paper towels.

2 Heat the remaining oil in a large heavy-based pan. Add the onion and cook over medium heat for 5 minutes, or until soft and golden. Add the garlic, carrot and celery, and cook for 3 minutes. Add the mushrooms and capsicum and cook for 3 minutes, or until the mushrooms are tender. Stir in the tomato, tomato paste, wine, vinegar and sugar. Bring to the boil, then reduce the heat and simmer for 1 hour. Add the basil.

3 To make the bechamel sauce, melt the butter in a pan and add the flour. Stir over low heat for 2 minutes, or until golden. Remove from the heat and gradually stir in the milk. Return to the heat and bring slowly to the boil, stirring, until the sauce boils and thickens. Simmer for 2 minutes, then add the ricotta and stir until smooth. Season with salt and pepper.

4 Preheat the oven to moderate 180°C (350°F/Gas 4). Lightly grease a 3-litre ovenproof dish. Spread a thin layer of vegetable sauce over the base of the dish and top with a layer of the lasagne sheets. Build up with a layer of vegetable sauce, spinach, eggplant and bechamel sauce. Continue layering, finishing with the bechamel sauce. Sprinkle the combined cheeses over the top and bake for 45–50 minutes, or until the lasagne is cooked and the cheese is golden brown. Leave for 10 minutes before cutting.

VEGETABLE STRUDEL is made with layers of filo pastry.

VEGETABLE STRUDEL

Preparation: 30 minutes + 20 minutes standing
Cooking: 50 minutes
Serves 6–8

1 large eggplant
1 red capsicum
3 zucchini, sliced lengthways
2 tablespoons olive oil
6 sheets filo pastry
50 g (1¾ oz) baby English spinach leaves
60 g (2 oz) feta cheese, sliced

1 Slice the eggplant lengthways. Sprinkle generously with salt and leave for 20 minutes (this draws out the bitterness). Rinse well and pat dry.
2 Cut the capsicum into large flat pieces and place, skin-side-up, under a hot grill until the skin blackens and blisters. Put in a plastic bag, then peel the skin away. Brush the eggplant and zucchini slices with some of the olive oil and grill for 5–10 minutes, or until golden brown. Set aside to cool. Preheat the oven to moderately hot 190°C (375°F/Gas 5).
3 Brush one sheet of filo pastry at a time with olive oil, then lay them on top of each other. Place half the eggplant slices lengthways down the centre of the filo and top with layers of zucchini, capsicum, spinach and feta cheese. Repeat the layers until the vegetables and cheese are used up. Tuck in the ends of the pastry, then roll up like a parcel. Brush lightly with oil, place on a baking tray and bake for 35 minutes, or until golden brown.

NOTE: Unopened filo can be stored in the fridge for up to a month. Once opened, use within 3 days or the pastry will dry out.

Make CHEESE SOUFFLES in small ramekins or one large one.

CHEESE SOUFFLES

Preparation: 35 minutes
Cooking: 20 minutes
Serves 6

1/4 cup (25 g/3/4 oz) dried breadcrumbs
20 g (3/4 oz) butter
3 tablespoons plain flour
1 cup (250 ml/8 fl oz) milk
1/4 cup (25 g/3/4 oz) grated Parmesan
3/4 cup (90 g/3 oz) grated Cheddar
1 teaspoon Dijon mustard
3 eggs, separated

1 Preheat the oven to moderate 180°C (350°F/Gas 4). Grease six 1/2 cup (125 ml/4 fl oz) soufflé dishes with melted butter. Coat the bases and sides evenly with the breadcrumbs, shaking off the excess.
2 Heat the butter in a small pan. Add the flour and stir over low heat for 2 minutes, or until lightly golden. Remove from the heat and add the milk gradually, stirring until smooth. Return to medium heat and stir until the sauce boils and thickens. Boil for 1 minute, then remove from the heat and add the Parmesan, Cheddar and mustard. Beat in the egg yolks, then transfer the mixture to a large bowl.
3 Place the egg whites in a small, clean dry mixing bowl. Beat until soft peaks form. Using a metal spoon, gradually fold the egg whites gently through the cheese mixture, then pour immediately into the soufflé dishes.
4 Bake for 10–15 minutes, or until the soufflés are puffed and golden. Serve the soufflés immediately because they quickly lose their volume once they leave the oven.

NOTE: If you would rather make one large soufflé, this mixture can be cooked in a 14 cm (6 inch) soufflé dish for approximately 45 minutes instead. Once your soufflé is cooking, try not to open the oven door before the cooking time is up. Soufflés should wobble slightly in the centre and should be moist when cooked. Soufflés can be prepared up to Step 2 ahead of time. Gently heat the base ingredients before adding the beaten egg whites.
HINT: Always use a clean dry bowl for whisking egg whites. The slightest hint of grease or moisture in the bowl (or yolk in the egg whites) will stop the whites foaming.

VEGETABLE FRITTATA

Preparation: 25 minutes
Cooking: 25 minutes
Serves 2 (or 4 as a snack)

1 tablespoon olive oil
2 cloves garlic, crushed
1 small red onion, chopped
1 small red capsicum, chopped
500 g (1 lb) roasted, boiled or steamed potatoes, thickly sliced
1/4 cup (15 g/1/2 oz) chopped fresh parsley
6 eggs, lightly beaten
1/4 cup (25 g/3/4 oz) grated Parmesan

1 Heat the oil in a large heavy-based, non-stick frying pan. Add the garlic, onion and capsicum and stir over medium heat for 2–3 minutes. Add the potato slices and cook for 2–3 minutes more. Stir in the parsley and spread the mixture evenly in the pan.
2 Beat the eggs with 2 tablespoons water, pour into the pan and cook over medium heat for 15 minutes, without burning the base.
3 Preheat the grill to high. Sprinkle the Parmesan over the frittata and grill for a few minutes to cook the egg and lightly brown. Cut into wedges to serve.

Leftover roast potatoes are ideal for a VEGETABLE FRITTATA.

GRATED VEGETABLE FRITTATA

Preparation: 25 minutes
Cooking: 30 minutes
Serves 2 (or 4 as a snack)

3 tablespoons olive oil
1 onion, finely chopped
1 small carrot, grated
1 small zucchini, grated
1 cup (125 g/4 oz) grated pumpkin
1/3 cup (45 g/1 1/2 oz) finely diced Jarlsburg or Cheddar cheese
5 eggs, lightly beaten

1 Heat 2 tablespoons of the oil in a pan and cook the onion for 5 minutes, or until soft. Add the carrot, zucchini and pumpkin and cook over low heat, covered, for 3 minutes. Transfer to a bowl and allow to cool. Stir in the cheese and plenty of salt and pepper. Add the eggs.
2 Heat the remaining oil in a small non-stick frying pan. Add the frittata mixture and shake the pan to spread it evenly. Reduce to low and cook for 15–20 minutes, or until set almost all the way through. Tilt the pan and lift the edges occasionally to allow the uncooked egg to flow underneath. Brown the top under a preheated hot grill. Cut into wedges and serve immediately.

HOT TOFU SALAD

Preparation: 20 minutes
Cooking: 10 minutes
Serves 4

1/4 cup (60 ml/2 fl oz) sweet chilli sauce
1 teaspoon crushed garlic
1 teaspoon grated ginger
2 tablespoons soy sauce
500 g (1 lb) firm tofu, cut into 1 cm (1/2 inch) cubes
2 tablespoons oil
2 carrots, sliced
2 zucchini, sliced
6 spring onions, sliced
100 g (3 1/2 oz) sugar snap peas, topped and tailed

1 Mix the sweet chilli sauce, garlic, ginger and soy sauce in a bowl. Add the tofu. Cover and marinate for 10 minutes.
2 Drain the tofu, reserving the marinade. Heat half the oil in a large frying pan. Add the tofu and cook in batches over high heat for 4 minutes, or until browned all over, turning often. Set aside.
3 Heat the remaining oil. Add the vegetables and toss over high heat for 2–3 minutes. Add the tofu and reserved marinade. Bring to the boil, stirring gently to combine the mixture. Remove from the heat and serve at once.

NOTE: Tofu is made from soy beans and is low in fat, high in calcium and an excellent source of protein. Use firm tofu for this recipe—this holds its shape well when marinated and cooked, as opposed to silken tofu which is soft and can be blended and used instead of dairy products when making dips, ice creams and desserts.
VARIATION: Cut the tofu into thick slices, marinate and then cook on the barbecue. Serve on a burger bun with lettuce and tomato.
STORAGE: To store tofu, place in an airtight container, cover it with water and store in the fridge.

STUFFED FIELD MUSHROOMS

Preparation: 20 minutes
Cooking: 25 minutes
Serves 4

4 large field mushrooms
30 g (1 oz) butter
1 leek, sliced
2–4 cloves garlic, crushed
2 teaspoons cumin seeds
1 teaspoon ground coriander
1/4–1/2 teaspoon chilli powder
2 tomatoes, chopped
2 cups (250 g/8 oz) mixed frozen vegetables
1/2 cup (95 g/3 oz) cooked white rice
1/3 cup (40 g/1 1/4 oz) grated Cheddar
1/4 cup (25 g/3/4 oz) grated Parmesan
1/4 cup (40 g/1 1/4 oz) cashews, chopped

1 Preheat the oven to moderately hot 200°C (400°F/Gas 6). Wipe the mushrooms with a paper towel. Remove the stalks and chop them finely.
2 Meanwhile, melt the butter in a pan. Add the chopped mushroom stalks and leek and cook for 2–3 minutes, or until soft. Mix in the garlic, cumin seeds, ground coriander and chilli powder and cook for 1 minute, or until the mixture is fragrant.
3 Stir in the tomato and frozen vegetables. Bring to the boil, reduce the heat and simmer for 5 minutes. Stir in the rice and season well.
4 Spoon the mixture into the mushroom caps, sprinkle with the Cheddar and Parmesan and bake for 15 minutes, or until the cheese has melted. Scatter with the cashews to serve.

Use any seasonal vegetables in the HOT TOFU SALAD (top). STUFFED FIELD MUSHROOMS (below).

LENTIL BURGERS

Preparation: 30 minutes
Cooking: 25 minutes
Makes 10 burgers

1 cup (250 g/8 oz) red lentils
1 tablespoon oil
2 onions, sliced
1 teaspoon ground cumin
1 teaspoon ground coriander
1 teaspoon garam masala
425 g (14 oz) can chickpeas, drained
1 egg
1/4 cup (15 g/1/2 oz) chopped fresh parsley
2 tablespoons chopped fresh coriander
2 1/4 cups (180 g/6 oz) stale breadcrumbs
plain flour, for dusting

Coriander garlic cream
1/2 cup (125 g/4 oz) sour cream
1/2 cup (125 ml/4 fl oz) cream
1 clove garlic, crushed
2 tablespoons chopped fresh coriander
2 tablespoons chopped fresh parsley

1 Add the lentils to a large pan of boiling water and simmer for 8 minutes, or until tender. Drain well. Heat the oil in pan and cook the onion for 3 minutes, or until soft. Add the ground spices and stir until fragrant. Cool the mixture slightly.
2 Place the chickpeas, egg, onion mixture and half the lentils in a food processor. Process for 20 seconds, or until smooth. Transfer to a bowl. Stir in the remaining lentils, parsley, coriander and breadcrumbs. Mix well. Divide into 10 portions.
3 Shape the portions into round patties. (If the mixture is too soft, chill for 15 minutes, or until firm.) Toss the patties in flour, shaking off the excess. Place on a lightly greased hot barbecue grill or flatplate. Cook for 3–4 minutes each side, or until browned.
4 To make the coriander garlic cream, mix together all the ingredients.

STORAGE: The patties can be made up to 2 days in advance and stored, covered, in the fridge. The coriander garlic cream can be kept, covered, in the fridge, for up to 3 days.
VARIATION: You could also use green lentils for this recipe, but they will take approximately 30 minutes to cook.

Serve LENTIL BURGERS with coriander garlic cream.

SPICY VEGETABLE COUSCOUS

Preparation: 30 minutes
Cooking: 1 hour
Serves 6

2 tablespoons olive oil
2 cloves garlic, crushed
1 small red chilli, diced
1 leek, thinly sliced
2 small fennel bulbs, sliced
2 teaspoons ground cumin
1 teaspoon ground coriander
1 teaspoon ground turmeric
1 teaspoon garam masala
350 g (11 oz) sweet potato, chopped
2 parsnips, sliced
1 1/2 cups (375 ml/12 fl oz) vegetable stock
2 zucchini, thickly sliced
250 g (8 oz) broccoli, cut into florets
2 tomatoes, peeled and chopped
1 large red capsicum, chopped
425 g (14 oz) can chickpeas, drained
2 tablespoons chopped fresh flat-leaf parsley
2 tablespoons chopped fresh lemon thyme

Couscous

1 1/4 cups (230 g/7 1/2 oz) instant couscous
30 g (1 oz) butter
1 cup (250 ml/8 fl oz) hot vegetable stock

SPICY VEGETABLE COUSCOUS.

1 Heat the oil in a large pan and add the garlic, chilli, leek and fennel. Cook over medium heat for 10 minutes, or until the leek and fennel are soft and golden brown.
2 Add the cumin, coriander, turmeric, garam masala, sweet potato and parsnip. Cook for 5 minutes, stirring to coat the vegetables with spices.
3 Add the vegetable stock and simmer, covered, for 15 minutes. Stir in the zucchini, broccoli, tomato, capsicum and chickpeas. Simmer, uncovered, for 30 minutes, or until the vegetables are tender. Stir in the herbs.
4 Put the couscous and butter in a bowl. Pour in the stock and leave to absorb for 5 minutes. Fluff gently with a fork to separate the grains. Make the couscous into a 'nest' on each plate and serve the spicy vegetables in the middle.

POTATO GNOCCHI WITH TOMATO AND BASIL SAUCE

Preparation: 1 hour
Cooking: 45 minutes
Serves 6

Tomato sauce

1 tablespoon oil
1 onion, chopped
1 celery stick, chopped
2 carrots, chopped
2 x 400 g (13 oz) cans crushed tomatoes
1 teaspoon sugar
½ cup (30 g/1 oz) fresh basil, chopped

Potato gnocchi

1 kg (2 lb) old potatoes
30 g (1 oz) butter
2 cups (250 g/8 oz) plain flour
2 eggs, beaten
grated Parmesan, to serve

1 To make the tomato sauce, heat the oil in a large frying pan, add the onion, celery and carrot, and cook for 5 minutes, stirring regularly. Add the tomato and sugar, and season with salt and pepper. Bring to the boil, then reduce the heat to low and simmer for 30 minutes. Add the basil, and set the sauce aside.
2 To make the potato gnocchi, peel the potatoes, chop roughly and steam or boil until very tender. Drain well and mash until smooth. Using a wooden spoon, stir in the butter and flour, then beat in the eggs. Allow to cool.
3 Turn the mixture out onto a floured surface and divide it in half. Roll each piece into a long sausage shape. Cut it into short pieces and press each piece with the back of a fork to make indentations.
4 Cook the gnocchi, in batches, in a large pan of boiling salted water for about 2 minutes, or until the gnocchi rise to the surface. Using a slotted spoon, remove and drain the gnocchi, and transfer to serving bowls. Serve with the tomato sauce and Parmesan. Garnish with fresh herbs if you like.

VARIATION: For a quick blue cheese sauce, put 150 g (5 oz) blue cheese and 2 cups (500 ml/16 fl oz) cream in a pan. Simmer for 10 minutes, or until slightly thickened.
NOTE: Potato gnocchi are traditionally made from baked rather than mashed potato. This gives a firmer, drier dough but is obviously more time-

POTATO GNOCCHI are good with both tomato- and cheese-based sauces.

Serve BEAN NACHOS topped with avocado, sour cream and sliced spring onions.

consuming. Bake 1 kg (2 lb) potatoes in the oven at 200°C (400°F/Gas 6) for 1 hour. Don't wrap in foil. Allow to cool, then peel and mash in a bowl with a masher. Add 150 g (5 oz) plain flour and work in with your hands. Knead gently on a floured surface, gradually adding another 50 g (1¾ oz) flour until you have a light soft dough that does not stick to the work surface but is still damp to touch. Roll out the dough into a long sausage shape, cut into short lengths and then press against a fork as above.

BEAN NACHOS

Preparation: 30 minutes
Cooking: 15 minutes
Serves 4

3 tomatoes, diced
1 small red onion, diced
¼ cup (15 g/½ oz) chopped fresh coriander
1 small red chilli, diced
2 x 400 g (13 oz) cans red kidney beans
2 x 230 g (7½ oz) packets corn chips
2 cups (250 g/8 oz) grated Cheddar
1 large avocado
⅓ cup (90 g/3 oz) sour cream
2 spring onions, sliced

1 Preheat the oven to moderate 180°C (350°F/Gas 4). Mix the tomato, onion, coriander and chilli. Put the rinsed kidney beans in a pan, cover with water and bring to the boil. Drain, return to the pan with ½ cup of tomato mixture and cook for 5 minutes.
2 Place the bean mixture on a baking tray and cover with the corn chips. Sprinkle with the cheese and bake for 3–5 minutes, or until the cheese melts. Transfer to serving plates.
3 Spread the tomato mixture over the cheese. Top with lightly mashed avocado, sour cream and spring onions.

PASTA AND RICE

Pasta is one of the easiest and most versatile ingredients to use. There are very few people who don't enjoy a bowl of pasta with a tomato or creamy sauce. Rice and noodles are also quick and simple to prepare and open to a thousand different variations on a delicious theme.

CLASSIC LASAGNE

Preparation: 40 minutes
Cooking: 1 hour 40 minutes
Serves 6–8

2 tablespoons oil
30 g (1 oz) butter
1 large onion, chopped
1 carrot, finely chopped
1 celery stick, chopped
650 g (1 lb 5 oz) minced beef
1 cup (250 ml/8 fl oz) Italian tomato passata
1/2 cup (125 ml/4 fl oz) red wine
2 tablespoons chopped fresh parsley
375 g (12 oz) dried lasagne sheets

Béchamel sauce
140 g (4 1/2 oz) butter
2 tablespoons plain flour
5 cups (1.25 litres) milk
1/2 teaspoon nutmeg
75 g (2 1/2 oz) Parmesan

1 Heat the oil and butter in a large frying pan. Cook the onion, carrot and celery, stirring, over medium heat until softened. Increase the heat, add the mince and brown well, breaking up any lumps with a fork. Add the tomato passata, wine and parsley, and season with salt and pepper. Bring to the boil, then reduce the heat and simmer for 35–40 minutes.
2 To make the béchamel sauce, melt the butter over low heat until foaming, then add the flour. Cook for 2 minutes, stirring constantly. Remove the pan from the heat and gradually stir in the milk. Return to the heat and bring to the boil, stirring, until thickened. When thick, simmer for 2 minutes. Season well with salt, pepper and nutmeg. Place a piece of baking paper on the surface of the sauce to prevent a skin forming.
3 Preheat the oven to moderate 180°C (350°F/Gas 4). Grease a 2-litre ovenproof dish. Spread a thin layer of the meat sauce over the base and top with a thin layer of béchamel. If the béchamel has cooled and become too thick, warm it gently to make spreading easier. Lay the lasagne sheets on top, gently pressing to push out any air. Continue the layers, finishing with the béchamel. Grate the Parmesan, sprinkle over the sauce and bake for 35–40 minutes, or until golden brown. Leave for 15 minutes before cutting.

NOTE: You can use 200 g (6 1/2 oz) fresh lasagne instead of the dried. Read the instructions—most do not need any precooking.

SPINACH AND RICOTTA CANNELLONI

Preparation: 45 minutes
Cooking: 1½ hours
Serves 4–6

2 tablespoons olive oil
1 large onion, chopped
2 cloves garlic, crushed
1 kg (2 lb) English spinach, finely chopped
650 g (1 lb 5 oz) ricotta cheese
2 eggs, lightly beaten
pinch of ground nutmeg
250 g (8 oz) dried cannelloni tubes
1 cup (150 g/5 oz) grated mozzarella
½ cup (50 g/1¾ oz) grated Parmesan

Tomato sauce

1 tablespoon olive oil
1 large onion, chopped
2 cloves garlic, crushed
800 g (1 lb 10 oz) can crushed tomatoes
½ cup (125 ml/4 fl oz) white wine
2 tablespoons tomato paste
1 teaspoon soft brown sugar
2 tablespoons chopped fresh basil

SPINACH AND RICOTTA CANNELLONI.

1 Heat the oil in a large heavy-based pan. Add the onion and cook for 3 minutes, or until golden. Stir in the garlic and cook for 1 minute. Add the spinach and cook for 2 minutes. Cover the pan and steam the spinach for 1–2 minutes, or until wilted. Allow to cool slightly. Transfer to a colander and squeeze to remove the moisture.

2 Mix the spinach with the ricotta, beaten eggs and nutmeg. Season to taste with salt and pepper. Preheat the oven to moderate 180°C (350°F/Gas 4) and grease a large ovenproof dish.

3 To make the tomato sauce, heat the oil in a large frying pan and cook the onion over low heat for 5 minutes, or until soft and golden. Add the garlic and cook for 1 minute. Add the tomato, wine, tomato paste, sugar and basil. Bring to the boil, reduce the heat and simmer for 30 minutes.

4 Spread a third of the tomato sauce in the dish. Spoon 2–3 tablespoons of the spinach mixture into each cannelloni tube and arrange neatly in the dish. Spoon the remaining tomato sauce over the top and sprinkle with the mozzarella and Parmesan. Bake for 40–45 minutes, or until the cannelloni is tender and the top is crisp and golden brown.

NOTE: This recipe can be made using fresh lasagne sheets instead of the dried cannelloni tubes. Cut the lasagne sheets into small rectangles, place the filling on the edge and roll up tightly. Place the filled tubes seam-side-down in the baking dish and cook as cannelloni tubes.

PASTA AND MEATBALLS

Preparation: 35 minutes
Cooking: 35 minutes
Serves 4

750 g (1 1/2 lb) pork and veal or beef mince
1 cup (80 g/2 3/4 oz) fresh breadcrumbs
1/4 cup (25 g/3/4 oz) grated Parmesan
1 onion, finely chopped
2 tablespoons chopped fresh parsley
1 egg, beaten
1 clove garlic, crushed
rind and juice of half a lemon
3 tablespoons plain flour
2 tablespoons olive oil
500 g (1 lb) fusilli

Sauce

425 g (14 oz) Italian tomato passata
1/2 cup (125 ml/4 fl oz) beef stock
1/2 cup (125 ml/4 fl oz) red wine
2 tablespoons chopped fresh basil
1 clove garlic, crushed

PASTA AND MEATBALLS, just like an Italian mama makes!

1 Mix together the mince, breadcrumbs, Parmesan, onion, parsley, egg, garlic, lemon rind and juice, and some salt and pepper. Roll tablespoons of the mixture into balls. Season the flour with salt and pepper and roll the meatballs in the seasoned flour.

2 Heat the oil in a large frying pan and fry the meatballs in batches until golden brown. Remove from the pan and drain on paper towels. Pour away the fat and meat juices from the pan.

3 To make the sauce, in the same pan, combine the tomato passata, stock, wine, basil, garlic and some salt and pepper. Bring to the boil. Reduce the heat, add the meatballs to the sauce and simmer for 10–15 minutes.

4 While the meatballs and sauce are cooking, add the fusilli to a large pan of rapidly boiling salted water and cook until just tender. Drain and serve with the meatballs and sauce over the top.

SPAGHETTI BOLOGNESE is an enduring family favourite.

SPAGHETTI BOLOGNESE

Preparation: 15 minutes
Cooking: 2¼ hours
Serves 6

2 tablespoons olive oil
1 large onion, chopped
1 carrot, chopped
1 celery stick, chopped
2 cloves garlic, crushed
500 g (1 lb) beef mince
1 cup (250 ml/8 fl oz) beef stock
2 x 425 g (14 oz) cans chopped tomatoes
1½ cups (375 ml/12 fl oz) red wine
1 teaspoon sugar
500 g (1 lb) spaghetti

1 Heat the olive oil in a large heavy-based pan and stir the onion, carrot and celery over medium heat for 5 minutes, or until softened. Add the garlic and cook for 1 minute.
2 Add the mince and cook over high heat until well browned, breaking up any lumps with a fork. Add the stock, tomato, wine and sugar.
3 Bring to the boil, reduce the heat and simmer for 2 hours, stirring occasionally. Cook the pasta in boiling water until just tender. Season the sauce and serve with the spaghetti. The sauce can be kept for up to 2 days in the fridge or frozen for up to 2 months.

SPAGHETTI CARBONARA

Preparation: 10 minutes
Cooking: 20 minutes
Serves 4–6

8 rashers bacon
500 g (1 lb) spaghetti
4 eggs
½ cup (50 g/1¾ oz) grated Parmesan
1¼ cups (315 ml/10 fl oz) cream

Don't overcook CARBONARA or you will make scrambled eggs.

VEGETABLE PILAF

Preparation: 20 minutes
Cooking: 30 minutes
Serves 6

60 g (2 oz) butter
2 onions, sliced
2 cloves garlic, crushed
1 large red capsicum, finely chopped
2 cups (400 g/13 oz) basmati rice
1.25 litres vegetable stock
1 fresh corn cob
1 1/2 cups (235 g/7 1/2 oz) peas
1/2 cup (50 g/1 3/4 oz) grated Parmesan
2 tablespoons chopped fresh chives
2 tablespoons chopped fresh coriander

VEGETABLE PILAF.

1 Melt the butter in a large pan. Add the onion and cook for 5 minutes over low heat, or until soft. Add the garlic and cook for 1 minute. Add the capsicum and rice and cook for 3 minutes, then stir in the stock. Bring to the boil, stirring once. Reduce the heat and simmer for 5 minutes, or until most of the stock has been absorbed.
2 Cut the corn kernels from the cob with a sharp knife (angle the knife and cut down the side of the cob). Stir the corn kernels and peas into the rice mixture. Cook, covered, over low heat for 10 minutes, or until the rice is tender.
3 Stir in the Parmesan and herbs. Season to taste with salt and pepper before serving.

Use arborio rice for a creamy RISOTTO PARMESAN.

SMOKED FISH KEDGEREE

Preparation: 20 minutes
Cooking: 35 minutes
Serves 4

600 g (1 1/4 lb) smoked haddock
50 g (1 3/4 oz) butter
1 onion, finely chopped
2 teaspoons curry powder
1 teaspoon ground cumin
1 teaspoon ground coriander
2 teaspoons seeded and finely sliced green chilli
1 cup (200 g/6 1/2 oz) basmati rice
3 cups (750 ml/24 fl oz) chicken or fish stock
1 cinnamon stick
1/3 cup (80 ml/2 3/4 fl oz) cream
2 hard-boiled eggs, chopped
2 tablespoons finely chopped fresh parsley
2 tablespoons finely chopped fresh coriander

1 Place the haddock in a large shallow pan, skin-side-up (the haddock must be in a single layer, so if you don't have a large enough pan you may need to poach the fish in a couple of batches). Cover with boiling water and simmer very gently for about 10 minutes. The fish is cooked when the flesh flakes easily when tested with a knife. Drain and pat dry with paper towels. Remove the skin and bones and flake into bite-sized chunks.
2 Heat the butter in a large pan and cook the onion for 5 minutes, or until soft and golden. Add the curry powder, cumin, coriander and chilli and cook, stirring, for 1 minute. Add the rice, stir well, then pour in the stock and add the cinnamon stick. Cover with a tight-fitting lid and simmer over gentle heat for about 15 minutes, or until the rice is tender.
3 Remove the cinnamon stick and gently stir in the flaked haddock. Fold in the cream, egg and herbs. Season to taste and serve immediately.

VARIATION: This dish is best made with smoked haddock, but if it is not available you could use smoked cod.
NOTE: The English adapted this recipe from the Indian 'khichiri' which was a dish of rice, spices and lentils. Kedgeree is now seen as a main meal, but it was originally a breakfast dish and is delicious for special occasion brunches.

KEDGEREE is an anglicized Indian dish.

FRIED RICE

Preparation: 15 minutes
Cooking: 10 minutes
Serves 4

2 eggs, lightly beaten
2 tablespoons peanut oil
1 onion, cut into wedges
250 g (8 oz) piece of ham, cut into thin strips
4 cups (740 g/1 1/2 lb) cold, cooked rice
1/4 cup (40 g/1 1/4 oz) frozen peas
2 tablespoons soy sauce
4 spring onions, diagonally sliced
250 g (8 oz) cooked small prawns, peeled

Use cold cooked rice for FRIED RICE, so the grains separate out.

1 Season the egg with salt and pepper. Heat half the oil in a wok or large frying pan and add the egg, pulling the set egg towards the centre and tilting the pan to let the uncooked egg run to the edge. When almost set, break the egg up into large pieces, so it looks like scrambled egg, and transfer to a plate.
2 Heat the remaining oil in the wok, swirling to coat the base and side. Add the onion and stir-fry over high heat until it starts to turn transparent. Add the ham and stir-fry for 1 minute. Add the rice and peas, and stir-fry for 3 minutes, or until the rice is heated through. Add the egg, soy sauce, spring onion and prawns. Heat through, then serve.

STORAGE: Cook the rice for frying a day in advance (this is an excellent recipe for using up leftovers). Cover and store in the refrigerator and the grains will separate. You will need to cook about 1 1/2 cups of rice to produce 4 cups of cooked.
VARIATION: Use barbecued pork, lap cheong (Chinese sausage) or bacon instead of ham.

There are many different rice varieties and they are all suited to different dishes. Brown long-grain are separate long grains with husks, best used for salads, rice cakes, pilaf and patties, or serving with stir-fries or curries as a healthy alternative to white long-grain. Brown short-grain rice is used for soups and patties. It has a nutty flavour and heavy texture—a healthy alternative to white short-grain. White rice has been processed to remove the outer hull and bran, then polished until it is white and glossy.

PAELLA

Preparation: 30 minutes
Cooking: 55 minutes
Serves 4

12 mussels, scrubbed, beards removed
1/2 cup (125 ml/4 fl oz) white wine
1 small red onion, chopped
1/2 cup (125 ml/4 fl oz) olive oil
1 chicken breast fillet, cut into cubes
275 g (9 oz) raw prawns, shelled and deveined
100 g (3 1/2 oz) calamari, cut into rings
100 g (3 1/2 oz) white boneless fish, cubed
1/2 small red onion, extra, finely chopped
1 rasher bacon, diced
4 cloves garlic, crushed
1 small red capsicum, finely chopped
1 tomato, peeled and chopped
1/2 cup (80 g/2 3/4 oz) fresh or frozen peas
90 g (3 oz) chorizo or pepperoni, thinly sliced
pinch of cayenne pepper
1 cup (200 g/6 1/2 oz) long-grain rice
1/4 teaspoon saffron threads
2 cups (500 ml/16 fl oz) chicken stock, heated
2 tablespoons finely chopped fresh parsley

Add the mussels to the Spanish PAELLA just before serving.

1 Discard any damaged mussels or any that are open and don't close when tapped on the work surface. Heat the wine and onion in a large pan. Add the mussels, cover and shake the pan for 3–5 minutes over high heat. After 3 minutes, start removing the opened mussels and set aside. At the end of 5 minutes discard any mussels that haven't opened. Reserve the cooking liquid.

2 Heat half the oil in a large frying pan. Pat the chicken dry with paper towels and fry for 5 minutes, or until golden brown. Remove from the pan. Add the prawns, calamari and fish to the pan and cook for 1 minute. Remove from the pan.

3 Heat the remaining oil in a pan and add the extra onion, bacon, garlic and capsicum. Cook for 5 minutes, or until the onion is soft. Add the tomato, peas, chorizo or pepperoni, cayenne pepper, and season with salt and pepper. Add the cooking liquid, and stir well. Add the rice and saffron and mix well.

4 Add the chicken stock and mix well. Bring slowly to the boil, then reduce the heat to low and simmer for 15 minutes, without stirring.

Fry the noodles, then serve topped with chicken and vegetables for CHICKEN CHOW MEIN.

5 Place the chicken pieces, prawns, calamari and fish on top of the rice. Using a wooden spoon, gently push the pieces into the rice, then cover and continue to cook over low heat for 10–15 minutes, or until the rice is tender and the seafood cooked. If the rice is not quite cooked, add a little extra stock and cook for a few minutes more. Serve in bowls, topped with the mussels and sprinkled with the parsley.

NOTE: It's a good idea to buy a few extra mussels to allow for any that do not open. Black- and green-lip mussels are both suitable for use in this recipe.

CHICKEN CHOW MEIN

Preparation: 25 minutes
Cooking: 30 minutes
Serves 4–6

2 teaspoons cornflour
1/2 cup (125 ml/4 fl oz) chicken stock
1/2 cup (125 ml/4 fl oz) hoisin sauce
375 g (12 oz) dried fine egg noodles
3 teaspoons sesame oil
oil, for cooking
1 clove garlic, crushed
1 teaspoon grated ginger
1 onion, cut into wedges
500 g (1 lb) chicken thigh fillets, cubed
1 red capsicum, sliced
1 green capsicum, sliced
12 leaves Chinese broccoli, chopped

1 Mix the cornflour, stock and half the hoisin sauce to make a sauce. Set aside.
2 Cook the noodles in boiling water according to the packet, or until tender. Drain well, pat dry and mix in the sesame oil and remaining hoisin sauce. Heat 2 tablespoons of oil in a wok. Fry the noodles over medium heat for 10 minutes until crispy. Drain and keep warm.
3 Heat some more oil and fry the garlic, ginger and onion for 2 minutes. Add the chicken and stir-fry in batches until tender. Add the capsicum, cook for 2 minutes. Add the sauce and stir until it boils and thickens. Add the broccoli and cook until just wilted. Serve the noodles with chicken and vegetables.

SINGAPORE NOODLES.

SINGAPORE NOODLES

Preparation: 40 minutes
Cooking: 15 minutes
Serves 4–6

150 g (5 oz) dried rice vermicelli
oil, for cooking
250 g (8 oz) Chinese barbecued pork, cut into small pieces
250 g (8 oz) raw prawn meat, chopped
2 tablespoons madras curry powder
2 cloves garlic, crushed
1 onion, thinly sliced
100 g (3 1/2 oz) shiitake mushrooms, thinly sliced
100 g (3 1/2 oz) green beans, thinly sliced
1 tablespoon soy sauce
4 spring onions, thinly sliced

1 Put the vermicelli in a large bowl, cover with boiling water and soak for 5 minutes. Drain well and dry on a clean tea towel.
2 Heat the wok until very hot, add 1 tablespoon of the oil and swirl to coat. Stir-fry the pork and prawns in batches over high heat, then remove.
3 Reheat the wok, add 2 tablespoons of the oil and stir-fry the curry powder and garlic for 1–2 minutes, or until fragrant. Add the onion and mushrooms, and stir-fry for 2–3 minutes, or until the onion and mushrooms are soft.
4 Return the pork and prawns to the wok, add the beans and 2 teaspoons water, and toss gently. Add the drained noodles, soy sauce and spring onion. Toss well.

FRIED NOODLES

Preparation: 30 minutes
Cooking: 25 minutes
Serves 4

1/4 cup (40 g/1 1/4 oz) sesame seeds
2 tablespoons oil
2 teaspoons sesame oil
4 spring onions, chopped
2 cloves garlic, crushed
150 g (5 oz) raw prawn meat
2 teaspoons finely chopped red chillies
150 g (5 oz) fresh firm tofu, cut into small cubes
100 g (3 1/2 oz) button mushrooms, thinly sliced
1 red capsicum, cut into thin strips
2 tablespoons soy sauce
2 teaspoons sugar
300 g (10 oz) packet Hokkien noodles

1 Dry-fry the sesame seeds over low heat for 3–4 minutes, shaking the pan gently, until the seeds are golden. Remove, allow to cool and then grind in a food processor or mortar and pestle.
2 Mix together the oils in a small bowl. Heat half the oil mixture in a wok or a large heavy-based frying pan, over medium-high heat. Add the spring onion, garlic and prawn meat and stir-fry for

1 minute. Add the chilli, stir for another minute, then remove the mixture from the wok and set aside. Add the tofu to the wok, tossing occasionally until lightly golden, then remove from the wok and set aside. Add the remaining oil to the wok, add the mushrooms and capsicum and stir-fry for 3 minutes, or until they are just crisp.

3 Add the soy sauce, sugar, noodles and 2 teaspoons water to the wok or pan. Toss gently to separate and coat the noodles in liquid. Cover and steam for 5 minutes, then toss well. Add the prawn mixture and tofu, and toss for 3 minutes over medium heat. Sprinkle with the crushed sesame seeds and serve.

NOTE: We have specified Hokkien noodles, but you could use a variety of different types of noodle for this dish as long as you prepare them correctly beforehand. Hokkien noodles have been cooked, then tossed in oil before packaging so they require no cooking before adding them to this dish. Fresh rice noodles have been prepared in the same way and can be added straight to the dish. Fresh egg noodles do however need to be cooked in boiling water first for 5 minutes. Dried noodles also need soaking or cooking before adding them to the dish—follow the instructions on the packet, drain well and add to the recipe as above. To drain the water thoroughly from noodles, place them in a salad spinner and spin until dry.

Leave out the prawn meat and FRIED NOODLES becomes an excellent vegetarian meal.

VEGETABLES AND SALADS

If your idea of vegetables is a packet of frozen peas, and your salad technique runs to a few limp lettuce leaves drowned in bottled dressing, it's time you became a little more creative on the 'green' front. Vegetables and salads shouldn't just be sad side dishes, they should be vibrant, crispy, crunchy stars.

STIR-FRIED VEGETABLES

Preparation: 15 minutes
Cooking: 10 minutes
Serves 4

- 1 tablespoon sesame seeds
- 2 spring onions
- 250 g (8 oz) broccoli
- 1 red capsicum
- 1 yellow capsicum
- 150 g (5 oz) button mushrooms
- 1 tablespoon oil
- 1 teaspoon sesame oil
- 1 clove garlic, crushed
- 2 teaspoons grated fresh ginger
- 1 tablespoon soy sauce
- 1 tablespoon honey
- 1 tablespoon sweet chilli sauce

1 Put the sesame seeds on a baking tray and toast under a hot grill until golden (or fry in a clean dry pan). Finely slice the spring onions. Cut the broccoli into small florets. Cut the capsicums into thin strips. Cut the mushrooms in half.
2 Heat the oils in a wok or large frying pan. Add the garlic, ginger and spring onion. Stir-fry over high heat for 1 minute. Add the broccoli, capsicum and mushrooms. Stir-fry for 2 minutes, or until the vegetables are just tender but still bright.
3 Mix together the soy sauce, honey and sweet chilli sauce in a jug. Pour the sauce over the cooked vegetables and toss lightly. Sprinkle with the toasted sesame seeds.

ASIAN GREENS

Preparation: 5 minutes
Cooking: 10 minutes
Serves 4

- 500 g (1 lb) baby bok choy
- 800 g (1 lb 10 oz) Chinese broccoli
- 1/3 cup (80 ml/2 3/4 fl oz) oyster sauce
- 1 teaspoon sesame oil

1 Wash the bok choy and broccoli thoroughly, and shake off the excess water. Trim the ends and roughly chop into large pieces. If the bok choy stems are particularly thick, cut them in half lengthways.
2 Place the broccoli in a steamer, preferably bamboo, over a pan half full of simmering water.

A mixture of healthy ASIAN GREENS (top) and STIR-FRIED VEGETABLES.

The bottom of the steamer should not be touching the water. Cover and steam the broccoli for 5–6 minutes. Add the bok choy, cover and steam for another 2 minutes.

3 Put the vegetables in a serving bowl. Pour in the oyster sauce and toss gently to coat the vegetables. Serve drizzled with the sesame oil.

NOTE: Bok choy is a variety of Chinese cabbage with long white stalks and large deep-green leaves. The leaves are crisp with a sweet cabbage-like flavour.

MASHED POTATO

Preparation: 10 minutes
Cooking: 30 minutes
Serves 4

4 large potatoes
3–4 tablespoons milk
60 g (2 oz) butter

1 Chop the potatoes and cook in boiling salted water until just tender, then drain.
2 Return the potato to the pan over low heat. Add the milk and quickly mash, adding more milk, if necessary, for fluffy potatoes. Beat in the butter and season well.

HERBED MASH

Add 2 tablespoons finely chopped chives or parsley.

CREAMY PARSNIP MASH

Cook equal quantities of potato and parsnip. Mash with milk, butter and 2 tablespoons sour cream.

CHEESY POTATO

Add 2 tablespoons sour cream instead of butter. Add 2–3 tablespoons finely grated Cheddar and 1 teaspoon Dijon mustard.

COLCANNON

Fry 200 g (6½ oz) shredded green cabbage and 8 chopped spring onions until brown and add to the mash.

Instead of plain mashed potato try CREAMY PARSNIP MASH.

CHIPS

Preparation: 5 minutes
Cooking: 20 minutes
Serves 4–6

5–6 large potatoes
oil, for deep-frying

1 Cut the potatoes lengthways into 1 cm (½ inch) wide chips. Soak for 10 minutes in cold water. Drain and pat dry. Half-fill a large heavy-based pan with oil (the oil will rise as the chips give off water). Heat the oil until a cube of bread dropped into the oil browns in 30 seconds. If it browns in less than 10 seconds, the oil is far too hot, so reduce the heat. Cook the chips in batches for 4–5 minutes, or until pale golden. Remove with tongs or a slotted spoon and drain on paper towels.
2 When you're almost ready to serve, reheat the oil until a cube of bread browns in 15 seconds. Add the chips in batches and cook for 2–3 minutes, or until golden and crisp. Drain on paper towels and serve sprinkled with salt.

NOTE: The best potatoes to use for perfect chips are floury varieties such as Spunta, King Edward and Russet (Idaho).

POTATO WEDGES

Preparation: 10 minutes
Cooking: 20 minutes
Serves 4

4–5 large potatoes
1 cup (125 g/4 oz) plain flour
3–4 teaspoons chicken seasoning salt
1 teaspoon white pepper
1 teaspoon sweet paprika
2 teaspoons garlic powder
oil, for deep-frying

1 Do not peel the potatoes, but wash and scrub them, leaving them wet to help the coating stick. Cut each potato into 10 wedges.
2 Mix together the flour, chicken seasoning salt, pepper, paprika and garlic powder. Dust the wedges in the seasoned flour: put the wedges and flour in a plastic bag and shake. Reserve the remaining seasoned flour.
3 Half-fill a large heavy-based pan with oil. Heat the oil to 160°C/315°F (if you have a deep-fryer with a thermometer), or until a cube of bread dropped into the oil browns in 30 seconds. If it browns in less than 10 seconds, the oil is too hot, so reduce the heat. Deep-fry the wedges in batches for 2–3 minutes each batch, or until pale golden. Remove with tongs or a slotted spoon. Drain on paper towels and cool a little.
4 Dust with a second coating of seasoned flour, pressing the flour onto the wedges. Return to the hot oil and cook for another 3–4 minutes, or until the wedges are dark golden and crispy. Remove and drain on paper towels. Sprinkle with a little extra chicken salt and serve hot, perhaps with sour cream and sweet chilli sauce.

Twice-fried CHIPS (top) and POTATO WEDGES.

NOTE: For Potato Skins, preheat the oven to moderately hot 200°C (400°F/Gas 6). Prick 1 kg (2 lb) unpeeled potatoes all over with a fork and place on a baking tray. Bake for 1–1½ hours, or until tender. Cool, then cut in half lengthways. Use a spoon to scoop out the flesh (use this to make mash, gnocchi or potato croquettes). Cut each half potato skin into three lengthways, then deep-fry in batches in hot oil (as for Potato Wedges).

BAKED JACKET POTATOES

Preparation: 5 minutes
Cooking: 1½ hours
Serves 4

4 even-sized potatoes

1 Preheat the oven to hot 220°C (425°F/Gas 7). Scrub the potatoes clean, dry and prick all over for even cooking. For crisp skins brush the potatoes with oil and sprinkle with salt. Bake directly on the oven rack for 1–1½ hours, or until tender when tested with a skewer. Alternatively, wrap the potatoes in paper towels and space evenly in the microwave. Cook on High for 8–10 minutes, or until soft. Leave to stand for about 2 minutes.
Cut a cross in the top of the cooked potato and squeeze from the base to open. Top with butter, or one of the following topping ideas:

Mix drained tuna with antipasto-style mixed beans. Add some chopped parsley and a squeeze of lemon juice and spoon into the potato with a little olive oil.

Toss a handful of peeled cooked prawns in a hot pan with a little olive oil and crushed garlic. Add some chopped fresh chives and a small amount of natural yoghurt, stir well and season to taste.

Fry some thinly sliced mushrooms in olive oil with a clove of crushed garlic and a little chopped fresh parsley. Season and top with a teaspoon of sour cream.

Finely chop a tomato and add to Greek-style yoghurt with grated cucumber, chopped mint and spring onion. Season and mix well.

Toss some small cooked cauliflower florets in a pan with chopped bacon until heated through and lightly browned. Mix a little wholegrain mustard and sour cream, spoon into the potato and top with the cauliflower.

Fill the potato with a large spoonful of herbed cream cheese and put back in the oven for 2 minutes. Meanwhile, toast a few pine nuts and scatter over the melted cream cheese.

Roughly purée some leftover cooked broccoli with a little sour cream and some cheese until you have a thick paste. Add a beaten egg and mix well. Spoon out some of the potato, refill with the soufflé, then return to the hot oven until the soufflé is golden and risen.

Mix some butter with ½ teaspoon grated lemon rind, 1 teaspoon lemon juice and 1 tablespoon finely chopped fresh dill. Chill before spooning onto the potato.

Put a small wedge of Camembert, Brie or creamy blue cheese in the potato and return to the oven for 2–3 minutes to soften the cheese.

Mash 1 small avocado with 1 teaspoon lemon juice and a dash of Tabasco to make guacamole. Top with sour cream, or mix in chopped bacon and chives.

Make a sweet corn salsa from a small tin of sweet corn, a chopped tomato, a finely sliced spring onion, half a chopped chilli and some chopped fresh coriander. Bind with a tablespoon of olive oil and a squeeze of lemon or lime juice.

Fry 2 crushed cloves of garlic and 2 chopped spring onions in a little butter and oil. Add 150 g (5 oz) sliced mushrooms and cook for 5 minutes.

SAUTEED HERB POTATOES

Preparation: 20 minutes
Cooking: 35 minutes
Serves 4–6

750 g (1 1/2 lb) baby new potatoes
30 g (1 oz) butter
2 tablespoons olive oil
1/2 teaspoon cracked black pepper
2 cloves garlic, crushed
1 tablespoon finely chopped fresh rosemary
1 teaspoon rock salt

1 Wash the potatoes, pat dry with paper towels and cut in half. Boil or steam until just tender. Drain.

2 Heat the butter and oil in a large heavy-based frying pan. When the mixture is foaming, add the potatoes and season with a little black pepper. Cook over medium heat for 5–10 minutes, or until golden and crisp, tossing regularly so that the potatoes brown evenly.
3 Stir in the garlic, rosemary and rock salt. Cook for 1 minute, or until well the potatoes are well coated. Add more cracked black pepper and mix well. Serve hot or warm.

NOTE: Fresh thyme would work nicely in this recipe, as would fresh parsley.

Use fresh rosemary for SAUTEED HERB POTATOES.

HASSELBACK POTATOES

Preparation: 20 minutes
Cooking: 45 minutes
Serves 4

60 g (2 oz) butter, melted
4 potatoes
2 tablespoons fresh white breadcrumbs
3 tablespoons grated Parmesan
1/2 teaspoon paprika

1 Preheat the oven to moderately hot 200°C (400°F/Gas 6). Brush a shallow baking tray with a little of the melted butter.
2 Peel the potatoes and cut in half. Put the potatoes, cut-side-down, on a board. Make thin evenly-spaced cuts about two-thirds of the way through, then place, flat-side-down, on the tray. Brush liberally with melted butter. Bake them for 30 minutes, brushing occasionally with butter.
3 Mix together the breadcrumbs and Parmesan and sprinkle evenly over the potatoes. Sprinkle with the paprika and bake for another 15 minutes, or until golden brown.

NOTE: Choose potatoes of a similar size so they cook evenly.

DUCHESS POTATOES

Preparation: 20 minutes + 40 minutes refrigeration
Cooking: 45 minutes
Serves 6

860 g (1 3/4 lb) floury potatoes
2 eggs, plus 1 extra yolk
3 tablespoons cream
2 tablespoons grated Parmesan
pinch of grated nutmeg

1 Peel the potatoes and cut into quarters, then boil or steam until just tender. Drain and return to the pan, turn the heat to very low and gently shake the pan for 1–2 minutes to dry the potato. Transfer to a bowl and mash.
2 Beat together the 2 eggs, cream, Parmesan, nutmeg and some salt and pepper. Add to the potato and mash until smooth. Cover and refrigerate for 40 minutes, or until cold. Preheat the oven to moderate 180°C (350°F/Gas 4).
3 Put the mashed potato into a piping bag with a wide star nozzle. Pipe in rosettes, not too close together as they might spread a little, onto greased oven trays. Brush lightly with the extra egg yolk, to give a golden, crisp finish. Bake for 15–20 minutes, or until golden. Serve hot, perhaps garnished with a little paprika.

DUCHESS (top) and HASSELBACK POTATOES.

Floury potatoes, such as Russet (Idaho) and King Edward have a high starch and low moisture content and are ideal for chips, baking, mash and gnocchi. Waxy potatoes have a high moisture content and are low in starch. They hold their shape well when boiled and steamed and are good in salads and stews, grate and slice well, but do not make particularly good chips or mash. Varieties are Desiree, Bintji, Tasmanian Pink Eye, Kipfler and Bison. Some potatoes, such as Sebago, Pontiac, Spunta, Nicola, Coliban and chats are good all-purpose varieties. Most bags of potatoes now specify their uses.

ROSTI *can be served as an accompaniment or as a filling lunch.*

BACON AND ONION ROSTI

Preparation: 30 minutes + 1 hour refrigeration
Cooking: 40 minutes
Serves 4

850 g (1 lb 12 oz) waxy potatoes, halved
60 g (2 oz) butter
6 thin bacon rashers, rind removed, chopped
1 small red onion, chopped
2 cloves garlic, crushed
2 tablespoons chopped fresh parsley
1 teaspoon each chopped fresh oregano and thyme

1 Boil or steam the potato until just tender. Drain, cover and refrigerate for 1 hour. Peel the potato and grate into a bowl.
2 Heat half the butter in a 23 cm (9 inch) heavy-based, non-stick frying pan. Add the bacon, onion and garlic and stir for 2 minutes, or until tender but not brown. Add to the potato. Add the herbs and mix well.
3 Add a little butter to the pan, spread the potato mixture over the base and press with a spatula. Cook over medium heat for 8 minutes, or until a crust forms on the base. Shake the pan occasionally to stop the potato sticking.
4 Slide the rosti onto a greased plate, add the remaining butter to the pan and when melted, flip the rosti back into the pan on its uncooked side. Cook for 6 minutes, or until the base is crusty.

RATATOUILLE

Preparation: 20 minutes + 20 minutes standing
Cooking: 40 minutes
Serves 4

250 g (8 oz) eggplant, chopped
4 tablespoons olive oil
250 g (8 oz) zucchini, thickly sliced
2 onions, cut in wedges
1 red capsicum, cubed
1 green capsicum, cubed
2 cloves garlic, crushed
500 g (1 lb) ripe tomatoes, chopped

1 Sprinkle the eggplant liberally with salt and leave for 20 minutes (this draws the bitterness from the eggplant). Rinse and pat dry with paper towels. Heat 3 tablespoons oil in a large heavy-based pan. Lightly brown the eggplant and zucchini in batches. Drain well.
2 Add the remaining oil to the pan and cook the onion over low heat for 3 minutes, or until golden. Add the capsicum and cook for 5 minutes, or until tender but not browned. Add the garlic and tomato and cook, stirring, for 5 minutes.
3 Stir in the eggplant and zucchini. Simmer for 15–20 minutes to reduce and thicken the sauce. Season to taste.

RATATOUILLE—a traditional French vegetable dish.

VEGETABLE FRITTERS are a great way to use up leftovers.

VEGETABLE FRITTERS

Preparation: 30 minutes
Cooking: 40 minutes
Makes 12

2 potatoes
1 carrot
2 zucchini
120 g (4 oz) sweet potato
1 small leek, white part only, thinly sliced
2 tablespoons plain flour
3 eggs, lightly beaten
oil, for shallow-frying

1 Finely grate the potatoes, carrot, zucchini and sweet potato. Put in a tea towel and squeeze out as much moisture as possible. Mix with the leek in a large bowl.
2 Sprinkle the flour over the vegetables and mix until coated. Add the eggs and mix well. Heat about 5 mm (1/4 inch) of oil in a frying pan and drop in 3 tablespoons of the mixture in a neat pile. Use a fork to gently press it into a 10 cm (4 inch) round patty. Fry two to three patties at a time over medium-high heat for 3 minutes on each side, or until golden and crispy. Drain on paper towels while cooking the remainder of the mixture.

ROAST VEGETABLES (top) and SCALLOPED POTATOES.

ROAST VEGETABLES

Preparation: 15 minutes
Cooking: 55 minutes
Serves 6–8

500 g (1 lb) pumpkin
1 large sweet potato
8 small onions
3 tablespoons olive oil
40 g (1 1/4 oz) butter

1 Preheat the oven to moderately hot 200°C (400°F/Gas 6). Peel the pumpkin and sweet potato and cut into large pieces. Peel the onions but leave whole. Pour the oil into a large baking dish and add the butter. Put in the oven to heat the oil and butter.
2 Add the vegetables to the dish and toss to coat with the hot oil. Bake for 45–50 minutes, or until the vegetables are crisp and golden and cooked through. Turn occasionally during cooking to coat with the oil and prevent sticking. Drain on paper towels before serving.

NOTE: A variety of vegetables are suitable for roasting, such as parsnips, turnips, fennel, carrots, garlic cloves, and, of course, potatoes. For par-boiled roast potatoes, cook them in boiling water for 10 minutes and drain thoroughly before putting in the baking dish or cooking in the tin with roast meat.

SCALLOPED POTATOES

Preparation: 20 minutes
Cooking: 40 minutes
Serves 4–6

4 waxy potatoes (Bintji, Desiree or Kipfler)
1 onion
1 cup (125 g/4 oz) grated Cheddar
1 1/2 cups (375 ml/ 12 fl oz) cream
2 teaspoons chicken stock powder

1 Preheat the oven to moderate 180°C (350°F/Gas 4). Peel the potatoes and thinly slice.

Slice the onion into rings.
2 Arrange a layer of overlapping potato slices in a baking dish and top with a layer of onion rings. Set aside half of the cheese to use as a topping. Sprinkle a little of the remaining cheese over the onion. Continue layering until all the potato and the onion have been used, finishing with a little of the grated cheese.
3 Gently whisk together the cream and stock powder, then pour over the potato and sprinkle the top with the rest of the grated cheese. Bake for 40 minutes, or until the potato is tender and the top is golden brown.

VARIATION: For boulangère potatoes, peel and thinly slice 1 kg potatoes (use all-purpose varieties). Preheat the oven to moderate 180°C (350°F/Gas 4) and grease a 1-litre casserole dish. Arrange a layer of potato in the base of the dish. Crush 2 cloves of garlic and sprinkle a little over the potato, with some salt and pepper. Continue the layers to use all the potato and garlic. Pour 400 ml (13 fl oz) chicken or vegetable stock over the potato and bake, uncovered, for 1 hour, or until the potato is tender and top is crisp.

STUFFED CAPSICUMS

Preparation: 20 minutes
Cooking: 1 hour
Serves 4

2 large red capsicums
1/2 cup (110 g/3 1/2 oz) short-grain rice
1 tablespoon olive oil
1 onion, finely chopped
2 cloves garlic, crushed
1 tomato, finely chopped
1/2 cup (60 g/2 oz) grated Cheddar
2 tablespoons finely grated Parmesan
1/4 cup (15 g/1/2 oz) chopped fresh basil
1/4 cup (15 g/1/2 oz) chopped fresh parsley

1 Preheat the oven to moderate 180°C (350°F/Gas 4). Cut the capsicums in half lengthways and remove the seeds and membrane. Cook the rice in boiling water for 12 minutes, or until tender. Drain well.
2 Heat the oil in a frying pan and cook the onion for 5–8 minutes, or until golden. Add the garlic and cook for 1 minute. Add to the rice with the tomato, cheeses, basil and parsley. Season well.
3 Spoon the filling into the capsicums and place on a baking tray. Bake for 30 minutes, or until the capsicums are soft and the filling is golden brown.

Stuff CAPSICUMS with a mixture of rice, cheese and herbs.

ASPARAGUS HOLLANDAISE

Preparation: 10 minutes
Cooking: 10 minutes
Serves 4–6

4 egg yolks
185 g (6 oz) butter, melted
2 tablespoons lemon juice
300 g (10 oz) asparagus

1 Put the egg yolks in a heatproof bowl over a pan of barely simmering water (don't let the base of the bowl touch the water). Add 1 tablespoon water and whisk until the eggs hold a trail. Remove from the heat and very slowly whisk in the butter (drop by drop at first). Whisk until thick and holding a trail. Stir in the lemon juice and season. (If you need to keep the sauce warm, replace the bowl over the hot water.)
2 Snap the woody ends from the asparagus and cook the spears in boiling water for 2–3 minutes, or until bright green and tender. Drain quickly and place on plates. Spoon the sauce over the top.

ASPARAGUS HOLLANDAISE (top) and CREAMED SPINACH.

CREAMED SPINACH

Preparation: 5 minutes
Cooking: 10 minutes
Serves 4

30 g (1 oz) butter
1 onion, thinly sliced
500 g (1 lb) English spinach, trimmed and roughly chopped
3 tablespoon cream
pinch of ground nutmeg
1/4 cup (30 g/1 oz) grated Cheddar

1 Heat the butter in a large heavy-based frying pan. Add the onion and cook over medium heat for 5 minutes, or until soft and golden. Add the spinach and cook for 3 minutes, or until wilted.
2 Stir in the cream and nutmeg and cook for 2 minutes, or until the spinach is tender and the cream heated through. Sprinkle with the cheese and serve immediately.

HONEY-GLAZED CARROTS

Preparation: 5 minutes
Cooking: 5 minutes
Serves 4

2 carrots, sliced
30 g (1 oz) butter
2 teaspoons honey
snipped chives, to serve

1 Boil or steam the carrots until tender. Place the butter and honey in a small pan and cook over low heat until warm.
2 Pour the butter and honey over the drained carrots and toss gently. Sprinkle with the snipped chives to serve.

CAULIFLOWER CHEESE

Preparation: 10 minutes
Cooking: 15 minutes
Serves 4–6

500 g (1 lb) cauliflower
30 g (1 oz) butter
3 teaspoons plain flour
1/2 cup (125 ml/4 fl oz) milk
3 tablespoons cream
1/3 cup (40 g/1 1/4 oz) grated Cheddar
1/4 teaspoon paprika
fresh chives, to serve

1 Cut the cauliflower into large florets and steam or boil until just tender.
2 Meanwhile, melt the butter in a pan. Stir in the flour and cook for 1 minute. Remove from the heat and gradually stir in the combined milk and cream. Return to the heat and stir until the mixture boils and thickens. Remove from the heat and stir in half the grated cheese. Season with salt and pepper to taste.
3 Put the drained cauliflower in a heatproof serving dish, spoon the cheese sauce over the top and sprinkle with the remaining grated cheese. Brown under a preheated hot grill for 3 minutes. Sprinkle with the paprika and snipped fresh chives to serve.

HONEY-GLAZED CARROTS (top) and CAULIFLOWER CHEESE.

Deep-fry POTATO CROQUETTES in batches for a crisp finish.

POTATO CROQUETTES

Preparation: 45 minutes + 2½ hours refrigeration
Cooking: 10 minutes
Makes 12

750 g (1½ lb) floury potatoes, chopped
2 tablespoons cream or melted butter
3 eggs, lightly beaten
¼ teaspoon nutmeg
plain flour, for coating
1½ cups (150 g/5 oz) dry breadcrumbs
oil, for deep-frying

1 Boil the potato in salted water until tender, drain, return to the hot pan and mash. Stir in the cream or butter, a third of the beaten egg and the nutmeg. Season. Spread on a tray, cover and leave in the fridge for at least 30 minutes.
2 Divide into 12 portions and roll each portion into a long sausage shape. Roll in flour, shaking off the excess. Dip in the remaining egg, coat evenly in the breadcrumbs and shake off the excess. Cover and refrigerate for at least 2 hours.
3 Half fill a deep heavy-based pan with oil and heat to 180°C/350°F (a cube of bread dropped in the oil will brown in 15 seconds). Cook in batches for 5 minutes, or until golden. Drain on paper towels and serve.

STUFFED PUMPKINS

Preparation: 30 minutes
Cooking: 1 hour
Serves 4

4 nugget pumpkins
60 g (2 oz) butter
1 tablespoon oil
1 leek, sliced
1 zucchini, chopped

Stuff PUMPKINS with a mixture of vegetables and rice.

1 red capsicum, chopped
100 g (3 1/2 oz) button mushrooms, sliced
1 tomato, chopped
1/2 cup (95 g/3 oz) cooked white rice
1 tablespoon chopped fresh parsley
1/2 cup (60 g/2 oz) grated Cheddar

1 Slice the top off each pumpkin and set it aside. Use a spoon to scoop out the pumpkin seeds.
2 Melt the butter and oil in a large frying pan, add the leek and cook over medium heat for 5 minutes, or until golden.
3 Add the zucchini, capsicum and mushrooms, and cook until tender. Remove from the heat and stir in the tomato, rice and parsley. Season with salt and pepper to taste.
4 Preheat the oven to moderate 180°C (350°F/ Gas 4). Spoon the filling into the pumpkin shells and place the shells into a clean ovenproof dish. Sprinkle with the grated Cheddar. Bake for 50 minutes, or until the pumpkins are tender. If you like, bake the pumpkin lids as well and replace to serve.

NOTE: To produce 1/2 cup (100 g/3 1/2 oz) cooked white rice you will need 1/4 cup (50 g/1 3/4 oz) uncooked rice.

CHAR-GRILLED VEGETABLES with a balsamic dressing.

CHAR-GRILLED VEGETABLES

Preparation: 15 minutes
Cooking: 15 minutes
Serves 4

2 large red capsicums
2 large sweet potatoes, sliced
6 zucchini, halved lengthways
4 large mushroom caps, thickly sliced

Dressing
3 cloves garlic, crushed
2 tablespoons balsamic vinegar
2 tablespoons chopped fresh rosemary
4 tablespoons olive oil

1 Remove the seeds and membrane from the capsicums and cut the flesh into thick strips.
2 To make the dressing, whisk together the garlic, vinegar, rosemary and oil.
3 Heat a char-grill pan or barbecue plate. Brush the capsicum, sweet potato, zucchini and mushrooms with the dressing and cook for 15 minutes, or until tender. Turn occasionally and brush with the dressing.

NOTE: For a full vegetarian meal, serve with chargrilled tofu or haloumi cheese, tossed in the dressing, and a mound of creamy polenta.

CAESAR SALAD is a modern café favourite.

CAESAR SALAD

Preparation: 15 minutes
Cooking: 20 minutes
Serves 4

4 slices white bread, crusts removed, cubed
3 rashers bacon, chopped
1 cos lettuce
60 g (2 oz) Parmesan shavings, plus extra, to serve
2–4 anchovies, chopped
1 egg
2 tablespoons lemon juice
1 clove garlic, crushed
1/2 cup (125 ml/4 fl oz) olive oil

1 Preheat the oven to moderately hot 190°C (375°F/Gas 5). Spread the bread cubes on a baking tray in a single layer and bake for 15 minutes, or until golden.
2 Fry the bacon until crisp, then drain on paper towels.
3 Tear the lettuce leaves into pieces and put in a bowl with the bread, bacon and Parmesan.
4 To make the dressing, whisk together the anchovies, egg, lemon juice and garlic until smooth. Start whisking in the oil, drop by drop at first, then in a thin stream, until the dressing is thick and creamy. Drizzle over the salad, sprinkle with extra Parmesan and serve.

WALDORF SALAD

Preparation: 20 minutes
Cooking: Nil
Serves 4–6

2 green apples
2 red apples
2 tablespoons lemon juice
1/4 cup (30 g/1 oz) walnut pieces
4 celery sticks, sliced
1 cup (250 g/8 oz) mayonnaise
lettuce, to serve

1 Quarter the apples, remove the seeds and cores, and cut the apples into small pieces.
2 Place the apple in a large bowl, drizzle with the lemon juice and toss to prevent the apples discolouring. Add the walnut pieces and celery and mix well.
3 Add the mayonnaise and toss well. Spoon into a lettuce-lined bowl and serve immediately.

COLESLAW

Preparation: 20 minutes
Cooking: Nil
Serves 8–10

1/2 green (Savoy) cabbage
1/4 red cabbage
3 carrots, coarsely grated
6 radishes, coarsely grated
1 red capsicum, chopped
4 spring onions, sliced
1/4 cup (15 g/1/2 oz) chopped fresh parsley
1 cup (250 g/8 oz) mayonnaise

1 Remove the hard cores from the cabbages and shred the leaves finely with a sharp knife. Place in a large bowl.
2 Add the carrot, radish, capsicum, spring onion and parsley. Add the mayonnaise, season with salt and freshly ground black pepper and toss the coleslaw well. Serve immediately (alternatively, cover and refrigerate the chopped vegetables for up to 3 hours, but serve immediately you have added the mayonnaise).

VARIATION: Instead of mayonnaise, dress the coleslaw with a mixture of sour cream, yoghurt, honey and mustard.

WALDORF SALAD.

COLESLAW.

GREEK SALAD

Preparation: 20 minutes
Cooking: Nil
Serves 6–8

6 ripe tomatoes, cut into thin wedges
1 red onion, cut into thin rings
2 Lebanese cucumbers, sliced
1 cup (185 g/6 oz) Kalamata olives
200 g (6 1/2 oz) feta cheese
1/2 cup (125 ml/4 fl oz) extra virgin olive oil
dried oregano, to serve

1 Put the tomato, onion, cucumber and olives in a large bowl and season.
2 Break the feta into large pieces and scatter over the top of the salad. Drizzle with olive oil and sprinkle with a little oregano.

GREEK SALAD—very simple, yet delicious.

HOT POTATO SALAD

Preparation: 20 minutes
Cooking: 30 minutes
Serves 6–8

4 rashers bacon
1 1/2 kg (3 lb) small Desiree potatoes (or other small, waxy, red-skinned potatoes)
4 spring onions, sliced
1/4 cup (7 g/1/4 oz) chopped fresh flat-leaf parsley
1/2 teaspoon salt

Dressing
2/3 cup (170 ml/5 1/2 fl oz) extra virgin olive oil
1 tablespoon Dijon mustard
1/3 cup (80 ml/2 3/4 fl oz) white wine vinegar

1 Trim the rind and fat from the bacon and grill

Dress HOT POTATO SALAD with a Dijon vinaigrette.

until crisp. Allow to cool. Chop into small pieces.
2 Simmer the potatoes in a large pan of water until just tender, trying not to let the skins break away too much. Drain and cool.
3 To make the dressing, whisk together the oil, mustard and white wine vinegar in a jug.
4 Cut the potatoes into quarters and put in a bowl with half the bacon, the spring onion, parsley, salt and some black pepper. Pour in the dressing and toss gently. Serve, sprinkled with the remaining bacon.

COLD POTATO SALAD

Preparation: 40 minutes
Cooking: 5 minutes
Serves 4

600 g (1 1/4 lb) waxy or salad potatoes
1 small onion, chopped
2 celery sticks, sliced
1 small green capsicum, chopped
2 tablespoons finely chopped fresh parsley

Dressing
3/4 cup (185 g/6 oz) mayonnaise
1–2 tablespoons vinegar or lemon juice
2 tablespoons sour cream

1 Wash the potatoes thoroughly, peeling them if you prefer, and cut into bite-sized pieces. Cook in boiling water for 5 minutes, or until just tender (pierce with a small sharp knife—the knife should come away easily). Drain and then leave to cool completely. Transfer to a large bowl.
2 Mix together the onion, celery, capsicum and parsley and add to the cooled potato. Mix together gently.
3 To make the dressing, mix together the mayonnaise, vinegar and sour cream, and season to taste. If you prefer a thinner dressing, add a little water. Pour over the salad and gently toss, being careful not to break up the pieces of potato.

VARIATIONS: Add chopped hard-boiled egg and crispy bacon.
Instead of a mayonnaise-based dressing, whisk together yoghurt and a little sweet chilli sauce (this is a good idea for anyone watching their fat intake).
For a Thai flavour, use coriander instead of parsley and top with peanuts or cashews.

Use waxy or salad potatoes for a COLD POTATO SALAD.

A RICE SALAD is perfect for barbecues or large gatherings.

RICE SALAD

Preparation: 30 minutes + 1 hour refrigeration
Cooking: 20 minutes
Serves 6–8

1 1/2 cups (300 g/10 oz) long-grain rice
1/2 cup (90 g/3 oz) peas
3 spring onions, sliced
1 green capsicum, diced
1 red capsicum, diced
310 g (10 oz) can corn kernels
1/4 cup (15 g/1/2 oz) chopped fresh mint

Dressing
1/2 cup (125 ml/4 fl oz) extra virgin olive oil
2 tablespoons lemon juice
1 clove garlic, crushed
1 teaspoon sugar

1 Bring a large pan of water to the boil and stir in the rice. Return to the boil and cook for 12–15 minutes, or until tender. Drain and cool (if possible, cook the rice a day in advance).
2 Cook the peas in boiling water for about 2 minutes. Rinse in cold water and drain well.
3 To make the dressing, whisk the oil, lemon juice, garlic and sugar together. Season to taste.
4 Mix the rice, peas, spring onion, capsicum, corn and mint in a bowl. Add the dressing and mix well. Cover and chill for 1 hour before serving.

TABBOULEH

Preparation: 20 minutes + 15 minutes standing
Cooking: Nil
Serves 8

3/4 cup (130 g/4 1/2 oz) burghul
300 g (10 oz) fresh flat-leaf parsley
1/2 cup (10 g/1/4 oz) mint leaves
4 spring onions, finely chopped
4 tomatoes, finely chopped
2 cloves garlic, crushed
1/3 cup (80 ml/2 3/4 fl oz) lemon juice
3 tablespoons olive oil

1 Put the burghul in a bowl with 185 ml (6 fl oz) water and leave for 15 minutes, or until all the water has been absorbed.
2 Finely chop the herbs with a large sharp knife or in a food processor—take care not to overprocess.

3 Place the burghul, herbs, spring onion, tomato, garlic, lemon juice and oil in a bowl and toss well. Refrigerate until required. Return to room temperature to serve.

TABBOULEH is a Middle Eastern mix of burghul and parsley.

PASTA SALAD

Preparation: 20 minutes
Cooking: 10 minutes
Serves 4

- 2 1/2 cups (225 g/7 oz) pasta spirals
- 150 g (5 oz) cherry tomatoes, halved
- 1 red or green capsicum, cubed
- 3 spring onions, sliced
- 100 g (3 1/2 oz) button mushrooms, sliced
- 1/2 barbecued chicken, shredded
- 1/2 cup (90 g/3 oz) cooked peas
- 3/4 cup (185 g/6 oz) whole egg mayonnaise

1 Bring a large pan of salted water to the boil, add the pasta and cook for 10 minutes, or until just tender. Drain, rinse under cold water and place in a large serving bowl.
2 Add the tomato, capsicum, spring onion, mushrooms, chicken, peas and mayonnaise and toss together well.

For speed, use a barbecued chicken in your PASTA SALAD.

THREE-BEAN SALAD

Preparation: 30 minutes
Cooking: 5 minutes
Serves 8–10

250 g (8 oz) green beans, topped and tailed
400 g (13 oz) can chickpeas, rinsed
425 g (13 1/2 oz) can red kidney beans, rinsed
400 g (13 oz) can cannellini beans, rinsed
270 g (9 oz) can corn kernels, rinsed
3 spring onions, sliced
1 red capsicum, chopped
3 celery sticks, chopped
4–6 gherkins, chopped
1/4 cup (15 g/1/2 oz) chopped fresh mint
1/4 cup (7 g/1/4 oz) chopped fresh flat-leaf parsley

Mustard vinaigrette
1/2 cup (125 ml/4 fl oz) olive oil
2 tablespoons white wine vinegar
1 teaspoon sugar
1 tablespoon Dijon mustard
1 clove garlic, crushed

1 Cut the green beans into short lengths. Bring a small pan of water to the boil, add the beans and cook for 2 minutes. Drain and rinse under cold water, then leave in iced water until cold. Drain.
2 Place the green beans, chickpeas, kidney beans, cannellini beans, corn, spring onion, capsicum, celery, gherkin, mint and parsley in a large bowl. Season and mix together.
3 To make the vinaigrette, whisk together all the ingredients, drizzle over the salad and toss gently.

STORAGE: The salad can be prepared up to 3 hours in advance and refrigerated, but don't add the dressing until just before serving.
NOTE: You can make this dish using dried beans and peas. Remember to soak the beans in cold water overnight, then cook in boiling water until tender. Check the packet for cooking times—some beans take longer than others and may need to be cooked separately.

Use green, cannellini and kidney beans for THREE-BEAN SALAD.

SALAD NICOISE

Preparation: 30 minutes
Cooking: 25 minutes
Serves 4–6

4 eggs
500 g (1 lb) baby new potatoes
250 g (8 oz) green beans, topped and tailed
6 artichoke hearts in oil, drained
350 g (11 oz) salad leaves
4 tomatoes, cut into wedges
425 g (14 oz) can tuna, drained and flaked
1 red capsicum, cut into strips
1 tablespoon bottled capers, drained
1 tablespoon coarsely chopped fresh tarragon
10 Niçoise (small) olives

Dressing
1 clove garlic, crushed
3 teaspoons Dijon mustard
2 anchovy fillets in oil, drained and chopped
1/4 cup (60 ml/2 fl oz) white wine vinegar
1/2 cup (125 ml/4 fl oz) extra virgin olive oil

1 Put the eggs in a pan of water and bring to the boil, stirring occasionally to centre the yolks. Boil for 10 minutes, drain and cool in cold water. Peel and cut into wedges.
2 Boil the potatoes until tender, drain and cool. Cut into thick slices. Cook the beans in a pan of boiling water until tender, then drain and rinse under cold water. Chill in a bowl of iced water. Halve or quarter the artichokes.
3 Arrange the salad leaves on a serving platter. Top with the potato, beans, tomato, artichoke, tuna, egg and capsicum. Sprinkle with the capers, tarragon and olives.
4 To make the dressing, whisk the garlic, mustard, anchovies and vinegar until smooth. Gradually add the oil and blend until smooth. Season with salt and pepper, and drizzle over the salad.

NOTE: Niçoise salad gets its name from the cuisine of Nice. All dishes described as 'niçoise' contain beans, tomatoes, olives and anchovies.

SALAD NICOISE, dressed with a garlic and anchovy vinaigrette.

SANDWICH FILLINGS

EGG AND MIXED CRESS

Combine 1/2 cup (125 g/4 oz) mayonnaise with 1 tablespoon chopped capers and 1 tablespoon wholegrain mustard. Spread half this mixture onto twelve slices of dark rye bread. Top six of the bread slices with 2 cups (60 g/2 oz) watercress, 6 thinly sliced hard-boiled eggs, 1 cup (45 g/1 1/2 oz) mustard cress or alfalfa sprouts, salt and freshly ground black pepper. Drizzle with the remaining mayonnaise mixture. Top with the other six slices. Serves 6.

COLD MEAT AND MUSTARD

Steam or boil 2 small carrots until tender. Cut into small dice and combine with 2 chopped spring onions, 1 thinly sliced celery stick including the leaves, 1 chopped gherkin and 140 g (4 1/2 oz) chopped cooked ham, corned beef or other cold meat. Mix 1 tablespoon Dijon mustard, 2 teaspoons lemon juice, 2 tablespoons mayonnaise, 2 tablespoons sour cream and 2 teaspoons chopped dill and add to the salad. Mix until combined. Season with salt and pepper. Put two thinly sliced tomatoes on lavash bread, top with the salad and roll up. Serves 4.

COTTAGE CHEESE, ASPARAGUS AND AVOCADO

Split open four bagels. Top with 2 cups (500 g/1 lb) cottage cheese combined with 1/2 cup (10 g/1/4 oz) chervil or parsley leaves. Blanch 155 g (5 oz) asparagus, drain well and cut into short lengths. Place 12 semi-dried tomatoes, 1 thinly sliced avocado and the asparagus on top of the cottage cheese, season to taste with salt and pepper, and replace the tops. Serves 4.

EGGPLANT AND ROCKET

Cut 400 g (13 oz) eggplant into quarters lengthways. Cut 1 red capsicum into quarters lengthways, removing the seeds and membrane. Bake the vegetables in a moderate 180°C (350°F/Gas 4) oven for 1 hour, or until soft and tender. Cool and cut into small pieces. Combine the vegetables with 100 g (3 1/2 oz) quartered cherry tomatoes, 2 chopped spring onions, 100 g (3 1/2 oz) crumbled feta cheese, 2 tablespoons each of coarsely chopped fresh flat-leaf parsley and mint leaves, 1 tablespoon chopped capers, 1 finely chopped clove garlic, 1/4 cup (60 ml/2 fl oz) lemon juice and 2 tablespoons olive oil. Season with salt and freshly ground black pepper. Split 4 slices of Turkish bread open. Fill with 150 g (5 oz) rocket leaves and the salad. Serves 4.

TUNA SALAD

Drain a 425 g (14 oz) can of tuna in oil. Break up the tuna with a fork and mix with 2 chopped hard-boiled eggs, 3 chopped spring onions, 2 teaspoons grated lemon rind, 1 chopped celery stick, 1 tablespoon chopped fresh flat-leaf parsley, 1/2 cup (125 g/4 oz) mayonnaise, 1/4 cup (60 g/2 oz) sour cream, salt and freshly ground black pepper to taste. Mix lightly with a fork. Serve with mixed lettuce leaves on bread rolls. Serves 4.

Clockwise from top left: EGG AND MIXED CRESS; COLD MEAT AND MUSTARD; COTTAGE CHEESE, ASPARAGUS AND AVOCADO; TUNA SALAD; EGGPLANT AND ROCKET.

SAVOURY PASTRIES

Savoury pastries can vary from sausage rolls for entertaining, to family dinners like chicken and leek cobbler. Perfect pastry, with a light buttery touch, can make any dish special. It has a reputation for difficulty, but once you've mastered the commonsense rules you'll probably find it rather easy.

QUICHE LORRAINE

Preparation: 35 minutes + 35 minutes refrigeration
Cooking: 1 hour
Serves 4–6

1 1/2 cups (185 g/6 oz) plain flour
90 g (3 oz) cold butter, chopped
1 egg yolk

Filling
20 g (3/4 oz) butter
1 onion, chopped
4 rashers bacon, cut into thin strips
2 tablespoons chopped fresh chives
2 eggs
3/4 cup (185 ml/6 fl oz) cream
1/4 cup (60 ml/2 fl oz) milk
100 g (3 1/2 oz) Swiss cheese, grated

1 Sift the flour into a bowl. Add the butter and, using your fingertips, rub the butter into the flour until it resembles fine breadcrumbs. Add the egg and mix with a knife, until the mixture just comes together. Add a little water if needed. Turn the mixture out onto a floured surface and gather together into a ball. Cover with plastic wrap and chill for at least 15 minutes.
2 Roll the pastry out between two sheets of baking paper until it is large enough to cover the base and side of a shallow loose-based round flan tin measuring 25 cm (10 inches) across the base. Lift the pastry into the tin and use a spare wad of pastry to press it firmly into the side of the tin. Trim off any excess pastry with a sharp knife or by rolling the rolling pin across the top. Place the pastry-lined flan tin in the refrigerator for 20 minutes. Preheat the oven to moderately hot 190°C (375°F/Gas 5).
3 Cover the pastry shell with crumpled baking paper, fill evenly with baking beads or uncooked rice or beans and bake for 15 minutes. Remove the paper and beads, and bake the pastry for 10 minutes, or until lightly golden and dried out. Reduce the oven to moderate 180°C (350°F/Gas 4).
4 To make the filling, heat the butter in a heavy-based pan. Add the onion and bacon and cook for 10 minutes, stirring frequently, until the onion is soft and the bacon cooked. Stir in the chives and set aside to cool.
5 Beat the eggs, cream and milk in a jug. Season with black pepper. Spread

QUICHE LORRAINE is the basic bacon-and-egg quiche.

the onion and bacon mixture evenly over the pastry shell. Pour in the egg mixture and sprinkle with the cheese. Bake for 30 minutes, or until golden and set.

VARIATION: To make a herb quiche, simply change the filling. Whisk together 3 eggs and 1 cup (250 ml/8 fl oz) cream. Stir in 1/2 cup of chopped fresh herbs (chives, parsley and dill all work well in a quiche) and 100 g (3 1/2 oz) grated cheese. Pour into the pastry case and bake for 30 minutes, or until set.

Use a can of red salmon for SALMON AND SPRING ONION QUICHE.

SALMON AND SPRING ONION QUICHE

Preparation: 20 minutes + 20 minutes refrigeration
Cooking: 1 hour
Serves 6

2 cups (250 g/8 oz) self-raising flour
160 g (5 1/2 oz) butter, melted
1/2 cup (125 ml/4 fl oz) milk

Filling

415 g (13 oz) can red salmon, drained and flaked
4 spring onions, sliced
1/3 cup (20 g/3/4 oz) chopped fresh parsley
4 eggs, lightly beaten
1/2 cup (125 ml/4 fl oz) milk
1/2 cup (125 ml/4 fl oz) cream
1/2 cup (60 g/2 oz) grated Cheddar

1 Sift the flour into a large bowl and make a well in the centre. Pour in the melted butter and milk and mix until the mixture comes together and forms a dough. Refrigerate for 20 minutes. Preheat the oven to moderately hot 200°C (400°F/Gas 6). Roll out the pastry between two sheets of baking paper until it is large enough to cover the base and side of a 26 cm (10 1/2 inch) round shallow loose-based fluted flan tin. Trim off any excess with a sharp knife or by rolling a rolling pin across the top of the tin.
2 Cover the pastry with crumpled baking paper and fill evenly with baking beads or uncooked rice or beans. Bake for 15 minutes. Remove the paper and beads and bake for 10 minutes, or until golden and dry. Allow to cool. Reduce the oven to moderate 180°C (350°F/Gas 4).
3 Place the salmon in the pastry base. Mix together the spring onion, parsley, eggs, milk, cream and cheese and pour over the salmon. Bake for 30 minutes, or until set.

CARAMELIZED ONION QUICHE

Preparation: 45 minutes + 20 minutes refrigeration
Cooking: 1¾ hours
Serves 6

1½ cups (185 g/6 oz) plain flour
125 g (4 oz) cold butter, chopped
1 egg yolk

Filling
75 g (2½ oz) butter
800 g (1 lb 10 oz) onions, thinly sliced
1 tablespoon soft brown sugar
¾ cup (185 g/6 oz) sour cream
2 eggs
40 g (1¼ oz) prosciutto, cut into strips
40 g (1¼ oz) grated mature Cheddar
2 teaspoons fresh thyme leaves

Cook the onions slowly for CARAMELIZED ONION QUICHE.

1 Sift the flour into a bowl, add the butter and rub between your fingertips until the mixture resemble fine breadcrumbs. Cut in the egg yolk with a knife and add 1–2 tablespoons of water until the dough just comes together. Add extra water if needed. Turn out and gather into a ball. Cover with plastic wrap and chill for 20 minutes.
2 Melt the butter in a pan and cook the onion over low heat for 25 minutes, or until soft and browned (this will produce sweet caramelized onions so do not be tempted to rush the process). Stir in the brown sugar and cook for 15 minutes, stirring occasionally to prevent burning. Preheat the oven to moderately hot 200°C (400°F/Gas 6). Grease a loose-based 22 cm (8¾ inch) round flan tin.
3 Roll out the pastry large enough to fit the flan tin. Fit the pastry into the tin, trimming off any excess with a sharp knife. Cover with crumpled baking paper and fill evenly with baking beads or uncooked rice or beans. Bake for 15 minutes, then remove the paper and beads and bake for 5 minutes. Cool slightly.
4 Lightly beat the sour cream and eggs. Add the prosciutto, cheese and thyme leaves. Season with salt and pepper. Stir in the onion and pour into the pastry shell. Bake for 40 minutes, or until set. If the pastry starts to over-brown, cover with foil.

CHICKEN AND LEEK COBBLER

Preparation: 1 hour
Cooking: 1 hour
Serves 4–6

50 g (1 3/4 oz) butter
1 kg (2 lb) chicken breast fillets, cut into strips
1 large leek, finely sliced
1 celery stick, sliced
1 tablespoon plain flour
1 cup (250 ml/8 fl oz) chicken stock
1 cup (250 ml/8 fl oz) cream
3 teaspoons Dijon mustard
3 teaspoons green peppercorns

Topping
400 g (13 oz) potatoes, quartered
1 1/3 cups (165 g/5 1/2 oz) self-raising flour
1/2 teaspoon salt
1/4 cup (30 g/1 oz) grated mature Cheddar
100 g (3 1/2 oz) cold butter, chopped
1 egg yolk, lightly beaten, to glaze

1 Melt half the butter in a pan. When foaming, add the chicken in batches and cook until golden. Remove from the pan. Add the remaining butter and cook the leek and celery until soft. Return the chicken to the pan.

Use a potato dough for the CHICKEN AND LEEK COBBLER.

2 Sprinkle the flour over the chicken and stir for 1 minute. Remove from the heat and stir in the stock and cream. Mix well, making sure that there are no lumps. Return to the heat and stir until it comes to the boil and thickens. Reduce the heat and simmer for 20 minutes. Add the mustard and peppercorns and season with salt and pepper. Transfer to a 1.5 litre casserole dish and cool. Preheat the oven to moderately hot 200°C (400°F/Gas 6).
3 To make the topping, cook the potatoes in boiling water until tender. Drain and mash until smooth. Rub together the flour, salt, cheese and butter with your fingertips until it resembles fine crumbs. Add to the potato and bring together with your hands into a dough.
4 Roll out the dough on a floured surface, until 1 cm (1/2 inch) thick. Cut into rounds with a 6 cm (2 1/2 inch) pastry cutter, re-rolling and cutting to use all the dough. Arrange the rounds overlapping on top of the cooled filling.
5 Brush the topping with the egg yolk, adding a little milk if more glaze is needed. Bake for 30 minutes, or until the filling is heated through and the topping golden.

COUNTRY VEGETABLE PIE

Preparation: 50 minutes + 30 minutes refrigeration
Cooking: 45 minutes
Serves 6

2 cups (250 g/8 oz) plain flour
125 g (4 oz) cold butter, chopped
2 egg yolks

Filling
2 new potatoes, cubed
350 g (11 oz) butternut pumpkin, cubed
100 g (3 1/2 oz) broccoli, cut into small florets
100 g (3 1/2 oz) cauliflower, cut into small florets
1 zucchini, grated
1 carrot, grated
3 spring onions, chopped
3/4 cup (90 g/3 oz) grated Cheddar
1/2 cup (125 g/4 oz) ricotta cheese
1/2 cup (50 g/1 3/4 oz) grated Parmesan
1/4 cup (15 g/1/2 oz) chopped fresh parsley
1 egg, lightly beaten
1 egg yolk, lightly beaten

1 Sift the flour into a bowl. Add the butter and, using your fingertips, rub in until it resembles fine breadcrumbs. Add the yolks and mix with a knife, until the dough just comes together. Add 3–4 tablespoons water if needed. Turn out onto a floured surface and gather together. Cover with plastic wrap and chill for at least 15 minutes.
2 To make the filling, steam or boil the potato and pumpkin for 10–15 minutes, or until tender. Drain and place in a large bowl to cool. Gently fold in the broccoli, cauliflower, zucchini, carrot, spring onion, cheeses, parsley and beaten egg. Season.
3 Grease a deep 18 cm (7 inch) loose-bottomed flan tin. Roll out two-thirds of the dough on a lightly floured surface to fit the base and side of the tin. Spoon the filling into the pastry base.
4 To make the lattice top, roll out the remaining dough a little larger than the pie. Cut the dough into thin strips and lay half on baking paper in one direction and the other half at right angles. Interweave the strips to make a lattice. Invert onto the pie and press the edge to seal. Cover and chill for 15 minutes. Brush with egg yolk. Place the tin on a baking tray. Preheat the oven to moderately hot 190°C (375°F/Gas 5). Bake for 25–30 minutes, or until the pastry is cooked and lightly golden.

Fold or plait the pastry top for COUNTRY VEGETABLE PIE.

DEEP-DISH CHICKEN PIE

Preparation: 45 minutes + refrigeration
Cooking: 1 hour 10 minutes
Serves 6

1 tablespoon olive oil
1 large onion, chopped
2 cloves garlic, crushed
600 g (1 1/4 lb) chicken thigh fillets, chopped
2 large carrots, chopped
2 large parsnips, chopped
1 large potato, chopped
2 bay leaves
2 celery sticks, sliced
3 tablespoons plain flour
1 1/4 cups (315 ml/ 10 fl oz) milk
1/2 cup (125 ml/4 fl oz) chicken stock
3 sheets frozen butterpuff pastry, thawed (see Note)
1 egg yolk, beaten

1 Heat the oil in a large deep frying pan and cook the onion and garlic for 3 minutes, or until the soft. Add the chicken and cook for 10 minutes, or until golden brown, turning regularly.
2 Add the chopped carrot, parsnip, potato, bay leaves and celery with 1/4 cup (60 ml/2 fl oz) water, and mix well. Cook over low heat, covered, for 10 minutes, or until the carrot, parsnip and potato are just tender.
3 Stir in the flour and cook for 2 minutes. Remove from the heat and add the milk and stock, stirring until blended and smooth. Return to the heat and stir until the sauce boils and thickens. Transfer to a large bowl, cover and refrigerate until completely cold.
4 Grease a deep 20 cm (8 inch) round springform tin. Using 1 sheet of the pastry, cut a circle to fit the base of the tin. Cut the second sheet of pastry into 3 strips and press each strip around the side of the tin, pressing the edges together gently with your fingertips. (Make sure the pastry is well sealed or the filling will leak.) Refrigerate for 20 minutes.
5 Preheat the oven to moderately hot 200°C (400°F/Gas 6). Spoon the cold filling into the pastry case and smooth with the back of the spoon. Using the last sheet of pastry, cut a circle 2 cm (3/4 inch) larger than the tin. Cut a 2 cm (3/4 inch) hole in the centre of the pastry. Gently place it over the pie and trim the edge. Pinch the edges together firmly to seal. Decorate with shapes cut from the pastry trimmings. Brush the top of the pie with the

Decorate your DEEP-DISH CHICKEN PIE with pastry trimmings.

beaten egg yolk. Bake for 35 minutes, or until crisp and golden. Leave in the tin for 10 minutes before removing and cutting.

NOTE: Butterpuff pastry will produce the best result for this pie. If you can't find butterpuff pastry, buy plain puff pastry and brush it with melted butter. The pastry sheets will take 5–10 minutes to defrost at room temperature.

SPINACH PIE

Preparation: 25 minutes
Cooking: 45 minutes
Serves 6–8

1 kg (2 lb) English spinach
1 tablespoon oil
6 spring onions, chopped
125 g (4 oz) feta cheese, crumbled
3/4 cup (90 g/3 oz) grated Cheddar
5 eggs, lightly beaten
16 sheets filo pastry
1/3 cup (80 ml/2 3/4 fl oz) olive oil
1 egg, lightly beaten
1 tablespoon poppy seeds

1 Preheat the oven to hot 210°C (415°F/Gas 6–7). Brush a 30 x 25 cm (12 x 10 inch) baking dish with oil. Wash the spinach thoroughly and shred finely. Place in a large pan with just the water clinging to the leaves, cover and cook over low heat for 2 minutes, or until just wilted. Cool, then wring the moisture from the spinach and spread out the strands.

2 Heat the oil in a small pan and cook the spring onion for 3 minutes, or until soft. Transfer to a large bowl and add the spinach, cheeses and eggs. Season with salt and pepper and mix well.

3 Place 1 sheet of pastry in the baking dish, letting the edges hang over. Cover the remaining pastry with a clean, damp tea towel to prevent it drying out. Brush the pastry in the dish with some of the oil. Repeat the process with another 7 layers of pastry, brushing each sheet lightly with the oil.

4 Spread the filling over the pastry and fold in the edges. Brush each remaining sheet of pastry lightly with oil and place on top of the pie. Tuck the edges of pastry down the sides, brush the top with the egg and sprinkle with the poppy seeds. Bake for 35–40 minutes, or until golden. Serve immediately.

Use layers of buttery filo pastry for SPINACH PIE.

Chill PORK PIE overnight, then cut into wedges to serve.

PORK PIE

Preparation: 45 minutes + overnight refrigeration
Cooking: 1 3/4 hours
Serves 6–8

3 cups (375 g/12 oz) plain flour
2 egg yolks
125 g (4 oz) lard
600 g (1 1/4 lb) boneless pork, cubed
4 rashers bacon, chopped
1 red onion, chopped
1/2 celery stick, chopped
1 tablespoon fresh thyme
1 cup (80 g/2 3/4 oz) fresh breadcrumbs
1 egg, lightly beaten
1 egg, lightly beaten, to glaze

Aspic
1/2 cup (125 ml/4 fl oz) apple juice or water
1 teaspoon chicken stock powder
2 teaspoons gelatine

1 Grease a deep 17 cm (6 3/4 inch) round springform tin. Sift the flour into a large bowl. Make a well in the centre and add the egg yolks. Cover the egg yolks with the flour and set aside. Place the lard and 2/3 cup (170 ml/5 1/2 fl oz) water in a small pan, and stir over medium heat until the lard has melted. Bring to the boil and then quickly pour it over the flour and eggs. Mix to a soft dough with a wooden spoon. Turn out onto a lightly floured surface and gather together into a smooth ball. Wrap in plastic wrap and refrigerate for 30 minutes.
2 Work the pork, in batches, in a processor until roughly chopped but not minced (or chop with a sharp knife). Transfer to a bowl. Add the bacon, onion, celery, thyme, breadcrumbs and egg. Mix well, cover and chill.
3 Roll out two-thirds of the pastry between two sheets of greaseproof paper and line the base and side of the tin. Trim the edge and brush with some of the egg. Spoon the filling into the tin and smooth the surface. Roll the remaining pastry out to a 20 cm (8 inch) circle. Cut a 2 cm (3/4 inch) hole in the centre. Fit over the filling, trim the pastry and press to seal the edges together. Decorate with the pastry scraps, then refrigerate for 30 minutes.
4 Preheat the oven to hot

210°C (415°F/Gas 6–7). Brush the pie with the egg. Bake for 45 minutes, then reduce the heat to moderate 180°C (350°F/Gas 4) and continue to cook for 1 hour. Cover with foil if the pastry is browning too much. Cool in the tin.

5 To make the aspic, mix the apple juice with the stock powder in a small pan. Sprinkle with the gelatine and stir over low heat until dissolved. Pour the aspic, a little at a time, into the pie hole, letting it soak in each time. Cover and refrigerate overnight. Serve cold, in wedges.

BACON AND EGG PIE

Preparation: 40 minutes
Cooking: 30 minutes
Serves 4–6

2 cups (250 g/8 oz) plain flour
125 g (4 oz) chilled butter, chopped
pinch of salt
2 teaspoons oil
6 rashers bacon, chopped
6 eggs
1 tablespoon chopped fresh parsley
1 egg, beaten

1 Lightly grease a 20 cm (8 inch) pie plate. Sift the flour into a bowl. Add the butter and, using your fingertips, rub the butter and salt into the flour until it resembles fine breadcrumbs. Add 3–4 tablespoons water and mix with a knife until the dough just comes together. Turn out onto a floured surface and gather together into a ball.

2 Roll out two thirds of the pastry and line the pie plate. Cover with plastic wrap and refrigerate for 20 minutes. Preheat the oven to moderately hot 200°C (400°F/Gas 6).

3 Heat the oil in a frying pan and cook the bacon for 5 minutes, or until soft and slightly golden. Remove from the heat and cool slightly. Arrange over the pastry base.

4 Crack the eggs into a cup, one at a time, then slide on top of the bacon at regular intervals (so, when the pie is sliced, each person will get some egg). Sprinkle with the parsley and season well. Roll out the remaining pastry and lay it over the top of the pie. Press the edges together and trim with a sharp knife. Pinch the edges in a decorative pattern, cut a steam hole in the top and decorate with pastry scraps. Brush with the egg and bake for 15–20 minutes. Serve hot.

BACON AND EGG PIE.

STEAK AND KIDNEY PUDDING

Preparation: 30 minutes
Cooking: 4 hours
Serves 4–6

200 g (6½ oz) lamb kidneys
500 g (1 lb) round or rump steak, cubed
2 tablespoons plain flour
30 g (1 oz) butter
1 tablespoon oil
1 onion, sliced
1 clove garlic, crushed
125 g (4 oz) button mushrooms, quartered
1 bay leaf
½ cup (125 ml/4 fl oz) red wine
1 cup (250 ml/8 fl oz) beef stock
2 tablespoons chopped fresh parsley

Suet pastry
1½ cups (185 g/6 oz) self-raising flour
90 g (3 oz) suet, finely grated

1 Peel the skin from the kidneys, cut into quarters and trim any fat or sinew. Toss the kidneys and steak cubes in the flour.
2 Heat the butter and oil in a heavy-based pan and cook the onion and garlic, stirring until soft; remove from the pan. Add the steak and kidneys to the pan in small batches and brown over high heat. Drain on paper towels.
3 Return the onion, garlic, steak and kidneys to the pan with the mushrooms, bay leaf, wine, stock and parsley and bring to the boil. Reduce the heat and simmer, covered, for 1 hour, or until the steak is tender, stirring occasionally. Cool.
4 To make the suet pastry, sift the flour into a bowl and stir in the suet. Add about ½ cup (125 ml/4 fl oz) water, or enough to mix to a firm dough. Turn out onto a lightly floured surface and gather together into a smooth ball. Roll out two-thirds of the pastry to line a 2-litre pudding basin. Brush the top edge with water.
5 Spoon the filling into the pastry. Roll the remaining pastry to cover the basin, then press the edges of the pastry firmly together to seal. Lay a sheet of foil on the work surface and cover with baking paper. Make a large pleat in the middle. Grease the paper with melted butter. Place, paper-side-down, on top of the basin and tie securely with string. Place the basin in a large pan. Add enough water to

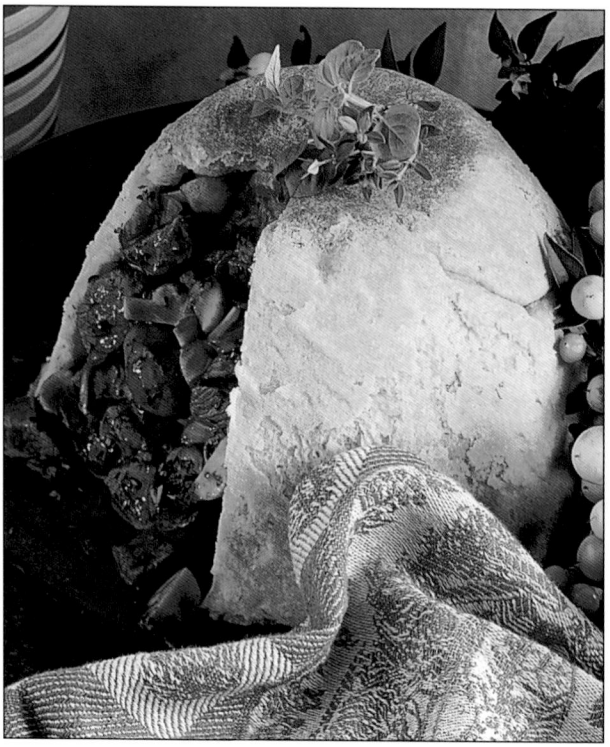

Use traditional suet pastry for STEAK AND KIDNEY PUDDING.

come halfway up the side of the basin. Bring to the boil, then reduce the heat to a simmer and cook, covered, for 3 hours, checking and replenishing the water when necessary. Serve immediately.

HINT: Suet gives the pastry a slightly crisp texture: it can be bought from your butcher. If you can't find it, use butter.
VARIATION: To make steak and kidney pie, place the cooled filling in a 23 cm (9 inch) pie dish and cover with a sheet of puff pastry. Press the edge to seal and cut a hole in the top to let the steam escape. Bake in a preheated moderately hot 200°C (400°F/Gas 6) oven for 25 minutes or until the top is golden brown and the filling has thoroughly heated through.

SAUSAGE ROLLS

Preparation: 35 minutes
Cooking: 25 minutes
Makes 48

1 teaspoon oil
1 onion, finely chopped
500 g (1 lb) sausage mince
1 cup (80 g/2¾ oz) fresh breadcrumbs
2 tablespoons tomato sauce
1 egg, lightly beaten
3 sheets frozen ready-rolled puff pastry, thawed
egg or milk, to glaze

Serve SAUSAGE ROLLS with extra tomato sauce.

1 Preheat the oven to moderately hot 200°C (400°F/Gas 6). Lightly grease a baking tray. Heat the oil in a frying pan and cook the onion over low heat until soft and transparent. Transfer to a bowl and mix with the mince, breadcrumbs, tomato sauce and egg.
2 Lay the pastry sheets on a lightly floured board and cut each sheet into two strips. Divide the filling into six equal portions and spoon across the long edge of the pastry. Roll up to make a long sausage shape. Brush lightly with a little beaten egg or milk. Cut the rolls into 4 cm (1½ inch) lengths and place on the tray, seam-side-down.
3 Bake for 20 minutes, or until the rolls are crisp and golden. Serve with tomato sauce.

NOTE: Sausage rolls can be frozen for up to 2 weeks after baking. Thaw and reheat in a preheated moderate 180°C (350°F/Gas 4) oven for 30 minutes.
VARIATION: This recipe can also be made using chicken mince.

PIZZA BASE

Preparation: 20 minutes
Cooking: 30 minutes
Makes one thick or two thin 30 cm (12 inch) bases

7 g (1/4 inch) sachet dry yeast
1/2 teaspoon salt
1/2 teaspoon sugar
2 1/2 cups (310 g/10 oz) plain flour
2 tablespoons olive oil
2 teaspoons semolina or polenta

1 Combine the yeast, salt, sugar and 1 cup (250 ml/8 fl oz) warm water in a small bowl. Leave, covered with plastic wrap, in a warm place for 10 minutes, or until the mixture is foamy.
2 Sift the flour into a large bowl. Make a well in the centre, add the yeast mixture and mix to a dough. Knead the dough on a lightly floured surface for 5 minutes, or until smooth and elastic. For thick pizza, roll the dough out to a 35 cm (14 inch) round. For thin pizza, divide the dough in half and roll out each portion to a 35 cm (14 inch) round.
3 Brush a 30 cm (12 inch) pizza tray with oil and sprinkle with semolina or polenta. Place the dough on the tray and tuck the edge underneath to make a rim. Spread with pizza sauce and then your choice of toppings. Bake at hot 210°C (415°F/Gas 6–7) for 30 minutes.

VARIATION: For wholemeal pizza base: Use 1 1/2 cups (185 g/6 oz) plain flour and 1 cup (150 g/5 oz) plain wholemeal flour.

PIZZA SAUCE

Preparation: 10 minutes
Cooking: 25 minutes
Makes sauce for two 30 cm (12 inch) pizzas

1 tablespoon olive oil
1 onion, finely chopped
2 cloves garlic, crushed
425 g (14 oz) can peeled tomatoes, crushed
1 teaspoon dried basil
1 teaspoon dried oregano
1 teaspoon sugar

1 Heat the oil in a pan and cook the onion over low heat for 5 minutes, or until soft. Add the garlic and cook for 1 minute.
2 Stir in the tomato, herbs and sugar and cook over high heat for 20 minutes, or until reduced and thickened. Season to taste and cool before using.

NOTE: The sauce can be made up to 2 days in advance. Refrigerate in an airtight container until required. The sauce may also be frozen for up to 2 months. You may like to make a double batch and freeze the remaining sauce for future use.

SUPER SUPREME

Preparation: 20 minutes
Cooking: 30 minutes
Serves 4

30 cm (12 inch) pizza base
3 tablespoons pizza sauce
1 cup (150 g/5 oz) grated mozzarella cheese
1 green capsicum, chopped
100 g (3 1/2 oz) small button mushrooms, sliced
45 g (1 1/2 oz) sliced ham, cut into strips
45 g (1 1/2 oz) cabanossi, thinly sliced
30 g (1 oz) sliced salami, cut into quarters
2 pineapple rings, sliced
pitted black olives, sliced

1 Preheat the oven to hot 210°C (415°F/Gas 6–7). Lightly oil a 35 cm (14 inch) pizza tray. Place the pizza base on the tray and spread evenly with the sauce.
2 Sprinkle three-quarters of the cheese over the

SUPER SUPREME pizza with all the toppings—or you can make up your own.

pizza base. Top with the capsicum and mushrooms. Arrange the ham, cabanossi, salami, pineapple and olives evenly over the top. Sprinkle with the remaining cheese.

3 Bake for 30 minutes, or until the base is crunchy and golden, and the cheese has melted. Cut into wedges and serve.

VARIATION: You can put pretty much anything on a pizza—try chilli, anchovies, ground beef, sun-dried tomatoes or cooked prawns.

For a simple vegetarian pizza, brush the base with a mixture of crushed garlic and olive oil, top with thin slices of potatoes and sprinkle with fresh herbs, salt and a little Parmesan.

For a special occasion antipasto pizza, spread with pizza sauce and top with marinated vegetables, sliced bocconcini and pesto.

SPRING ROLLS

Preparation: 35 minutes
Cooking: 30 minutes
Makes about 20

4 dried Chinese mushrooms
1 clove garlic, crushed
3/4 teaspoon finely grated fresh ginger
6 spring onions, chopped
3 cups (135 g/4 1/2 oz) shredded Chinese cabbage
1 large carrot, grated
150 g (5 oz) can water chestnuts, chopped
1 tablespoon oyster sauce
1 packet spring roll wrappers
oil, for deep-frying
sweet chilli sauce, to serve

1 Soak the mushrooms in boiling water for 10 minutes. Drain and squeeze out the liquid. Remove the stems and chop the caps finely.
2 Heat a little oil in a wok or frying pan and cook the garlic, ginger, spring onion, cabbage, carrot, water chestnuts and mushrooms for 5 minutes over high heat, or until softened. Stir in the oyster sauce and leave to cool.
3 Work with one wrapper at a time, keeping the rest covered with a damp tea towel. Place 2 tablespoons filling on each wrapper and fold one point over. Fold in the two side points and roll up towards the last point, making a parcel. Seal with a little flour and water paste.
4 Half-fill the wok with oil and heat until a cube of bread browns in 15 seconds. Deep-fry the rolls, four at a time, for about 3 minutes, or until golden. Drain the rolls on paper towels and serve with sweet chilli sauce.

Serve SPRING ROLLS with sweet chilli sauce, for dipping.

MEAT PIE

Preparation: 30 minutes + overnight refrigeration
Cooking: 3 hours
Serves 4

1/3 cup (40 g/1 1/4 oz) plain flour, seasoned
750 g (1 1/2 lb) gravy beef, cut into chunks
1/3 cup (80 ml/2 3/4 fl oz) oil
3 onions, sliced
2 cups (500 ml/16 fl oz) beef stock
1 tablespoon Worcestershire sauce
2 tablespoons chopped fresh parsley
1 sheet ready-rolled shortcrust pastry
1 egg yolk, to glaze
1 sheet ready-rolled puff pastry

Glazing the MEAT PIE with egg yolk will give it a lovely crisp and shiny crust.

1 Put the seasoned flour in a plastic bag, add the meat and shake to coat with the flour. Remove the meat and shake off the excess flour. Heat a little oil in a large heavy-based pan and fry the meat, in batches, until golden brown. Remove all the meat from the pan.

2 Add the onion to the pan and cook over medium heat until it is golden and translucent. Return the meat to the pan, add the stock and Worcestershire sauce and stir until it boils and thickens. Reduce the heat, cover and simmer for 2 hours, or until the meat is very tender, stirring every 30 minutes to prevent sticking. Stir in the parsley. Cool, then refrigerate (preferably overnight—most meat stew mixtures are better left overnight for the flavours to develop).

3 Place a baking tray in the oven and preheat the oven to hot 220°C (425°F/Gas 7). Grease a deep 20 cm (8 inch) round pie plate. Line the base and side of the dish with the shortcrust pastry. You may need to roll the square of pastry a little larger to fit into the dish. Place the cold filling into the pastry shell.

4 Mix the egg yolk with 2 teaspoons of water and brush the pastry edge. Place the puff pastry over the top, press the edge gently to seal, then trim away the extra pastry. Pinch or crimp the edges to decorate. Cut two small slits in the pastry to allow the steam to escape during cooking. Brush with the egg yolk glaze. Put on the preheated tray and bake for 20 minutes. Reduce the heat to moderate 180°C (350°F/Gas 4) and cook for 15–20 minutes. Check the pastry during cooking and cover with foil if overbrowning.

CORNISH PASTIES

Preparation: 30 minutes
Cooking: 30 minutes
Makes 6 pasties

Shortcrust pastry

2 1/2 cups (310 g/10 oz) plain flour
1/2 teaspoon dry mustard
120 g (4 oz) butter, chopped

Filling

250 g (8 oz) round or blade steak, finely chopped
2 small floury potatoes, finely chopped
1 onion, finely chopped
1/4 cup (15 g/1/2 oz) chopped fresh parsley
1/4 cup (60 ml/2 fl oz) beef or chicken stock
1/4 teaspoon English mustard
1 teaspoon grated horseradish
beaten egg, to glaze

1 Preheat the oven to hot 210°C (415°F/Gas 6–7) and grease a baking tray. Put the flour, mustard and butter in a bowl and rub in the butter with your fingertips until the mixture resembles fine breadcrumbs. Add 2 tablespoons water and mix with a knife until the mixture comes together, adding more water if necessary. Gather into a ball, wrap in plastic wrap and refrigerate.

2 To make the filling, mix together the steak, potato, onion and parsley. Add the stock, mustard and horseradish, and season with salt and white pepper. Mix well.

3 Roll the pastry out to 3 mm (1/8 inch) thickness. Cut out six 16 cm (6 1/2 inch) rounds, using a saucer as a guide. Spoon the filling into the centres of the six pastry rounds.

4 Glaze the edge of the pastry with egg and bring up two sides over the filling to make a half circle. Pinch the edges together to form a frill. Brush with the egg and bake on a baking tray for 10 minutes. Reduce the heat to moderate 180°C (350°F/Gas 4) and cook for a further 20 minutes. Serve hot or cold.

NOTE: Cold pasties are excellent for work or school lunches. They were originally baked for farmers who worked outside all day, and for miners. Family members would have their own preferences for fillings, and each pasty would be marked with its owner's initials. The pasty has the frill so that it can easily be held to eat.

CORNISH PASTIES can be served hot from the oven, or cold.

CHEESE AND PINE NUT FILO TRIANGLES

Preparation: 30 minutes
Cooking: 15 minutes
Makes 28 triangles

125 g (4 oz) feta cheese
125 g (4 oz) ricotta cheese
2 tablespoons chopped fresh basil
1/4 cup (40 g/1 1/4 oz) pine nuts, toasted
1 egg, lightly beaten
14 sheets filo pastry
125 g (4 oz) butter, melted

CHEESE AND PINE NUT FILO TRIANGLES.

1 Preheat the oven to moderately hot 200°C (400°F/Gas 6). Mix together the cheeses, basil, pine nuts and egg. Season well with salt and black pepper.
2 Place a sheet of pastry on a work surface and brush all over with the melted butter. Top with another sheet of pastry and brush with the butter. Cut the pastry lengthways into four strips.
3 Place 3 level teaspoons of the mixture on the end of each strip. Fold the pastry diagonally over and up to enclose the filling and make a triangle. Brush the triangles with butter and place on a baking tray. Repeat with the remaining pastry and filling. Bake the triangles for 15 minutes, or until golden brown. Serve hot.

STORAGE: The triangles can be made several hours ahead and kept in the fridge under a damp tea towel. Bake just before serving. Cooked triangles can be frozen in a single layer on a baking tray until firm, then transferred to an airtight container in the freezer.
HINT: Handle filo pastry quickly and carefully as it becomes brittle when exposed to air. To prevent it drying out, cover the spare sheets with a damp tea towel while assembling the triangles.

VARIATION: For prawn and crab triangles, melt 30 g (1 oz) butter in a small pan and cook 3 finely chopped spring onions for 2 minutes. Stir in 1 tablespoon plain flour, then 1/2 cup (125 ml/4 fl oz) milk. Stir until thickened then remove from the heat, add 1 tablespoon each of cream and lemon juice and 3 tablespoons finely chopped parsley. Squeeze dry 170 g (5 1/2 oz) canned white crab meat and 200 g (6 1/2 oz) canned prawns and stir into the sauce. Use to fill the filo triangles as before.

BREAD AND BUNS

Baking your own bread is one of the most satisfying skills in cooking. It is a shame the 'baking day' has fallen from favour—there are few smells as wonderful as those from fresh-baked bread. We've selected recipes for everything from everyday breads to special occasion hot cross buns.

BRIOCHE

Preparation: 1 hour + 3 hours standing
Cooking: 30 minutes
Makes 6 small and 1 medium brioche

7 g (1/4 oz) sachet dried yeast
1/2 cup (125 ml/4 fl oz) warm milk
1 teaspoon caster sugar
4 cups (500 g/1 lb) unbleached plain flour
1 teaspoon salt
2 tablespoons caster sugar, extra
4 eggs, lightly beaten
175 g (6 oz) butter, chopped and softened
extra flour, for kneading
1 egg yolk, to glaze
1 tablespoon cream

1 Grease six small brioche moulds and a 21 x 11 cm (8 1/2 x 4 1/2 inch) bread or loaf tin. (If you don't have brioche moulds you could bake the dough as two medium loaves.) Dissolve the yeast in the warm milk. Stir in the sugar, cover with plastic wrap and leave for 5 minutes, or until frothy. Sift the flour, salt and extra sugar into a bowl and make a well in the centre. Pour in the eggs and yeast mixture. Using a wooden spoon, beat well until the mixture forms a rough ball.
2 Turn the dough out onto a lightly floured surface and knead for 5 minutes, or until it is smooth and firm. Gradually incorporate small amounts of the softened butter into the dough. Pull and stretch the dough until all the butter has been incorporated: do this with your hand with the fingers slightly apart, using a slapping motion from the wrist. It will take about 10 minutes and the dough will be very sticky.
3 Clean your working surface and hands, and sprinkle the surface, hands and dough with a small amount of the extra flour. Knead the dough lightly for 10 minutes, or until it is smooth and elastic. Place in a large buttered bowl, brush the surface of the dough with oil and cover with plastic wrap. Leave in a warm place for 1 1/2–2 hours, or until the dough has doubled.
4 Punch down the dough (give it one good hard punch in the centre with your fist) and divide it in half. Cover one half with plastic wrap. Divide the other half into six even-sized pieces. Remove a quarter of the dough from each piece. Mould the larger pieces into rounds and place in the brioche

The BRIOCHE dough makes enough for six small rolls and a medium-sized loaf.

moulds. Brush with a glaze made of the mixed egg yolk and cream. Shape the small pieces into balls and place on top of each roll.

5 Push a floured wooden skewer through the centre of the top ball to the base of the roll, then pull the skewer out. This secures the ball to the roll. Brush again with the glaze, cover and leave in a warm place for 45 minutes, or until well risen. Preheat the oven to hot 210°C (415°F/Gas 6–7) and bake for 10 minutes. Reduce the heat to moderate 180°C (350°F/Gas 4) and bake for 10 minutes, or until golden and cooked. Turn out immediately onto a wire rack to cool.

6 Meanwhile place the other half of the dough in the bread tin and brush with the glaze. Cover and leave to rise for 1 hour. Bake in a hot 210°C (415°F/Gas 6–7) oven for 15 minutes. Reduce the heat to moderate 180°C (350°F/Gas 4) and bake for 15 minutes, or until golden and cooked. Turn out immediately onto a wire rack to cool.

CHELSEA BUNS

Preparation: 25 minutes + 1½ hours standing
Cooking: 25 minutes
Makes 8

7 g (¼ oz) sachet dried yeast
1 teaspoon sugar
1 tablespoon plain flour
½ cup (125 ml/4 fl oz) milk, warmed
2½ cups (310 g/10 oz) plain flour, sifted, extra
125 g (4 oz) butter, chopped
1 tablespoon sugar, extra
1 teaspoon mixed spice
1 egg, lightly beaten
2 teaspoons grated lemon rind
60 g (2 oz) butter, extra
¼ cup (45 g/1½ oz) soft brown sugar
1 cup (185 g/6 oz) mixed dried fruit

Glaze
1 tablespoon milk
2 tablespoons sugar

Glacé icing
½ cup (60 g/2 oz) icing sugar
1–2 tablespoons milk

CHELSEA BUNS are glazed, then drizzled with glacé icing.

1 Grease a large baking tray. Combine the yeast, sugar and flour in a small bowl. Gradually add the milk and blend until smooth. Cover with plastic wrap and leave in a warm place for 5 minutes, or until foamy. Place the extra flour, butter, sugar and half the mixed spice in a bowl and rub in the butter with your fingertips until the mixture is fine and crumbly. Add the egg, lemon rind and yeast mixture, and mix together until the mixture almost forms a dough.

2 Turn onto a lightly floured surface and knead for 2 minutes, or until the dough is smooth. Shape into a ball and place in a large, lightly oiled bowl. Cover with plastic wrap and leave in a warm place for 1 hour, or until well risen. Punch down the dough (give it a hard punch in the centre with your fist) and knead for 2 minutes, until smooth.

3 Using electric beaters, beat the extra butter and brown sugar in a small bowl until light and creamy. Roll the dough out to 40 x 25 cm (16 x 10 inches). Spread the butter and sugar all over the dough, leaving a small border along one of the longer sides. Spread with the combined fruit and remaining mixed spice. Roll the dough lengthways, firmly and evenly into a log, swiss-roll style. Cut the roll into eight slices. Arrange the slices, close together, on the baking tray. Place the seams inwards and flatten the pieces slightly. Cover with plastic wrap and leave in a warm place for 30 minutes to rise. Preheat the oven to hot 210°C (415°F/Gas 6–7).

4 Bake the buns for 20 minutes, or until well browned and cooked through. To make the glaze, put the milk and sugar in a small pan. Stir over low heat until the sugar dissolves and the mixture is almost boiling. Remove from the heat, brush liberally over the buns and transfer them to a wire rack to cool.

5 To make the glacé icing, mix together the icing sugar and milk, and stir until smooth. Drizzle over the glazed and cooled buns.

DAMPER

Preparation: 20 minutes
Cooking: 25 minutes
Makes 1 damper

3 cups (375 g/12 oz) self-raising flour
1–2 teaspoons salt
90 g (3 oz) butter, melted
1/2 cup (125 ml/4 fl oz) milk plus a little extra, to glaze

1 Preheat the oven to hot 210°C (415°F/Gas 6–7) and grease a baking tray. Sift the flour and salt into a large mixing bowl, and make a well in the centre. Combine the butter, milk and 1/2 cup (125 ml/4 fl oz) water, and add it to the flour. Stir with a knife until just combined.

2 Turn onto a lightly floured surface and knead for 20 seconds, or until smooth. Transfer the dough to the tray and press out to a 20 cm (8 inch) round.

3 Use the tip of a knife to score the damper into eight sections, with cuts 1 cm (1/2 inch) deep. Brush with a little milk, to glaze, and dust with a little extra flour. Bake for 10 minutes.

4 Reduce the heat to moderate 180°C (350°F/Gas 4). Bake for 15 minutes, or until the damper is golden and sounds hollow when tapped. Serve with butter and golden syrup.

VARIATIONS: The damper can be made into individual rolls. Use wholemeal self-raising flour for a more healthy version. For a savoury damper, ideal for eating with soup, add grated cheese and chopped mixed herbs, or sliced sun-dried tomatoes and finely sliced ham to the mixture. Simply add to the bowl with the flour and salt at the beginning of the recipe.

Serve DAMPER with butter and golden syrup (cocky's joy).

FINGER BUNS

Preparation: 45 minutes + 1½ hours standing
Cooking: 15 minutes
Makes 12

4 cups (500 g/1 lb) unbleached plain flour
⅓ cup (35 g/1¼ oz) full cream milk powder
2 x 7 g (¼ oz) sachets dried yeast
½ teaspoon salt
½ cup (125 g/4 oz) caster sugar
½ cup (60 g/2 oz) sultanas
60 g (2 oz) butter, melted
1 egg, lightly beaten
1 egg yolk, extra

Glacé icing
1¼ cups (155 g/5 oz) icing sugar
20 g (¾ oz) butter, melted
2–3 teaspoons water
pink food colouring

1 Brush two large baking trays with melted butter or oil. Put 3 cups (375 g/12 oz) of the flour in a large bowl with the milk powder, yeast, salt, sugar and sultanas. Mix well and make a well in the centre. Mix together the butter, egg and 1 cup (250 ml/8 fl oz) warm water and then pour into the well. Stir for 2–3 minutes to combine. Add enough of the remaining flour to make a soft dough.
2 Turn out onto a lightly floured surface and knead for 10 minutes, or until smooth and elastic. Place the dough in a large, lightly oiled bowl and brush the surface with oil. Cover with plastic wrap and leave in a warm place for 1 hour, or until well risen.
3 Punch the down dough (give it one firm punch in the centre with your fist) and knead for 1 minute. Divide into twelve pieces. Shape each piece into a 15 cm (6 inch) oval and place on the trays, spaced 5 cm (2 inches) apart. Cover with plastic wrap and leave in a warm place for 20 minutes, or until well risen.
4 Preheat the oven to moderate 180°C (350°F/Gas 4). Brush the buns well with the combined egg yolk and 1 tablespoon water. Bake for 12–15 minutes, or until cooked through. Cool on a rack.
5 To make the glacé icing, mix the icing sugar and butter with 2–3 teaspoons water. Stir until smooth. Mix in the colouring. Use a knife to spread the icing over the buns.

NOTE: Can be kept for two days in an airtight container. They can be frozen, before icing, for up to a month.

Use unbleached plain flour to make FINGER BUNS.

HOT CROSS BUNS

Preparation: 30 minutes + 1 hour standing
Cooking: 25 minutes
Makes 12

2 x 7 g (1/4 oz) sachets dry yeast or 30 g (1 oz) fresh yeast
4 cups (500 g/1 lb) plain flour
2 tablespoons caster sugar
1 teaspoon mixed spice
1 teaspoon ground cinnamon
40 g (1 1/4 oz) butter
1 1/4 cups (155 g/5 oz) sultanas

Paste for crosses
1/4 cup (30 g/1 oz) plain flour
1/4 teaspoon caster sugar

Glaze
1 1/2 tablespoons caster sugar
1 teaspoon gelatine

Pipe the crosses on the HOT CROSS BUNS, then glaze.

1 Place the yeast, 2 teaspoons of the flour, 1 teaspoon of the sugar and 1/2 cup (125 ml/ 4 fl oz) water in a small bowl. Leave in a warm place until foamy.
2 Sift the remaining flour and spices into a large bowl, stir in the sugar and rub in the butter with your fingertips. Stir in the sultanas. Make a well in the centre, stir in the yeast mixture and up to 3/4 cup (185 ml/6 fl oz) water to make a soft dough. Turn the dough out onto a lightly floured surface and knead for 5 minutes or until smooth, adding more flour to prevent sticking if neccessary.
3 Put the dough in a large floured bowl, cover loosely with plastic and leave in a warm place for 30–40 minutes, or until doubled in size.
4 Preheat the oven to 200°C (400°F/Gas 6). Turn the dough out onto a lightly floured surface and knead gently to deflate. Divide into 12 portions and roll each one into a ball. Place the balls on a lightly greased oven tray, just touching each other, in a rectangle 3 rolls wide and 4 rolls long. Cover loosely with a tea towel and leave in a warm place for 20 minutes, or until nearly doubled in size.
5 To make the crosses, mix the flour, sugar and 2 1/2 tablespoons water into a paste. Spoon into a paper piping bag and pipe crosses on the buns.
6 Bake for 20 minutes, or until golden brown. Put the sugar, gelatine and 1 tablespoon water in a small pan and stir over the heat until dissolved. Brush over the hot buns and allow to cool.

Make a variety of different shaped WHITE DINNER ROLLS.

WHITE DINNER ROLLS

Preparation: 15 minutes
+ 1½ hours standing
Cooking: 20 minutes
Makes 12 rolls

- 1 teaspoon dried yeast
- ½ teaspoon caster sugar
- 2 cups (250 g/8 oz) plain flour
- ½ teaspoon salt
- 1 tablespoon dried whole milk powder
- 2 teaspoons caster sugar, extra
- 1½ tablespoons oil
- 1 tablespoon milk
- poppy seeds, sesame seeds, caraway seeds, sea salt flakes or plain flour, to decorate

1 Combine the yeast, sugar and 3 tablespoons warm water in a bowl. Cover and leave in a warm place for 10 minutes until foamy.
2 Mix the flour, salt, milk powder and extra sugar in a bowl. Make a well in the centre and pour in the oil, yeast and ½ cup (125 ml/4 fl oz) warm water. Mix to a soft dough and knead for 10 minutes, or until smooth and elastic. Add a little extra flour if needed.
3 Put in a lightly oiled bowl, cover loosely with greased plastic wrap and leave in a warm place for 1 hour, or until the dough has doubled in size.
4 Punch down the dough (give it one firm punch with your fist in the centre), knead for 1 minute and divide into twelve portions. Make a variety of different shaped rolls. To make spiral rolls, roll each portion into a 30 cm (12 inch) rope, coil tightly and tuck under the end to seal. Alternatively, tie the ropes to make knot rolls. Or simply shape the dough into ovals and leave plain or slash diagonally with a knife.
5 Arrange the rolls apart on lightly greased trays and cover loosely with a damp tea towel. Leave to rise for 20 minutes. Preheat the oven to moderate 180°C (350°F/Gas 4). Brush the dinner rolls with the milk and then sprinkle with your choice of seeds, sea salt flakes or plain flour topping. Bake for 15–20 minutes, or until lightly browned.

Use a mixture of sultanas, currants, mixed peel and pecans in FRUIT AND NUT BREAD.

FRUIT AND NUT BREAD

Preparation: 30 minutes + 1¼ hours standing
Cooking: 30 minutes
Makes 1 loaf

- 2¼ cups (280 g/9 oz) plain unbleached flour
- 7 g (¼ oz) sachet dried yeast
- 1 teaspoon ground mixed spice
- 2 tablespoons caster sugar
- 2 teaspoons grated orange rind
- ⅓ cup (40 g/1¼ oz) sultanas
- ¼ cup (35 g/1¼ oz) currants
- 1 tablespoon mixed peel
- ¼ cup (30 g/1 oz) chopped pecans
- 1 egg
- ⅓ cup (80 ml/2¾ fl oz) orange juice
- 30 g (1 oz) butter, melted
- oil or melted butter, for brushing
- 1 tablespoon milk
- 1 tablespoon sugar

1 Sift the flour into a large bowl. Add the yeast, mixed spice, caster sugar, orange rind, sultanas, currants, mixed peel and pecans and mix well. Make a well in the centre.
2 Combine the egg, orange juice, butter and ⅓ cup (80 ml/2¾ fl oz) warm water and pour into the well. Using a wooden spoon, mix to a soft dough. Turn onto a lightly floured surface and knead for 10 minutes, or until the dough is smooth and elastic, adding extra flour, if needed. Place in a large oiled bowl and brush with oil. Cover and leave in a warm place for 45 minutes, or until well risen. Preheat the oven to moderate 180°C (350°F/Gas 4).
3 Punch down the dough and knead for 1 minute. Shape into an oblong or round and place either in an oiled 21 x 11 cm (9 x 5 inch) loaf tin or on a greased tray and pat out to a 23 cm (9 inch) circle.
4 Brush the loaf with oil or melted butter. Cover and leave in a warm place for 30 minutes. Bake for 20–30 minutes, or until cooked through. Turn out onto a wire rack. While still hot, brush with the combined milk and sugar. Serve warm or cold.

SOUR CREAM POLENTA BREAD

Preparation: 15 minutes
Cooking: 50 minutes
Makes 1 loaf

1 1/2 cups (225 g/7 oz) fine polenta
1/2 cup (60 g/2 oz) plain flour
2 tablespoons soft brown sugar
1 teaspoon baking powder
1/2 teaspoon bicarbonate of soda
1/2 teaspoon salt
1 egg
1/3 cup (80 ml/2 3/4 fl oz) milk
1 1/4 cups (310 g/10 oz) sour cream
2 tablespoons vegetable oil
1/2 teaspoon poppy seeds

1 Preheat the oven to moderately hot 200°C (400°F/Gas 6) and grease an 11 x 18 cm (5 x 7 inch) loaf tin.
2 Mix together the polenta, flour, sugar, baking powder, bicarbonate of soda and salt in a large bowl.
3 Whisk together the egg, milk, sour cream and oil, and add them to the dry ingredients, mixing just long enough for them to be evenly combined. Pour the mixture into the tin and sprinkle with the poppy seeds.
4 Bake for 30 minutes, then reduce the temperature to moderate 180°C (350°F/Gas 4) and continue baking for a further 15–20 minutes, or until the loaf is golden. Delicious served warm with butter.

NOTE: There are different grades of polenta, some finer than others, and it is worth checking brands before you buy. The fine polenta is best for this recipe—it produces a less coarse and gritty bread.

Use fine-textured polenta for this SOUR CREAM POLENTA BREAD.

WHOLEMEAL BREAD

Preparation: 40 minutes + 2 hours rising
Cooking: 40 minutes
Makes 4 small or 2 large loaves

15 g (1/2 oz) fresh yeast or 7 g (1/4 oz) sachet dried yeast
1 tablespoon caster sugar
1/2 cup (125 ml/4 fl oz) warm milk
4 cups (600 g /1 1/4 lb) wholemeal plain flour
1 teaspoon salt
1/4 cup (60 ml/2 fl oz) oil
1 egg, lightly beaten

1 Lightly grease four 13 x 6.5 cm (5 x 3 inch) loaf tins, or two 11 x 18 cm (4 x 7 inch) loaf tins. Mix the yeast, sugar and milk in a small bowl. Cover and leave in a warm place until frothy.
2 Mix the flour and salt in a large bowl. Make a well in the centre and pour in the oil, frothy yeast and 1 cup (250 ml/ 8 fl oz) warm water. Mix to a soft dough and gather into a ball; turn out onto a floured surface and knead for 10 minutes. Add a little extra flour if the dough is too sticky. Put in a large oiled bowl, cover loosely with greased plastic wrap and leave in a warm place for 1 hour, or until well risen.
3 Punch down the dough (give it one firm punch in the centre), turn out onto a floured surface and knead for 1 minute, or until smooth: push the dough away from you with the palm of your hand, roll it and turn it; continue pushing, rolling and turning. Divide into four or two; knead into shape and put in the tins. Cover with a damp tea towel and leave in a warm place for 45 minutes, or until risen. Preheat the oven to hot 210°C (415°F/Gas 6–7).
4 Brush the tops with the egg. Bake for 10 minutes, reduce the oven to 180°C (350°F/Gas 4) and bake for 30 minutes, or until the base sounds hollow when tapped. Cover with foil if overbrowning.

This recipe for WHOLEMEAL BREAD makes four small loaves.

CAKES AND BISCUITS

Cakes and biscuits are an excellent start for the novice cook. Beat together the ingredients and spoon them into a tin, or roll out a dough and cut out biscuits with a cookie-cutter—either way, it's not too difficult and the results are usually appreciated by all. Top with buttercream or a sticky icing and you could find yourself rather popular!

CHOCOLATE MUD CAKE

Preparation: 20 minutes
Cooking: 2¼ hours
Serves 8

1 ½ cups (185 g/6 oz) self-raising flour
½ cup (60 g/2 oz) plain flour
⅓ cup (40 g/1 ¼ oz) cocoa powder
250 g (8 oz) butter, chopped
1 tablespoon oil
200 g (6½ oz) dark chocolate, chopped
1 ½ cups (375 g/12 oz) caster sugar
1 tablespoon instant coffee powder
2 eggs, lightly beaten

Chocolate topping
150 g (5 oz) butter, chopped
150 g (5 oz) dark chocolate, chopped

1 Preheat the oven to warm 160°C (315°F/Gas 2–3). Grease a deep 20 cm (8 inch) round cake tin and line with baking paper. Sift the flours and cocoa powder into a large mixing bowl and make a well in the centre.
2 Combine the butter, oil, chocolate, sugar and coffee powder with 1 cup (250 ml/8 fl oz) water in a pan. Stir over low heat until the chocolate and butter are melted and the sugar has dissolved. Pour into the well in the dry ingredients. Whisk until just combined. Add the eggs and mix well, but do not overbeat.
3 Pour the mixture into the tin and bake for 2 hours, or until a skewer comes out clean when inserted into the centre of the cake. Leave in the tin to cool completely, then turn out onto a wire rack.
4 To make the topping, combine the butter and chocolate in a pan. Stir over low heat until melted. Remove from the heat to cool slightly.
5 Trim the top of the cake so it will sit flat, then place it upside down on a wire rack over a baking tray. Pour the topping over the cake, letting it run down the side. This cake is delicious served with cream or ice cream.

SPONGE CAKE

Preparation: 15 minutes
Cooking: 25 minutes
Serves 8

75 g (2½ oz) plain flour
150 g (5 oz) self-raising flour
6 eggs
220 g (7 oz) caster sugar
2 tablespoons boiling water
½ cup (160 g/5½ oz) strawberry jam
1 cup (250 ml/8 fl oz) cream, whipped
icing sugar, to dust

1 Preheat the oven to moderate 180°C (350°F/Gas 4). Brush two deep 23 cm (9 inch) round cake tins with melted butter and line the bases with baking paper. Dust lightly with flour, shaking off the excess.
2 Sift the flours three times onto greaseproof paper. Beat the eggs in a small bowl with electric beaters for 7 minutes, or until thick and pale.
3 Gradually add the sugar to the eggs, beating well after each addition. Transfer to a large bowl and, using a metal spoon, fold in the sifted flour and hot water. Spread evenly into the tins and bake for 25 minutes, or until the sponge is lightly golden and shrinks slightly from the side of the tin. Leave the sponges in their tins for 5 minutes before turning out onto a wire rack to cool.
4 Spread the jam evenly over one of the sponges, top with the whipped cream and sandwich with the second sponge. Dust the top with icing sugar.

STORAGE: This sponge is best eaten on the day it is made as it only contains a very small amount of fat. Alternatively, it can be frozen, immediately after cooling, for up to 1 month.

Sandwich the two SPONGE CAKES together with a jam and cream filling.

Use orange or apricot jam in the mixture for ORANGE POPPY SEED CAKE.

ORANGE POPPY SEED CAKE

Preparation: 40 minutes
Cooking: 1 hour
Serves 8

1 1/2 cups (185 g/6 oz) self-raising flour
1/3 cup (60 g/2 oz) ground almonds
1/4 cup (40 g/1 1/4 oz) poppy seeds
185 g (6 oz) butter
2/3 cup (160 g/5 1/2 oz) caster sugar
1/4 cup (80 g/2 3/4 oz) orange or apricot jam
2–3 teaspoons finely grated orange rind
1/3 cup (80 ml/2 3/4 fl oz) orange juice
3 eggs

Icing
100 g (3 1/2 oz) butter
100 g (3 1/2 oz) cream cheese
1 cup (125 g/4 oz) icing sugar, sifted
1–2 teaspoons lemon juice or vanilla essence

1 Preheat the oven to moderate 180°C (350°F/Gas 4). Grease a deep 20 cm (8 inch) round cake tin and line the base and side with baking paper. Sift the flour into a large bowl and add the almonds and poppy seeds. Make a well in the centre.
2 Put the butter, sugar, jam, orange rind and juice in a pan. Stir over low heat until melted and smooth. Gradually pour into the well in the dry ingredients, stirring with a whisk until smooth. Add the eggs and whisk until combined.
3 Pour into the tin and bake for 50–60 minutes, or until a skewer comes out clean when inserted into the centre of the cake. Leave in the tin for at least 15 minutes before turning out onto a wire rack to cool.
4 To make the icing, beat the butter and cream cheese until smooth. Add the icing sugar and lemon juice or vanilla gradually, and beat until thick and creamy. Spread the icing over the cooled cake.

CARROT CAKE

Preparation: 30 minutes
Cooking: 45 minutes
Serves 8

3 eggs
1 cup (250 ml/8 fl oz) oil
1 1/4 cups (230 g/7 1/2 oz) soft brown sugar
1 1/2 cups (185 g/6 oz) self-raising flour
1 teaspoon bicarbonate of soda
pinch of salt
2 teaspoons ground cinnamon
3/4 cup (90 g/3 oz) chopped pecans
1 2/3 cups (255 g/8 oz) grated carrot
125 g (4 oz) cream cheese, softened
30 g (1 oz) butter
1 cup (125 g/4 oz) icing sugar
2 teaspoons orange juice

1 Preheat the oven to moderate 180°C (350°F/Gas 4). Grease a deep 23 cm (9 inch) square cake tin and line the base and sides with baking paper.
2 Combine the eggs, oil and brown sugar in a large bowl. Add the sifted flour, soda, salt and cinnamon, and beat with electric beaters until the mixture is smooth. Add the nuts and carrot and stir well.
3 Pour the mixture into the tin and bake for 45 minutes, or until a skewer comes out clean when inserted into the centre of the cake. Leave for at least 20 minutes before turning out onto a wire rack to cool.
4 To make a cream cheese topping, put the cream cheese, butter, sugar and orange juice in a bowl and beat together until the mixture is spreadable. Spread over the cake and perhaps sprinkle with a few extra chopped pecans to serve.

COCONUT CAKE

Preparation: 15 minutes
Cooking: 55 minutes
Serves 8

185 g (6 oz) butter, chopped and softened
1 cup (250 g/8 oz) caster sugar
1 cup (90 g/3 oz) desiccated coconut
1/2 cup (125 ml/4 fl oz) buttermilk or plain yoghurt
2 teaspoons vanilla essence
3 eggs, lightly beaten
1 1/2 cups (185 g/6 oz) self-raising flour
1/3 cup (40 g/1 1/4 oz) cornflour
1 tablespoon caster sugar, extra
2 tablespoons desiccated coconut, extra

1 Preheat the oven to moderate 180°C (350°F/Gas 4). Lightly grease a 23 x 13 x 7 cm (9 x 5 x 3 inch) loaf tin with melted butter or oil. Line the base and sides with baking paper.
2 Beat the butter, sugar, coconut, buttermilk or yoghurt, vanilla and eggs briefly with electric beaters until combined. Add the sifted flours and beat on low speed to combine. Beat on medium speed for 1 minute, or until the mixture is smooth and creamy. Do not overbeat.
3 Carefully spoon the mixture into the tin and smooth the surface with a spatula. Sprinkle the combined extra sugar and coconut over the top. Bake for 50–55 minutes, or until a skewer comes out clean when inserted into the centre of the cake. Cover the cake loosely with foil during the last 15 minutes of cooking to prevent the coconut topping from overbrowning. Leave the cake in the tin for 5 minutes before turning out onto a wire rack to cool.

CARROT CAKE (top) with a cream cheese icing, and COCONUT CAKE.

A CHRISTMAS FRUIT CAKE can be stored for up to 3 months.

CHRISTMAS FRUIT CAKE

Preparation: 30 minutes + 4 hours standing
Cooking: 3 hours
Serves 10

1 kg (2 lb) mixed dried fruit
1 1/2 cups (280 g/9 oz) chopped dried dates
1 cup (185 g/6 oz) chopped dried apricots
1/2 cup (95 g/3 oz) mixed peel
1/2 cup (60 g/2 oz) chopped glacé fruits
3/4 cup (185 ml/6 fl oz) brandy
1 cup (185 g/6 oz) soft brown sugar
250 g (8 oz) butter
5 eggs
1 1/2 cups (185 g/6 oz) plain flour
1/3 cup (40 g/1 1/4 oz) self-raising flour
1 teaspoon ground cinnamon
1 teaspoon mixed spice

1 Preheat the oven to slow 150°C (300°F/ Gas 2). Grease a 23 cm (9 inch) round cake tin and line the base and sides with a double thickness of baking paper. In a bowl, mix the mixed fruit, dates, apricots, mixed peel, glacé fruits and brandy, cover with plastic wrap and leave at room temperature for at least 4 hours.

2 Using electric beaters, beat the sugar and butter in a small bowl until just combined (overbeating will result in a crumbly cake). Add the eggs gradually, beating after each addition. Transfer to a large bowl.

3 Stir in the fruits and brandy. Fold in the sifted flours and spices. Stir gently, but don't overbeat.

4 Spoon into the tin and smooth the surface. Bake for 3 hours, or until firm to the touch and golden brown. Cool completely in the tin. Turn out and wrap tightly in plastic wrap. Store for up to 3 months in an airtight container in the fridge.

BOILED FRUIT CAKE

Preparation: 30 minutes
Cooking: 1½ hours
Serves 10

250 g (8 oz) butter
1 cup (185 g/6 oz) soft brown sugar
1 kg (2 lb) mixed dried fruit
½ cup (125 ml/4 fl oz) sweet sherry
½ teaspoon bicarbonate of soda
1½ cups (185 g/6 oz) self-raising flour
1 cup (125 g/4 oz) plain flour
1 teaspoon mixed spice
4 eggs, lightly beaten

1 Preheat the oven to moderate 180°C (350°F/Gas 4). Lightly grease a 22 cm (9 inch) round cake tin. Line the base and side with greaseproof paper.
2 Put the butter, sugar, mixed fruit, sherry and ¾ cup (185 ml/6 fl oz) water in a pan. Stir over low heat until the butter has melted and the sugar dissolved. Bring to the boil, reduce the heat and simmer for 10 minutes. Remove from the heat, stir in the soda and cool.
3 Sift the flours and mixed spice into a large bowl and make a well in the centre. Add the eggs to the fruit mixture and mix together. Pour into the well and mix well. Pour into the tin and smooth the surface. Bake for 1–1¼ hours, or until a skewer comes out clean when inserted into the centre of the cake. Leave in the tin for at least an hour before turning out. The flavour of this cake improves if left for 3 days before eating. Can be kept for up to 2 months.

NOTE: The colour of your fruit cake will largely depend on the dried fruit you use. If you prefer a dark cake, use raisins, currants and sultanas. For a lighter coloured cake, mix in chopped glacé fruit.

The flavour of a BOILED FRUIT CAKE actually improves on keeping.

MADEIRA CAKE

Preparation: 20 minutes
Cooking: 55 minutes
Serves 8

150 g (5 oz) butter
3/4 cup (185 g/6 oz) caster sugar
3 eggs, lightly beaten
2 teaspoons finely grated orange or lemon rind
1/2 cup (95 g/3 oz) ground almonds
1 3/4 cups (215 g/7 oz) self-raising flour
icing sugar, to dust

1 Preheat the oven to moderate 180°C (350°F/ Gas 4). Grease a 23 x 13 x 7 cm (9 x 5 x 3 inch) loaf tin and line the base and sides with baking paper. Using electric beaters, beat the butter and caster sugar in a small mixing bowl until light and creamy. Add the eggs gradually, beating thoroughly after each addition. Add the orange or lemon rind and beat until combined.
2 Transfer the mixture to a large bowl. Using a metal spoon, fold in the ground almonds and sifted flour. Stir until the mixture is combined and smooth.
3 Spoon into the tin and smooth the surface. Bake for 55 minutes, or until a skewer comes out clean when inserted into the centre of the cake.
4 Leave the cake in the tin for 10 minutes before turning out onto a wire rack. Lightly dust the top with icing sugar before serving.

STORAGE: Cake will keep for up to four days in an airtight container.

DATE AND NUT ROLLS

Preparation: 25 minutes
Cooking: 1 hour
Serves 8

3/4 cup (90 g/3 oz) self-raising flour
3/4 cup (90 g/3 oz) plain flour
1/2 teaspoon bicarbonate of soda
1 teaspoon mixed spice
1 cup (125 g/4 oz) chopped walnuts
100 g (3 1/2 oz) butter
3/4 cup (140 g/4 1/2 oz) soft brown sugar
1 1/2 cups (280 g/9 oz) chopped dates
1 egg, lightly beaten

1 Preheat the oven to moderate 180°C (350°F/ Gas 4). Grease two 17 x 8 cm (7 x 3 inch) tube tins (nut roll tins) and lids. Sift the flours, bicarbonate of soda and mixed spice into a large mixing bowl. Add the walnuts, stir to combine and make a well in the centre.
2 Combine the butter, sugar, 1/2 cup (125 ml/ 4 fl oz) water and dates in a pan. Stir over low heat until the butter has melted and the sugar has dissolved. Remove from the heat and leave to cool slightly.
3 Pour the butter mixture and the egg into the well in the dry ingredients, and stir until combined. Spoon the mixture evenly into the tins. Bake with the tins upright for 1 hour, or until a skewer comes out clean when inserted into the centre. Leave the cakes in the tins, with the lids on, for 10 minutes, then turn onto a wire rack. Serve sliced, with butter.

STORAGE: This is a very moist cake that will keep fresh in an airtight container for a week.
NOTE: If you don't have nut roll tins, bake this mixture in a 23 x 13 cm (9 x 5 inch) loaf tin.
HINT: Store walnuts in the freezer to prevent them becoming rancid.

MADEIRA CAKE (top) and DATE AND NUT ROLLS.

CHOCOLATE CAKE topped with glossy chocolate buttercream.

CHOCOLATE CAKE

Preparation: 25 minutes
Cooking: 50 minutes
Serves 8

125 g (4 oz) butter
1/2 cup (125 g/4 oz) caster sugar
1/3 cup (40 g/1 1/4 oz) icing sugar, sifted
2 eggs, lightly beaten
1 teaspoon vanilla essence
1/4 cup (80 g/2 3/4 oz) blackberry jam
1 1/4 cups (155 g/5 oz) self-raising flour
1/2 cup (60 g/2 oz) cocoa powder
1 teaspoon bicarbonate of soda
1 cup (250 ml/8 fl oz) milk

Chocolate buttercream

50 g (1 3/4 oz) dark chocolate, finely chopped
25 g (3/4 oz) butter
3 teaspoons cream
1/4 cup (30 g/1 oz) icing sugar, sifted

1 Preheat the oven to moderate 180°C (350°F/Gas 4). Grease the base and sides of a deep 20 cm (8 inch) square cake tin and line with baking paper.

2 Beat the butter, caster sugar and icing sugar with electric beaters in a small mixing bowl until the mixture is light and creamy. Add the eggs gradually, beating thoroughly after each addition. Add the vanilla essence and jam and beat until combined.

3 Transfer the mixture to a large bowl. Using a metal spoon, fold in the combined sifted flour, cocoa and soda alternately with the milk. Stir until the mixture is just combined and almost smooth.

4 Pour into the tin and smooth the surface. Bake for 45 minutes, or until a skewer comes out clean when inserted into the centre of the cake. Leave in the tin for 15 minutes, then cool on a wire rack.

5 To make the buttercream, combine the chopped chocolate, butter, cream and icing sugar in a small pan. Stir over low heat until the mixture is smooth and glossy. Spread the chocolate buttercream over the top of the cake with a flat-bladed knife.

BANANA CAKE

Preparation: 20 minutes
Cooking: 1 hour
Serves 8

125 g (4 oz) butter
1/2 cup (125 g/4 oz) caster sugar
2 eggs, lightly beaten
1 teaspoon vanilla essence
1 1/2 cups (360 g/12 oz) mashed ripe banana (about 4 bananas)
1 teaspoon bicarbonate of soda
1/2 cup (125 ml/4 fl oz) milk
2 cups (250 g/8 oz) self-raising flour

Butter frosting

125 g (4 oz) butter
3/4 cup (90 g/3 oz) icing sugar
1 tablespoon lemon juice
1/4 cup (15 g/1/2 oz) flaked coconut

1 Preheat the oven to moderate 180°C (350°F/Gas 4). Grease a 20 cm (8 inch) round cake tin and line the base with baking paper. Using electric beaters, beat the butter and sugar in a small mixing bowl until light and creamy. Add the eggs gradually, beating well after each addition. Add the vanilla essence and mashed banana, and beat until combined.

Use very ripe bananas to make a flavoursome BANANA CAKE.

2 Transfer the mixture to a large mixing bowl. Dissolve the bicarbonate of soda in the milk. Using a metal spoon, fold in the sifted flour alternately with the milk. Stir until all the ingredients are just combined and the mixture is smooth. Spoon into the tin and smooth the surface. Bake for 1 hour, or until a skewer comes out clean when inserted into the centre of the cake. Leave the cake in the tin for 10 minutes before turning out onto a wire rack.

3 To make the frosting, beat the butter, icing sugar and lemon juice with electric beaters until smooth and creamy. Spread onto the cooled cake. Toast the coconut flakes in a moderate 180°C (350°F/Gas 4) oven for 5 minutes and sprinkle around the edge of the top of the cake.

STORAGE: The un-iced cake can be kept for one week in an airtight container. Alternatively, freeze for up to a month before icing.
HINT: Very ripe bananas are best for this recipe as they have the best developed flavour.

BLACK FOREST GATEAU

Preparation: 45 minutes
Cooking: 15 minutes
Serves 8

1/3 cup (40 g/1 1/4 oz) plain flour
1/3 cup (40 g/1 1/4 oz) self-raising flour
2 tablespoons cocoa powder
4 eggs, separated
1/2 cup (125 g/4 oz) caster sugar
1/4 cup (60 ml/2 fl oz) Kirsch (see Note)
3 1/2 cups (875 ml/28 fl oz) cream, whipped
700 g (1 lb 6 oz) jar morello cherries or two 425 g (14 oz) cans pitted dark cherries, well drained (see Note)
250 g (8 oz) dark chocolate
maraschino cherries, to garnish
icing sugar, to dust

1 Preheat the oven to moderate 180°C (350°F/Gas 4). Grease two shallow 20 cm (8 inch) round sandwich tins and line with baking paper. Sift the flours and cocoa powder onto greaseproof paper three times.
2 Beat the egg whites in a small, clean, dry mixing bowl until firm peaks form. Add the sugar gradually, beating constantly until the sugar has dissolved and the mixture is thick and glossy. Add the yolks and beat for 20 seconds. Transfer the mixture to a larger bowl.
3 Fold in the flours and cocoa quickly and lightly in 2–3 batches. Spread the mixture evenly into the tins and bake for 15 minutes, or until the cakes are springy to the touch. Leave them in the tins for 5 minutes before turning out onto wire racks to cool. Cut each cake in half horizontally.
4 Brush the top of one round of cake with some of the Kirsch. Spread with a layer of the whipped cream and top with one third of the cherries. Place another round of cake on top. Repeat brushing with the Kirsch and layering with the cream and cherries, finishing with the last round of cake. Spread the rest of the cream all over the cake, keeping a little aside for decorating the top.
5 Using a potato peeler, shave curls from the edge of the chocolate. Press some of the curls lightly onto the cream around the side of the cake. Decorate the top with

BLACK FOREST GATEAU.

rosettes of whipped cream and the maraschino cherries. Pile some more chocolate curls in the centre and dust the cake with icing sugar.

NOTES: Kirsch is a cherry-flavoured liqueur. Black Forest gateau is traditionally made with fresh morello cherries, poached in a sugar syrup and pitted. Bottled morello cherries or canned, pitted cherries are a good substitute. Drain the cherries well on paper towels to prevent their juices staining the whipped cream.

HUMMINGBIRD CAKE

Preparation: 20 minutes
Cooking: 1 hour
Serves 8

1 cup (125 g/4 oz) plain flour
1/2 cup (60 g/2 oz) self-raising flour
1 teaspoon ground cinnamon
1/2 teaspoon bicarbonate of soda
3/4 cup (185 g/6 oz) caster sugar
2 eggs, lightly beaten
1/2 cup (125 ml/4 fl oz) vegetable oil
1 1/2 cups (360 g/12 oz) mashed ripe banana
3/4 cup (195 g/6 1/2 oz) undrained crushed unsweetened pineapple
100 g (3 1/2 oz) cream cheese, softened
3/4 cup (90 g/3 oz) icing sugar, sifted

Use banana and pineapple in a HUMMINGBIRD CAKE.

1 Preheat the oven to moderate 180°C (350°F/Gas 4). Lightly grease a 20 cm (8 inch) square cake tin. Sift the flours, cinnamon and bicarbonate of soda into a bowl. Stir in the sugar and make a well in the centre.

2 Stir together the eggs, oil, banana and pineapple and pour into the well in the dry ingredients. Stir until just combined, then spoon into the tin.

3 Bake for 1 hour or until a skewer inserted into the centre of the cake comes out clean. Leave in the tin for 10 minutes before turning out and cooling on a wire rack.

4 Beat the cream cheese and icing sugar until smooth and fluffy. Spread over the cake.

PINEAPPLE UPSIDE-DOWN CAKE

Preparation: 20 minutes
Cooking: 40 minutes
Serves 8

20 g (3/4 oz) butter, melted
2 tablespoons soft brown sugar
440 g (14 oz) can pineapple slices in natural juice
90 g (3 oz) butter
1/2 cup (125 g/4 oz) caster sugar
2 eggs, lightly beaten
1 teaspoon vanilla essence
1 cup (125 g/4 oz) self-raising flour

1 Preheat the oven to moderate 180°C (350°F/Gas 4). Grease a 20 cm (8 inch) ring tin. Pour the melted butter into the tin and tip to coat the base evenly. Sprinkle the brown sugar over the butter. Drain the pineapple, reserving 1/3 cup (80 ml/2 3/4 fl oz) of the juice. Cut the pineapple pieces into halves and arrange over the brown sugar.
2 Using electric beaters, beat the butter and sugar in a small bowl until light and creamy. Add the eggs gradually, beating well after each addition. Beat in the vanilla essence.
3 Transfer the mixture to a large bowl. Using a metal spoon, fold in the flour alternately with the reserved pineapple juice.
4 Spoon the mixture evenly over the pineapple and smooth the surface. Bake for 35–40 minutes, or until a skewer comes out clean when inserted into the centre. Leave in the tin for 10 minutes, then cool on a wire rack.

JAM SWISS ROLL

Preparation: 30 minutes
Cooking: 12 minutes
Makes one roll

1/2 cup (60 g/2 oz) self-raising flour
1/4 cup (30 g/1 oz) plain flour
3 eggs
1/2 cup (125 g/4 oz) caster sugar
2 tablespoons caster sugar, extra
1/2 cup (160 g/5 1/2 oz) strawberry jam
1/2 cup (125 ml/4 fl oz) cream, whipped

1 Preheat the oven to hot 210°C (415°F/Gas 6–7). Grease a 30 x 25 cm (12 x 10 inch) swiss roll tin and line the base with baking paper, leaving the paper to hang over the two long sides (this will help you lift the cake out of the tin after cooking). Sift the flours three times onto greaseproof paper.
2 Beat the eggs with electric beaters for 5 minutes, or until thick, frothy and pale. Add the sugar gradually, beating constantly until it has completely dissolved and the mixture is pale and glossy. Using a metal spoon, fold in the flour quickly and lightly.
3 Spread the mixture evenly into the tin and smooth the surface. Bake for 12 minutes, or until lightly golden and springy to the touch. Turn the cake out onto a dry, clean tea towel covered with greaseproof paper that has been sprinkled with the extra caster sugar. Leave for 1 minute, then use the tea towel as a guide to carefully roll the cake up from the short side, with the paper. Leave the cake for 5 minutes, or until it is cool.
4 Unroll the cake and remove the paper. Spread the cake with the jam and cream and re-roll. Trim the ends with a knife and cut into slices to serve.

PINEAPPLE UPSIDE-DOWN CAKE (top) and JAM SWISS ROLL.

SEMOLINA LEMON SYRUP CAKE

Preparation: 30 minutes
Cooking: 45 minutes
Serves 6

150 g (5 oz) butter
3/4 cup (185 g/6 oz) caster sugar
2 eggs, lightly beaten
2 teaspoons finely grated lemon rind
1 1/2 cups (185 g/6 oz) fine semolina
1 cup (185 g/6 oz) ground almonds
1 1/2 teaspoons baking powder
1/4 cup (60 ml/2 fl oz) milk
icing sugar, to dust

Lemon syrup
1/2 cup (125 ml/4 fl oz) lemon juice
rind of 1 lemon
1/2 cup (125 g/4 oz) caster sugar

1 Preheat the oven to moderate 180°C (350°F/Gas 4). Grease a deep 23 cm (9 inch) fluted ring tin with oil or melted butter. Using electric beaters, beat the butter and sugar in a small bowl until light and creamy. Add the eggs gradually, beating well after each addition. Add the grated lemon rind and beat until well combined.

Use finely ground semolina in your LEMON SEMOLINA CAKE.

2 Transfer the mixture to a large bowl. Using a metal spoon, fold in the combined semolina, almonds and baking powder alternately with the milk. Stir the mixture until smooth.
3 Spoon into the tin and smooth the surface. Bake for 45 minutes, or until a skewer comes out clean when inserted into the centre of the cake. Leave the cake in the tin for 5 minutes, then turn onto a serving plate.
4 To make the lemon syrup, combine the lemon juice, rind and sugar in a small pan. Stir over medium heat without boiling until the sugar has dissolved. Bring to the boil, then reduce the heat and simmer for 5 minutes. Brush the syrup over the top and sides of the cake. Dust with sifted icing sugar to serve.

LAMINGTONS

Preparation: 1 hour
Cooking: 1 hour
Makes 25

1 1/2 cups (185 g/6 oz) self-raising flour
1/3 cup (40 g/1 1/4 oz) cornflour
185 g (6 oz) butter, softened
1 cup (250 g/8 oz) caster sugar
2 teaspoons vanilla essence
3 eggs, lightly beaten

1/2 cup (125 ml/4 fl oz) milk
3/4 cup (185 ml/6 fl oz) thick cream

Icing
4 cups (500 g/1 lb) icing sugar
1/3 cup (40 g/1 1/4 oz) cocoa powder
30 g (1 oz) butter, melted
2/3 cup (170 ml/ 5 1/2 fl oz) milk
3 cups (270 g/9 oz) desiccated coconut, approximately

1 Preheat the oven to moderate 180°C (350°F/ Gas 4). Grease a shallow 23 cm (9 inch) square cake tin and line the base and sides with baking paper. Sift the flour and cornflour into a large bowl. Add the butter, sugar, vanilla essence, eggs and milk. Using electric beaters, beat on low speed for 1 minute, or until the ingredients are just lightly moistened. Beat on high speed for 3 minutes, or until the mixture is free of lumps and has increased in volume.
2 Pour the mixture into the tin and smooth the surface. Bake for 1 hour, or until a skewer comes out clean when inserted into the centre of the cake. Leave the cake in the tin for 3 minutes before turning out onto a wire rack to cool.
3 Using a serrated knife, trim the top of the cake until it is flat. Trim the crusts from the sides of the cake. Cut the cake in half horizontally. Using electric beaters, beat the cream in a small mixing bowl until stiff peaks form. Place the first layer of cake on a board and spread evenly with the cream. Top with the other cake layer. Cut the cake into 25 squares.
4 To make the icing, sift the icing sugar with the cocoa. Combine with the butter and milk in a heatproof bowl. Stand the bowl over a pan of simmering water, stirring until the icing is smooth and glossy. Remove from the heat. Place 1 cup (90 g/3 oz) of the coconut on a sheet of greaseproof paper. Using two forks, roll a piece of cake in the icing. Hold the cake over the bowl and allow the excess to drain. Roll the cake in the coconut, then put on a wire rack. Repeat with the remaining cake, adding extra coconut for rolling as needed.

LAMINGTONS are a welcome family treat.

Sprinkle CINNAMON TEA CAKE with a mixture of sugar and ground cinnamon.

CINNAMON TEA CAKE

Preparation: 20 minutes
Cooking: 30 minutes
Serves 8

60 g (2 oz) butter
1/2 cup (125 g/4 oz) caster sugar
1 egg, lightly beaten
1 teaspoon vanilla essence
3/4 cup (90 g/3 oz) self-raising flour
3 tablespoons plain flour
1/2 cup (125 ml/4 fl oz) milk
20 g (3/4 oz) butter, melted
1 tablespoon caster sugar, extra
1 teaspoon ground cinnamon

1 Preheat the oven to moderate 180°C (350°F/Gas 4). Grease a 20 cm (8 inch) round cake tin and line the base with baking paper. Beat the butter and sugar until light and creamy. Add the egg gradually, beating well after each addition. Beat in the vanilla.
2 Fold in the sifted flours alternately with the milk. Stir until smooth. Spoon into the tin and smooth the top. Bake for 30 minutes, or until a skewer comes out clean when inserted into the centre. Cool in the tin for 5 minutes, then on a wire rack. Brush with melted butter while still warm and sprinkle with the sugar and cinnamon.

ROCK CAKES

Preparation: 25 minutes
Cooking: 15–20 minutes
Makes about 20

2 cups (250 g/8 oz) self-raising flour, sifted
90 g (3 oz) butter, cubed
1/2 cup (125 g/4 oz) caster sugar
1/2 cup (95 g/3 oz) mixed dried fruit
1 tablespoon chopped mixed nuts
1/2 teaspoon ground ginger
1 egg
3 tablespoons milk

1 Preheat the oven to moderately hot 200°C (400°F/Gas 6). Place the flour in a large bowl and

rub in the butter with your fingertips until fine and crumbly.
2 Mix in the sugar, fruit, nuts and ginger. Whisk the egg into the milk and add to the mixture. Mix to a stiff dough.
3 Spoon in small heaps onto greased baking trays. Bake for 15–20 minutes, or until golden brown. Transfer to a wire rack to cool. Serve buttered.

ROCK CAKES are ideal for a cup of tea with friends.

MERINGUES

Preparation: 10 minutes
Cooking: 25 minutes
Makes about 30

2 egg whites
1/2 cup (125 g/4 oz) caster sugar

1 Preheat the oven to slow 150°C (300°F/Gas 2). Beat the egg whites until stiff peaks form. Gradually add the sugar, beating well after each addition. Beat until thick and glossy, and the sugar has dissolved.
2 Spoon into a piping bag and pipe into shapes on baking trays lined with baking paper. Bake for 20–25 minutes, or until the meringues are just crisp. Turn off the oven, leaving the meringues inside with the door ajar to cool.

MERINGUES can be piped into shapes, rounds or nests.

BUTTERCAKE

Preparation: 20 minutes
Cooking: 45 minutes
Serves 8

125 g (4 oz) butter
3/4 cup (185 g/6 oz) caster sugar
2 eggs, lightly beaten
1 teaspoon vanilla essence
2 cups (250 g/8 oz) self-raising flour
1/2 cup (125 ml/4 fl oz) milk

Buttercream
60 g (2 oz) butter
1/3 cup (40 g/1 1/4 oz) icing sugar
1 teaspoon vanilla essence

1 Preheat the oven to moderate 180°C (350°F/Gas 4). Grease a 20 cm (8 inch) round cake tin and line the base with baking paper. Using electric beaters, beat the butter and sugar in a small mixing bowl until light and creamy. Add the eggs gradually, beating well after each addition. Add the vanilla essence and beat until combined.
2 Transfer the mixture to a large bowl. Using a metal spoon, fold in the sifted flour alternately with the milk. Stir until the mixture is just combined and almost smooth. Spoon the mixture into the tin and smooth the surface. Bake for 45 minutes, or until a skewer comes out clean when inserted into the centre of the cake. Leave in the tin for 10 minutes, then cool on a wire rack.
3 To make the buttercream, beat the butter and sifted icing sugar with electric beaters until light and creamy. Add the vanilla essence and beat for another 2 minutes, or until the mixture is quite smooth and fluffy. Spread over the top of the cake with a flat-bladed knife. Decorate with chopped almonds, or other nuts.

You can add many variations to the basic BUTTERCAKE mix.

STORAGE: Buttercake will keep, iced, for two days in an airtight container in the fridge. It can be frozen, un-iced and wrapped tightly in plastic wrap, for up to a month.
VARIATIONS: For lemon cake, add 2 tablespoons grated lemon rind to the basic buttercake mixture. To make coffee cake,

dissolve a tablespoon of instant coffee in the milk before adding to the dry ingredients.
For chocolate cake, add 3 tablespoons cocoa to the dry ingredients and an extra tablespoon of milk at the end.
For ginger cake, add a teaspoon of ground ginger to the dry ingredients.

CUSTARD ORANGE CAKE

Preparation: 15 minutes
Cooking: 50 minutes
Serves 6–8

2 cups (250 g/8 oz) self-raising flour
1/3 cup (40 g/1 1/4 oz) custard powder
80 g (2 3/4 oz) butter, chopped
1 1/3 cups (340 g/11 oz) caster sugar
3 eggs
2 teaspoons finely grated orange rind
1 cup (250 ml/8 fl oz) orange juice
125 g (4 oz) cream cheese, softened
2 tablespoons icing sugar

1 Preheat the oven to moderate 180°C (350°F/Gas 4). Grease a deep 23 cm (9 inch) round cake tin and line the base with baking paper. Sift the flour and custard powder into a bowl and add the butter and sugar. Rub in the butter with your fingertips until the mixture resembles fine crumbs.
2 Add the eggs, orange rind and juice and mix until smooth. Spoon into the tin and smooth the surface. Bake for 50 minutes, or until a skewer comes out clean when inserted into the centre of the cake.
3 Leave the cake in the tin for 5 minutes before turning out onto a wire rack to cool.
4 Mix together the cream cheese and icing sugar and spread over the top of the cake. If you like, decorate with thin strips of orange rind.

CUSTARD ORANGE CAKE has a tang of fresh orange.

CAKE ICINGS

Many of our recipes have their own icings and buttercreams included. But for when you've just made a plain buttercake or muffin and want to turn it into something special, try one of the following:

CITRUS FROSTING

100 g (3½ oz) cream cheese, softened
¾ cup (90 g/3 oz) icing sugar, sifted
1–2 teaspoons finely grated lemon rind (or orange, lime or mandarin rind)
2 teaspoons milk

Beat the cream cheese and icing sugar until light and creamy. Add the rind and milk. Beat for 2 minutes, or until the frosting is smooth and fluffy. Spread over the cake.

HONEY FROSTING

100 g (3½ oz) cream cheese, softened
¾ cup (90 g/3 oz) icing sugar, sifted
1–2 teaspoons honey, warmed
2 teaspoons milk

Beat the cream cheese and icing sugar until light and creamy. Add the honey and milk and beat for 2 minutes, or until the frosting is smooth and fluffy. Spread the frosting over the cake.

PASSIONFRUIT FROSTING

100 g (3½ oz) cream cheese, softened
¾ cup (90 g/3 oz) icing sugar, sifted
1–2 tablespoons passionfruit pulp

Beat the cream cheese and icing sugar until light and creamy. Add the passionfruit pulp and beat for 2 minutes, or until smooth and fluffy. Spread over the cake.

RICH CHOCOLATE ICING

60 g (2 oz) butter
100 g (3 1/2 oz) dark chocolate, chopped
1 tablespoon cream

Put the butter, chocolate and cream in a small heatproof bowl. Bring a pan, half full of water, to the boil and remove from the heat. Place the bowl over the pan (don't let the base of the bowl sit in the water) and stir until the butter and chocolate have melted and the mixture is smooth. Leave to cool slightly until the icing is spreadable.

GINGER ICING

60 g (2 oz) butter
1 tablespoon golden syrup
1 tablespoon finely chopped glacé ginger
1/3 cup (60 g/2 oz) soft brown sugar
2 tablespoons milk
1 1/2 cups (185 g/6 oz) icing sugar, sifted

Put the butter, golden syrup, ginger and sugar in a pan. Stir over low heat until the mixture is melted and smooth. Using a wooden spoon, beat in 1 tablespoon of the milk and enough icing sugar to make a stiff but spreadable icing. Use the extra milk if necessary to reach the right consistency.

CHOCOLATE SOUR CREAM ICING

200 g (6 1/2 oz) milk chocolate, chopped
1/3 cup (90 g/3 oz) sour cream

Combine the chocolate and sour cream in a small pan. Whisk over low heat until the chocolate has melted and the mixture is smooth. Remove from the heat and allow to cool slightly until spreadable.

SCONES

Preparation: 25 minutes
Cooking: 20 minutes
Makes 12

2 1/4 cups (280 g/9 oz) self-raising flour
pinch of salt
1 tablespoon sugar
20 g (3/4 oz) butter, chopped
1 egg
3/4 cup (185 ml/6 fl oz) milk
extra milk, for glazing

1 Preheat the oven to hot 220°C (425°F/Gas 7). Sift the flour, salt and sugar into a large bowl. Rub in the butter, using your fingertips, until the mixture is fine and crumbly. Make a well in the centre of the mixture.
2 Lightly beat the egg and milk in a small bowl. Pour almost all the egg mixture into the well. Mix lightly with a flat-bladed knife to form a soft dough, adding the remaining egg mixture if needed.
3 Gather the dough together and turn it out onto a lightly floured surface. Press out the dough until it is 2.5 cm (1 inch) thick. Cut out rounds with a floured 5 cm (2 inch) cutter.
4 Heat a baking tray in the oven for 5 minutes. Place the rounds on the heated tray, leaving a little room for spreading. Brush with the extra milk. Bake on the middle shelf of the oven for 15–20 minutes, or until golden brown on top. If you are serving the scones warm, straight from the oven, wrap them in a clean tea towel while still hot. Serve warm or cold, with butter or with cream and jam or strawberries.

VARIATIONS: For sultana scones, add 1 cup (125 g/4 oz) sultanas in step 1 when you sift the flour into the bowl.
For date scones, add 1 cup (185 g/6 oz) finely chopped pitted dates to the flour in step 1.
For wholemeal scones, replace one of the cups of flour with wholemeal self-raising flour.
For cheese scones, add 1 cup (125 g/4 oz) grated Cheddar cheese to the flour in step 1.

The secret to making perfect scones is to use a light touch and handle the dough as little as possible. Do not knead the dough. Merely turn it out onto a floured surface and then press out before cutting into rounds.

For a Devonshire tea, serve SCONES with jam and cream.

Butternut pumpkin is excellent for PUMPKIN SCONES as it is less watery than some.

PUMPKIN SCONES

Preparation: 20 minutes
Cooking: 15 minutes
Makes about 15

2 1/2 cups (310 g/10 oz) self-raising flour
1/4 teaspoon dried mixed herbs
60 g (2 oz) butter, chopped
1 egg, lightly beaten
1 cup (250 g/8 oz) cooked, mashed pumpkin (350 g/11 oz raw pumpkin)
1–2 tablespoons milk
milk, extra, for glazing

1 Preheat the oven to hot 210°C (415°F/Gas 6–7). Grease a 28 x 18 cm (11 x 7 inch) shallow tin. Sift the flour into a large mixing bowl. Stir in the mixed herbs and add the chopped butter. Using your fingertips, rub in the butter until the mixture is fine and crumbly.
2 Combine the egg, mashed pumpkin and milk. Add to the flour mixture and stir with a knife until just combined.
3 Gather the dough together and turn it out onto a lightly floured surface. Press out gently until the dough is about 2 cm (3/4 inch) thick. Cut out rounds with a floured 5 cm (2 inch) cutter.
4 Place the rounds in the tin and brush the tops with the extra milk. Bake for 15 minutes, or until the tops of the scones are lightly golden. Turn out onto a wire rack to cool. Serve warm or cold, with butter.

MUFFINS

Preparation: 15 minutes
Cooking: 20 minutes
Makes 12

3 cups (375 g/12 oz) self-raising flour
1 cup (250 g/8 oz) caster sugar
2 eggs, lightly beaten
1 cup (250 ml/8 fl oz) milk
90 g (3 oz) butter, melted

1 Preheat the oven to hot 210°C (415°F/Gas 6–7). Lightly grease a 12-hole, 1/2-cup (125 ml/4 fl oz) muffin tin. Sift the flour into a large bowl and stir in the sugar. Make a well in the centre.
2 Mix together the eggs, milk and butter and pour into the well all at once. Using a wooden spoon, stir until just mixed. Do not overbeat—the batter should be lumpy.
3 Spoon the mixture into the muffin holes. Bake for 15–20 minutes, or until puffed and golden. Cool on a wire rack.

VARIATION: For a low-fat muffin, use skim milk and use orange juice instead of half the butter.

Use very ripe bananas for the best BANANA MUFFINS.

BANANA MUFFINS

Preparation: 15 minutes
Cooking: 15 minutes
Makes 12

2 cups (250 g/8 oz) self-raising flour
1 cup (150 g/5 oz) oat bran
3/4 cup (185 g/6 oz) caster sugar
2 eggs, lightly beaten
3/4 cup (185 ml/6 fl oz) milk
60 g (2 oz) butter, melted
2 ripe bananas, mashed

1 Preheat the oven to hot 210°C (415°F/Gas 6–7). Lightly grease a 12-hole, 1/2-cup (125 ml/4 fl oz) muffin tin. Sift the flour into a large bowl and stir in the oat bran and sugar. Make a well in the centre.
2 Mix together the eggs, milk, butter and mashed banana and pour into the well all at once. Using a wooden spoon, stir until just mixed. Do not overbeat—the batter should be lumpy.
3 Spoon the mixture into the muffin holes. Bake for 15 minutes, or until the muffins are puffed and golden brown. Transfer to a wire rack to cool.

We've decorated our CHOCOLATE MUFFINS with chocolate buttercream and icing sugar.

CHOCOLATE MUFFINS

Preparation: 15 minutes
Cooking: 15 minutes
Makes 6 large muffins

- 2 cups (250 g/8 oz) plain flour
- 2 1/2 teaspoons baking powder
- 3 tablespoons cocoa powder
- 2 tablespoons caster sugar
- 1 cup (175 g/6 oz) dark choc bits
- 1 egg, lightly beaten
- 1/2 cup (125 g/4 oz) sour cream
- 3/4 cup (185 ml/6 fl oz) milk
- 90 g (3 oz) butter, melted

1 Preheat the oven to hot 210°C (415°F/Gas 6–7). Lightly grease a 6-hole, 1-cup (250 ml/8 fl oz) muffin tin. Sift the flour, baking powder and cocoa powder into a large bowl and stir in the sugar and choc bits. Make a well in the centre.

2 Mix together the egg, sour cream, milk and butter and pour into the well all at once. Using a wooden spoon, stir until just mixed. Do not overbeat—the batter should be lumpy.

3 Spoon the mixture into the muffin holes. Bake for 12–15 minutes, or until the muffins are firm. Loosen from the tin with a flat-bladed knife and transfer to a wire rack to cool completely.

HONEY ROLL

Preparation: 40 minutes
Cooking: 12 minutes
Serves 6–8

3/4 cup (90 g/3 oz) self-raising flour
2 teaspoons mixed spice
3 eggs
2/3 cup (125 g/4 oz) soft brown sugar
1/4 cup (25 g/3/4 oz) desiccated coconut

Honey cream
125 g (4 oz) butter
1/3 cup (90 g/3 oz) caster sugar
2 tablespoons honey

1 Preheat the oven to hot 210°C (415°F/Gas 6–7). Grease a 30 x 25 cm (12 x 10 inch) swiss roll tin and line the base with baking paper, leaving the paper to hang over two sides. Sift the flour and spice onto greaseproof paper three times.
2 Using electric beaters, beat the eggs in a large mixing bowl for 5 minutes, or until thick, frothy and pale. Add the sugar gradually, beating constantly until it has dissolved and the mixture is pale and glossy. Use a metal spoon to fold in the flour quickly and lightly.
3 Spread the mixture evenly in the tin and smooth the surface. Bake for 12 minutes, or until the cake is lightly golden and springy to touch. Lay out a clean, dry tea towel, cover with greaseproof paper and sprinkle the paper with the coconut. Turn the cooked cake onto the coconut and leave for 1 minute.
4 Using the tea towel as a guide, carefully roll the cake, along with the paper, up from the short side. Leave for 5 minutes, or until cool. Unroll the cake and discard the paper.
5 To make the honey cream, beat the butter, sugar and honey in a small mixing bowl with electric beaters until light and creamy. Remove the bowl from the electric mixer. Cover the mixture with cold water, swirl the water around, then pour it off. Beat the mixture again with electric beaters for another 2 minutes. Repeat this process six times, or until the cream is white and fluffy, and the sugar has completely dissolved. Spread the honey cream over the cake, re-roll and trim the ends with a knife. Serve sliced.

Make HONEY ROLL like a swiss roll, with a creamy honey filling.

AFGHANS

Preparation: 20 minutes
Cooking: 20 minutes
Makes 20

150 g (5 oz) butter
1/3 cup (60 g/2 oz) soft brown sugar
1 egg, lightly beaten
1 teaspoon vanilla essence
1 cup (125 g/4 oz) plain flour
2 tablespoons cocoa powder
1/3 cup (30 g/1 oz) desiccated coconut
1 1/2 cups (75 g/2 1/2 oz) lightly crushed cornflakes
1/2 cup (90 g/3 oz) choc bits

Spread melted chocolate topping over AFGHANS.

1 Preheat the oven to moderate 180°C (350°F/Gas 4). Grease a 32 x 28 cm (13 x 11 inch) baking tray and line with baking paper.
2 Using electric beaters, beat the butter and sugar in a small bowl until the mixture is light and creamy. Add the egg and vanilla essence a little at a time, beating thoroughly after each addition. Transfer the mixture to a large bowl and add the sifted combined flour and cocoa with the coconut and cornflakes. Using a metal spoon, fold in gently until just combined.
3 Drop level tablespoons of the mixture onto the tray. Bake for 20 minutes, or until lightly browned. Allow the biscuits to cool on the tray.
4 Put the choc bits in a heatproof bowl. Half fill a saucepan with water and bring it to the boil. Remove from the heat and place the bowl over the pan, making sure the base of it is not sitting in the water. Stir occasionally until the chocolate has melted. Remove from the heat. Spread the biscuit tops thickly with chocolate and leave for the topping to set.

VARIATIONS: Afghans can be sprinkled with toasted shredded coconut. To toast coconut, spread it on a baking tray and toast in a preheated moderate 180°C (350°F/Gas 4) oven for 5 minutes. Alternatively, top the Afghans with finely chopped walnuts or pecans. You may prefer to use dark chopped chocolate instead of choc bits.

FLORENTINES

Preparation: 25 minutes
Cooking: 20 minutes
Makes 24

1/4 cup (30 g/1 oz) plain flour
2 tablespoons chopped walnuts
2 tablespoons chopped flaked almonds
2 tablespoons finely chopped glacé cherries
2 tablespoons finely chopped mixed peel
75 g (2 1/2 oz) butter
1/4 cup (45 g/1 1/2 oz) soft brown sugar
180 g (6 oz) dark compound chocolate, chopped

1 Preheat the oven to moderate 180°C (350°F/ Gas 4). Line a 32 x 28 cm (13 x 11 inch) baking tray with baking paper. Sift the flour into a mixing bowl. Add the walnuts, almonds, cherries and mixed peel. Stir and make a well in the centre.
2 Combine the butter and sugar in a small pan. Stir over low heat until the butter has melted and the sugar has dissolved. Pour into the well in the dry ingredients. Using a wooden spoon, stir until just combined, but do not overbeat. Drop heaped teaspoons of the mixture onto the tray, leaving plenty of room between each one. Press into neat 5 cm (2 inch) rounds. Bake for 7 minutes. While the florentines are still soft, use a flat-bladed knife to push them into neat rounds. Cool on the tray for 5 minutes before transferring to a wire rack to cool completely.
3 Put the chocolate in a heatproof bowl. Half fill a pan with water and bring it to the boil. Remove from the heat and place the bowl of chocolate over the pan, making sure it is not touching the water. Stir occasionally until the chocolate is melted. Using a flat-bladed knife, carefully spread the chocolate on the underside of the florentines. Place the biscuits chocolate-side-up on a wire rack to set. Best eaten on the same day.

COCONUT JAM SLICE

Preparation: 30 minutes + 10 minutes refrigeration
Cooking: 35 minutes
Makes 25 squares

1 1/2 cups (185 g/6 oz) plain flour
150 g (5 oz) butter, cubed
1/2 cup (60 g/2 oz) icing sugar

Topping
1/3 cup (90 g/3 oz) caster sugar
2 eggs
2 cups (180 g/6 oz) desiccated coconut
1/3 cup (105 g/3 1/2 oz) blackberry jam

1 Preheat the oven to moderate 180°C (350°F/ Gas 4). Grease a 23 cm (9 inch) square cake tin and line with baking paper, extending over two sides.
2 Put the flour, butter and sugar in a bowl and, with your fingertips, rub in the butter until crumbly. Turn out onto a lightly floured surface and gather together. Press the dough into the tin and refrigerate for 10 minutes. Bake for 15 minutes, or until just golden. Cool.
3 To make the topping, whisk the sugar and eggs until combined. Stir in the coconut.
4 Spread the jam over the cooled base. Spread the topping over the jam, pressing down with the back of a spoon, and bake for 20 minutes, or until light golden. Cut into squares when cool.

STORAGE: Store for up to 3 days in an airtight container.

FLORENTINES (top) and COCONUT JAM SLICE.

CHOCOLATE CHIP COOKIES

Preparation: 15 minutes
Cooking: 15 minutes
Makes about 24

150 g (5 oz) unsalted butter
1/4 cup (45 g/1 1/2 oz) soft brown sugar
1/3 cup (90 g/3 oz) caster sugar
1 egg yolk
1 teaspoon vanilla essence
1 1/2 cups (185 g/6 oz) self-raising flour
1/2 cup (90 g/3 oz) dark choc bits
1/2 cup (90 g/3 oz) milk choc bits

1 Preheat the oven to moderate 180°C (350°F/Gas 4). Grease two baking trays and line with non-stick baking paper. Using electric beaters, beat the butter, sugars and egg yolk in a small bowl until light and creamy. Add the vanilla and beat until combined.
2 Transfer the mixture to a large bowl and add the flour and half the choc bits. Using a metal spoon, stir until just combined. Use your hands to press the mixture together to form a soft dough.
3 Roll level tablespoons of the mixture into balls. Press the remaining chocolate bits firmly onto the tops of the balls. Arrange the balls on the tray, leaving room for spreading. Bake for 15 minutes, or until crisp and lightly browned, and then cool on the trays.

Press chocolate bits into the CHOCOLATE CHIP COOKIES.

PEANUT BUTTER BISCUITS

Preparation: 20 minutes
Cooking: 15 minutes
Makes 36

125 g (4 oz) butter
155 g (5 oz) soft brown sugar
1/2 cup (125 g/4 oz) peanut butter
2 teaspoons vanilla essence
1 egg
1 3/4 cups (215 g/7 oz) plain flour
1 cup (160 g/5 1/2 oz) raw peanuts

1 Preheat the oven to moderate 180°C (350°F/Gas 4). Line two or three baking trays with baking paper. Using electric beaters, beat the butter and sugar until light and creamy. Beat in the peanut butter, vanilla essence and egg.
2 Transfer the mixture to a large bowl. Sift in the flour and add the peanuts. Stir until combined, using a large metal spoon.
3 Place tablespoons of the mixture on the trays, leaving room for spreading. Bake for 15 minutes, or until golden. Leave the biscuits on the trays for at least 2 minutes before transferring them to a wire rack to cool.

NOTE: Try adding 90 g (3 oz) chopped chocolate or choc bits to the dough. For neater biscuits, roll the mixture into balls and flatten on the tray.

JAM DROPS

Preparation: 20 minutes
Cooking: 15 minutes
Makes 32

80 g (2¾ oz) butter
⅓ cup (90 g/3 oz) caster sugar
2 tablespoons milk
½ teaspoon vanilla essence
1 cup (125 g/4 oz) self-raising flour
⅓ cup (40 g/1¼ oz) custard powder
2 tablespoons raspberry jam

1 Preheat the oven to moderate 180°C (350°F/Gas 4). Line two baking trays with baking paper. Beat the butter and sugar until light and creamy. Beat in the milk and vanilla. Add the sifted flour and custard powder and mix to form a soft dough.
2 Roll 2 teaspoonfuls at a time into balls and put on the trays. Press the centre of each ball with your thumb. Fill the hole with jam. Bake for 15 minutes, then cool on a wire rack.

Use raw peanuts in your PEANUT BUTTER BISCUITS.

JAM DROPS are simple for children to make, and fun too.

MONTE CREAMS

Preparation: 30 minutes
Cooking: 20 minutes
Makes 25

125 g (4 oz) butter
1/2 cup (125 g/4 oz) caster sugar
3 tablespoons milk
1 1/2 cups (185 g/6 oz) self-raising flour
1/4 cup (30 g/1 oz) custard powder
1/3 cup (30 g/1 oz) desiccated coconut

Filling
75 g (2 1/2 oz) butter
2/3 cup (85 g/3 oz) icing sugar
2 teaspoons milk
1/3 cup (105 g/3 1/2 oz) strawberry jam

1 Preheat the oven to moderate 180°C (350°F/Gas 4). Line two baking trays with baking paper. Using electric beaters, beat the butter and sugar until light and creamy. Add the milk and beat until combined. Sift the flour and custard powder and add to the bowl with the coconut. Mix to form a soft dough.
2 Roll two teaspoons of the mixture into balls. Place on the trays and press with a fork. Dip the fork in custard powder occasionally to prevent it from sticking. Bake for 15–20 minutes, or until just golden. Transfer to a wire rack to cool completely before filling.
3 To make the filling, beat the butter and sugar with electric beaters until light and creamy. Beat in the milk. Spread one biscuit with about half a teaspoon of the filling and one with about half a teaspoon of the jam, and sandwich the halves together.

STORAGE: These will keep for up to 4 days in an airtight container.

Sandwich the MONTE CREAMS together with filling and jam.

Decorate MELTING MOMENTS with half a glacé cherry in the middle of each one.

MELTING MOMENTS

Preparation: 30 minutes
Cooking: 15 minutes
Makes 40

180 g (6 oz) butter
1/3 cup (40 g/1 1/4 oz) icing sugar
1 teaspoon vanilla essence
1/3 cup (40 g/1 1/4 oz) cornflour
1 cup (125 g/4 oz) plain flour
100 g (3 1/2 oz) glacé cherries

1 Preheat the oven to moderate 180°C (350°F/Gas 4). Grease a 32 x 28 cm (13 x 11 inch) baking tray and line with baking paper.
2 Using electric beaters, beat the butter, sugar and vanilla essence in a small bowl until light and creamy. Beat in the sifted cornflour and flour gradually, beating until the mixture is just combined and smooth.
3 Spoon into a piping bag fitted with a 1 cm (1/2 inch) fluted nozzle. Pipe the mixture in rosettes 4 cm (1 1/2 inches) in diameter onto the tray. Top each biscuit with half a glacé cherry. Bake for 15 minutes, or until lightly golden and crisp. Cool on a wire rack.

VARIATION: Sandwich the biscuits together with jam and a creamy filling. To make the filling, beat 60 g (2 oz) butter with electric beaters until creamy. Gradually add 1/2 cup (60 g/2 oz) icing sugar alternately with 2 teaspoons milk. Beat until the mixture is light and fluffy. Sandwich the biscuits together with a little filling and jam. Dust with icing sugar to serve.

ANZAC BISCUITS

Preparation: 12 minutes
Cooking: 20 minutes
Makes 26

1 cup (125 g/4 oz) plain flour
2/3 cup (160 g/5 1/2 oz) sugar
1 cup (100 g/3 1/2 oz) rolled oats
1 cup (90 g/3 oz) desiccated coconut
125 g (4 oz) butter
1/4 cup (90 g/3 oz) golden syrup
1/2 teaspoon bicarbonate of soda

1 Preheat the oven to moderate 180°C (350°F/Gas 4). Line two baking trays with baking paper. Sift the flour and sugar into a large mixing bowl. Add the rolled oats and coconut and make a well in the centre of the dry ingredients.
2 Put the butter and syrup in a small pan. Stir over low heat until melted and smooth. Dissolve the soda in 1 tablespoon boiling water, then add immediately to the butter mixture. It will foam up instantly. Pour into the well in the dry ingredients. Stir well with a wooden spoon.
3 Drop level tablespoons of the mixture onto the tray. Flatten gently with your fingers, leaving room for spreading. Bake for 20 minutes, or until just browned. Remove from the oven and transfer to a wire rack to cool.

STORAGE: Will keep in an airtight container for up to three days.
VARIATION: Use treacle or honey instead of syrup.
HINT: Instant or 1-minute oats are quite suitable for this recipe.

You can use instant or 1-minute oats for ANZAC BISCUITS.

GINGERBREAD PEOPLE

Preparation: 1 hour + 15 minutes refrigeration
Cooking: 10 minutes
Makes about 16

125 g (4 oz) butter
1/3 cup (60 g/2 oz) soft dark brown or soft brown sugar
1/3 cup (115 g/4 oz) golden syrup
1 egg, lightly beaten
2 cups (250 g/8 oz) plain flour
1/3 cup (40 g/1 1/4 oz) self-raising flour
1 tablespoon ground ginger
1 teaspoon bicarbonate of soda

Use tinted icing to pipe faces and clothing onto GINGERBREAD PEOPLE.

Icing

1 egg white
1/2 teaspoon lemon juice
1 cup (125 g/4 oz) pure icing sugar, sifted
assorted food colourings

1 Preheat the oven to moderate 180°C (350°F/Gas 4). Grease two or three baking trays and line with baking paper. Using electric beaters, beat the butter, sugar and syrup until light and creamy. Add the egg gradually, beating well after each addition.
2 Sift the flours, ginger and bicarbonate of soda onto the butter mixture and use a knife to mix until just combined. Use a well-floured hand to combine the dough thoroughly, then turn onto a floured surface and knead for 1–2 minutes, or until smooth.
3 Line a large board with baking paper. Roll out the dough on the board to 5 mm (1/4 inch) thickness. (Flour the rolling pin, if necessary, to prevent the dough sticking.) Put the dough on the board in the fridge for 15 minutes, or until firm enough to cut.
4 Cut out the dough with people-shaped biscuit cutters. Press any remaining dough together, then re-roll and cut out again. Put on the trays and bake for 10 minutes, or until lightly browned. Cool the biscuits on trays, and then ice.
5 To make the icing, put the egg white in a small dry bowl and beat with electric beaters until foamy. Add the lemon juice and icing sugar gradually, and beat until thick and creamy. Divide the icing among several bowls and tint with food colourings. Spoon into small paper icing bags and pipe faces and clothing onto the biscuits.

COCONUT MACAROONS

Preparation: 15 minutes
Cooking: 20 minutes
Makes about 60

3 egg whites
1 1/4 cups (310 g/10 oz) caster sugar
1/2 teaspoon coconut essence
1 teaspoon grated lemon rind
2 tablespoons cornflour
3 cups (270 g/9 oz) desiccated coconut
3 tablespoons shredded coconut, to sprinkle
60 g (2 oz) dark chocolate, chopped

1 Preheat the oven to warm 160°C (315°F/ Gas 2–3). Grease two baking trays and line with baking paper. Place the egg whites in a small, dry bowl. Using electric beaters, beat the egg whites until firm peaks form. Add the sugar gradually, beating constantly until the mixture is thick and glossy and all the sugar has dissolved. Add the coconut essence and lemon rind, and beat until just combined.

2 Transfer the mixture to a large bowl and add the sifted cornflour and the coconut. Using a metal spoon, stir until just combined. Drop 1 or 2 level teaspoons of the mixture onto the prepared trays about 3 cm (1 1/4 inches) apart. Sprinkle with shredded coconut and bake for 15–20 minutes, or until golden. Transfer to a wire rack to cool.

3 Put the chocolate in a heatproof bowl. Bring a pan of water to a simmer, remove from the heat and place the bowl over the pan (make sure the base of the bowl isn't sitting in the water). Stir occasionally until the chocolate has melted. Dip the cooled macaroons in the melted chocolate and return to the wire rack to set.

VARIATION: To make plain almond macaroons, beat 115 g (4 oz) ground almonds with 1 cup (250 g/8 oz) caster sugar and 2 egg whites for 5 minutes. Add 1 tablespoon plain flour and 2 teaspoons vanilla essence and beat until smooth. Add a little finely grated orange or lemon rind, if you like, and then bake as directed above. Makes 25–30.

Decorate MACAROONS with coconut and melted chocolate.

BRANDY SNAPS

Preparation: 15 minutes
Cooking: 45 minutes
Makes 25

60 g (2 oz) butter
2 tablespoons golden syrup
1/3 cup (60 g/2 oz) soft brown sugar
1/4 cup (30 g/1 oz) plain flour
1 1/2 teaspoons ground ginger
60 g (2 oz) dark chocolate, chopped

1 Preheat the oven to moderate 180°C (350°F/Gas 4). Lightly grease two baking trays and line with baking paper.
2 Combine the butter, golden syrup and sugar in a small pan. Stir over low heat until the butter has melted and the sugar has dissolved, then remove from the heat. Add the sifted flour and ginger to the pan. Use a wooden spoon to stir the mixture until well combined, taking care not to overbeat.
3 Using 3 level teaspoons of the mixture for each brandy snap, drop the mixture onto the trays about 12 cm (5 inches) apart. Bake for 5–6 minutes, or until lightly browned. Leave the biscuits on the trays for 30 seconds then, while still hot, lift off the tray and wrap around the handle of a thin wooden spoon. Slide off the spoon and set aside to cool while you curl the remaining brandy snaps.
4 Put the chocolate in a heatproof bowl. Bring a pan of water to a simmer, remove from the heat and place the bowl over the pan (make sure the base of the bowl isn't sitting in the water). Stir occasionally until the chocolate has melted. Dip the ends of the brandy snaps in the melted chocolate and leave on a foil-lined tray to dry.

Dip the ends of the BRANDY SNAPS in melted dark chocolate.

HINT: There is a real art to working with these biscuits: work quickly, as they harden and crack when cooled. Use a large flat knife or spatula to lift them off the tray. If they cool too much, return to the oven for a few minutes to warm, then try again.

CUSTARD TARTS

Preparation: 30 minutes + 20 minutes refrigeration
Cooking: 45 minutes
Makes 12

2 cups (250 g/8 oz) plain flour
1/3 cup (60 g/2 oz) rice flour
1/4 cup (30 g/1 oz) icing sugar
120 g (4 oz) butter, chopped
1 egg yolk
3 tablespoons iced water
1 egg white, lightly beaten

Filling
3 eggs
1 1/2 cups (375 ml/12 fl oz) milk
1/4 cup (60 g/2 oz) caster sugar
1 teaspoon vanilla essence
1/2 teaspoon ground nutmeg

1 Place the flours, icing sugar and butter in a bowl. Rub in the butter with your fingertips until the mixture is fine and crumbly. Add the egg yolk and almost all of the iced water, and stir with a knife until the mixture comes together, adding more water if necesary. Turn onto a lightly floured surface and press together until smooth. Divide the dough into 12 equal portions. Roll out and line twelve 10 cm (4 inch) fluted tart tins. Refrigerate for 20 minutes.
2 Preheat the oven to moderate 180°C (350°F/Gas 4). Cover each pastry-lined tin with a crumpled sheet of baking paper and fill with a layer of baking beads or rice. Place the tins on a large baking tray and bake for 10 minutes. Discard the baking paper and beads or rice and bake the pastry for a further 10 minutes, or until lightly golden and dry. Allow to cool. Brush the base and side of each pastry case with beaten egg white.
3 To make the filling, reduce the oven to slow 150°C (300°F/Gas 2). Combine the eggs and milk in a mixing bowl, and whisk to combine. Add the sugar gradually, whisking to dissolve completely. Stir in the vanilla, strain the mixture into a jug, then pour into the pastry cases. Sprinkle with the nutmeg and bake for 25 minutes, or until the filling is just set. Serve the custard tarts at room temperature.

NOTE: For blind baking, if you don't have baking beads, use raw rice or dried beans. They can be kept and used again.

CHOCOLATE BROWNIES

Preparation: 20 minutes
Cooking: 40 minutes
Makes 24

150 g (5 oz) butter, chopped
125 g (4 oz) dark chocolate, chopped
3 eggs, lightly beaten
1 1/2 cups (375 g/12 oz) caster sugar
1 teaspoon vanilla essence
1 cup (125 g /4 oz) plain flour
1/4 cup (30 g/1 oz) cocoa power
icing sugar, to dust

1 Preheat the oven to moderate 180°C (350°F/Gas 4). Grease a 20 cm (8 inch) square tin with oil or melted butter Line the base with baking paper, extending over two opposite sides (to help you lift the brownies out).
2 Bring a small pan of water to a simmer. Remove from the heat. Put the butter and chocolate in a heatproof bowl, place over the pan (don't let the base of the bowl sit in the hot water) and stir occasionally until smooth. Remove from the heat and cool slightly.
3 Use a whisk to beat the eggs, sugar and vanilla together in a large bowl.

CUSTARD TARTS (top) and CHOCOLATE BROWNIES.

Add the melted chocolate mixture and whisk together. Stir in the combined sifted flour and cocoa. Do not overbeat.

4 Pour into the tin and bake for 40 minutes, or until slightly risen and just firm. Leave to cool in the tin (the brownie will sink back down on cooling). Lift out and cut into squares. Dust with icing sugar to serve.

STORAGE: Can be stored in an airtight container for two days.

VARIATIONS: For nut brownies, add 1 cup (125 g/4½ oz) of chopped roasted macadamias, walnuts or pecans to the mixture.

For white chocolate brownies, use white chocolate melts instead of the dark chocolate.

For marshmallow brownies, add 1 cup (45 g/1½ oz) of mini marshmallows to the raw mixture.

To make a brownie ice cream sandwich, cut brownies into small squares and sandwich two squares together with vanilla ice cream. Serve with a hot chocolate fudge sauce as a dessert.

CHOCOLATE CARAMEL SLICE.

CHOCOLATE CARAMEL SLICE

Preparation: 15 minutes
Cooking: 20 minutes
Makes 24 triangles

125 g (4 oz) plain sweet biscuits, crushed
80 g (2¾ oz) butter, melted
2 tablespoons desiccated coconut
400 g (13 oz) can sweetened condensed milk
125 g (4 oz) butter, extra
⅓ cup (90 g/3 oz) caster sugar
⅓ cup (115 g/4 oz) golden syrup
250 g (8 oz) milk chocolate melts
1 tablespoon vegetable oil

1 Grease a shallow 30 x 20 cm (12 x 8 inch) cake tin, line the base and sides with foil and grease the foil. Mix together the biscuits, melted butter and coconut. Press the mixture evenly into the tin and smooth the surface.
2 Combine the condensed milk, extra butter, sugar and golden syrup in a small pan. Stir over low heat for 15 minutes, or until the sugar has dissolved and the caramel is smooth, thick and lightly browned. Remove from the heat and leave to cool slightly. Pour the caramel over the biscuit base and smooth the surface.
3 Put the milk chocolate melts and oil in a heatproof bowl. Half fill a saucepan with water and bring it to the boil. Remove from the heat and place the bowl of chocolate over the pan, making sure the base of the bowl is not sitting in the water. Stir occasionally until the chocolate has melted and the mixture is smooth. Spread the chocolate mixture over the caramel. Allow to partially set before marking into 24 triangles. Refrigerate until firm.

STORAGE: The slice can be stored in an airtight container in a cool place for up to two days.
VARIATION: Use dark chocolate melts in place of milk chocolate.

FRUIT MINCE PIES

Preparation: 30 minutes
Cooking: 30 minutes
Makes 24

2 cups (250 g/8 oz) plain flour
2/3 cup (85 g/3 oz) icing sugar
150 g (5 oz) butter
2–3 tablespoons iced water
icing sugar, to dust

Fruit mince

1/3 cup (40 g/1 1/4 oz) raisins, chopped
1/3 cup (60 g/2 oz) soft brown sugar
1/4 cup (30 g/1 oz) sultanas
1/4 cup (45 g/1 1/2 oz) mixed peel
1 tablespoon currants
1 tablespoon chopped almonds
1 small apple, grated
1 teaspoon lemon juice
1/2 teaspoon finely grated orange rind
1/2 teaspoon finely grated lemon rind
1/2 teaspoon mixed spice
pinch of nutmeg
25 g (3/4 oz) melted butter
1 tablespoon brandy

1 To make the fruit mince, combine the ingredients in a bowl and then spoon into a sterilized jar. You can use the fruit mince straight away but the flavours develop if kept for a while. You can keep it in a cool dark place for up to 3 months. (You can use shop-bought fruit mince if you are short for time.)

2 Preheat the oven to moderate 180°C (350°F/Gas 4). Brush two 12-hole shallow patty tins lightly with melted butter. Place the flour, sugar and butter in a bowl and rub in the butter with your fingertips until fine and crumbly. Add almost all the water and mix with a knife until it just comes together.

3 Turn out onto a lightly floured surface and gather into a ball. Roll out two thirds of the pastry and cut out 24 rounds with a biscuit cutter. Fit the rounds into the tins.

4 Divide the fruit mince among the pastry cases. Roll out the remaining pastry and cut out 12 rounds with the same cutter. Using a smaller, fluted cutter, cut a circle from the centre of each. Place the large circles on top of half the pies and press the edges to seal. Place the smaller circles on the remainder. Bake for 25 minutes, or until golden. Leave in the tins for 5 minutes, then lift out with a knife and cool on wire racks. Dust lightly with icing sugar.

Make decorative pastry tops for Christmas FRUIT MINCE PIES.

VANILLA SLICE

Preparation: 40 minutes
Cooking: 15 minutes
Makes 9

2 sheets ready-rolled puff pastry
1 cup (250 g/8 oz) caster sugar
3/4 cup (90 g/3 oz) cornflour
1/2 cup (60 g/2 oz) custard powder
3 cups (750 ml/24 fl oz) milk
1 cup (250 ml/8 fl oz) cream
60 g (2 oz) butter
2 teaspoons vanilla essence
3 egg yolks

Icing

1 1/2 cups (185 g/6 oz) icing sugar
1/4 cup (60 g/2 oz) passionfruit pulp
2 teaspoons lemon juice
15 g (1/2 oz) butter, softened

1 Preheat the oven to very hot 240°C (475°F/Gas 9). Grease two baking trays with oil. Line the base and sides of a shallow 23 cm (9 inch) square cake tin with foil, leaving the foil to hang over two sides. Place the pastry sheets on the baking trays. Prick all over with a fork and bake for 8 minutes, or until golden. Remove from the oven and trim each pastry sheet to a 23 cm (9 inch) square. Place one sheet in the tin, top-side-down.
2 Combine the sugar, cornflour and custard powder in a pan. Gradually add the milk and cream and stir until smooth. Stir the mixture constantly over medium heat for 2 minutes, or until it boils and thickens. Add the butter and vanilla essence, and stir until smooth.
3 Remove the mixture from the heat. Whisk in the egg yolks until combined. Spread the custard over the pastry in the tin and cover with the remaining pastry, top-side-down. Allow to cool.
4 To make the icing, combine the icing sugar, passionfruit pulp, lemon juice and butter in a heatproof bowl. Place the bowl over a pan of simmering water and stir until the icing is smooth and glossy. Remove from the heat. Lift the slice out of the cake tin, using the foil 'handles' to help you. Spread the icing over the top of the slice and leave it to set before cutting into squares with a sharp serrated knife.

Top the VANILLA SLICE with a passionfruit icing.

CHOCOLATE ECLAIRS

Preparation: 50 minutes
Cooking: 25 minutes
Makes 12

60 g (2 oz) butter
1/2 cup (60 g/2 oz) plain flour, sifted
2 eggs, lightly beaten
100 g (3 1/2 oz) dark chocolate, chopped

Cream filling
300 ml (10 fl oz) chilled cream
1 tablespoon icing sugar

CHOCOLATE ECLAIRS are made using choux pastry.

1 Preheat the oven to hot 210°C (415°F/Gas 6–7). Line a tray with baking paper and mark with 10 cm (4 inch) lines, as a piping guide.
2 Put the butter in a pan with 3/4 cup (185 ml/ 6 fl oz) water. Stir over medium heat until the mixture comes to the boil. Immediately remove from the heat and beat in the flour. Return to the heat and beat until the mixture comes together and leaves the side of the pan. Allow to cool slightly and then transfer to a bowl.
3 Beat the mixture to release any more heat. Gradually add the egg, a little at a time, beating well after each addition, until thick and glossy. You may not need to add all the egg. A wooden spoon should stand up in the mixture—if it is too runny, the egg has been added too quickly. Beat for several minutes more, or until thickened.
4 Spoon into a piping bag fitted with a 1 cm (1/2 inch) plain nozzle. Pipe twelve 10 cm (4 inch) fingers, a little apart, onto the tray, cutting off with a wet knife. Bake for 10 minutes, then reduce the heat to moderate 180°C (350°F/ Gas 4) and bake for 15–20 minutes. Pierce for the steam to escape, and cool on a wire rack.
5 Put the chocolate in a heatproof bowl. Half fill a saucepan with water and bring it to the boil. Remove from the heat and place the bowl of chocolate over the pan, making sure the base of the bowl isn't sitting in the water. Stir until the chocolate has melted. Cut each eclair in half with a serrated knife and spread chocolate along the top half. Leave on a wire rack until set.
6 To make the filling, put the cream and icing sugar in a bowl and beat until stiff. Spoon or pipe into the bottom half of each eclair and top with a chocolate lid.
Serve immediately.

BAKLAVA is a traditional Greek sweet pastry.

BAKLAVA

Preparation: 15 minutes
Cooking: 30 minutes
Serves 8

3 1/2 cups (435 g/14 oz) walnuts, finely chopped
1 cup (155 g/5 oz) almonds, finely chopped
1/2 teaspoon ground cinnamon
1/2 teaspoon ground mixed spice
1 tablespoon caster sugar
16 sheets filo pastry
40 g (1 1/4 oz) butter, melted
1 tablespoon olive oil

Syrup
1 cup (250 g/8 oz) sugar
3 whole cloves
3 teaspoons lemon juice

1 Preheat the oven to moderate 180°C (350°F/Gas 4). Grease a shallow 18 x 28 cm (7 x 11 inch) tin. Mix together the walnuts, almonds, spices and sugar in a bowl.
2 Divide the mixture into three portions. Place one sheet of pastry on a work surface. Brush half the sheet with the combined butter and oil, then fold in half along the width. Trim the edges of the pastry to fit the dish. Place in the base of the dish. Repeat the process with another three sheets of pastry.
3 Sprinkle one portion of the walnut mixture over the pastry. Repeat the pastry process with four more sheets. Sprinkle with the second portion of walnut mixture. Continue with another four sheets of pastry, the remaining walnut mixture and the final four sheets of pastry. Trim the edges.
4 Brush the top of the pastry with the remaining butter and oil mixture. Score the slice evenly into four lengthways, but not cut through to the base.

Bake for 30 minutes or until golden and crisp.
5 Meanwhile, make the syrup. Combine the sugar, cloves, lemon juice and 2/3 cup (170 ml/5 1/2 fl oz) water in a small pan. Stir constantly over low heat until the mixture boils and the sugar has dissolved. Reduce the heat and leave to simmer, without stirring, for 10 minutes. Allow to cool.
6 Pour the cooled syrup over the hot slice. When cold, cut the slice into squares or diamonds.

CRUNCHY MUESLI SLICE

Preparation: 10 minutes
Cooking: 50 minutes
Makes 18 fingers

250 g (8 oz) butter
1 cup (250 g/8 oz) caster sugar
2 tablespoons honey
2 1/4 cups (225 g/7 oz) rolled oats
3/4 cup (65 g/2 1/4 oz) desiccated coconut
1 cup (30 g/1 oz) cornflakes, lightly crushed
1/3 cup (30 g/1 oz) flaked almonds
1 teaspoon mixed spice
1/2 cup (95 g/3 oz) finely chopped dried apricots
1 cup (185 g/6 oz) mixed dried fruit

CRUNCHY MUESLI SLICE makes a good lunchbox filler.

1 Preheat the oven to warm 160°C (315°F/ Gas 2–3). Grease a shallow 30 x 20 cm (12 x 8 inch) cake tin, line the base and sides with paper, and grease the paper.
2 Combine the butter, sugar and honey in a small pan. Stir over low heat for 5 minutes, or until the butter has melted and the sugar has dissolved.
3 Place the oats, coconut, cornflakes, almonds, mixed spice and fruit in a large bowl, and stir to combine. Make a well in the centre. Pour the butter and sugar mixture into the well and stir thoroughly.
4 Press the mixture firmly into the tin. Using a sharp knife, score the slice into 18 fingers. (Do not cut through to the base.) Bake for 45 minutes, or until golden. Leave in the tin for 15 minutes before turning out onto a board to cool. Cut into fingers when cool.

STORAGE: Store in an airtight container for up to three days.
VARIATION: You can use golden syrup instead of honey.

SHORTBREAD

Preparation: 20 minutes
Cooking: 40 minutes
Makes 8 wedges

1 cup (125 g/4 oz) plain flour
1/2 cup (90 g/3 oz) rice flour
150 g (5 oz) butter, chopped
1/4 cup (60 g/2 oz) caster sugar, plus 1 teaspoon to sprinkle

1 Preheat the oven to warm 160°C (315°F/ Gas 2–3). Using a bowl as a guide, draw an 18 cm (7 inch) circle on a sheet of baking paper. Sift the flours into a large mixing bowl and add the chopped butter and sugar.
2 Using your fingertips, rub the butter into the flour until the mixture resembles fine breadcrumbs. Turn out onto a lightly floured surface and gather into a smooth ball.
3 Turn the paper pencil-side-down and press out the dough to fit the circle. Pinch the edges to decorate. Score into eight wedges, sprinkle with the extra caster sugar and bake for 40 minutes. Cool on a wire rack and break into wedges to serve.

STORAGE: Will keep for up to 4 days in an airtight container.
HINT: Shortbread will come out of the oven soft and will firm up when left to cool.

Pinch the edges of the SHORTBREAD to decorate.

LITTLE LEMON TARTS

Preparation: 40 minutes + 10 minutes refrigeration
Cooking: 15 minutes
Makes about 24

2 cups (250 g/8 oz) plain flour
pinch of salt
125 g (4 oz) butter, chopped
2 teaspoons caster sugar
1 teaspoon lemon rind
1 egg yolk
2–3 tablespoons iced water

Filling
125 g (4 oz) cream cheese, softened
1/2 cup (125 g/4 oz) caster sugar
2 egg yolks
2 tablespoons lemon juice
1/2 cup (160 g/5 1/2 oz) sweetened condensed milk
candied lemon, to garnish

1 Preheat the oven to moderate 180°C (350°F/ Gas 4). Brush two 12-hole patty tins with oil. Sift the

You can use the basic recipe for LITTLE LEMON TARTS, to make jam tarts.

flour and salt into a bowl, add the butter and rub in with your fingertips until the mixture resembles fine breadcrumbs. Add the sugar, lemon rind, egg yolk and water, and mix with a knife until the mixture just starts to come together. Turn out onto a lightly floured surface and gather together in a ball. Cover in plastic wrap and refrigerate for 10 minutes.

2 To make the filling, beat the cream cheese, sugar and egg yolks with electric beaters until smooth and thickened. Add the lemon juice and condensed milk and beat until well combined.

3 Roll out the dough between sheets of baking paper to 3 mm (1/8 inch) thick. Using a 7 cm (2 3/4 inch) fluted, round cutter, cut rounds from the pastry. Gently press the pastry into the patty tins. Lightly prick each one three times with a fork and bake for 10 minutes, or until the pastry is just starting to turn golden.

4 Spoon 2 teaspoons of the filling into each pastry case. Bake for another 5 minutes, or until the filling has set. Leave to cool slightly before removing from the tins. Garnish with candied lemon strips.

VARIATION: For jam tarts, place 1 tablepoon strawberry, apricot or fruit conserve into the unfilled tart shells and bake for 10–15 minutes, or until the jam has melted. Allow to cool before serving.

BASIC BISCUITS

Preparation: 20 minutes
Cooking: 15 minutes
Makes about 50 biscuits

125 g (4 oz) butter, cubed
1/2 cup (125 g/4 oz) caster sugar
1 egg
1/4 teaspoon vanilla essence
1 cup (125 g/4 oz) plain flour
1 cup (125 g/4 oz) self-raising flour

1 Preheat the oven to warm 160°C (315°F/ Gas 2–3). Line two baking trays with baking paper. Beat together the butter and sugar until creamy. Add the egg and vanilla, and beat well. Fold in the sifted flours to form a soft dough.

2 Turn the dough out onto a sheet of baking paper and cover with another sheet. Roll out to 5 mm (1/4 inch) thick. Using biscuit cutters, cut out shapes and place on the trays.

3 Bake in batches for 10–15 minutes, or until lightly golden. Cool on a wire rack. Make up one of the following fillings and use to sandwich the biscuits together. Or simply spread the biscuits with one of our icings.

CARAMEL FILLING

Melt 30 g (1 oz) butter, 1/2 cup (95 g/3 oz) soft brown sugar and 1/2 cup (160 g/5 1/2 oz) condensed milk in a pan, then bring to the boil. Boil for 1 minute, or until the mixture thickens. Cool, then spread on the biscuits. For a variation, stir in 1 tablespoon chopped glacé ginger.

LIME BUTTER FILLING

Beat 60 g (2 oz) softened butter and 1 cup (125 g/ 4 oz) icing sugar until smooth. Add the finely shredded rind of a lime and 1–2 teaspoons of lime juice. Beat until the filling is spreadable.

CHOCOLATE AND PEANUT FILLING

Beat together 50 g (1¾ oz) softened butter and 1 cup (125 g/4 oz) sifted icing sugar until well combined. In a separate bowl, mix ⅓ cup (90 g/3 oz) peanut butter with 100 g (3½ oz) melted chocolate. Beat into the butter mixture, then beat in 1 tablespoon boiling water.

ORANGE CREAM CHEESE FILLING

Beat ¾ cup (185 g/6 oz) cream cheese with ¼ cup (30 g/1 oz) sifted icing sugar. Add the finely grated rind of an orange and beat until creamy.

MARSHMALLOW FILLING

Put the biscuits on a plate with a marshmallow on top of each one. Cook for 10 seconds in the microwave, then sandwich with another biscuit. Alternatively, lay the biscuits on a baking tray with a marshmallow on top of each one and bake in a moderate 180°C (350°F/Gas 4) oven for 1 minute. Sandwich with another biscuit.

PEPPERMINT FILLING

Mix 2 cups (250 g/8 oz) sifted icing sugar with 5–6 teaspoons hot water and a few drops of peppermint essence.

VANILLA ICING

Mix 1¼ cups (155 g/5 oz) sifted icing sugar with 1 tablespoon softened butter, ½ teaspoon vanilla essence and 2 tablespoons boiling water.

CHOCOLATE FLECK ICING

Make vanilla icing as above and gently mix in 2 tablespoons grated dark chocolate.

PASSIONFRUIT GLACE ICING

Mix 1¼ cups (155 g/5 oz) sifted icing sugar with 2 tablespoons passionfruit pulp in a heatproof bowl. Stir over simmering water until smooth and glossy.

HEDGEHOG SLICE is crunchy with pieces of biscuit.

HEDGEHOG SLICE

Preparation: 20 minutes + 1 hour refrigeration
Cooking: 5 minutes
Makes 20

125 g (4 oz) butter
1/2 cup (125 g/4 oz) caster sugar
125 g (4 oz) plain sweet biscuits, crushed
1 cup (100 g/3 1/2 oz) walnuts, chopped
1/2 cup (60 g/2 oz) cocoa powder
1 egg, lightly beaten
125 g (4 oz) cooking chocolate, chopped
30 g (1 oz) butter

1 Line the base and sides of a 20 cm (8 inch) square cake tin with foil, leaving the foil to hang over two sides. Combine the butter and sugar in a large heavy-based pan. Stir over medium heat until the butter has melted and the sugar has dissolved. Reduce the heat to low, add the crushed biscuits, walnuts and cocoa, and stir until well combined.
2 Remove the mixture from the heat and cool slightly. Add the egg and stir until thoroughly combined. Press the mixture into the tin, using the back of a spoon to smooth the surface.
3 Place the chocolate and butter in a small heatproof bowl. Bring a pan of water to a simmer, then remove from the heat and place the bowl over the pan (don't let the base of the bowl sit in the water). Stir until the mixture is melted and smooth.
4 Spread the topping over the slice and make a swirling pattern if you wish. Refrigerate for 1 hour. Use the foil 'handles' to lift the slice from the tin. Cut into squares to serve.

STORAGE: Store in an airtight container in a cool dark place, or in the refrigerator if the weather is warm.

MATCHSTICKS

Preparation: 40 minutes + 1 hour refrigeration
Cooking: 15 minutes
Makes 12

2 cups (250 g/8 oz) plain flour
pinch of salt
180 g (6 oz) butter
1 teaspoon lemon juice

Chocolate icing
1/2 cup (60 g/2 oz) icing sugar, sifted
1 tablespoon cocoa powder

Vanilla icing

2 cups (250 g/8 oz) icing sugar, sifted

1/2 teaspoon vanilla essence

Filling

3/4 cup (250 g/8 oz) raspberry jam

1 1/4 cups (315 ml/10 fl oz) cream, whipped

1 Sift the flour and salt into a large bowl. Add the butter and, with a knife, cut in the butter until just coated with the flour. Combine 3/4 cup (185 ml/ 6 fl oz) cold water with the lemon juice and add most of it to the bowl. Cut in with a knife, without breaking up the butter. Add more of the liquid if necessary.

2 With floured fingers, gently bring the mixture together into a rough ball. Turn out onto a floured surface and form into a rectangle. Do not knead. Roll the dough out to a 45 x 15 cm (18 x 6 inch) neat rectangle.

3 Fold the dough into three layers by folding the bottom third up and then the top third down. Seal the edges lightly with a rolling pin. Give a quarter turn clockwise: the top edge will now be to the right as if it were a book. Cover and refrigerate for 15 minutes. Repeat rolling, folding and turning four more times. Refrigerate between rollings if the dough becomes too soft. Chill for at least 30 minutes after the final rolling.

4 Divide the dough in half and roll each half out to 30 x 20 cm (12 x 8 inches), then cut into twelve 10 x 5 cm (4 x 2 inch) pieces.

5 Grease two baking trays and line with baking paper. Put the pastry on the trays, cover and chill for 20 minutes. Preheat the oven to moderately hot 200°C (400°F/Gas 6). Bake for 10 minutes, or until puffed and golden. Cool on a wire rack.

6 To make the chocolate icing, mix the sugar and cocoa with 1 tablespoon hot water. Spoon into a paper icing bag.

7 To make the vanilla icing, mix the sugar and vanilla with 3 tablespoons hot water in a heatproof bowl. Place the bowl over a pan of barely simmering water and stir until the icing is smooth and glossy. Spread the icing over half of the pastry pieces. Pipe diagonal lines with the chocolate icing and drag a skewer along the icing at intervals to give a feathered effect. Leave on a wire rack until the icing has set.

8 Spread the jam and cream over the un-iced halves of the pastry and then sandwich together with the iced tops.

NOTE: You can use ready-rolled puff pastry.

Use a skewer to give MATCHSTICKS feathered icing.

DESSERTS

Desserts are a wonderful starting point for the novice cook. It is difficult to go far wrong once sugar, chocolate and cream are involved... Desserts can range from a simple piece of poached fruit or bowl of home-made sorbet, to fabulous creations of pastry, meringue and summer berries. If you, or any of your friends and family, have a sweet tooth then this is the chapter for you.

PROFITEROLES

Preparation: 30 minutes
Cooking: 50 minutes
Serves 8–10

Choux pastry

50 g (1 3/4 oz) butter
3/4 cup (90 g/3 oz) plain flour, sifted twice
3 eggs, lightly beaten

Filling

1 1/2 cups (375 ml/12 fl oz) milk
4 egg yolks
1/3 cup (90 g/3 oz) caster sugar
3 tablespoons plain flour
1 teaspoon vanilla essence

110 g (3 1/2 oz) good-quality dark chocolate
2 teaspoons vegetable oil

1 Preheat the oven to hot 210°C (415°F/Gas 6–7). Put the butter in a large heavy-based pan with 3/4 cup (185 ml/6 fl oz) water and stir over medium heat until coming to the boil. Remove from the heat and quickly beat in the flour. Return to the heat and continue beating until the mixture comes together, forms a ball and leaves the side of the pan. Allow to cool slightly.
2 Transfer to a bowl and beat to release any more heat. Gradually add the beaten egg about 3 teaspoons at a time, beating well after each addition, until all the egg has been added and the mixture is thick and glossy—a wooden spoon should stand upright in it. (If it is too runny, the egg has been added too quickly. Beat for several more minutes, or until thickened.)
3 Spoon heaped teaspoons of the mixture onto two baking trays, leaving room for spreading. Sprinkle the baking trays with water—this creates steam, helping the puffs to rise. Bake for 20–30 minutes, or until browned and hollow sounding, then remove and make a small hole in the base of each one with a skewer. Return to the oven for 5 minutes to dry out. Cool on a wire rack.
4 To make the filling, put the milk in a small pan and bring to the boil. Set aside while quickly whisking the yolks and sugar in a bowl, until combined. Whisk in the

PROFITEROLES are a little fiddly to make, but fabulous for a special occasion.

flour. Pour the hot milk slowly onto the egg mixture, whisking constantly. Wash out the pan, return the milk mixture and bring to the boil, stirring with a wooden spoon until the mixture comes to the boil and thickens. Transfer to a bowl and stir in the vanilla essence. Lay plastic wrap directly over the surface to prevent a skin forming, then refrigerate until cold.

5 Pipe the filling into the profiteroles through the hole in the base, using a piping bag and nozzle. Melt the chocolate and oil gently, stir until smooth and dip the profiterole tops in the chocolate.

BAKED CHEESECAKE

Preparation: 30 minutes + refrigeration
Cooking: 55 minutes
Serves 6–8

250 g (8 oz) butternut cookies
1 teaspoon mixed spice
100 g (3 1/2 oz) butter, melted
500 g (8 oz) cream cheese, softened
2/3 cup (160 g/5 1/2 oz) caster sugar
1 teaspoon vanilla essence
1 tablespoon lemon juice
4 eggs

Topping
1 cup (250 g/8 oz) sour cream
1/2 teaspoon vanilla essence
3 teaspoons lemon juice
1 tablespoon caster sugar
nutmeg, to sprinkle

1 Line the base of a 20 cm (8 inch) round springform tin with foil and brush it with oil. Finely crush the biscuits in a food processor for 30 seconds, or put in a plastic bag and roll with a rolling pin. Transfer to a bowl and add the mixed spice and butter. Stir until the crumbs are all moistened, then spoon the mixture into the tin and press it firmly into the base and side. Refrigerate for 20 minutes, or until firm.
2 Preheat the oven to moderate 180°C (350°F/Gas 4). Beat the cream cheese until smooth. Add the sugar, vanilla and lemon juice, and beat until smooth. Add the eggs, one at a time, beating well after each addition.
3 Pour the mixture into the tin and bake for 45 minutes, or until just firm to the touch.
4 To make the topping, combine the sour cream, vanilla, lemon juice and sugar in a bowl. Spread over the hot cheesecake, sprinkle with the nutmeg and return to the oven for a further 7 minutes. Cool, then refrigerate until firm.

VARIATION: To make a baked chocolate cheesecake, make the crumb base with butter, plain chocolate biscuits, a pinch of ground cinnamon and 1/2 teaspoon instant coffee powder. For the filling, mix together 500 g (1 lb) cream cheese, 2 eggs, 125 g (4 oz) sugar, 1/2 teaspoon vanilla essence, 1 tablespoon cocoa powder, 225 g (7 oz) melted cooking chocolate, 375 g (12 oz) sour cream and 45 g (1 1/2 oz) melted butter. Pour into the crust and

Our BAKED CHEESECAKE has a sour cream topping.

CHEESECAKES made with gelatine do not require cooking. Just leave in the fridge to set.

bake as above. You will not need a separate topping. Chill for 6 hours before serving.

CHEESECAKE

Preparation: 30 minutes + refrigeration
Cooking: 5 minutes
Serves 6–8

250 g (8 oz) plain sweet biscuits
125 g (4 oz) butter, melted
3 teaspoons gelatine
250 g (8 oz) cream cheese
1/3 cup (80 ml/23/4 fl oz) lemon juice
1 teaspoon grated lemon rind
1/2 cup (125 g/4 oz) caster sugar
1 cup (250 ml/8 fl oz) cream, whipped

1 Lightly grease a 20 cm springform tin with oil or melted butter. Line the base with baking paper. Finely crush the biscuits in a food processor or in a bag with a rolling pin. Mix together with the melted butter. Press into the base and side of the tin and refrigerate for 10 minutes.

2 Sprinkle the gelatine over 2 tablespoons water in a small bowl. Place over a pan or bowl of hot water and leave until spongy. Stir until dissolved. Beat the cream cheese, lemon juice, rind and sugar with electric beaters for 4–5 minutes, or until smooth. Add the cooled gelatine to the bowl and beat well.

3 Using a large metal spoon, fold the whipped cream into the cream cheese mixture. Spoon evenly into the tin, carefully smooth the surface and refrigerate until set.

The furrows in the side of the FRESH FRUIT PAVLOVA stop it crumbling and give a decorative look.

FRESH FRUIT PAVLOVA

Preparation: 15 minutes
Cooking: 40 minutes
Serves 6–8

4 egg whites
1 cup (250 g/8 oz) caster sugar
1 1/2 cups (375 ml/ 12 fl oz) cream, whipped
1 banana, sliced
125 g (4 oz) raspberries
125 g (4 oz) blueberries

1 Preheat the oven to slow 150°C (300°F/ Gas 2). Line a large baking tray with baking paper and draw a 20 cm (8 inch) circle on the paper. Beat the egg whites with electric beaters in a large dry bowl until soft peaks form—any hint of grease will prevent the egg whites foaming. Gradually add the sugar, beating well after each addition. Beat for 5–10 minutes, or until all the sugar has completely dissolved.
2 Spread the meringue mixture onto the tray inside the circle. Shape the meringue evenly, running the flat side of a flat-bladed knife along the edge and over the top.
3 Run the knife up the edge of the meringue all the way round, making furrows. This strengthens the pavlova, stops the edge crumbling and gives it a decorative finish.
4 Bake for 30 minutes, or until the pavlova is pale and crisp. Reduce the heat to very slow 120°C (250°F/Gas 1/2) and bake for a further 10 minutes. Turn off the oven and leave the pavlova inside to cool, using a wooden spoon to keep the door ajar. Top with the whipped cream and arrange the banana, raspberries and blueberries on top.

STORAGE: Pavlova is best eaten on the day it is made. Serve immediately once the pavlova is topped with the cream and fruit.

GRANDMA'S PAVLOVA

Preparation: 30 minutes
Cooking: 1 hour
Serves 6–8

4 egg whites
pinch of salt
1 cup (250 g/8 oz) sugar
2 teaspoons cornflour
1 teaspoon white vinegar
1 cup (250 ml/8 fl oz) cream, whipped
pulp from 3 passionfruit
strawberries, for decoration

1 Preheat the oven to very hot 240°C (475°F/ Gas 9) and lightly grease a 32 x 28 cm (13 x 11 inch) baking tray. Line the tray with a very wet piece of brown paper.
2 Place the egg whites and salt in a small, dry mixing bowl. Using electric beaters, beat until stiff peaks form. Add the sugar gradually, beating constantly after each addition. Beat until the mixture is thick and glossy, and all the sugar has dissolved.
3 Using a metal spoon, fold in the cornflour and vinegar. Spoon the mixture into a mound on the tray. Lightly flatten the top of the pavlova and smooth the sides. (This pavlova should have a cake shape and be about 2.5 cm/1 inch high.)
4 Reduce the oven to warm 160°C (315°F/ Gas 2–3). Bake the pavlova for 1 hour, or until it is pale cream and crisp. Remove the pavlova from the oven while it is warm, then carefully turn it upside down onto a plate and peel away the paper. (If the pavlova is cold, the paper will stick. It may crack slightly underneath but this is normal.) Leave the pavlova to cool.
5 Spread the soft centre of the pavlova with whipped cream. Decorate with the passionfruit pulp and some whole strawberries. Cut into wedges to serve.

GRANDMA'S PAVLOVA has a more chewy, less brittle meringue.

FRUIT FOOL

Preparation: 15 minutes + refrigeration
Cooking: Nil
Serves 4

2 red pawpaw or papaya, about 1 kg (2 lb)
1–2 tablespoons lime juice
3 tablespoons vanilla sugar
1 1/4 cups (315 ml/10 fl oz) cream

1 Peel and seed the pawpaw and mash the flesh until smooth. Do not do this in a food processor or it will be too runny.
2 Add the lime juice and vanilla sugar, to taste—according to the sweetness of the fruit.
3 Whisk the cream until soft peaks form, then fold through the mashed pawpaw. Spoon into serving glasses and chill until ready to serve.

VARIATIONS: For rhubarb fool, use 500 g (1 lb) stewed rhubarb instead of the pawpaw. For mango fool, purée 3 large mangoes in a food processor, process with 1 cup (250 ml/8 fl oz) custard, then fold in 1 2/3 cups (410 ml/13 fl oz) whipped cream.

FRUIT FOOL, made using pawpaw and lime juice.

BLACKBERRY JELLY

Preparation: 10 minutes + 4 hours refrigeration
Cooking: 20 minutes
Serves 6–8

300 g (10 oz) fresh blackberries, or thawed frozen blackberries
3/4 cup (185 g/6 oz) caster sugar
3 tablespoons vodka, optional
3 tablespoons gelatine

1 Place the blackberries (with any juice), caster sugar, vodka and 1 litre water in a pan. Stir over low heat until the sugar has dissolved. Cover and bring to the boil, then reduce the heat and simmer for 15 minutes. Uncover and cool for 10 minutes.
2 Place the fruit in a muslin-lined sieve and strain into a bowl without pushing any fruit through. Put a little of the juice in a small pan, sprinkle the gelatine in an even layer over the surface, leave to go spongy, then stir over low heat until dissolved. Do not boil. Combine with the remaining juice.
3 Wet a 1.25 litre jelly mould and pour in the jelly mixture. Refrigerate for 4 hours, or until set.

PEACH MELBA

Preparation: 25 minutes
Cooking: 10 minutes
Serves 4

300 g (10 oz) fresh raspberries, or thawed frozen raspberries
2 tablespoons icing sugar
1 1/2 cups (375 g/12 oz) sugar
1 vanilla bean, split lengthways
4 firm ripe peaches
vanilla ice cream, to serve

1 Put the raspberries and icing sugar in a food processor and purée. Pass through a strainer and discard the seeds. Stir the sugar, vanilla bean and 2 1/2 cups (600 ml/20 fl oz) water in a pan over low heat until the sugar has completely dissolved.
2 Bring the sugar syrup to the boil and add the peaches, ensuring they are covered with the syrup. Simmer for 5 minutes, or until tender, then remove the peaches with a slotted spoon and carefully remove the skin.
3 Put a scoop of ice cream on a plate, add a peach then spoon the raspberry purée over the top.

BLACKBERRY JELLY, with optional vodka for the adults!

PEACH MELBA—named in honour of Dame Nellie Melba.

LEMON DELICIOUS

Preparation: 20 minutes
Cooking: 1 hour
Serves 4

60 g (2 oz) butter
3/4 cup (185 g/6 oz) caster sugar
3 eggs, separated
1 teaspoon grated lemon rind
1/3 cup (40 g/1 1/4 oz) self-raising flour, sifted
1/4 cup (60 ml/2 fl oz) lemon juice
3/4 cup (185 ml/6 fl oz) milk
icing sugar, to dust

1 Preheat the oven to moderate 180°C (350°F/Gas 4). Brush a 1 litre ovenproof dish with oil. Using electric beaters, beat the butter, sugar, egg yolks and lemon rind in a small bowl until the mixture is light and creamy. Transfer to a larger mixing bowl.
2 Add the flour and stir with a wooden spoon until just combined. Add the lemon juice and milk, and stir in gently.
3 Place the egg whites in a clean, dry bowl. Using electric beaters, beat until firm peaks form. Add to the lemon mixture and gently fold in until just combined, using a metal spoon.
4 Spoon the mixture into the dish. Place the dish in a deep baking tray and pour boiling water into the tray to come a third of the way up the side of the dish. Bake for 1 hour. Sprinkle with the sifted icing sugar. Serve with some of the sauce spooned over the top.

NOTE: It is important to beat egg whites in a clean dry bowl. The slightest hint of grease or moisture will prevent the egg whites foaming. Any yolk in the whites will do likewise.

Sprinkle the LEMON DELICIOUS with icing sugar to serve.

CLAFOUTIS is a classic French batter pudding, and very simple to make.

CHERRY CLAFOUTIS

Preparation: 15 minutes
Cooking: 35 minutes
Serves 6–8

500 g (1 lb) fresh cherries, or 800 g (1 lb 10 oz) can pitted cherries, well drained
1/2 cup (60 g/2 oz) plain flour
1/3 cup (90 g/3 oz) sugar
4 eggs, lightly beaten
1 cup (250 ml/8 fl oz) milk
25 g (3/4 oz) butter, melted
icing sugar, to dust

1 Preheat the oven to moderate 180°C (350°F/Gas 4). Brush a 23 cm (9 inch) glass or ceramic shallow pie plate with melted butter.
2 Pit the cherries and spread into the dish in a single layer. If using canned cherries, drain them thoroughly in a sieve before spreading in the dish. If they are still wet, they will leak into the batter.
3 Sift the flour into a bowl, add the sugar and make a well in the centre. Gradually add the combined eggs, milk and butter, whisking until smooth and free of lumps.
4 Pour the batter over the cherries and bake for 30–35 minutes. The batter should be risen and golden. Dust with icing sugar. Serve immediately, with cream.

NOTE: A clafoutis (pronounced 'clafootee') is a classic French batter pudding, a speciality of the Limousin region. Clafoutis comes from 'clafir', a dialect verb meaning 'to fill'. It is traditionally made with cherries but you could use blueberries, blackberries, raspberries, or small, well-flavoured strawberries may be used. Use a shallow pie dish or the top will not brown.

RICH CHOCOLATE SELF-SAUCING PUDDING

Preparation: 20 minutes
Cooking: 55 minutes
Serves 6–8

1 1/2 cups (185 g/6 oz) self-raising flour
1/4 cup (30 g/1 oz) cocoa powder
3/4 cup (1850 g/6 oz) caster sugar
90 g (3 oz) butter, melted
3/4 cup (185 ml/6 fl oz) milk
2 eggs, lightly beaten

Sauce
1 1/2 cups (375 ml/12 fl oz) milk
185 g (6 oz) dark chocolate, chopped

1 Preheat the oven to moderate 180°C (350°F/Gas 4) and grease a deep 2.25 litre ovenproof dish. Sift the flour and cocoa into a large mixing bowl. Add the sugar and make a well in the centre.
2 Add the butter and combined milk and eggs. Using a wooden spoon, stir until all the ingredients are just combined and the mixture is smooth, but do not overbeat. Pour the mixture into the prepared dish.
3 To make the sauce, put the milk, chocolate and 1 cup (250 ml/8 fl oz) water in a small pan. Stir over low heat until the chocolate has melted and the mixture is smooth.
4 Pour the sauce gently over the pudding mixture. Bake for 45–50 minutes, or until the pudding is firm to the touch. Serve with cream or ice cream and fresh fruit, if desired.

STORAGE: Self-saucing puddings are best served immediately.

RICH CHOCOLATE SELF-SAUCING PUDDING.

STICKY DATE PUDDING

Preparation: 30 minutes
Cooking: 1 hour 10 minutes
Serves 6–8

2 cups (370 g/12 oz) chopped pitted dates
1 1/2 teaspoons bicarbonate of soda
1 teaspoon grated fresh ginger
90 g (3 oz) butter
1 cup (250 g/8 oz) caster sugar
3 eggs
1 1/2 cups (185 g/6 oz) self-raising flour
pinch of ground cloves
1/2 teaspoon mixed spice

Caramel sauce

150 g (5 oz) butter
1 cup (185 g/6 oz) soft brown sugar
1/3 cup (115 g/4 oz) golden syrup
3/4 cup (185 ml/6 fl oz) cream

1 Preheat the oven to moderate 180°C (350°F/Gas 4). Grease and line the base of a deep 23 cm (9 inch) round cake tin. Put the dates in a pan with 1 3/4 cups (440 ml/14 fl oz) water, bring to the boil, then remove from the heat. Add the bicarbonate of soda and ginger, and leave for 5 minutes. Coarsely mash with a potato masher.
2 Cream the butter, sugar and 1 egg. Beat in the remaining eggs one at a time. Fold in the sifted flour and spices, add the date mixture and stir until well combined. Pour into the tin and bake for 1 hour, or until a skewer comes out clean when inserted into the middle of the pudding. Cover with foil if the pudding is overbrowning. Leave to stand for 5 minutes before turning out onto a plate.
3 To make the caramel sauce, put all the ingredients in a pan and stir over low heat until the sugar has dissolved. Simmer for about 3 minutes, or until the sauce has thickened slightly. Brush some sauce over the top and sides of the pudding until it is well glazed. Serve immediately with the sauce and cream.

VARIATION: For a quick-mix steamed pudding, grease the base and side of a 1 litre pudding basin. Place a round of baking paper in the bottom of the basin. Put the empty basin in a large pan on a trivet or upturned saucer and pour in enough cold water to come halfway up the side of the basin. Remove the basin and put the water on to boil. Sift 150 g (5 oz) self-raising flour into a bowl. Add a pinch of salt, 120 g (4 oz) softenened butter, 150 g (5 oz) sugar and 3 eggs and beat to combine. For chocolate pudding, add 2 tablespoons cocoa and 90 g (3 oz) choc bits. For treacle pudding, add 2 tablespoons treacle. Pour into the basin. Lay a sheet of foil on a work surface, cover with a sheet of baking paper and make a pleat in the middle. Grease the paper and place over the top of the basin. Tie string around the rim and over the top. Lower the basin into the boiling water and cover tightly. Cook for 1 3/4 hours, topping up the water as necessary.

Serve STICKY DATE PUDDING with cream or crème fraîche.

CREME CARAMEL

Preparation: 25 minutes + 6 hours refrigeration
Cooking: 35 minutes
Serves 8

1 cup (250 g/8 oz) sugar

Custard
1 litre milk, warmed
1/2 cup (125 g/4 oz) sugar
6 eggs
1 1/2 teaspoons vanilla essence

1 Preheat the oven to moderate 180°C (350°F/ Gas 4). Grease eight 1/2 cup (125 ml/4 fl oz) ramekins.
2 Put the sugar in a pan with 1/4 cup (60 ml/2 fl oz) water. Stir over low heat until the sugar has dissolved. Bring to the boil, then reduce the heat and simmer until the mixture turns golden brown. To avoid a burnt flavour, remove the pan from the heat just before the caramel reaches the desired colour. It will continue to darken even after cooking has finished. Pour a little hot mixture into each ramekin and swirl to cover the base. Set aside.
3 To make the custard, put the milk and sugar in a pan and stir gently over low heat until the sugar has dissolved. Whisk together the eggs and vanilla for 2 minutes, then stir in the warm milk. Strain the mixture into a jug and pour it into the ramekins.
4 Place the ramekins in a deep baking dish. Pour hot water into the baking dish to come halfway up the sides of the ramekins. Bake for 30 minutes, or until the custard is set and a knife comes out clean when inserted into the centre. Allow to cool, then refrigerate for at least 6 hours. To unmould, run a knife around the edge of each custard and gently upturn onto a serving plate. Shake gently to remove, if necessary. Serve with whipped cream, fresh fruit and wafers, if desired.

STORAGE: Can be kept in the fridge for up to 1 day.
VARIATIONS: The custard for crème caramel can be flavoured with spices such as cardamom, cinnamon and nutmeg, with lemon or orange rind, or with your favourite spirit or liqueur.

Chill CREME CARAMEL for six hours before serving.

CHOCOLATE MOUSSE

Preparation: 20 minutes + 2 hours refrigeration
Cooking: 5 minutes
Serves 4

250 g (8 oz) good-quality dark chocolate, chopped
3 eggs
1/4 cup (60 g/2 oz) caster sugar
1 cup (250 ml/8 fl oz) cream, softly whipped

1 Put the chocolate in a heatproof bowl. Half fill a saucepan with water and bring to a simmer. Remove from the heat and place the bowl over the pan, making sure it is not sitting in the water. Stir occasionally until the chocolate has melted. Set aside to cool slightly.
2 Meanwhile, using electric beaters, beat the eggs and sugar in a small bowl for 5 minutes, or until the mixture is thick, pale and increased in volume.
3 Transfer the mixture to a large bowl. Using a metal spoon, fold in the melted chocolate and then leave the mixture to cool. Fold in the whipped cream until just combined.
4 Spoon into four 250 ml (8 fl oz) ramekins or dessert glasses and refrigerate for 2 hours, or until set, before serving.

Use good-quality chocolate for CHOCOLATE MOUSSE.

VARIATION: For a rich chocolate mousse without using cream, try this simple variation. It will make enough for six people. Break 175 g (6 oz) dark chocolate into pieces and place it in a heatproof bowl. Bring a small pan of water to a simmer, remove from the heat and place the bowl over the pan (don't let the base of the bowl sit in the water). Stir until the chocolate melts. Separate 5 eggs and put the whites in a large clean glass bowl. Cool the chocolate a little and gently stir in the egg yolks. Whisk the egg whites with a balloon whisk or electric beaters until they are stiff, add one tablespoon of the egg whites to the chocolate mixture and mix it in well. Add the chocolate mixture to the remaining egg whites and fold the whites into the chocolate, making sure you do not lose too much volume. Divide the mixture among six 150 ml (5 oz) ramekins. Chill in the refrigerator for 4 hours, or until set.

Serve POACHED PEARS with thick cream or mascarpone.

POACHED PEARS

Preparation: 10 minutes
Cooking: 1 hour 10 minutes
Serves 4

4 large beurre bosc or Josephine pears
1 1/2 cups (375 ml/12 fl oz) sweet dessert wine (Sauternes; Muscat)
3/4 cup (185 g/6 oz) sugar
1 vanilla pod, split lengthways
1 cinnamon stick

1 Peel the pears, keeping the stalks attached. Put 1 1/2 cups (375 ml/12 fl oz) water in a large pan with the wine, sugar, vanilla pod and cinnamon. Stir over medium heat until the sugar has dissolved. Bring to the boil and simmer for 5 minutes. Stand the pears upright in the syrup and gently spoon over a little syrup to coat them.
2 Cover and simmer gently for 30–40 minutes, or until tender. Test if they are cooked by piercing with a sharp knife. Remove from the pan with a slotted spoon.
3 Remove the vanilla pod and cinnamon stick. Bring the syrup to the boil, then boil rapidly for 15 minutes, or until reduced by half. Pour over the pears to serve.

APPLE STRUDEL

Preparation: 20 minutes
Cooking: 25 minutes
Serves 6

30 g (1 oz) butter
4 green cooking apples, peeled and thinly sliced
2 tablespoons orange juice
1 tablespoon honey
3 tablespoons sugar
1/2 cup (60 g/2 oz) sultanas
2 sheets ready-rolled puff pastry
3 tablespoons ground almonds
1 egg, lightly beaten
2 tablespoons soft brown sugar
1 teaspoon ground cinnamon

1 Preheat the oven to hot 220°C (425°F/Gas 7). Brush two oven trays with melted butter. Heat the butter in a pan and cook the apples for 2 minutes, or until lightly golden. Add the orange juice, honey, sugar and sultanas and stir until the sugar dissolves and the apples are just tender. Leave to cool completely.
2 Place a sheet of pastry on the work surface. Fold in half and make small cuts in the folded edge at 2 cm (1 inch) intervals. Open out and sprinkle with half the almonds.

APPLE STRUDEL.

BAKED APPLES.

Drain the apples and place half in the centre of the pastry. Brush the edges with egg and fold together, pressing firmly.
3 Place the strudel on the baking tray, seam-side-down. Brush with egg and sprinkle with half the sugar and cinnamon. Repeat with the other sheet and filling. Bake for 20–25 minutes until crisp.

HINT: For quick strudel, spread canned apple along one edge of a sheet of puff pastry. Sprinkle with sugar and sultanas, fold over the pastry to enclose, brush with egg yolk, cut holes in the top and bake for 20 minutes.

BAKED APPLES

Preparation: 20 minutes
Cooking: 40 minutes
Serves 4

4 Granny Smith apples, peeled and cored
1/4 cup (55 g/2 oz) raw sugar
1/4 cup (40 g/1 1/4 oz) dried figs, chopped
1/4 cup (45 g/1 1/2 oz) dried apricots, chopped
1/4 cup (30 g/1 oz) slivered almonds
1 tablespoon apricot jam
1/4 teaspoon ground cardamom
1/4 teaspoon ground cinnamon
30 g (1 oz) butter

1 Preheat the oven to moderate 180°C (350°F/Gas 4). Brush a deep ovenproof dish with melted butter.
2 Gently roll the apples in the sugar. Mix together the figs, apricots, almonds, jam and spices, stuff into the apples and put in the dish. Dot with butter. Bake for 35–40 minutes, or until tender. Serve immediately.

NOTE: This is an excellent quick stand-by dessert for emergencies. You do not even need to peel the apples.

ENGLISH TRIFLE

Preparation: 15 minutes + overnight refrigeration
Cooking: 10 minutes
Serves 6

85 g (3 oz) packet port wine jelly crystals
2 tablespoons custard powder
1 tablespoon caster sugar
2 cups (500 ml/16 fl oz) milk
250 g (8 oz) Madeira cake, cut into cubes
1/3 cup (80 ml/2 3/4 fl oz) sherry
425 g (14 oz) can sliced peaches in syrup
whipped cream and toasted flaked almonds

1 Dissolve the jelly in 2 cups (500 ml/16 fl oz) boiling water. Pour into a shallow dish and refrigerate until set. Cut into bite-sized cubes.
2 Combine the custard powder and sugar, and gradually stir in the milk until smooth. Stir over medium heat for 5 minutes, or until the mixture boils and thickens. Remove from the heat and cover the surface with baking paper to prevent a skin forming.
3 Put the cake cubes in a 1-litre glass bowl. Sprinkle with the sherry. Drain the peaches, reserving half the syrup. Brush the syrup over the cake. Pour half the custard over the cake. Top with the jelly, peaches and remaining custard. Top with the whipped cream and almonds. Leave in the fridge overnight.

VARIATION: It is very easy to vary the base of a trifle. Instead of the Madeira cake, try sliced jam roll, swiss roll or chocolate cake. Alternatively, soak crushed biscuits such as sponge fingers or macaroons in sherry or sweet wine and use instead of the cake.

Use cubed Madeira cake as the base for your ENGLISH TRIFLE.

LATTICE BERRY PIE

Preparation: 20 minutes + 20 minutes refrigeration
Cooking: 55 minutes
Serves 6

- 2 cups (250 g/8 oz) plain flour
- 150 g (5 oz) cold butter, cubed
- 1 egg, lightly beaten
- 3 tablespoons ground almonds
- 2 tablespoons caster sugar
- 1 teaspoon ground cinnamon
- 1 kg (2 lb) fresh or frozen mixed berries
- 1 egg, lightly beaten, extra

You could also use canned peaches or apples in a LATTICE PIE.

1 Place the flour and butter in a bowl and rub in the butter with your fingertips until fine and crumbly. Add the egg and mix with a knife until the dough just comes together, adding a little chilled water if necessary. Turn out onto a lightly floured surface and gather together.

2 Roll out half the dough to line a deep 19 cm (7½ inch) fluted flan tin. Chill for 20 minutes. Roll out the other portion to a 24 cm (10 inch) circle. Cut into 1.5 cm (⅝ inch) wide strips with a fluted pastry wheel. Lay half the strips 2 cm (1 inch) apart on a sheet of baking paper. Interweave the remaining strips to make a lattice. Slide onto a baking tray, cover with plastic wrap and chill.

3 Preheat the oven to moderate 180°C (350°F/Gas 3). Line the pastry shell with crumpled baking paper, fill with baking beads or rice and bake for 10 minutes. Remove the paper and beads and bake the pastry for 10 minutes, or until golden. Leave to cool.

4 Mix together the almonds, sugar and cinnamon and sprinkle into the pastry shell. Spread the berries over the top. Brush the edge of the pastry with egg. Using the baking paper to help, invert the lattice over the top of the tart and trim the edge. Press the edge lightly to seal to the cooked pastry. Brush the top with egg and bake for 35 minutes, or until golden.

LEMON MERINGUE PIE

Preparation: 40 minutes
Cooking: 25 minutes
Serves 8

185 g (6 oz) packet shortcrust pastry mix

Lemon filling

1 cup (250 g/8 oz) sugar
1/2 cup (60 g/2 oz) cornflour
2 teaspoons grated lemon rind
3/4 cup (185 ml/6 fl oz) lemon juice
60 g (2 oz) butter, chopped
3 egg yolks

Meringue

3 egg whites
1/2 cup (125 g/4 oz) caster sugar

1 Preheat the oven to hot 210°C (415°F/Gas 6–7). Prepare the pastry according to the instructions on the packet (you will probably have to buy a 340 g/11 oz packet of pastry mix and use half of it). Roll the pastry out thinly to cover the base and side of a 23 cm (9 inch) pie plate. Cut a sheet of greaseproof paper large enough to cover the pastry-lined plate. Spread a layer of baking beads or rice over the paper. Bake for 7 minutes, then discard the paper and beads. Bake the pastry for a further 7 minutes, or until lightly golden. Allow to cool.

2 To make the filling, combine the sugar, cornflour and lemon rind in a pan. Blend in the lemon juice and 1 1/2 cups (375 ml/12 fl oz) water, and stir until smooth. Stir over medium-high heat for 2 minutes, or until the mixture boils and becomes very thick. Add the butter and stir over the heat for 1 minute, or until the butter has melted. Remove from the heat, quickly add the egg yolks and whisk until combined. Place a piece of baking paper over the surface of the filling and leave to cool. Spread evenly into the pastry shell.

3 To make the meringue, put the egg whites in a small dry bowl (any hint of grease in the bowl will prevent the whites foaming). Using electric beaters, beat until soft peaks form. Add the sugar gradually, beating until the mixture is thick and glossy, and the sugar has dissolved. Spread over the filling. Bake for 5 minutes, then cool before serving.

LEMON MERINGUE PIE.

APPLE PIE

Preparation: 35 minutes
Cooking: 1 hour
Serves 6

2 cups (250 g/8 oz) plain flour
1/4 cup (30 g/1 oz) icing sugar
185 g (6 oz) cold butter, cubed
2 egg yolks
milk, for glazing
caster sugar, for sprinkling

Filling
4–5 green cooking apples, sliced
3/4 cup (160 g/5 1/2 oz) caster sugar
1/2 teaspoon ground cinnamon
6 whole cloves
1 tablespoon marmalade
30 g (1 oz) butter

1 Grease a 23 cm (9 inch) pie dish. Place the flour, icing sugar and butter in a bowl and rub in the butter with your fingertips until fine and crumbly. Add the egg and mix with a knife until the dough just comes together, adding a little chilled water if necessary. Turn out onto a lightly floured surface and gather together into a ball.
2 Divide the dough into two portions, one slightly larger than the other. Roll the larger portion between two sheets of baking paper to fit the pie dish, then trim the edge. Roll the remaining pastry on a sheet of baking paper to fit the top of the dish. Cover both pastries and refrigerate while making the filling.
3 To make the filling, combine the apple, sugar, cinnamon and cloves with 2 tablespoons water in a large pan. Cover and cook over low heat, stirring occasionally, for 20 minutes, or until the apple has just softened. Remove from the heat and pour off any juice. Remove the cloves. Add the marmalade and butter to the pan, mix and cool.
4 Preheat the oven to hot 210°C (415°F/Gas 6–7). Pile the apple into the pastry-lined pie dish. Brush the pie rim with milk or water. Place the pastry lid over the apple and seal the edge with a fork, trimming any excess. Cut shapes from the leftover pastry trimmings and place on top of the pie. Slash a couple of small holes in the pastry to allow steam to escape. Brush the pie with milk and sprinkle with caster sugar. Bake for 10 minutes. Reduce the oven to moderate 180°C (350°F/Gas 4) and bake for 30 minutes, or until golden brown.

APPLE PIE is delicious hot from the oven, or as cold picnic food.

FARMHOUSE RHUBARB PIE

Preparation: 40 minutes + refrigeration
Cooking: 50 minutes
Serves 6

1 1/2 cups (185 g/6 oz) plain flour, sifted
125 g (4 oz) chilled butter, chopped
2 tablespoons icing sugar
1 egg yolk
1 cup (250 g/8 oz) sugar
6 cups (750 g/1 1/2 lb) chopped rhubarb
2 cups (220 g/7 oz) sliced apple
2 teaspoons grated lemon rind
3 pieces preserved ginger, sliced
2 teaspoons sugar, extra
sprinkle of cinnamon
icing sugar, to dust

1 Place the flour, butter and icing sugar in a bowl and rub in the butter with your fingertips until fine and crumbly. Add the egg yolk and mix with a knife until the dough just comes together, adding a little chilled water if necessary.
2 Turn out onto a lightly floured surface and gather together. Wrap in plastic wrap and refrigerate for 15 minutes if very soft. Preheat the oven to moderately hot 190°C (375°F/Gas 5). Roll the pastry out to a 35 cm (14 inch) circle and fit into a greased 20 cm (8 inch) pie plate, leaving the pastry hanging over the edge. Chill while you make the filling.
3 Heat the sugar and 1/2 cup (125 ml/4 fl oz) water in a pan for 5 minutes, or until syrupy. Add the rhubarb, apple, lemon rind and ginger, then cover and simmer for 5 minutes, or until the rhubarb is cooked but still holds its shape.
4 Drain off the liquid and cool the rhubarb. Spoon into the pastry base and sprinkle with the extra sugar and the cinnamon. Fold the overhanging pastry roughly over the fruit and bake for 40 minutes, or until golden. Dust with icing sugar to serve. Delicious with ice cream or custard.

FARMHOUSE RHUBARB PIE is a simple, freeform pastry pie.

SUMMER BERRY FLAN

Preparation: 35 minutes + 20 minutes refrigeration
Cooking: 35 minutes
Serves 4–6

1 cup (125 g/4 oz) plain flour
90 g (3 oz) butter
2 tablespoons icing sugar

We used strawberries, blueberries and raspberries for our SUMMER BERRY FLAN.

Filling

3 egg yolks
2 tablespoons caster sugar
2 tablespoons cornflour
1 cup (250 ml/8 fl oz) milk
1 teaspoon vanilla essence
250 g (8 oz) strawberries, halved
125 g (4 oz) blueberries
125 g (4 oz) raspberries
1–2 tablespoons baby apple gel

1 Preheat the oven to moderate 180°C (350°F/Gas 4). Place the flour, butter and icing sugar in a bowl and rub in the butter with your fingertips until fine and crumbly. Add 1–2 tablespoons chilled water and mix with a knife until the dough just comes together. Turn out onto a lightly floured surface and gather together.

2 Roll the pastry out to fit a 20 cm (8 inch) fluted flan tin. Trim and refrigerate for 20 minutes. Cover with crumpled greaseproof paper. Spread a layer of baking beads or rice evenly over the paper. Bake for 15 minutes, then discard the paper and beads. Bake for another 15 minutes, or until the pastry is lightly golden.

3 To make the filling, put the egg yolks, sugar and cornflour in a bowl, and whisk until pale. Heat the milk in a small pan until it is almost boiling, then remove from the heat. Add to the egg mixture gradually, beating constantly. Strain into a pan. Stir over low heat for 3 minutes, or until it boils and thickens. Add the vanilla, transfer to a bowl and cover the surface with plastic wrap. Cool.

4 Spread the filling into the cooled pastry shell. Top with the strawberries, blueberries and raspberries. Heat the apple gel in a pan of simmering water, or in the microwave, until it liquefies and brush over the fruit to glaze.

PECAN PIE

Preparation: 30 minutes + 20 minutes refrigeration
Cooking: 1¼ hours
Serves 6

1½ cups (185 g/6 oz) plain flour
125 g (4 oz) butter, chopped
2–3 tablespoons iced water

Filling
2 cups (200 g/6½ oz) pecans
3 eggs, lightly beaten
50 g (1¾ oz) butter, melted and cooled
⅔ cup (125 g/4 oz) brown sugar
⅔ cup (170 ml/5½ fl oz) light corn syrup
1 teaspoon vanilla essence
pinch of salt

Bourbon cream
1 cup (250 ml/8 fl oz) cream
1 tablespoon icing sugar
2 tablespoons Bourbon

1 Preheat the oven to moderate 180°C (350°F/Gas 4). Place the flour and butter in a bowl and rub in the butter with your fingertips until fine and crumbly. Add the iced water and mix with a knife until the dough just comes together. Turn out onto a lightly floured surface and gather together.
2 Roll out the pastry to fit a 23 cm (9 inch) flan tin. Trim the edge and refrigerate for 20 minutes. Pile the pastry trimmings together and roll out on a sheet of baking paper to a rectangle about 2 mm (⅛ inch) thick. Refrigerate until needed.
3 Cut a sheet of greaseproof paper large enough to cover the pastry-lined tin. Crumple the paper, lay over the pastry base and spread with a layer of baking beads or uncooked rice. Bake for 15 minutes. Discard the paper and baking beads and bake the pastry base for another 15 minutes, or until lightly golden. Allow to cool completely.
4 To make the filling, spread the pecans over the pastry base. In a large jug, whisk together the eggs, butter, brown sugar, corn syrup, vanilla and salt until well combined. Pour the mixture over the nuts.
5 Using a fluted pastry wheel or small sharp knife, cut narrow strips from half the pastry. Cut out small stars with a biscuit cutter from the remaining pastry. Place over the filling. Bake for 45 minutes, or until firm. Cool completely and serve at room temperature.

PECAN PIE is a traditional American favourite.

6 To make the bourbon cream, put the cream and icing sugar in a small bowl. Using electric beaters, whip until soft peaks form. Add the Bourbon and fold through with a metal spoon until it is just combined with the cream. Serve with the Pecan pie.

STORAGE: The pie can be kept refrigerated for up to a day.
NOTE: The pecan is native to North America and is much used in the cooking of the American South.

TIRAMISU

Preparation: 30 minutes + 2 hours refrigeration
Cooking: Nil
Serves 6–8

- **3 cups (750 ml/24 fl oz) strong black coffee, cooled**
- **3 tablespoons dark rum**
- **2 eggs, separated**
- **1/4 cup (60 g/2 oz) caster sugar**
- **250 g (8 oz) mascarpone**
- **1 cup (250 ml/8 fl oz) cream, whipped**
- **16 large savoyardi (sponge finger) biscuits**
- **2 teaspoons dark cocoa powder**

TIRAMISU means 'pick-me-up' in Italian.

1 Put the coffee and rum in a bowl. Using electric beaters, beat the egg yolks and sugar in a small bowl for 3 minutes, or until thick and pale. Add the mascarpone and beat until just combined. Fold in the whipped cream with a metal spoon.
2 Beat the egg whites until soft peaks form. Fold quickly and lightly into the cream mixture with a metal spoon, trying not to lose the volume.
3 Dip half the biscuits, one at a time, into the coffee mixture (don't leave them to soak or they will become soggy and break up). Drain off any excess liquid and arrange the biscuits in the base of a deep serving dish. Spread half the mascarpone cream mixture over the biscuits.
4 Dip the remaining biscuits in the coffee mixture and repeat the layers. Smooth the surface and dust liberally with cocoa powder. Refrigerate for at least 2 hours (and up to a day) to let the flavours develop.

CREPES SUZETTE is a traditional French dessert.

CREPES SUZETTE

Preparation: 30 minutes + 30 minutes resting
Cooking: 30–40 minutes
Serves 4

1 cup (125 g/4 oz) plain flour
1 cup (250 ml/8 fl oz) milk
1 egg
30 g (1 oz) butter, melted

Orange butter
200 g (6½ oz) softened butter
2 tablespoons finely grated orange rind
⅓ cup (90 g/3 oz) sugar
2 tablespoons icing sugar
½ cup (125 ml/4 fl oz) orange juice
¼ cup (60 ml/2 fl oz) Grand Marnier

1 Sift the flour into a bowl and make a well in the centre. Mix together the milk, egg and butter and pour into the well in the flour. Whisk together until the batter is smooth and free of lumps. Pour into a jug, cover and leave for at least 30 minutes.
2 To make the orange butter, beat the butter with electric beaters or a wooden spoon until creamy. Add the rind, sugar and icing sugar, and beat well. Add the combined orange juice and Grand Marnier, ½ teaspoon at a time, beating well after each addition.
3 Heat a small crepe pan and lightly grease with melted butter. Pour in just enough batter, swirling, to thinly cover the base of the pan. Cook for about 20 seconds, or until the edges just begin to curl. Turn the crepe over and lightly brown the other side. Cook the rest of the crepes, greasing the pan when necessary.
4 Place the orange butter in a large frying pan and heat until foaming. Working quickly with tongs, dip the crepes, one at a time, into the pan, then fold into quarters. Serve with ice cream.

NOTE: For traditional Crêpes Suzette, dip each crepe in the orange butter and fold in the pan, then push to one side, continuing until all crepes are folded in the pan. Pour over a little liqueur and flambé with a match.
VARIATION: This is a basic crepe batter. The crepes can be used for other recipes or simply served with lemon and icing sugar.

SUMMER PUDDING

Preparation: 30 minutes + overnight refrigeration
Cooking: 5 minutes
Serves 4–6

200 g (6½ oz) strawberries, hulled and quartered or halved
150 g (5 oz) blackcurrants
150 g (5 oz) redcurrants
150 g (5 oz) raspberries
150 g (5 oz) blackberries
caster sugar, to taste
6–8 slices good-quality white bread
fresh berries and cream, to serve

SUMMER PUDDING can also be made as individual puddings.

1 Put all the berries except the strawberries in a large pan with ½ cup (125 ml/4 fl oz) water and heat gently until the berries begin to collapse. Add the strawberries and turn off the heat. Add sugar, to taste (how much you need will depend on how ripe the fruit is and how sweet your tooth). Set aside to cool.
2 Line a 1-litre pudding basin or six 150 ml (5 fl oz) moulds with the bread. For the large basin, cut a large circle out of one slice for the bottom and cut the rest of the bread into fingers. For the small moulds, use 1 slice of bread for each, cutting a circle to fit the bottom and strips to fit the sides. Drain a little of the juice off the fruit mixture. Dip one side of each piece of bread in the juice before fitting it, juice-side-down, into the mould, leaving no gaps. Do not squeeze it or flatten it or it will not absorb the juices as well.
3 Fill the centre of the mould with the fruit and add a little juice—keep any fruit mixture which won't fit, for serving with the pudding. Cover the top with a layer of dipped bread, juice-side-up, and cover with plastic wrap. Place a plate which fits inside the dish onto the plastic wrap, then weigh it down so that it presses on the pudding. Refrigerate overnight. Carefully turn out the pudding and serve with any extra fruit filling, or berries and cream.

BAKED RICE CUSTARD

Preparation: 20 minutes
Cooking: 1 hour
Serves 4

1/4 cup (55 g/2 oz) short-grain rice
2 eggs
1/4 cup (60 g/2 oz) caster sugar
1 1/2 cups (375 ml/12 fl oz) milk
1/2 cup (125 ml/4 fl oz) cream
1–2 teaspoons grated lemon rind
1 teaspoon vanilla essence
1/4 cup (30 g/1 oz) sultanas or currants
1/4 teaspoon ground nutmeg or cinnamon

1 Preheat the oven to warm 160°C (315°F/Gas 2–3). Grease a deep 20 cm (8 inch) round ovenproof dish (1.5 litre capacity).
2 Cook the rice in a pan of boiling water until it is just tender, then drain.
3 Whisk the eggs, sugar, milk, cream, rind and vanilla essence for about 2 minutes. Fold in the cooked rice and sultanas or currants. Pour the mixture into the dish and sprinkle with nutmeg or cinnamon.
4 Put the ovenproof dish in a deep baking tray. Pour enough water into the tray to come halfway up the side of the dish. Bake for 50 minutes, or until the custard is set and a knife comes out clean when inserted into the centre. Remove from the baking tray immediately, but leave for 5 minutes before serving. Serve with cream or stewed fruits.

CLASSIC BAKED EGG CUSTARD

Preparation: 5 minutes
Cooking: 30 minutes
Serves 4–6

3 eggs, lightly beaten
1/3 cup (90 g/3 oz) caster sugar
2 cups (500 ml/16 fl oz) milk
1 teaspoon vanilla essence
1/4 teaspoon ground nutmeg

1 Preheat the oven to moderate 180°C (350°F/Gas 4). Grease a deep 1 litre ovenproof dish.
2 Whisk the eggs, sugar, milk and vanilla essence for 2 minutes. Strain into the dish and sprinkle with the nutmeg.
3 Place the dish in a baking tray and pour enough hot water into the baking tray to come halfway up the side of the dish. Bake for 30 minutes, or until the custard is set and a knife comes out clean when inserted into the centre.

CREAMED RICE

Preparation: 15 minutes
Cooking: 1 hour 10 minutes
Serves 4–6

90 g (3 oz) short-grain rice
1 litre milk
1/2 cup (125 g/4 oz) caster sugar
1 teaspoon vanilla essence

1 Rinse the rice in a colander until the water runs clear. Drain well.
2 Place the milk in a pan, add the sugar and vanilla and heat until it is about to boil.
3 Add the rice and stir for 1 minute, or until the mixture returns to the boil. Reduce the heat and simmer for 1 hour, or until the rice is tender.

VARIATION: Add 2 tablespoons of sultanas or 2 teaspoons grated orange rind with the rice.

From the top: CLASSIC BAKED EGG CUSTARD; CREAMED RICE; BAKED RICE CUSTARD

ICE CREAM

Preparation: 30 minutes + chilling and freezing
Cooking: 15 minutes
Serves 4

1 cup (250 ml/8 fl oz) milk
1 cup (250 ml/8 fl oz) cream
1 vanilla pod, split lengthways
6 egg yolks
1/2 cup (125 g/4 oz) caster sugar

1 Combine the milk and cream in a pan and add the vanilla pod. Bring to the boil, then remove from the heat and set aside for 10 minutes.
2 Using a wire whisk, beat the yolks and sugar together in a bowl for 2–3 minutes, until thick, creamy and pale, then whisk in the warm milk. Scrape the seeds from the vanilla pod into the mixture. Discard the pod.
3 Wash the pan, and pour the mixture into it. Stir over very low heat until thickened. This will take about 5–10 minutes. To test, run a finger across the back of the wooden spoon—if it leaves a clear line, the custard is ready.
4 Pour the custard into a bowl and cool to room temperature, stirring frequently to hasten the cooling process.
5 Pour into a shallow metal container, cover the surface of the custard with plastic wrap or baking paper and freeze for about 2 hours, or until almost frozen. Scoop into a chilled bowl and beat with electric beaters until smooth, then return to the tray and freeze again. Repeat this step twice more before transferring to a storage container. Cover the surface with baking paper or plastic wrap to stop ice crystals forming on the surface, then a lid.
6 To serve, transfer the ice cream to the refrigerator for about 30 minutes to soften slightly. Ice cream will keep, well sealed, in the freezer for up to 1 month.

VARIATIONS: To make strawberry ice cream, chop 250 g (8 oz) strawberries in a food processor just until smooth. Stir into the custard mixture after the

VANILLA ICE CREAM (top) and CHOCOLATE ICE CREAM.

first freezing and beating, then continue the recipe as directed.

To make banana ice cream, thoroughly mash 3 ripe bananas (or for a finer texture, purée in a food processor). Stir into the custard mixture when it has first been frozen and beaten, along with 1 tablespoon lemon juice. Continue as directed. This will serve 6.

To make chocolate ice cream, make the custard using 2 cups (500 ml/16 fl oz) milk, 1 cup (250 ml/8 fl oz) cream and a split vanilla pod. Whisk 8 egg yolks with the sugar and then stir in 2 tablespoons sifted cocoa powder. Gently whisk the hot milk into the egg yolk mixture and make the custard as before. Meanwhile, chill a deep 20 cm (8 inch) square cake tin in the freezer. Add 250 g (8 oz) warm melted chocolate to the warm custard and stir constantly until the chocolate has mixed through. Allow to cool, then pour into the chilled cake tin and freeze and beat as for vanilla ice cream.

PASSIONFRUIT AND ORANGE SORBET.

PASSIONFRUIT AND ORANGE SORBET

Preparation: 15 minutes + churning and freezing
Cooking: Nil
Serves 4

3 cups (750 ml/24 fl oz) orange juice
3/4 cup (185 g/6 oz) passionfruit pulp
1/2 cup (125 g/4 oz) caster sugar
2 egg whites, lightly beaten

1 Combine the orange juice, passionfruit pulp and sugar in a large bowl. Pour into a metal tray and freeze until just firm around the edges. Do not allow to become too firm.

2 Transfer to a bowl or food processor and beat with electric beaters or process. Refreeze. Repeat this step twice more, adding the egg white the final time, with the beaters or motor running. Return to the tray, cover with greaseproof paper and freeze for 3 hours, or until firm.

3 Alternatively, pour the mixture into an ice cream machine and churn for about 30 minutes.

RHUBARB CRUMBLE

Preparation: 15 minutes
Cooking: 40 minutes
Serves 4–6

1 kg (2 lb) rhubarb
2/3 cup (160 g/5 1/2 oz) sugar
1 cup (125 g/4 oz) plain flour
1/2 cup (95 g/3 oz) soft brown sugar
3/4 teaspoon ground cinnamon
100 g (3 1/2 oz) butter

1 Preheat the oven to moderately hot 200°C (400°F/Gas 6). Trim the rhubarb, cut into short lengths and put in a pan with the sugar. Stir over low heat until the sugar has dissolved, then cover and simmer for 10 minutes, or until the rhubarb is soft but still chunky. Spoon into a deep, round ovenproof dish.
2 Put the flour, brown sugar and cinnamon in a bowl, add the butter and rub in with just your fingertips until the mixture resembles coarse breadcrumbs.
3 Sprinkle the crumble over the stewed rhubarb and bake for 25 minutes, or until the topping is golden brown.

RHUBARB CRUMBLE (top) and APPLE BETTY.

VARIATION: For an apple crumble, peel and core 8 green cooking apples and cut each one into 8 wedges. Place in a pan with 3 tablespoons water, bring to the boil, then reduce the heat to low and cover. Cook for about 15 minutes, or until the apples are just soft. Remove from the heat, drain and then stir in 2 tablespoons caster sugar. Spoon into a dish and make the crumble topping as above.

APPLE BETTY

Preparation: 15 minutes
Cooking: 45 minutes
Serves 4–6

5 cooking apples, peeled, cored and chopped
100 g (3 1/2 oz) butter
1/2 cup (95 g/3 oz) soft brown sugar, plus 1 tablespoon
grated rind of 1 lemon
1/4 teaspoon ground cinnamon
pinch of ground nutmeg
3 cups (240 g/7 1/2 oz) fresh breadcrumbs

1 Cook the apples with 1 tablespoon of the butter, 1 tablespoon sugar and the rind, cinnamon and nutmeg, for 15 minutes, until the apples are soft enough to beat to a purée.
2 Preheat the oven to moderate 180°C (350°F/ Gas 4). Melt the remaining butter in a frying pan over low heat and add the breadcrumbs and the remaining brown sugar. Toss until all the crumbs are coated and then fry, tossing, until golden brown.
3 Spread one-third of the crumbs in a 1 litre ovenproof dish and layer with half the apple purée. Repeat with layers, then finish with the final portion of crumbs. Bake for 20 minutes, or until crisp and golden brown.

PLUM COBBLER has a scone dough topping.

PLUM COBBLER

Preparation: 15 minutes
Cooking: 45 minutes
Serves 6–8

750 g (1 1/2 lb) fresh blood plums, quartered
1/4 cup (60 g/2 oz) caster sugar

Topping
1 cup (125 g/4 oz) self-raising flour
1/2 cup (60 g/2 oz) plain flour
1/4 cup (60 g/2 oz) caster sugar
125 g (4 oz) butter, chopped
1 egg
1/2 cup (125 ml/4 fl oz) milk
icing sugar, to dust

1 Preheat the oven to moderate 180°C (350°F/ Gas 4). Lightly grease a 2 litre ovenproof dish.
2 Put the plums in a pan with the sugar and 1 tablespoon water. Stir over low heat for 5 minutes, or until the sugar dissolves and the fruit softens slightly. Spread into the ovenproof dish.
3 To make the topping, sift the flours into a bowl, add the sugar and stir to combine. Add the butter, Using your fingertips, rub in the butter until the mixture resembles fine breadcrumbs. Combine the egg and milk, whisk until smooth, then stir into the dough mixture.
4 Place large spoonfuls of the dough on top of the layer of plums. Bake for 30–40 minutes, or until the cobbler topping is golden and cooked through. Dust with icing sugar and serve immediately.

GOLDEN SYRUP DUMPLINGS

Preparation: 15 minutes
Cooking: 30 minutes
Serves 4

1 cup (125 g/4 oz) self-raising flour
40 g (1 1/4 oz) butter, chopped
1 egg
1 tablespoon milk

Syrup
1 cup (250 g/8 oz) sugar
40 g (1 1/4 oz) butter
2 tablespoons golden syrup
1/4 cup (60 ml/2 fl oz) lemon juice

1 Sift the flour and a pinch of salt into a bowl. Using your fingertips, rub in the butter until the mixture is fine and crumbly, and make a well in the centre. Using a flat-bladed knife, stir the combined egg and milk into the flour mixture to form a soft dough.
2 To make the syrup, put 2 cups (500 ml/16 fl oz) water in a large pan with the sugar, butter, golden syrup and lemon juice. Stir over medium heat until combined and the sugar has dissolved.
3 Bring to the boil, then gently drop dessertspoons of the dough into the syrup. Cover and reduce the heat to a simmer. Cook for 20 minutes, or until a knife inserted into a dumpling comes out clean. Spoon onto serving plates and drizzle with some of the syrup. Serve the dumplings immediately with whipped cream.

GOLDEN SYRUP DUMPLINGS.

HOT PASSIONFRUIT SOUFFLE

Preparation: 15 minutes
Cooking: 25 minutes
Serves 4–6

2 egg yolks
1/2 cup (125 g/4 oz) passionfruit pulp (about 6 passionfruit)
2 tablespoons lemon juice
3/4 cup (90 g/3 oz) icing sugar
6 egg whites
icing sugar, to dust

1 Preheat the oven to hot 210°C (415°F/Gas 6–7). Lightly grease four 1-cup (250 ml/8 fl oz) ramekins or 1 large soufflé dish. Sprinkle the base and side with caster sugar. Place a collar of baking paper around the dishes, secure with string and lightly grease the paper.
2 Combine the egg yolks, passionfruit pulp, lemon

Bake HOT PASSIONFRUIT SOUFFLE with a collar around the dish, then remove before serving.

juice and half the icing sugar in a large bowl and whisk well.

3 Using electric beaters, beat the egg whites in a large bowl until soft peaks form. Gradually add the remaining icing sugar, beating well after each addition.

4 Using a large metal spoon, fold the egg white mixture through the passionfruit mixture in batches. Spoon into the dishes. Using a flat-bladed knife, cut through the mixture in a circular motion 2 cm (1 inch) from the edge. Place the dishes on a large oven tray and bake for 20–25 minutes, or until the soufflés are well risen and cooked through. Cut the collars from the dishes and serve the soufflés immediately, sprinkled with sifted icing sugar.

VARIATION: To make Chilled berry soufflés, prepare six 125 ml (4 fl oz) soufflé dishes by wrapping a double strip of baking paper around the outside of each, extending 2 cm (3/4 inch) above the rim, then tying with string. Brush the collar and dish with oil or butter, sprinkle with sugar, shake to coat evenly, then tip out any excess. Place 3 tablespoons water in a small heatproof bowl. Sprinkle with 3 teaspoons gelatine and leave to go spongy. Bring a large pan with 4 cm (2 inches) water to the boil, remove from the heat and carefully lower the gelatine bowl into the water. Stir until dissolved; cool slightly. Purée 150 g (5 oz) raspberries and push through a sieve. Mash another 150 g (5 oz) and mix both lots together. Fold in the cooled gelatine mixture. Beat 1 1/4 cups (315 ml/ 10 fl oz) cream into soft peaks. In a separate bowl, beat 4 egg whites into stiff peaks, then gradually beat in 2 tablespoons of sugar until dissolved. Fold the cream into the raspberries, followed by the egg white. Spoon into the dishes and chill for several hours, until set. Remove the collars to serve.

CHRISTMAS PUDDING

Preparation: 40 minutes + 2 nights standing
Cooking: 7 hours 20 minutes
Serves 10–12

500 g (1 lb) mixed sultanas, currants and raisins
300 g (10 oz) mixed dried fruit, chopped
50 g (1 3/4 oz) mixed peel
1/2 cup (125 ml/4 fl oz) brown ale
2 tablespoons rum or brandy
juice and rind 1 orange
juice and rind 1 lemon
225 g (7 oz) suet, grated
1 1/3 cups (250 g/8 oz) soft brown sugar
3 eggs, lightly beaten
2 1/2 cups (200 g/6 1/2 oz) fresh white breadcrumbs
3/4 cup (90 g/3 oz) self-raising flour
1 teaspoon mixed spice
1/4 teaspoon freshly grated nutmeg
60 g (2 oz) blanched almonds,chopped

1 Put the dried fruit, mixed peel, ale, rum, orange and lemon juice and rind into a large bowl, cover and leave overnight.
2 Mix the fruit mixture, suet, sugar, eggs, breadcrumbs, flour, spices, almonds and good pinch of salt in a large bowl. Leave for 10 minutes so the breadcrumbs absorb any extra liquid and the mixture thickens.
3 Cut an 80 cm (32 inch) square from a clean piece of calico or an old tea towel and boil it for 20 minutes. Remove, wring out (wearing rubber gloves to prevent scalding) and spread on a clean work surface. Dust the calico with a thick, layer of sifted plain flour, leaving a border around the edge. Spread the flour out with your hands—it is important that you get an even covering as the flour forms a seal to prevent the pudding absorbing any water. Place the pudding mixture in the centre of the calico and bring the points of the material together. (Drape the calico over a bowl if you find it easier.) Gather in all the excess, trying to make the folds neat and even (they will leave an imprint on the finished pudding). Tie the top as tightly as possible with a piece of unwaxed string—there must be no gap between the calico to let water in. Tie a loop into the end of one of the pieces of string—this will act as a handle for getting the pudding in and out of the water.
4 Hook a wooden spoon handle through the loop of string and lower the pudding into a large pan of boiling water with a trivet at the bottom—the pan should be large enough for the pudding to move around. Cover the pan and boil for 5 hours. If the water level drops, add a little more boiling water around the edge of the pudding. The pudding should not rest on the base of the pan. Remove from the water and hang in a well-ventilated, dry place where it will not touch anything else. Make sure the calico ends all hang to one side so they do not drip all over the pudding. Leave overnight.
5 Untie the cloth and, if there are still damp patches, spread it out to make sure the calico dries ,all over. When ,dry, re-wrap and tie with a new piece of unwaxed string and store hanging in a cool, dry place for up to 4 months. When you wish to serve, boil for 2 hours, hang for 15 minutes, then remove it from its cloth.

VARIATION: The mixture can also be put into a greased pudding basin, covered with a layer of greaseproof paper and foil and steamed in a pan of water for 8 hours. For instructions on preparing the basin and steaming, see page 309.

CREME BRULÉE

Preparation: 15 minutes + 3 hours refrigeration
Cooking: 15 minutes
Serves 6

1 1/4 cups (315 ml/10 fl oz) cream
1 1/4 cups (315 ml/10 fl oz) thick cream
1 vanilla pod
5 egg yolks
2 tablespoons caster sugar
1/4 cup (60 ml/2 fl oz) caster sugar, extra

1 Place the cream and thick cream in a pan and stir to combine. Split the vanilla pod lengthways and add it to the pan. Bring slowly to the boil over low heat. Beat the egg yolks and sugar with a wire whisk for 1 minute, or until pale and thickened slightly.
2 Pour the just-boiled cream into the yolk mixture, whisking continuously, then discard the vanilla bean. Return to the pan and place over low heat. Cook, stirring, for 5 minutes, or until the custard thickens—do not allow it to boil. Pour into six 3/4-cup (185 ml/6 fl oz) ramekins. Cool slightly, then refrigerate for at least 3 hours, or until the custard has set.
3 Preheat the grill until very hot. Sprinkle the extra caster sugar evenly onto the surface of each custard, then grill under high heat for 3 minutes, or until the sugar on top has dissolved and caramelized. Cool completely before serving. (Do not put them in the fridge or the sugar will soften.)

STORAGE: Crème brûlées can be kept in the fridge for up to a day without the toffee topping. Serve them within 30 minutes of caramelizing the sugar. It is important that the brûlées are not refrigerated after this step.
HINT: Restaurants use an extremely hot commercial grill called a salamander, or a special brûlée iron (something like a branding iron), to achieve a hard toffee topping on this dessert. It is difficult to recreate this at home. However, good results can be had by melting the sugar with a small butane blowtorch, available from hardware stores. Follow the manufacturer's directions for use and be extremely careful if you decide to try this.

CREME BRULEE.

Use all sorts of leftover bread to make BREAD AND BUTTER PUDDING.

BREAD AND BUTTER PUDDING

Preparation: 20 minutes + 1½ hours soaking
Cooking: 40 minutes
Serves 4

60 g (2 oz) mixed raisins and sultanas
2 tablespoons orange juice or brandy
30 g (1 oz) butter
4 slices good-quality white bread or brioche loaf
3 eggs
3 tablespoons caster sugar
3 cups (750 ml/24 fl oz) milk
3 tablespoons cream
¼ teaspoon vanilla extract
¼ teaspoon ground cinnamon
1 tablespoon demerara sugar

1 Soak the raisins and sultanas in the orange juice or brandy for 30 minutes. Butter the slices of bread or brioche (remove the crusts or leave them on, whichever you prefer) and cut each piece into 8 triangles. Arrange the bread in a 1 litre ovenproof dish.
2 Combine the eggs with the sugar, add the milk, cream, vanilla and cinnamon and mix well. Drain the raisins and sultanas and add any liquid to the custard.
3 Scatter the soaked raisins and sultanas over the bread and pour the custard over the top. Cover with plastic wrap and refrigerate for 1 hour.
4 Preheat the oven to moderate 180°C (350°F/Gas 4). Sprinkle the pudding with the demerara sugar and then bake for 35–40 minutes, or until the custard has set and the top of the pudding is crunchy and golden.

NOTE: Use good-quality bread. Ordinary sliced white will tend to become soggy when it soaks up the milk.
VARIATION: You can use all sorts of bread or cake leftovers. Try Danish pastries, croissant and any fruit loaves or buns.

SWEET TREATS

For a children's party or a rainy afternoon when it's fun to be in the kitchen, fudge or rocky road are ideal treats. All our sweet treats are easy to make, with a little parental guidance, and perfect for wrapping up in cellophane and pretty boxes and giving away as Christmas presents.

VANILLA FUDGE

Preparation: 10 minutes + cooling
Cooking: 25 minutes
Makes 12 pieces

2 cups (500 g/1 lb) caster sugar
1 cup (250 ml/8 fl oz) cream
1 teaspoon vanilla essence

1 Lightly grease a 21 x 11 cm (9 x 5 inch) loaf tin with melted butter or oil. Line the base with baking paper, extending over two sides. Place the caster sugar, cream and a pinch of salt in a heavy-based pan. Stir over low heat, without boiling, until all the sugar has dissolved. Increase the heat slightly, until the mixture is just simmering. Cover and cook for 3 minutes.

2 Remove the lid and clean the sugar from the side of the pan with a wet pastry brush. Do not stir the mixture. Continue to boil the fudge for about 10 minutes, or until it reaches 115°C (240°F) on a sugar thermometer. If you don't have a thermometer, drop a little of the mixture into a glass of cold water. It should form a 'soft ball' when squeezed between your thumb and forefinger.

3 Remove from the heat, cool slightly and stir in the vanilla essence. Beat with electric beaters for 1–2 minutes, or until the mixture loses its gloss and begins to thicken. Quickly pour into the tin and smooth the surface. Cover and leave to set. Cut into small squares, or shapes. Shown here dusted with cocoa powder. Refrigerate for up to 1 week.

CHOCOLATE FUDGE

Preparation: 15 minutes + cooling
Cooking: 20 minutes
Makes 12 pieces

2 1/2 cups (310 g/10 oz) pure icing sugar
1/2 cup (125 ml/4 fl oz) milk
30 g (1 oz) butter
2 tablespoons cocoa powder, sifted
1 teaspoon vanilla essence

1 Lightly grease a 21 x 11 cm (9 x 5 inch) loaf tin. Line the base with baking paper, extending over two sides. Place the icing sugar, milk, butter and cocoa in a heavy-based pan. Stir over low heat without boiling until the mixture is smooth and the sugar has

Cut VANILLA and CHOCOLATE FUDGE into pieces, or into shapes with a biscuit cutter.

dissolved. Brush the mixture from the sides of the pan with a wet pastry brush.

2 Bring the mixture to the boil. Boil, without stirring, for 8 minutes, or until it reaches 115°C (240°F) on a sugar thermometer. If you don't have a thermometer, drop a little of the mixture into a glass of cold water. It should form a 'soft ball' when squeezed between your thumb and forefinger. Leave to cool slightly, add the vanilla and beat with electric beaters until the mixture starts to thicken and loses its gloss. Pour into the tin, cover and leave to set. Cut into pieces when set.

Instead of RUM BALLS, you can flavour with brandy or whisky.

RUM BALLS

Preparation: 20 minutes + 50 minutes refrigeration
Cooking: 5 minutes
Makes about 25

200 g (6 1/2 oz) dark cooking chocolate, finely chopped
1/4 cup (60 ml/2 fl oz) cream
30 g (1 oz) butter
50 g (1 3/4 oz) chocolate cake crumbs
2 teaspoons dark rum
1/2 cup (90 g/3 oz) chocolate sprinkles

1 Line a baking tray with foil. Place the chocolate in a bowl. Combine the cream and butter in a small pan and stir over low heat until the butter melts and the mixture is just boiling. Pour the hot cream mixture over the chocolate, and stir until the chocolate melts and the mixture is smooth.
2 Stir in the cake crumbs and rum. Refrigerate for 20 minutes, stirring occasionally, or until just firm enough to handle. Roll heaped teaspoons of the mixture into balls.
3 Spread the chocolate sprinkles on a sheet of greaseproof paper. Carefully roll each rum ball in the sprinkles, then place on the tray. Refrigerate for 30 minutes, or until firm. Serve in paper cases.

HARD CARAMELS

Preparation: 15 minutes + setting
Cooking: 25 minutes
Makes 50

1 cup (250 g/8 oz) sugar
90 g (3 oz) butter
2 tablespoons golden syrup
1/3 cup (80 ml/2 3/4 fl oz) liquid glucose
1/2 cup (160 g/5 1/2 oz) condensed milk
250 g (8 oz) dark chocolate, chopped

HARD CARAMELS are perfect for wrapping up as a gift.

1 Grease a 20 cm (8 inch) square cake tin. Line the base and sides with baking paper, and grease the paper. Put the sugar, butter, syrup, glucose and condensed milk in a heavy-based pan. Stir over medium heat without boiling, until the butter has melted and the sugar has dissolved completely. Brush the sugar crystals from the side of the pan with a wet pastry brush.
2 Bring to the boil, then reduce the heat slightly and boil, stirring, for about 10–15 minutes, until the mixture reaches 122°C (250°F) on a sugar thermometer. If you don't have a thermometer, drop a little mixture into a glass of cold water. It should be brittle but sticky between your thumb and finger.
3 Remove from the heat immediately. Pour into the tin and leave to cool. While the caramel is still warm, score squares with an oiled knife. Snap into squares when cold.
4 Line two 32 x 28 cm (13 x 11 inch) baking trays with foil. Put the chocolate in a heatproof bowl. Half fill a pan with water and bring it to the boil. Remove from the heat and place the bowl over the pan, making sure it is not sitting in the water. Stir until melted. Cool slightly, then dip the caramels one at a time into the chocolate and set on the trays. Store in an airtight container for up to a month.

Serve WHITE CHRISTMAS during the party season.

WHITE CHRISTMAS

Preparation: 10 minutes + 30 minutes setting
Cooking: 5 minutes
Makes 24

1 1/2 cups (45 g/1 1/2 oz) rice bubbles
1 cup (100 g/3 1/2 oz) powdered milk
1 cup (125 g/4 oz) icing sugar
1 cup (90 g/3 oz) desiccated coconut
1/3 cup (80 g/2 3/4 oz) chopped red glacé cherries
1/3 cup (80 g/2 3/4 oz) chopped green glacé cherries
1/3 cup (40 g/1 1/4 oz) sultanas
250 g (8 oz) white vegetable shortening (Copha)

1 Line the base and sides of a shallow 28 x 18 cm (11 x 7 inch) tin with foil.
2 Combine the rice bubbles, powdered milk, sugar, coconut and fruit in a large mixing bowl. Make a well in the centre.
3 Melt the shortening over low heat. Cool slightly, then stir into the dry ingredients.
4 Spoon into the tin and smooth the surface. Chill for 30 minutes, or until set. Cut into pieces to serve. Store in the fridge for up to 10 days.

PEANUT BRITTLE

Preparation: 20 minutes + cooling
Cooking: 15 minutes
Makes about 500 g (1 lb)

2 cups (500 g/1 lb) sugar
1 cup (185 g/6 oz) soft brown sugar
1/2 cup (175 g/6 oz) golden syrup
60 g (2 oz) butter
2 1/2 cups (390 g/13 oz) roasted, unsalted peanuts

1 Line the base and sides of a shallow 30 x 25 cm (12 x 10 inch) swiss roll tin with foil or baking paper. Grease the foil with melted butter or oil.
2 Combine the sugars, golden syrup and 1/2 cup (125 ml/4 fl oz) water in a large heavy-based pan. Stir over medium heat without boiling until the sugar has completely dissolved. Brush the sugar crystals from the side of the pan with a wet pastry brush. Add the butter and stir until melted. Bring to the boil, reduce the heat slightly and boil without stirring for 15–20 minutes. The mixture must reach 150°C (250°F) on a sugar thermometer, or a little dropped in cold water will be brittle and not sticky. Remove from the heat.
3 Add the peanuts and fold in lightly, tilting the pan to help mix—don't overmix or it will crystallize. Pour into the tin and smooth the surface with a buttered spatula. Leave the tin on a wire rack for the brittle to cool. Break into pieces when almost set. Store in an airtight container for up to 3 weeks.

Use roasted unsalted nuts to make PEANUT BRITTLE.

TOFFEE APPLES

Preparation: 10 minutes + setting
Cooking: 20 minutes
Makes 12

12 small red or green apples, very crisp
4 cups (1 kg/2 lb) sugar
2 tablespoons white vinegar
red or green food colouring

1 Line two 32 x 28 cm (13 x 11 inch) baking trays with foil. Grease the foil lightly with oil.
2 Wipe the apples well with a clean, dry towel. Push a wooden lolly stick or thick skewer into the stem end of each apple.
3 Combine the sugar, vinegar and 2 cups (500 ml/16 fl oz) water in a large, heavy-based pan. Stir over medium heat, without boiling, until the sugar has completely dissolved. Brush the sugar crystals from the side of the pan with a wet pastry brush. Add the food colouring. Bring to the boil and boil without stirring for 15–20 minutes. The mixture must reach 138°C (275°F) on a sugar thermometer. If you don't have a sugar thermometer, test by dropping a little mixture into cold water. It will be

brittle ('small-crack' stage). Remove from the heat immediately.

4 Dip the apples, one at a time, into the toffee to coat. Lift out and twist quickly to coat evenly. Drain, then place on the trays. Leave to set at room temperature. When set, wrap each toffee apple in cellophane and tie with ribbon. Can be kept for up to two days.

HINT: It is important that the apples are at room temperature when they are dipped into the hot toffee. If they are too cold, the toffee will form bubbles on the surface.

TOFFEE APPLES (top) and COCONUT ICE.

COCONUT ICE

Preparation: 20 minutes + 1 hour setting
Cooking: Nil
Makes 30 pieces

2 cups (250 g/8 oz) icing sugar
1/4 teaspoon cream of tartar
400 g (13 oz) can condensed milk
3 1/2 cups (315 g/10 oz) desiccated coconut
2–3 drops pink food colouring

1 Brush a 20 cm (8 inch) square cake tin with oil or melted butter. Line the base with baking paper.

2 Sift the icing sugar and cream of tartar into a large bowl. Make a well in the centre and add the condensed milk. Stir in the coconut, half at a time. Mix with your hands until well combined.

3 Divide the mixture in half. Tint one half with pink food colouring. Using your hands, knead the colour through evenly.

4 Press the pink mixture over the base of the tin, cover with the white mixture and press down firmly to even the surface. Refrigerate the coconut ice for 1 hour, or until it is firm. Remove from the tin and cut into squares or bars to serve. Can be stored in an airtight container in a cool place for up to three weeks.

SMALL TOFFEES (left) and TOASTED MARSHMALLOWS.

SMALL TOFFEES

Preparation: 10 minutes + setting
Cooking: 25 minutes
Makes 24

4 cups (1 kg/2 lb) sugar
1 tablespoon vinegar
hundreds and thousands or desiccated coconut, for decoration

1 Line two deep 12-cup patty tins with paper cases. Combine the sugar and vinegar with 1 cup (250 ml/8 fl oz) water in a large, heavy-based pan.
2 Stir over medium heat without boiling until the sugar has completely dissolved. Brush the sugar crystals from the side of the pan with a wet pastry brush. Bring to the boil, then reduce the heat slightly and boil without stirring for 15–20 minutes. The mixture must reach 150°C (300°F) on a sugar thermometer. If you don't have a sugar thermometer, test by dropping a little mixture into cold water. It will be brittle but not sticky. Remove the pan from the heat immediately.
3 Pour into patty cases and decorate with hundreds and thousands or desiccated coconut. Leave to set at room temperature. Store in an airtight container in a cool dry place for up to a week.

TOASTED MARSHMALLOWS

Preparation: 25 minutes + overnight setting
Cooking: 3 minutes
Makes 36

1 1/2 cups (375 g/12 oz) caster sugar
5 teaspoons gelatine
1 teaspoon vanilla essence
3/4 cup (65 g/2 oz) desiccated coconut

1 Line a 30 x 20 cm (12 x 8 inch) shallow cake tin with foil and brush with melted butter or oil.
2 Using electric beaters, beat the sugar and 1/2 cup (125 ml/4 fl oz) water for 3 minutes.

3 Combine the gelatine with 1/2 cup (125 ml/ 4 fl oz) water in a small bowl. Stand the bowl in hot water until the gelatine becomes spongy, then stir until dissolved. Add to the sugar mixture and beat with electric beaters for 10 minutes, or until thick and white. Add the vanilla essence. Pour into the tin and spread out evenly. Leave overnight to set at room temperature.
4 Preheat the oven to moderate 180°C (350°F/ Gas 4). Spread the coconut evenly on a flat baking tray. Bake for about 3 minutes, or until golden (watch the coconut carefully when toasting as it can quickly burn). Pour onto a plate to cool.
5 Turn the marshmallow out of the tin and cut it into cubes. Place the toasted coconut in a plastic bag and add a few cubes of marshmallow at a time. Shake to coat. Store in a single layer in an airtight container in a cool dark place for up to a week. Keep flat.

ROCKY ROAD

Preparation: 20 minutes + refrigeration
Cooking: 5 minutes
Makes 30 pieces

250 g (8 oz) pink and white marshmallows, halved
1 cup (160 g/5 1/2 oz) unsalted peanuts, roughly chopped
1/2 cup (105 g/3 1/2 oz) glacé cherries, halved
1 cup (60 g/2 oz) shredded coconut
350 g (11 oz) dark chocolate, chopped

1 Line the base of a shallow 20 cm (8 inch) square cake tin with foil, leaving it to hang over two sides. Mix together the marshmallows, peanuts, cherries and shredded coconut.
2 Put the chocolate in a heatproof bowl. Half fill a pan with water and bring to the boil. Remove from the heat and place the bowl over the pan, making sure it is not sitting in the water. Stir occasionally until the chocolate has melted.
3 Add the chocolate to the marshmallow mixture, and mix. Press evenly into the tin. Refrigerate for several hours, or until set. Lift out and cut into small pieces. Store in an airtight container in the fridge for up to two weeks.

ROCKY ROAD is a favourite for children's parties.

JAMS AND PICKLES

For anyone who has a fruit tree or a vegetable patch, making your own jams, marmalades and pickles is a skill well worth having. Kept in properly sterilized jars, jams and pickles will keep for six months, in a cool dark place. Once opened, they can be stored in the fridge for up to a month.

THREE-FRUIT MARMALADE

Preparation: 30 minutes + overnight soaking
Cooking: 2¼ hours
Fills twelve 250 ml (8 fl oz) jars

1 grapefruit
2 oranges
2 lemons
3 kg (6 lb) sugar

1 Scrub the grapefruit, oranges and lemons under hot running water with a soft bristle brush, to remove the wax coating. Slice the quartered grapefruit and halved oranges and lemons very thinly and place in a large non-metal bowl. Put the pips in a piece of muslin, tied securely with string. Add to the bowl with 2.5 litres water, cover and leave overnight.
2 Put two small plates in the freezer. Transfer the fruit and water to a large pan. Bring slowly to the boil, then reduce the heat and simmer, covered, for 1 hour, or until the fruit is tender. Meanwhile, 'warm' the sugar by spreading in a large baking dish and heating in a very slow 120°C (250°F/Gas ½) oven for 10 minutes, stirring occasionally.
3 Add the warmed sugar to the fruit all at once. Stir over low heat, without boiling, for 5 minutes, or until all the sugar has dissolved. Return to the boil and boil rapidly for 50–60 minutes. When the marmalade reaches 104°C on the sugar thermometer, start testing for setting point: remove from the heat and place a little marmalade on one of the plates. A skin will form on the surface and the marmalade will wrinkle when pushed with your finger when setting point is reached. Leave to cool for 10 minutes, then remove any scum from the surface. Remove the muslin bag.
4 Spoon the cooled marmalade into hot, sterilized jars and seal. Turn upside-down for 2 minutes, then turn back again and leave to cool completely. Label and date for storage.

Jars must always be sterilized before jams are put in them for storage, or bacteria will multiply. To sterilize your jars and lids, rinse with boiling water, then do not dry with a towel (even a clean tea towel may have germs on it) but place in a warm oven for 20 minutes, or until completely dry.

STRAWBERRY JAM

Preparation: 30 minutes
Cooking: 1½ hours
Fills six 250 ml (8 fl oz) jars

5 cups (1.25 kg) sugar
1.5 kg (3 lb) strawberries
½ cup (125 ml/4 fl oz) lemon juice

1 'Warm' the sugar by spreading in a large baking dish and heating in a very slow 120°C (250°F/Gas ½) oven for 10 minutes, stirring occasionally. Put two plates in the freezer. Hull the strawberries and put in a large pan with the lemon juice, sugar and ½ cup (125 ml/4 fl oz) water. Warm gently, without boiling, stirring carefully with a wooden spoon. Try not to break up the fruit too much.
2 Increase the heat and, without boiling, continue stirring for 10 minutes, until the sugar has thoroughly dissolved. Increase the heat and boil, without stirring, for 20 minutes. Start testing for setting point: place a little jam on one of the cold plates; a skin will form on the surface and the jam will wrinkle when pushed with your finger. It could take up to 40 minutes to reach setting point. Remove from the heat and leave for 5 minutes before removing any scum that forms on the surface. Pour into hot sterilized jars, seal and label.

LEMON CURD

Preparation: 15 minutes
Cooking: 20 minutes
Fills two 250 ml (8 fl oz) jars

1½ tablespoons finely grated lemon rind
¾ cup (185 ml/6 fl oz) lemon juice
185 g (6 oz) soft butter, chopped
1 cup (250 g/8 oz) caster sugar
12 egg yolks

1 Combine the rind, juice, butter and sugar in a heatproof bowl over a pan of simmering water. Stir until the butter has melted and the sugar dissolved.
2 Add the egg yolks to the bowl and stir until the mixture thickens to coat the back of the spoon. This will take about 15–17 minutes and the heat must be low or the mixture will curdle.
3 Strain the curd into a jug, then pour into cooled sterilized jars. Seal immediately. Store in the fridge for up to 3 weeks, unopened. Use within a week of opening.

MIXED BERRY JAM

Preparation: 20 minutes
Cooking: 30 minutes
Fills four 250 ml (8 fl oz) jars

1 kg (2 lb) mixed berries (we used strawberries, raspberries, blackberries, blueberries, mulberries but any combination of fresh berries will do)
⅓ cup (80 ml/2¾ oz) lemon juice
1 kg (2 lb) sugar
25 g (¾ oz) jam setting mixture

1 Put two small plates in the freezer. Place the berries and lemon juice in a saucepan and gently cook for 10 minutes. Add the sugar and stir over low heat until it dissolves.
2 Boil for 15 minutes and then remove from the heat. Add the jam setting mixture and boil rapidly for a further 5 minutes. Test for setting point: place a little jam on a cold plate; a skin should form on the surface and the jam will wrinkle when pushed with your finger.
3 Pour into hot sterilized jars. Seal and label.

Clockwise from top right: STRAWBERRY JAM; MIXED BERRY JAM; LEMON CURD.

APRICOT AND ALMOND JAM

Preparation: 20 minutes + overnight soaking
Cooking: 1 1/4 hours
Fills eight 250 ml (8 fl oz) jars

500 g (1 lb) dried apricots
6 cups (1.5 kg/3 lb) sugar
1/2 cup (45 g/1 1/2 oz) flaked almonds

1 Place the apricots in a large non-metal bowl. Add 2 litres water and leave to soak overnight.
2 Place two small plates in the freezer. Pour the apricots and water into a large pan. Bring slowly to the boil, then reduce the heat and simmer, covered, for 45 minutes, or until the fruit is soft. 'Warm' the sugar by spreading in a large baking dish and heating in a very slow 120°C (250°F/Gas 1/2) oven for 10 minutes, stirring occasionally.
3 Add the sugar to the fruit. Stir over low heat, without boiling, for 5 minutes, or until all the sugar has dissolved. Return to the boil and boil, uncovered, for 20 minutes, stirring occasionally. When the jam reaches 104°C on the sugar thermometer, start testing for setting point: place 1/4 teaspoon jam on one of the plates. A skin will form on the surface and the jam will wrinkle when pushed with your finger when setting point is reached. Allow the jam to cool for 5 minutes, then remove any scum from the surface.
4 Spoon into hot, sterilized jars and seal. Turn upside-down for 2 minutes, then invert and leave to cool.

LIME MARMALADE

Preparation: 40 minutes + overnight soaking
Cooking: 1 1/4 hours
Fills ten 250 ml (8 fl oz) jars

1 kg (2 lb) limes
2.25 kg (4 1/2 lb) sugar

1 Scrub the limes under hot, running water to remove the wax coating. Cut them in half lengthways, then slice thinly. Place in a large non-metal bowl with 2 litres water. Cover with plastic wrap and leave overnight.
2 Place two small plates in the freezer. Place the fruit and water in a large pan. Bring slowly to the boil, then reduce the heat and simmer, covered, for 45 minutes, or until the fruit is tender. 'Warm' the sugar by spreading in a large baking dish and heating in a very slow 120°C (250°F/Gas 1/2) oven for 10 minutes, stirring occasionally.
3 Add the sugar to the fruit and stir over low heat, without boiling, for 5 minutes, or until all the sugar has dissolved. Then boil rapidly, without stirring, for 20 minutes. When the marmalade reaches 104°C on the sugar thermometer, start testing for setting point: place 1/4 teaspoon marmalade on one of the plates. A skin will form and the marmalade will wrinkle when pushed with your finger when setting point is reached. Cool for 5 minutes, then remove any scum.
4 Spoon the marmalade into hot, sterilized jars. Turn upside down for 2 minutes, then invert and cool. Label and date.

RASPBERRY JAM

Preparation: 20 minutes
Cooking: 35 minutes
Fills seven 250 ml (8 fl oz) jars

1.5 kg (3 lb) raspberries
1/3 cup (80 ml/2 3/4 oz) lemon juice
6 cups (1.5 kg/3 lb) sugar

Clockwise from top left: LIME MARMALADE; APRICOT AND ALMOND JAM; RASPBERRY JAM.

1 Place the raspberries and lemon juice in a large pan. Gently stir over low heat for 10 minutes, or until the raspberries have softened. 'Warm' the sugar by spreading in a large baking dish and heating in a very slow 120°C (250°F/Gas ½) oven for 10 minutes, stirring occasionally.
2 Add the sugar to the pan and stir, without boiling, for 5 minutes or until the sugar has completely dissolved.
3 Put 2 small plates in the freezer. Bring the jam to the boil and boil for 20 minutes, then start testing for setting point: place ¼ teaspoon jam on a cold plate. A skin will form on the surface and the jam will wrinkle when pushed with your finger when setting point is reached. Cool for 5 minutes, then remove any scum from the surface. Pour into hot sterilized jars and label.

SPICY DRIED FRUIT CHUTNEY

Preparation: 30 minutes
Cooking: 1 1/2 hours
Fills seven 250 ml (8 fl oz) jars

400 g (13 oz) dried apricots
200 g (6 1/2 oz) dried peaches
200 g (6 1/2 oz) dried pears
250 g (8 oz) raisins
200 g (6 1/2 oz) dried dates, pitted
250 g (8 oz) onions
250 g (8 oz) green apples, peeled and cored
4 cloves garlic, finely chopped
2 teaspoons salt
1 teaspoon ground cumin
1 teaspoon ground coriander
1 teaspoon ground cloves
1 teaspoon ground cayenne pepper
3 1/4 cups (600 g/1 1/4 lb) soft brown sugar
2 1/2 cups (600 ml/ 20 fl oz) malt vinegar

1 Finely chop the apricots, peaches, pears, raisins, dates, onions and apples. Place in a large stainless steel or enamel pan. Add the garlic, salt, cumin, coriander, cloves, cayenne pepper, brown sugar, vinegar and 3 cups (750 ml/24 fl oz) water.
2 Stir over low heat until the sugar has dissolved. Bring to the boil, then reduce the heat and simmer over medium heat for 1 1/2 hours, or until the mixture has thickened and the fruit is soft and pulpy. Don't increase the heat or the liquid will evaporate too quickly and the flavours won't develop.
3 Spoon the chutney into hot, sterilized jars, and seal. Turn upside-down for 2 minutes, then invert and cool. Label and store for 1 month before serving to let the flavours develop.

TOMATO SAUCE

Preparation: 25 minutes
Cooking: 2 hours
Fills six 250 ml (8 fl oz) jars

2 teaspoons black peppercorns
2 teaspoons whole cloves
2 teaspoons allspice
2.5 kg (5 lb) firm ripe tomatoes, roughly chopped
1 large onion, chopped
50 g (1 3/4 oz) tomato paste
4 cloves garlic, crushed
2 teaspoons ground ginger
1 teaspoon salt
1/4 teaspoon cayenne pepper
600 ml (20 fl oz) white wine or cider vinegar
500 g (1 lb) sugar

1 Place the black peppercorns, cloves and allspice in a small muslin bag and tie securely.
2 Place the muslin bag in a large heavy-based pan with the chopped tomatoes, onion, tomato paste, garlic, ginger, salt, cayenne pepper and vinegar. Bring slowly to the boil, then reduce the heat and simmer for 45 minutes.
3 Add the sugar and stir for 5 minutes to dissolve. Bring to the boil then reduce the heat and simmer for 1 hour, or until thickened and pulpy. Stir frequently during cooking and watch the mixture does not burn.
4 Remove the muslin bag. Cool a little, then place in batches into a coarse sieve. Use a wooden spoon to press the juice firmly from the pulp. Discard the pulp and return the juice to the cleaned out pan. Reheat gently for 10 minutes then pour into hot sterilized jars and seal while hot. Label and store for a month before using, to let the flavours develop.

NOTE: Allspice is also known as pimento.

TOMATO SAUCE (top) and SPICY DRIED FRUIT CHUTNEY.

RICH MINT JELLY

Preparation: 20 minutes + overnight standing
Cooking: 40 minutes
Fills three 250 ml (8 fl oz) jars

1 kg (2 lb) green apples
1/2 cup (125 ml/4 fl oz) lemon juice
3 cups (60 g/2 oz) fresh mint leaves
sugar
2–3 drops green food colouring

1 Wash and cut the apples into thick slices, without peeling or coring. Put the apple, lemon juice, 2 1/2 cups of the mint leaves and 1 litre water in a large heavy-based pan, and bring to the boil. Reduce the heat and cook for 10 minutes, or until the apple is a soft pulp. Break up any large pieces with a wooden spoon.
2 Strain through a piece of muslin into a bowl—do not press the liquid through or it will become cloudy. Leave overnight.
3 Put two plates in the freezer. Measure the strained juice and return it to the pan. Add 1 cup (250 g/8 oz) of sugar for each cup of liquid. Stir over low heat without boiling until the sugar has dissolved completely. Bring to the boil, then reduce the heat slightly and simmer on low heat for 20 minutes, or until a little mixture on a cold plate forms a skin and wrinkles when pushed.
4 Finely chop the remaining mint and add with the colouring. Stir well. Remove from the heat and leave for 5 minutes. Pour into hot, sterilized jars and seal.

PICCALILLI

Preparation: 30 minutes + overnight soaking
Cooking: 20 minutes
Fills six 250 ml (8 fl oz) jars

400 g (13 oz) cauliflower, chopped
1 small cucumber, chopped
200 g (6 1/2 oz) green beans, chopped
1 onion, chopped
2 carrots, chopped
2 celery sticks, chopped
4 tablespoons salt
1 cup (250 g/8 oz) sugar
1 tablespoon mustard powder
2 teaspoons ground turmeric
1 teaspoon ground ginger
1 fresh red chilli, seeded and finely chopped
1 litre white vinegar
200 g (6 1/2 oz) frozen broad beans, peeled
1/2 cup (60 g/2 oz) plain flour

1 Combine the cauliflower, cucumber, beans, onion, carrot, celery and salt in a large bowl. Add enough water to cover the vegetables, and cover with an upturned small plate to keep the vegetables submerged. Leave to soak overnight.
2 Drain the vegetables well and rinse under cold running water. Drain again and put in a pan. Add the sugar, mustard, turmeric, ginger, chilli and all but 3/4 cup (185 ml/6 fl oz) of the vinegar. Bring to the boil, then reduce the heat and simmer for 3 minutes. Stir in the broad beans.
3 Blend the flour with the remaining vinegar and stir it into the piccalilli. Stir until the mixture boils and thickens. Stand hot, sterilized jars on a wooden board or cloth-covered surface and spoon the piccalilli into the jars, then seal while hot. Turn the jars upside-down onto their lids. Leave for 2 minutes, then invert the jars. Label. Store for a month before using, to give the flavours time to develop fully.

RICH MINT JELLY (top) and PICCALILLI.

DILL PICKLES

Preparation: 15 minutes + overnight standing
Cooking: 5 minutes
Fills one 750 ml (24 fl oz) jar

500 g (1 lb) small firm Lebanese cucumbers, quartered lengthways
salt, to sprinkle
3 cups (750 ml/24 fl oz) white vinegar
3 tablespoons caster sugar
2 tablespoons yellow mustard seeds
2 tablespoons dill seeds
2 tablespoons black peppercorns
6 sprigs of fresh dill

1 Place the cucumber in a colander and sprinkle with salt. Cover with a dry cloth and leave overnight. Rinse under cold water and drain thoroughly.
2 Put the vinegar, caster sugar, mustard seeds, dill seeds and black peppercorns in a pan. Bring to the boil, then reduce the heat and simmer for 5 minutes. Pack the cucumbers with 6 sprigs of dill in a warm sterilized jar. Pour in the liquid with the seeds. Press gently to remove any air bubbles. Seal the jar, label and store in a cool dark place for at least a month before serving, shaking occasionally.

NOTE: Make sure the cucumbers are kept completely covered in the vinegar solution.

PICKLED BEETROOT

Preparation: 30 minutes
Cooking: 30 minutes
Fills one 750 ml (24 fl oz) jar

8 beetroot
6 sprigs of fresh rosemary
1 onion, thinly sliced
zest of 1 orange
1 cup (250 ml/8 fl oz) white vinegar
1 cup (250 ml/8 fl oz) malt vinegar
1/2 cup (125 g/4 oz) caster sugar

1 Cook the beetroot in a large pan of boiling water for 20 minutes, or until tender. Drain and leave to cool. Remove the skin from the beetroot and discard. (Wear rubber gloves to do this to prevent your hands from being stained.)
2 Cut the beetroot into thick slices and layer in a large warm sterilized jar with the rosemary, onion and orange zest. Leave 2 cm (3/4 inch) at the top of the jar empty.
3 Combine the vinegars with the sugar in a pan. Stir over low heat until the sugar dissolves. Bring to the boil, then reduce the heat and simmer for 5 minutes. Allow to cool before pouring over the beetroot. Seal, label and store in a cool dark place.

NOTE: To make zest, cut strips of rind from the orange with a sharp knife. Remove the white pith from the rind and cut the rind into fine strips.

PICKLED ONIONS

Preparation: 20 minutes
Cooking: 5 minutes
Fills one 1 litre jar

1 kg (2 lb) pickling onions
1 litre malt vinegar
2 tablespoons allspice
2 teaspoons sea salt
2 tablespoons black peppercorns
6 cloves
3 bay leaves

1 Peel the onions and rinse well. Pat dry and pack into sterilized jars.
2 Put the remaining ingredients in a pan. Bring to the boil, then reduce the heat and simmer for 2 minutes. Cool slightly and pour over the onions.

From the top: DILL PICKLES; PICKLED BEETROOT; PICKLED ONIONS.

BASIC RECIPES

There are some basic recipes that you will find you use over and over again for a variety of different dishes. A white sauce (béchamel) can be layered and baked in lasagne, served over vegetables, mixed with seafood to make a creamy pie, or flavoured with cheese or herbs. Similarly, a shortcrust pastry will usually be the same whether it's filled with berries, a creamy quiche mixture or meat and sauce.

Many of the following basic recipes will have appeared within this book, but as part and parcel of a whole dish. But, for when you need a quick reference, turn to these pages for your basic pastries, stocks, dressings, savoury and sweet sauces.

PASTRIES

Whether it is shortcrust, Danish, choux or puff, beautiful pastry with a light buttery touch can raise any dish to sublime heights. Perfect pastry that melts in the mouth is one of the hallmarks of a great cook—follow a few commonsense rules and you'll probably find it all rather easy.

PLAIN SHORTCRUST PASTRY

2 cups (250 g/8 oz) plain flour
125 g (4 oz) cold butter, chopped
1 egg yolk
3–4 tablespoons cold water

1 Sift the flour into a large mixing bowl and add the butter. Rub the butter into the flour with your fingertips until the mixture resembles fine breadcrumbs.
2 Add the combined egg yolk and 3 tablespoons of the water. Cut the liquid in with a knife to form a dough, adding the remaining water if necessary. Turn onto a lightly floured surface and gather together into a smooth ball (do not knead, or you will have tough pastry). Cover with plastic wrap and refrigerate if not immediately required. If the weather is hot, chill for at least 30 minutes, before proceeding with the recipe as directed.

NOTE: Shortcrust pastry can be made very easily in the food processor, but care must be taken not to overwork it. 'Rub' the butter into the flour by processing in short bursts, using the pulse button if you have one, until the mixture is fine and crumbly. Add most of the liquid and, again, process in short bursts until the mixture just comes together in small particles, adding more liquid if necessary.

If you continue to process until the mixture forms a ball, you will find that it is overworked and the pastry will be tough. Instead, turn the mixture out onto a lightly floured surface and press together to form a clump, before rolling out as required.

SWEET SHORTCRUST PASTRY

2 cups (250 g/8 oz) plain flour
125 g (4 oz) cold butter, chopped
1/4 cup (60 g/2 oz) caster sugar
2 egg yolks
1 teaspoon vanilla essence
2–3 tablespoons cold water

1 Sift the flour into a large mixing bowl and add the butter. Using your fingertips, rub the butter into the flour until the mixture resembles fine breadcrumbs. Stir in the sugar.
2 Add the combined egg yolks, vanilla essence and 2 tablespoons of the water. Cut with a knife to form a dough, adding the remaining water if necessary. Turn out onto a lightly floured surface and gather into a smooth ball.

DANISH PASTRY

1/2 cup (125 ml/4 fl oz) warm milk
7 g (1/4 oz) sachet dried yeast
1 teaspoon caster sugar
2 cups (250 g/8 oz) plain flour
1/2 teaspoon salt
1/4 cup (60 g/2 oz) caster sugar, extra
1 egg, lightly beaten
1 teaspoon vanilla essence
250 g (8 oz) cold unsalted butter

1 In a small bowl, mix together the milk, yeast and sugar. Cover and leave in a warm place for 5 minutes, or until the mixture is frothy.
2 Sift the flour into a large bowl with the salt and stir in the extra sugar. Make a well in the centre and add the yeast mixture, egg and vanilla essence all at once. Mix to a firm dough. Turn out onto a floured surface and knead for 10 minutes to form a smooth, elastic dough.
3 Place the dough in a lightly greased bowl, cover and set aside in a warm place for 1 hour, or until doubled in size. Meanwhile roll the cold butter between two sheets of baking paper to a 15 x 20 cm (6 x 8 inch) rectangle and then refrigerate until required.
4 Punch down the dough (give it one good punch with your fist) and knead for 1 minute. Roll out to a rectangle 25 x 30 cm (10 x 12 inches). Place the butter in the centre of the dough and fold up the bottom and top of the dough over the butter to join in the centre. Seal the edges with a rolling pin.
5 Give the dough a quarter turn clockwise then roll out to a 20 x 45 cm (8 x 18 inch) rectangle. Fold over the top third of the pastry, then the bottom third and then give another quarter turn clockwise. Cover and refrigerate for 30 minutes. Repeat the rolling, folding and turning four more times. Wrap in plastic wrap and refrigerate for at least 2 hours before using.

CHOUX PASTRY

60 g (2 oz) butter
1/2 cup (125 ml/4 fl oz) water
1/2 cup (60 g/2 oz) plain flour, sifted
2 eggs, lightly beaten

1 Chop the butter and put in a pan with the water. Stir over low heat until melted.
2 Bring to the boil then immediately remove from the heat and add the flour all at once. Beat with a wooden spoon until smooth. Return to the heat and continue to beat for 2 minutes, or until the mixture forms a mass and leaves the side of the pan.
3 Remove from the heat and transfer to the bowl. Cool for 5 minutes. Add the egg, a little at a time, beating well between each addition, until thick and glossy. You may not need to add all the egg.
4 Shape the pastry onto trays and cook as directed in the recipe. If not completely dried out, return to a slow 150°C (300°F/Gas 2) oven for 5–10 minutes.

ROUGH PUFF PASTRY

90 g (3 oz) unsalted butter
90 g (3 oz) cooking margarine or lard
2 cups (250 g/8 oz) plain flour
pinch of salt
3/4 cup (185 ml/6 fl oz) cold water
1 teaspoon lemon juice

1 Place the butter and margarine together on a large plate. Using two knives, roughly chop the fats together, then cover and chill. When cold and hard, chop the combined fats into small cubes.
2 Sift the flour and salt

into a large bowl. Add the cubes of fat to the flour. Using a knife, cut in the fat until just coated with the flour. Combine the water and lemon juice and add most of it to the bowl. Cut into the flour with a dinner knife, without breaking up the fat. Add more of the liquid if necessary.

3 With floured fingers, bring together into a rough ball. Turn out onto a floured surface. Do not knead. Roll the dough out into a 45 x 15 cm (18 x 6 inch) rectangle, keeping the sides and ends straight.

4 Fold the dough into three layers by folding the bottom third up and then the top third down. Seal the edges lightly with a rolling pin. Give a quarter turn clockwise: the top edge will now be to the right as if it were a book. Cover and refrigerate for 15 minutes. Repeat rolling, folding and turning clockwise four more times. Refrigerate between rollings if the dough becomes too soft. Chill for at least 30 minutes after the final rolling.

5 Roll and shape or cut the pastry as required in the recipe.

PUFF PASTRY

200–250 g (6½–8 oz) unsalted butter
2 cups (250 g/8 oz) plain flour
½ teaspoon salt
⅔ cup (170 ml/ 5½ fl oz) chilled water

1 We've given a range of fat quantities—if you've never made puff pastry before, you'll find it easier to use the lower amount. Melt 30 g (1 oz) butter in a pan. Sift the flour and salt onto a work surface and make a well in the centre. Add the butter and water. Blend with your fingertips, drawing in the flour. You should end up with a crumb mixture—if it seems a little dry, add extra drops of water before bringing it all together to form a dough.

2 Cut the dough with a pastry scraper, using a downward cutting action, then turn and repeat in the opposite direction. The dough should now come together to form a soft ball. Score a cross in the top to prevent shrinkage, wrap and chill for 15–20 minutes.

3 Soften the remaining butter by pounding it between 2 sheets of baking paper with a rolling pin. Then, still between the sheets of baking paper, roll it into a 10 cm (4 inch) square. The butter must be the same consistency as the dough or the pastry layers will not be even.

4 Put the pastry on a well floured surface. Roll it out to form a cross, leaving the centre slightly thicker than the arms. Place the butter in the centre and fold over each of the arms to make a parcel. Turn the dough so that it looks like a book with the spine to the left. Tap and roll out the dough to form a 15 x 45 cm (6 x 18 inch) rectangle. Square off the corners—otherwise, every time you fold, the edges will become less neat and the layers will be uneven.

5 Fold the dough like a letter, the top third down and the bottom third up, to form another square, brushing off any excess flour. Turn the dough 90° to bring the spine side to your left and press the seam sides down with the rolling pin to seal. Re-roll and fold as before to complete two turns. Wrap the dough and chill again.

6 Re-roll and fold twice more, chill, then repeat to complete six turns. On a hot day, you may need to chill after each turn. The pastry should now be yellow and ready to use—if it looks a little streaky, roll and fold once more. Chill until required.

STOCKS

The secret to great soups and stews is good stock. Home-made stock will give your dishes a richer, more flavoursome base and, although the cooking time is long, the preparation couldn't be easier. Browning meat bones beforehand adds flavour and colour.

BEEF STOCK

2 kg (4 lb) beef bones
2 unpeeled carrots, chopped
2 unpeeled onions, quartered
2 tablespoons tomato paste
2 sticks celery, leaves included, chopped
1 bouquet garni
12 black peppercorns

1 Preheat the oven to hot 210°C (415°F/Gas 6–7). Put the bones in a baking dish and bake for 30 minutes, turning occasionally. Add the carrot and onion and cook for a further 20 minutes. Allow to cool.
2 Put the bones, carrot and onion in a large, heavy-based pan. Drain the excess fat from the baking dish and pour 1 cup (250 ml/8 fl oz) of water into the dish. Stir to dissolve any pan juices; add the liquid to the pan.
3 Add the tomato paste, celery and 10 cups (2.5 litres) water. Bring to the boil, skimming the surface as required and add the bouquet garni and peppercorns. Reduce the heat to low and simmer gently for 4 hours. Skim the froth from the surface regularly.
4 Ladle the stock in batches into a fine sieve sitting over a bowl. Gently press the solids with a ladle to extract all the liquid. Discard the bones and vegetables and set aside to cool. Refrigerate until cold and spoon off any fat that has set on the top. At this stage you can reduce the stock to concentrate its flavour (dilute before using) and store in the refrigerator for up to 2 days or in the freezer for up to 6 months. Makes 1.75 litres (7 cups).

CHICKEN STOCK

2 kg (4 lb) chicken bones
2 unpeeled onions, quartered
2 unpeeled carrots, chopped
2 sticks celery, leaves included, chopped
1 bouquet garni
12 black peppercorns

1 Put the chicken bones, onion, carrot, celery and 14 cups (3.5 litres) of water in a large, heavy-based pan. Bring slowly to the boil. Skim the surface as required and add the bouquet garni and peppercorns. Reduce the heat to low and simmer gently for 3 hours. Skim the froth from the surface regularly.
2 Ladle the stock in batches into a fine sieve sitting over a bowl. Gently press the solids with a ladle to extract all the liquid. Let the stock cool, then refrigerate until cold and spoon off any fat

that has set on the top. At this stage you can reduce the stock to concentrate its flavour (dilute before using) and store in the refrigerator for up to 2 days or in the freezer for up to 6 months. Makes 2.5 litres (10 cups).

FISH STOCK

2 kg (4 lb) chopped fish bones, heads and tails
1 stick celery, leaves included, roughly chopped
1 onion, chopped
1 unpeeled carrot, chopped
1 leek, sliced
1 bouquet garni
12 black peppercorns

1 Place the fish bones, celery, onion, carrot, leek and 8 cups (2 litres) of water in a large, heavy-based pan. Bring slowly to the boil. Skim the surface as required and add the bouquet garni and peppercorns. Reduce the heat to low and simmer very gently for 20 minutes. Skim off any froth regularly.
2 Ladle the stock in batches into a sieve lined with damp muslin sitting over a bowl. To keep a clear fish stock, do not press the solids, but simply allow the stock to strain undisturbed. Allow to cool, then store in the refrigerator for up to 2 days or in the freezer for up to 6 months. Makes about 7 cups (1.75 litres)

VEGETABLE STOCK

1 tablespoon oil
1 onion, chopped
2 leeks, chopped
4 carrots, chopped
2 parsnips, chopped
4 sticks celery, leaves included, chopped
2 bay leaves
1 bouquet garni
4 unpeeled cloves garlic
8 black peppercorns

1 Heat the oil in a large, heavy-based pan and add the onion, leek, carrot, parsnip and celery. Cover and cook for 5 minutes without colouring. Add 12 cups (3 litres) of water. Bring to the boil. Skim the surface if required and add the bay leaves, bouquet garni, garlic and peppercorns. Reduce the heat to low and simmer for 1 hour. Skim the froth from the surface of the stock regularly.
2 Ladle the stock in batches into a fine sieve sitting over a bowl. Gently press the solids to extract all the liquid.
3 Leave to cool, then refrigerate until cold and spoon off any fat that has set on the top. At this stage you can reduce the stock to concentrate its flavour (dilute before using) and store in the refrigerator for up to 2 days or in the freezer for up to 6 months. Makes 2 litres (8 cups).

NOTE: Unpeeled garlic adds a subtle flavour and will not cloud the stock.

FREEZING STOCK

Once you are making stock you may as well make a large amount and freeze some for another time. Simply pour the stock into a measuring jug lined with a plastic bag, so you can measure how much you have, and then divide it up and freeze it in convenient portions. Remove the bag from the jug, label, seal securely and freeze.
Alternatively, keep simmering the stock until it is reduced, pour into ice cube trays and freeze. You will now have quite concentrated stock 'cubes' that can be diluted to use.

BOUQUET GARNI

To make a bouquet garni, wrap the green part of a leek loosely around a bay leaf, sprig of thyme, some celery leaves and a few stalks of parsley, then tie with string. Leave enough string for easy removal.

DRESSINGS

Dressing, mayonnaises and vinaigrettes are really very simple to make, so there should be no excuse for reaching for the bottled varieties. Learn how to dress your salads in style at home. Home-made mayonnaise is always a vast improvement on the commercial varieties.

MAYONNAISE

2 egg yolks
1 teaspoon Dijon mustard
1 tablespoon lemon juice
3/4 cup (185 ml/6 fl oz) olive oil

1 Whisk together the egg yolks, mustard and lemon juice for 30 seconds, or until light and creamy. Add the oil, a teaspoon at a time, whisking continuously. You can add the oil more quickly as the mayonnaise thickens. Season to taste with salt and white pepper. Alternatively, place the egg yolks, mustard and lemon juice in a food processor and mix for 10 seconds. With the motor running, add the oil in a slow, thin stream. Season to taste with salt and white pepper. Makes about 1 cup (250 ml/8 fl oz).

AIOLI (GARLIC MAYONNAISE)

1 cup (250 ml/8 fl oz) mayonnaise
3 cloves of garlic, crushed

1 Mix together the mayonnaise and garlic. Season to taste with salt and pepper. Makes about 1 cup (250 ml/8 fl oz).

THOUSAND ISLAND DRESSING

1/2 cup (125 ml/4 fl oz) mayonnaise
1 tablespoon tomato paste
1 teaspoon Worcestershire sauce
1 teaspoon French mustard
2 teaspoons chilli sauce

1 Mix together the mayonnaise, tomato paste, Worcestershire sauce, mustard and chilli sauce. Season with salt. Makes about 1/2 cup (125 ml/4 fl oz).

GREEN GODDESS DRESSING

1 1/2 cups (375 ml/12 fl oz) mayonnaise
4 mashed anchovy fillets
4 finely chopped spring onions
1 clove garlic, crushed
1/4 cup (7 g/1/4 oz) chopped flat-leaf parsley
1/4 cup (15 g/1/2 oz) finely chopped chives
1 teaspoon tarragon vinegar

1 Mix together the mayonnaise, anchovies, spring onions, garlic, parsley, chives and vinegar. Delicious with seafood. Makes about 2 cups (500 ml/16 fl oz).

BASIC VINAIGRETTE

1/2 cup (125 ml/4 fl oz) extra virgin olive oil
2 tablespoons white wine vinegar
1 teaspoon sugar

1 Put the oil, vinegar and sugar in a small jug. Whisk with a small wire whisk or fork until well blended and season with salt and freshly ground black pepper. Makes about 2/3 cups (170 ml/5 1/2 fl oz).

BALSAMIC DRESSING

2 tablespoons balsamic vinegar
1 teaspoon French mustard
1/3 cup (80 ml/2 3/4 fl oz) extra virgin olive oil
1 small clove garlic

1 Whisk the vinegar and mustard in a small jug. Gradually beat in the oil. Season with salt and freshly ground black pepper. Cut the garlic in half, skewer onto a toothpick and leave in the dressing to infuse for at least 1 hour. Makes about 1/2 cup (125 ml/4 fl oz).

ITALIAN DRESSING

3 tablespoons white wine vinegar
3 tablespoons olive oil
1/2 teaspoon sugar
1 tablespoon chopped fresh basil

1 Place the vinegar, olive oil and sugar in a bowl and whisk to combine. Stir in the basil and leave to stand for 15 minutes before serving. Makes about 1/2 cup (125 ml/4 fl oz).

CREAMY SALAD DRESSING

1 tablespoon white wine vinegar
1 teaspoon Dijon mustard
1 crushed clove garlic
1/4 cup (60 ml/2 fl oz) oil
1/4 cup (60 ml/2 fl oz) cream

1 Whisk together the vinegar, mustard and garlic in a bowl. Slowly add the oil and cream and whisk until combined. Serve immediately. Makes about 2/3 cup (170 ml/5 1/2 fl oz).

THAI STYLE DRESSING

1 tablespoon fish sauce
2 tablespoon sweet chilli sauce
2 tablespoon lime juice
1 clove garlic, crushed
1/4 cup peanut oil
1 tablespoon chopped fresh coriander

1 Whisk together the fish sauce, chilli sauce, lime juice and garlic. Slowly add the oil and whisk to combine. Stir in the coriander. Serve immediately. Makes about 3/4 cup (185 ml/6 fl oz).

TARTARE SAUCE

1 1/2 cups (375 ml/12 fl oz) mayonnaise
1 tablespoon finely chopped onion
1 teaspoon lemon juice
1 tablespoon chopped gherkins
1 teaspoon chopped capers
1/4 teaspoon Dijon mustard
1 tablespoon finely chopped parsley

1 Mix together the mayonnaise, onion, lemon juice, gherkins, capers, mustard and parsley. Season with salt and white pepper. Top with a few capers to serve. Makes about 2 cups (500 ml/16 fl oz).

BLUE CHEESE DRESSING

80 g (2 3/4 oz) blue cheese
1/4 cup (60 g/2 oz) sour cream
1/2 cup (125 g/4 oz) whole egg mayonnaise
1 tablespoon chopped chives
1 teaspoon white wine vinegar

1 Mash the blue cheese with a fork to a chunky paste. Add the sour cream, mayonnaise and white pepper to taste. Stir in chives and vinegar. Makes about 1 1/4 cups (315 ml/10 fl oz).

SAVOURY SAUCES

Sauces are a quick and easy way to brighten up any meal. Hot savoury sauces can be served over meat (both hot and cold), chicken, seafood, vegetables and even eggs. Asparagus with a buttery hollandaise is a wonderfully stylish dish, and here we give you instructions for an even easier version.

CLASSIC WHITE SAUCE

1 cup (250 ml/8 fl oz) milk
slice of onion
1 bay leaf
6 peppercorns
30 g (1 oz) butter
1 tablespoon plain flour

1 Put the milk, onion, bay leaf and peppercorns in a small pan. Bring to the boil, remove from the heat and leave to infuse for 10 minutes. Strain the milk, discarding the flavourings.
2 Melt the butter in a small pan and stir in the flour. Cook, stirring, for 1 minute until the mixture is golden and bubbling. Remove from the heat and gradually add the milk, stirring until completely smooth. Return to the heat and stir until the mixture boils. Continue cooking for 1 minute or until thick, remove from the heat and season with salt and white pepper. Serve with steamed cauliflower and broccoli. Also good with fish or corned beef. Serves 2–4.

MORNAY SAUCE

1 1/3 cups (350 ml/11 fl oz) milk
slice of onion
1 bay leaf
6 peppercorns
30 g (1 oz) butter
1 tablespoon plain flour
1/2 cup (60 g/2 oz) finely grated Cheddar
1/4 teaspoon mustard powder

1 Put the milk, onion, bay leaf and peppercorns in a small pan. Bring to the boil, remove from the heat and leave to infuse for 10 minutes. Strain the milk, discarding the flavourings.
2 Melt the butter in a small pan and add the flour. Cook, stirring, for 1 minute until the mixture is golden and bubbling. Add the infused milk, a little at a time, stirring between each addition until completely smooth. Continue stirring until the mixture boils and thickens. Boil for 1 minute more and then remove from the heat. Add the cheese and mustard and stir until the cheese has melted and the sauce is smooth. Season to taste with salt and pepper. Serve with grilled lobster (lobster mornay). Also good with grilled oysters, steamed or poached fish or vegetables. Mornay sauce is often poured over the top of dishes and then grilled or baked. Serves 4.

HINT: When preparing sauces such as these, if you don't want to serve them immediately, lay plastic wrap directly onto the surface to prevent a skin forming.

GREEN PEPPERCORN SAUCE

4 steaks or chicken breast fillets
1 cup (250 ml/8 fl oz) beef or chicken stock
1 cup (250 ml/8 fl oz) cream
2–3 teaspoons canned green peppercorns, rinsed and drained
1 tablespoon brandy

1 Pan-fry the steak or chicken in oil or butter. Remove from the pan and keep warm.
2 Add the stock to the juices in the pan. Stir over low heat until boiling. Add the cream and peppercorns. Boil for 8–10 minutes, stirring until slightly thickened. Add the brandy and boil for 1 minute. Serves 4.

SPEEDY HOLLANDAISE

You can make hollandaise in a food processor: blend 4 egg yolks, 2 tablespoons water and 1 tablespoon lemon juice in the processor for 10 seconds. With the motor running, add 175 g (6 oz) cooled, melted butter in a thin stream.
To make hollandaise in the microwave: melt the butter on high for 1 minute. Beat the yolks, water and lemon juice together and whisk in the butter. Cook for 1 minute 20 seconds on medium, whisking every 20 seconds. Season well. Serve with fish, eggs or vegetables. Serves 4.

VELOUTE SAUCE

30 g (1 oz) butter
3 tablespoons plain flour
1 1/2 cups (375 ml/ 12 fl oz) chicken, fish or veal stock
lemon juice, to taste
1 tablespoon cream

1 Melt the butter in a pan, add the flour and cook over medium heat for 2 minutes, or until a thick paste has formed—be careful not to brown the mixture or it will colour your sauce.
2 Whisk in the stock a little at a time to prevent the mixture becoming lumpy. Cook the sauce, whisking continuously, for 3–5 minutes—it should be quite thick and not have a floury taste.
3 Season with salt, pepper and lemon juice, adding a little at a time. Finally, stir in the cream. Serve immediately, as this sauce will quickly thicken if left to stand. If necessary, add a little extra stock to thin it down. Serve with chicken, seafood or veal. Serves 4.

CUMBERLAND SAUCE

2 oranges
1 lemon
225 g (7 oz) redcurrant jelly
2 teaspoons Dijon mustard
2 tablespoons red wine vinegar
1 cup (250 ml/8 fl oz) port

1 Remove the orange and lemon rind with a zester. Place the rind in a small pan with 1 cup (250 ml/8 fl oz) water and bring to the boil. Cook for 5 minutes, then drain the rind.
2 Squeeze the juice from the oranges and lemon and place in a pan. Add the jelly, mustard, vinegar, port and reserved rind. Slowly bring to the boil, stirring as the jelly melts. Reduce the heat to simmer gently for 15 minutes. Season to taste and serve at room temperature or cover with plastic wrap and refrigerate for up to a week. Serve with ham, turkey, venison or game meats. Serves 8.

SWEET AND SOUR SAUCE

2 tablespoons dry sherry
1 cup (250 ml/8 fl oz) pineapple juice
3 tablespoons white wine vinegar
2 teaspoons soy sauce
2 tablespoons soft brown sugar
2 tablespoons tomato sauce
1 small red capsicum, finely diced
1 tablespoon cornflour

1 Mix together the sherry, pineapple juice, vinegar, soy sauce, brown sugar and tomato sauce in a pan. Cook, stirring constantly, over low heat until the sugar has dissolved. Bring to the boil and add the capsicum.
2 Mix the cornflour in 1 tablespoon water. Add to the pan and cook, stirring, until the mixture boils and thickens. Reduce the heat and simmer for 2 minutes. Serve at once. Serve with spring rolls, pan-fried, grilled or deep-fried fish and pan-fried pork or lamb. Serves 6–8.

SATAY SAUCE

1 tablespoon oil
1 large onion, finely chopped
2 cloves garlic, finely chopped
2 red chillies, finely chopped
1 teaspoon shrimp paste
250 g (8 oz) peanut butter
1 cup (250 ml/8 fl oz) coconut milk
2 teaspoons kecap manis or thick soy sauce
1 tablespoon tomato sauce

1 Heat the oil in a pan and cook the onion and garlic for 8 minutes over low heat, stirring regularly. Add the chilli and shrimp paste, cook for 1 minute and remove from the heat.
2 Add the peanut butter, return to the heat and stir in the coconut milk and 1 cup (250 ml/8 fl oz) water. Bring to the boil over low heat, stirring so that it does not stick. Add the kecap manis and tomato sauce and simmer for 1 minute. Cool. Serve with chicken skewers, meat or fish skewers, or vegetables. Serves 8.

BREAD SAUCE

2 cloves
1 onion
1 cup (250 ml/8 fl oz) milk
1 bay leaf
50 g (1 3/4 oz) fresh breadcrumbs (made using about 3 slices of day-old bread)
3 tablespoons cream

1 Push the cloves into the onion and put in a pan with the milk and bay leaf. Bring to the boil, then remove from the heat, cover and leave for 10 minutes. Remove the onion and leaf.
2 Add the breadcrumbs to the pan and season. Return to the heat, cover and simmer gently for 10 minutes, stirring occasionally. Stir in the cream. Serve warm with roasted spatchcock, chicken, turkey, goose or game meat. Serves 4.

DEMI-GLACE

Beef Stock

1 kg (2 lb) beef bones
1 tablespoon oil
1 onion, chopped
2 carrots, chopped
5 parsley stalks
2 bay leaves
6 peppercorns

Espagnole

2 tablespoons oil
2 carrots, finely chopped
1 onion, finely chopped
1 stalk celery, finely chopped
1 tablespoon flour
1/2 teaspoon tomato paste
bouquet garni

1 To make the beef stock, preheat the oven to hot 220°C (440°F/Gas 7). Roast the bones for 1 hour, or until browned. Heat the oil in a large pan and brown the vegetables, being careful not to burn them. Add the bones, parsley, bay leaves and peppercorns and cover with cold water. Bring to the boil, reduce the heat and simmer for 3–4 hours, skimming off the fat as it rises to the surface. Add a little more cold water if needed. You should have about 3 1/2 cups (875 ml/28 fl oz) of stock—if you have more, continue reducing; if less, add a little water. Strain and cool. Remove any fat which sets on the surface.

2 To make the espagnole, heat the oil in a pan and brown the vegetables. Add the flour and cook, stirring, until browned. Add 2 1/2 cups (600 ml/20 fl oz) of the beef stock with the tomato paste and bouquet garni and bring to the boil. Reduce the heat, half-cover the pan and simmer, skimming off any fat, for 30 minutes, or until reduced to 1 cup (250 ml/8 fl oz). Sieve and leave to cool.

3 To make the demi-glace, put the espagnole and the remaining cup of stock in a pan and simmer until reduced by half. Strain thoroughly through a fine mesh sieve or muslin. Serve with beef tournedos, but good with any type of beef steak. Serves 8.

NOTE: Don't use ready-made stock—it is far too salty for this recipe.
VARIATION: To make a beef glace, reduce the strained stock to a thick sticky liquid which will set to a jelly when cold. This gives a rich flavour when added to sauces.

BEARNAISE SAUCE

1/3 cup (80 ml/2 1/2 fl oz) white wine vinegar
2 spring onions, roughly chopped
2 teaspoons chopped fresh tarragon
2 egg yolks
125 g (4 oz) butter, cubed

1 Put the white wine vinegar, spring onion and tarragon in a small pan. Bring to the boil, then reduce the heat slightly and simmer until the mixture has reduced by a third. Allow to cool completely and then strain the vinegar into a heatproof bowl.

2 Add the egg yolks to the bowl, then place the bowl over a pan of barely simmering water. Whisk until the mixture is thick and pale. Add the butter, a cube at a time, whisking between each addition until the mixture is thick and smooth. Season to taste with salt and pepper and serve immediately with pan-fried steak, roast beef or lamb, or poached salmon. Serves 4.

SWEET SAUCES

Custard and creme anglaise can be served over sticky and steamed pudding, simple apple pies or pastries, crumbles and cobblers and just about any baked pudding you can think of. Our rich butterscotch and chocolate sauces are ideal for drizzling over ice cream. Berry coulis is wonderful with plain sponges or ice cream. And zabaglione is perfect with fruit, biscuits or on its own, at any time!

EASY VANILLA CUSTARD

1 cup (250 ml/8 fl oz) milk
1/4 cup (60 ml/2 fl oz) cream
3 egg yolks
1/3 cup (90 g/3 oz) caster sugar
2 teaspoons cornflour
1 teaspoon vanilla essence

1 Put the milk and cream in a pan and heat until almost at boiling point. Immediately remove the pan from the heat.
2 Whisk the egg yolks together with the sugar and cornflour in a heatproof bowl. Slowly pour the hot milk and cream over the egg mixture, whisking continuously. Return the mixture to the clean pan and stir over low heat for 5 minutes, or until the custard boils and thicken. Remove from the heat immediately. Whisk in the vanilla essence. Serve with apple pie, or any sweet pie, pastry or pudding you can think of. Serves 6.

CREME ANGLAISE

3 egg yolks
2 tablespoons caster sugar
1 1/2 cups (375 ml/12 fl oz) milk
1/2 teaspoon vanilla essence

1 Whisk the yolks and sugar in a heatproof bowl for 2 minutes, or until light and creamy. Heat the milk in a small pan until almost boiling, then pour onto the mixture, whisking constantly.
2 Return the mixture to the pan and stir over low heat for about 5 minutes, or until slightly thickened, enough to coat the back of a spoon. Do not allow to boil or the custard will curdle. Remove the pan from the heat, stir in the vanilla essence and transfer to a jug. Serve immediately, or lay a piece of plastic wrap directly on the surface of the custard to prevent it forming a skin. Serve with fruit tart. Good with all fruit pastries and warmed cakes, and anything you would serve with ordinary custard. Serves 4.

HINT: Any thick sauces, such as custard, which aren't going to be served immediately, should be kept with a sheet of plastic wrap directly over the surface to prevent a skin forming on top.

BUTTERSCOTCH SAUCE

125 g (4 oz) butter
1/2 cup (90 g/3 oz) soft brown sugar
2 tablespoons golden syrup
1/2 cup (125 ml/4 fl oz) cream
1 teaspoon vanilla essence

1 Put the butter and sugar in a pan and stir over low heat until the butter has melted and the sugar has dissolved.
2 Bring to the boil and add the golden syrup and cream. Reduce the heat and simmer for 10 minutes, or until slightly thickened. Remove from the heat and add the vanilla essence. Serve hot or cold with grilled bananas, grilled peaches, nectarines or other fruit, puddings, waffles and crepes. Serves 6.

DARK CHOCOLATE SAUCE

150 g (5 oz) chopped dark chocolate
300 ml (10 fl oz) cream
2 tablespoons caster sugar

1 Put chocolate in a bowl. Bring the cream to the boil in a pan. Stir in the sugar, then pour over the chocolate. Leave for 2 minutes, then stir until smooth. Serve warm. Serves 6.

CHOCOLATE FUDGE SAUCE

1 cup (250 ml/8 fl oz) cream
30 g (1 oz) butter
1 tablespoon golden syrup
200 g (6 1/2 oz) chopped dark chocolate

1 Put the cream, butter, golden syrup and chocolate in a pan. Stir over low heat until melted and smooth. Serve hot or warm. Serves 6.

BERRY COULIS

250 g (8 oz) mixture of berries (strawberries, raspberries or blackberries)
2–4 tablespoons icing sugar, or to taste
1 tablespoon lemon juice
1–2 tablespoons Cointreau or Grand Marnier

1 Hull the berries. Place the fruit in a food processor and add the sugar and lemon juice. Blend until smooth. Stir in the liqueur. Serve with sorbet or fresh or poached fruit, soufflés, ice cream, pies and tarts. Serves 6.

VARIATION: Make mango coulis using 2 mangoes, peeled, seeded and puréed, or frozen mango purée.

ZABAGLIONE

8 egg yolks
1/3 cup (90 g/3 oz) caster sugar
1 1/4 cups (315 ml/10 fl oz) Marsala

1 Beat the egg yolks and sugar in a heatproof bowl until pale yellow.
2 Put the bowl over a gently simmering pan of water and beat, adding the Marsala gradually—don't let the base of the bowl touch the water. Beat for 5 minutes, or until thick and frothy. To test if it is ready, dip a metal spoon into the zabaglione, hold it up and if the mixture slides down the back it is not yet thickened enough. If you can draw a line through the zabaglione with a spoon and leave a trail, it is ready. Serve immediately or keep refrigerated for up to 1 day. Serve chilled with fresh blueberries and strawberries or just about any poached or grilled fruits (pears, nectarines, peaches) or with sponge fingers (langues de chats). Serves 10–12.

MAKING PASTA

Our basic pasta dough makes enough to serve 6 as a starter or 4 as a main meal. All the ingredients should be at room temperature before you start. Oil makes the dough easier to work with but you don't have to use it. Use plain or unbleached flour to give a well-textured light dough.

BASIC PASTA DOUGH

300 g (10 oz) plain flour
3 large (60 g/2 oz) eggs
30 ml (1 fl oz) olive oil
a pinch of salt

1 To mix the dough by hand, sift and mound the flour on a work surface or in a large bowl and make a well in the centre.
2 Break the eggs into the well and add the oil and salt. Begin to whisk the eggs and oil together with a fork, incorporating the flour as you do so. Gradually blend the flour with the eggs, working from the centre out. Use your free hand to hold the mound in place and stop leakage if any of the egg escapes.
3 Knead the dough on a lightly floured surface with smooth, light strokes, turning it as you fold and press. It should be soft and pliable, but dry to the touch. If sticky, knead in a little flour.
4 It will take at least 6 minutes kneading to achieve a smooth and elastic texture with a slightly glossy appearance. Put the dough in a plastic bag without sealing, or cover with a tea towel or an upturned bowl. Allow to rest for 30 minutes. (The dough can also be mixed in a food processor.)

ROLLING AND CUTTING BY HAND

1 Divide the dough into three or four manageable portions and cover them.
2 Lightly flour a large work surface. Flatten one portion of dough onto the surface and, using a long, floured rolling pin, roll out the dough from the centre to the outer edge.
3 Continue rolling, always from in front of you outward, and rotating the dough often. Keep the work surface dusted with just enough flour to prevent sticking. When you have rolled a well-shaped circle, fold the dough in half and roll it out again. Continue in this way seven or eight times to give a smooth circle of pasta about 5 mm (1/4 inch) thick.
4 Roll the sheet quickly and smoothly to a thickness of 2.5 mm (1/8 inch). Patch any tears with a piece of dough from the edge and a little water to help it stick.
5 As each sheet is done, transfer it to a dry tea towel. If the pasta is to be used to make filled pasta keep the sheets covered, but if it is to be cut into lengths or shapes, leave

them uncovered while the others are being rolled, so that the surface moisture will dry slightly.

6 For lasagne sheets, simply cut the pasta into the sizes required. The best way to cut lengths such as fettucine is to roll each pasta sheet up like a swiss roll, then cut this into uniform widths with a long, sharp knife. For tagliatelle, cut at 8 mm (4/10 inch) intervals, 5 mm (1/4 inch) for fettucine, or about 3 cm (1 1/4 inches) for pappardelle. Discard the offcuts. Place the lengths in a single layer on a tea towel to surface dry for no more than 10 minutes. Or hang long pasta strips to surface dry on floured broom handles or long wooden spoons between two chairs. Lengths can also be cut from the flat sheet, using a long, sharp knife or a pastry wheel. You may find it easier to run the wheel beside a ruler for straight cutting. A zig-zag pastry wheel will give an interesting edge to pasta shapes such as lasagnette and farfalle.

Don't leave pasta to dry in a cold place or in a draught or it may become brittle. Pasta is better if it allowed to dry slowly.

ROLLING AND CUTTING WITH A PASTA MACHINE

1 Clamp the machine securely onto the edge of your work surface. Divide the dough into three or four portions and shape each into a rough log. Keeping the unworked portions covered, take one and flatten it by one or two rolls with a rolling pin. Dust lightly with plain flour.

2 With the machine's rollers at their widest setting, crank the dough through two or three times. Fold it in thirds, turn the dough 90 degrees and feed through again. If the dough feels damp or tends to stick, lightly flour the outside surfaces each time it is rolled until it passes through cleanly. Repeat this folding and rolling process eight to ten times, or until the dough is a smooth and elastic sheet with a velvety appearance. From now on the dough is not folded.

3 Reduce the width of the rollers by one setting and pass the dough through. Repeat, setting the rollers one notch closer each time until you have rolled to the desired thickness. Some machines may roll the sheets too thinly on their last setting, tearing them. A way around this is to stop at the second last setting and roll the dough through several times. It will come out a little thinner each time. This step also applies to machines that don't roll the pasta thinly enough on the last setting.

4 As each sheet is completed, place it on a dry tea towel. Leave uncovered to surface dry for 10 minutes if the sheets are to be cut, but cover them if they are to be used for filled pasta.

5 For lasagne sheets, cut the pasta to the desired size. For narrower lengths, select the appropriate cutters on the machine and crank each pasta sheet through it. Spread them on the tea towel until ready to be cooked, only covering them if they appear to be drying too much. Long pasta such as tagliatelle can be hung to surface dry on floured broom handles or long wooden spoons balanced between chairs.

INDEX

Afgans, 273
Aioli, 362
almonds
  Apricot Jam with, 348
  Chicken and, 138–9
  Trout with, 144
Anzac Biscuits, 280
apple
  Baked, 313
  Pie, 317
  Sauce, 112, 113
  Strudel, 312–13
  Waldorf Salad, 207
Apple Betty, 328–9
Apples, Toffee, 340–1
Apricot and Almond Jam, 348
Apricot Chicken, 139
arborio, 46
artichokes, 40
Asian Greens, 190–1
asparagus, 40
  Cottage Cheese and Avocado sandwich filling with, 214
  Cream of Asparagus Soup, 86–7
  Hollandaise, 202
  preparation of, 38
Aspic, 224
avocado, 40
Avocado, Cottage Cheese and Asparagus sandwich filling, 214

bacon
  Caesar Salad, 206
  Coq au Vin, 132
  Creamy Boscaiola, 181
  Filet Mignon, 96
  Hamburger with the Works, 102
  Lamb's Fry and, 61
  Macaroni Cheese, 182
  Minestrone, 68
  Paella, 186–7
  Pork and Veal Terrine, 118
  Quiche Lorraine, 216–17
  Roast Chicken with Breadcrumb Stuffing, 124–5
  Seafood Crepes, 149
  Spaghetti Carbonara, 178–9
Bacon and Egg Pie, 225
Bacon and Onion Rosti, 198
Baked Apples, 313
Baked Cheesecake, 300–1
Baked Egg Custard, Classic, 324
Baked Jacket Potatoes, 194
Baked Rice Custard, 324
Baked Snapper with Garlic and Tomatoes, 144–5
baking dishes, 13
Baklava, 290–1
Balsamic Dressing, 363
banana
  Cream, 255
  Muffins, 270
  Smoothie, 58
Barbecue Marinade, 114
barbecuing, 15
Basic Biscuits, 294–5
Basic Vinaigrette, 362–3
basil, 42
basmati, 46
bay leaf, 42
Bean Nachos, 173
beans, 38, 40
Beans, Chilli, 163
Béchamel Sauce, 164, 174
beef
  Black Bean Sauce and, 98–9
  Bombay Curry, 98
  Chilli con Carne, 103
  Classic Lasagne, 174
  Consomme, 84
  Cornish Pasties, 232
  cuts of, 18–19
  Filet Mignon, 96
  Hamburger with the Works, 102
  Hot Beef Borscht, 82
  Meat Loaf, 97
  Meat Pie, 230–1
  Nachos, 105
  Pasta and Meatballs, 177
  Pepper Steak, 94
  Pot Roast, 100–1
  Rissoles with Gravy, 100
  Roast Beef and Yorkshire Puddings, 88
  Spaghetti Bolognese, 178
  Steak and Kidney Pudding, 226–7
  Steak Diane, 95

Steak Sandwich, 96
Stock, 360
Thai Beef Salad, 104
Traditional Corned Beef and Vegetables, 92–3
Beef Bourguignon, 93
Beef Stroganoff, 91
Beef Wellington, 90
beetroot, 40
Hot Beef Borscht, 82
Pickled, 354
preparation of, 38
Belgian endive, 40
Bernaise Sauce, 367
Berry Coulis, 369
Berry Flan, Summer, 318–19
Berry Jam, Mixed, 346
Berry Pie, Lattice, 315
beverages
Banana Smoothie, 58
Breakfast Shake, 58
biscuits
Afghans, 273
Anzac, 280
basic, 294–5
Brandy Snaps, 283
Chocolate Chip Cookies, 276
Coconut Macaroons, 282
Florentines, 274
Gingerbread People, 280
Jam Drops, 277
Melting Moments, 279
Monte Creams, 278
Peanut Butter, 276
Shortbread, 292
Black Bean Sauce, Beef in, 98–9
Black Forest Gateau, 256–7
Blackberry Jelly, 304
Blue Cheese Dressing, 363
Blueberry Pancakes, 55
Boiled Eggs, 52
Boiled Fruit Cake, 251
bok choy, 40
Bombay Curry, 98
Borscht, Hot Beef, 82
Boscaiola, Creamy, 181
Boulangère Potatoes, 201
Bourbon Cream, 320, 321
Bourguignon Beef, 93
bowls, mixing, 13
Brandy Butter, 332
Brandy Snaps, 283
bread
Brioche, 234–5
Damper, 237
Fruit and Nut, 241
Sour Cream Polenta, 242
White Dinner Rolls, 240
Wholemeal, 243
Bread and Butter Pudding, 335
Bread Sauce, 366
Breadcrumb Stuffing, Roast Chicken with, 124–5
Breakfast Shake, 58
bream, 36
Brioche, 234–5
broccoli, 38, 40
Broccoli Soup, Cream of, 79
brussels sprouts, 38, 40
buns
Chelsea, 236–7
Finger, 238
Hot Cross, 239
Burgers, Lentil, 170
Buttercake, 264–5
Buttercream, 264
Butterscotch Sauce, 369

cabbage, 40
Coleslaw, 207
preparation of, 38
Caesar Salad, 206
cakes
Banana, 255
Banana Muffins, 270
Black Forest, 256
Boiled Fruit, 251
Buttercake, 264
Carrot, 248
Chocolate, 254
Chocolate Mud, 244
Chocolate Muffins, 271
Christmas Fruit, 250
Cinnamon Tea, 262
Coconut, 248
Custard Orange, 265
Date and Nut Rolls, 252
Honey Roll, 272
Hummingbird, 257
icings, 266–7
Jam Swiss Roll, 258
Lamingtons, 260–1
Madeira, 252
Orange Poppy Seed, 247
Pineapple Upside-down, 258
Pumpkin Scones, 268
Rock Cakes, 262
Scones, 268
Semolina Lemon Syrup, 260
Sponge, 246
Meringues, 263
Muffins, 270
calamari, 35, 36
Chilli Plum Sauce with, 158
Paella, 186–7
Spaghetti Marinara, 151
cannelloni, 46
Cannelloni, Spinach and Ricotta, 176–7
capsicums, 38–9, 40

Capsicums, Stuffed, 201
Caramel, Crème, 310
Caramel Filling, 294
Caramel Sauce, 309
Caramel Slice, Chocolate, 286
Caramelized Onion Quiche, 219
Caramels, Hard, 338–9
Carrot Cake, 248
carrots, 39, 40
Carrots, Honey-glazed, 203
Cashew Stuffing, Roast Turkey with, 126–7
casserole dishes, 13
casseroles
  chicken, 26
  meat, 16
cauliflower, 39, 40
Cauliflower Cheese, 203
celery, 39, 40
Char-grilled Baby Octopus, 159
Char-grilled Vegetables, 205
cheese
  Caesar Salad, 206
  Cauliflower Cheese, 203
  Fettucine Alfredo, 181
  Greek Salad, 208
  Herb Omelette, 54
  Macaroni Cheese, 182
  Risotto Parmesan, 182
  Mornay Sauce, 364
Spinach and Ricotta Cannelloni, 176–7
Cheese and Pine Nut Filo Triangles, 233
Cheese Soufflés, 166
Cheesecake, 301
Cheesecake, Baked, 300–1
Cheesy Potato, 192
Chelsea Buns, 236–7
Cherry Clafoutis, 307
chervil, 42
chicken
  Almonds and, 138–9
  Apricot Chicken, 139
  buying, 24
  carving, 26
  cooking, 26
  Coq au Vin, 132
  Corn Chowder and, 86
  Cream of Chicken Soup, 78
  cuts of, 28–9
  Deep Dish Pie, 222–3
  jointing and boning of, 24
  Leek and Chicken Cobbler, 220
  livers, 27
  mince, 27
  Mulligatawny, 85
  Nuggets with Dipping Sauce, 137
  Paella, 186–7
  preparation of, 26–7
  Roast with Breadcrumb Stuffing, 124–5
  Southern Fried, 136–7
  Stock, 360–1
  storing and freezing, 9, 24
  stuffing and trussing, 27
  Sweet Chilli Wings, 135
  Tandoori Chicken, 128–9
  Teriyaki Chicken, 139
  Thai Green Chicken Curry, 134
  Tom Kha Gai, 83
  Vegetable Soup and, 70–1
Chicken Chasseur, 130–1
Chicken Chow Mein, 187
Chicken Cordon Bleu, 130
Chicken Kief, 131
Chicken Laksa, 81
Chicken Liver Pâté, 133
Chicken Noodle Soup, 69
Chicken Satay, 128
chickpeas
  Felafel, 162
  Lentil Burgers, 170
  Three-Bean Salad, 212
Chilli Beans, 163
Chilli Chicken Wings, Sweet, 135
Chilli con Carne, 103
Chilli Marinade, 114
Chilli Plum Sauce, 158
chillis, 40
Chinese broccoli, 40
Chips, 192
chives, 42
chocolate
  Brownies, 284–5
  Buttercream, 254
  Cake, 254
  Eclairs, 289
  Fudge, 336–7
  Mousse, 311
  Mud Cake, 244
  Muffins, 271
  Rich Icing, 267
  Rich Self-saucing Pudding, 308
  Sauce, 369
  Sour Cream Icing, 267
  Topping, 244
Chocolate and Peanut Filling, 295
Chocolate Caramel Slice, 286
Chocolate Chip Cookies, 276
Chocolate Fleck Icing, 295
Choux Pastry, 298, 359
chowder
  Chicken and Corn, 86
  Smoked Haddock, 72
Christmas Fruit Cake, 250
Christmas Pudding, 332

Chutney, Spicy Dried Fruit, 350
Cinnamon Tea Cake, 262
Citrus Frosting, 266
Citrus Summer Salad, 62
clams, 31, 36
Classic Baked Egg Custard, 324
Classic White Sauce, 264
Cobbler, Chicken and Leek, 220
Coconut Cake, 248
Coconut Ice, 341
Coconut Jam Slice, 274
Coconut Macaroons, 282
colanders, 13
Colcannon, 192
Cold Meat and Mustard sandwich filling, 214
Cold Potato Salad, 209
Coleslaw, 207
Compote, Dried Fruit, 62
Consomme, Beef, 84
cookery terms, 10–11
Coq au Vin, 132
Coquilles Saint Jacques, 153
coriander, 42
Coriander Garlic Cream, 170
corn, 39, 40
Corn Chowder, Chicken and, 86
Corned Beef and Vegetables, Traditional, 92–3
Cornish Pasties, 232
Cornmeal Breads, 64
Cottage Cheese, Asparagus and Avocado sandwich filling, 214
Country Rabbit in Red Wine, 136
Country Vegetable Pie, 221
couscous, 46
Couscous, Spicy Vegetable, 171
crab, 30, 31, 34, 36
Cream of Asparagus Soup, 86–7
Cream of Broccoli Soup, 79
Cream of Chicken Soup, 78
Cream of Mushroom Soup, 87
Cream of Tomato Soup, 74–5
Creamed Rice, 324
Creamed Spinach, 202
Creamy Boscaiola, 181
Creamy Parsnip Mash, 192
Creamy Salad Dressing, 363
Crème Anglaise, 368
Crème Brûlée, 334
Crème Caramel, 310
Crepes, Seafood, 149
Crepes Suzette, 322
Crumbed Lamb Cutlets, 109
Crumble, Rhubarb, 328
Crunchy Muesli Slice, 291
cucumber, 40
Cumberland Sauce, 365
curry
  Bombay, 98
  Thai Green Chicken, 134
  Thai Vegetable, 163
custard
  Baked Rice, 324
  Classic Baked Egg, 324
  Easy Vanilla, 368
Custard Orange Cake, 265
Custard Tarts, 284

Damper, 237
Danish Pastry, 358–9
dates
  Date and Nut Rolls, 252
  Oat and Date Muffins, 64
  Sticky Date Pudding, 308–9
Deep-dish Chicken Pie, 222–3
Demi Glace, 367
dill, 42
Dill Pickles, 354
Dipping Sauce, 137
dressings
  Aioli, 362
  Balsamic, 363
  Basic Vinaigrette, 362
  Blue Cheese, 363
  Creamy Salad, 363
  Green Goddess, 362
  Italian, 363
  Mayonnaise, 362
  Tartare Sauce, 363
  Thai Style, 363
  Thousand Island, 362
Dried Fruit Compote, 62
drinks
  Banana Smoothie, 58
  Breakfast Shake, 58
Duchess Potatoes, 197
Duck with Orange Sauce, Roast, 127
Dumplings, Golden Syrup, 330

Easy Vanilla Custard, 368
Eclairs, Chocolate, 289
eggplant, 40
  preparation of, 39
  Ratatouille, 198
  Rocket sandwich filling with, 214
  Vegetable Lasagne, 164–5
  Vegetable Strudel, 165

eggs
Bacon and Egg Pie, 225
Boiled, 52
Fried, 52
Herb Omelette, 54
Mixed Cress sandwich filling with, 214
Omelette, 54
Poached, 53
Scrambled, 52
Eggs Benedict, 53
Eggs Florentine, 53
English spinach, 40
English Trifle, 314

farfalle, 46
Farmhouse Rhubarb Pie, 318
Felafel, 162
fennell, 40
fettucine, 46
Fettucine Alfredo, 181
Field Mushrooms, Stuffed, 168
Filet Mignon, 96
Finger Buns, 238
fish, 30, 31–2, 36–7
see also seafood
Fish and Chips, 142–3
Fish Cakes, Thai, 142
Fish Stock, 361
Fisherman's Pie, 140
Flan, Summer Berry, 318–19
Florentines, 274
flounder, 36
Fool, Fruit, 304
freezing chart, 48–9
French Dressing, 363
French Onion Soup, 71
French Toast, 60
Fresh Fruit Pavlova, 302
Fried Eggs, 52
Fried Noodles, 188–9
Fried Rice, 185
frittata
Grated Vegetable, 167
Vegetable, 167
Fritters, Vegetable, 199
frosting, 266
frozen food, 8, 9
fruit
Breakfast Shake, 58
Citrus Summer Salad, 62
Fresh Fruit Pavlova, 302
Fruit Fool, 304
see also under fruit
eg banana
Fruit and Nut Bread, 241
fruit cake
Boiled, 251
Christmas, 250
Fruit Chutney, Spicy Dried, 350
Fruit Mince Pies, 287
frying pans, 13
fudge
Chocolate, 236–7
Vanilla, 336
fusilli, 46

garlic chives, 42
Garlic Mayonnaise, 362
Garlic Prawns, 150
ginger, 40
Ginger Icing, 267
Ginger Marinade, 114
Gingerbread People, 280–1
Glacé Icing, 236, 238
gnocchi, fresh, 46
Gnocchi with Tomato and Basil Sauce, Potato, 172–3
Golden Syrup Dumplings, 330
Grandma's Pavlova, 303
grapefruit
Citrus Summer Salad, 62
Toasted, 57
Grated Vegetable Frittata, 167
Gravy, Rissoles with, 100
Greek Salad, 208
Green Goddess Dressing, 362
Green Peppercorn Sauce, 365
Gremolata, 120, 121
grilling, 15
Guacamole, 105

haddock
Smoked Fish Kedgeree, 184
Smoked Haddock Chowder, 72
ham
Chicken Cordon Bleu, 130
Fried Rice, 185
Orange-glazed, 116–17
Pea and Ham Soup, 75
Super Supreme, 228–9
Hamburger with the Works, 102
Hard Caramels, 338–9
Hash Browns, 60–1
Hasselback Potatoes, 196
Hedgehog Slice, 296
Herb Omelette, 54
Herb Potatoes, Sauteed, 196
Herbed Mash, 192
herbs, 42–3
Hollandaise, Asparagus, 202
Hollandaise in a Processor, 365
Hollandaise Sauce, 146
holy basil, 42
Home-made Yoghurt, 58
Honey Cream, 272
Honey Frosting, 266
Honey-glazed Carrots, 203
Honey Roll, 272
Hot Beef Borscht, 82

Hot Cross Buns, 239
Hot Passionfruit Soufflé, 230–1
Hot Potato Salad, 208–9
Hot Tofu Salad, 168
Hotpot, Lancashire, 111
Hummingbird Cake, 257
Hummus, 162

Ice Cream, 326–7
icing
  biscuit, 295
  cake, 266–7
  Chocolate, 296
  Glacé, 236, 238
  Vanilla, 297
Irish Stew, 112
Italian Dressing, 363

Jacket Potatoes, Baked, 194
Jam Drops, 277
Jam Swiss Roll, 258
jams
  Apricot and Almond, 348
  Mixed Berry, 346
  Raspberry, 348–9
  Strawberry, 346
  see also marmalade
jasmine rice, 46
jelly
  Blackberry, 304
  Rich Mint, 352
John Dory, 36

Kedgeree, Smoked Fish, 184
kitchen equipment, 12–13
knives, 12

ladles, 12
Laksa, Seafood, 80–1
lamb
  Bombay Curry, 98
  Crumbed Cutlets, 109
  cuts of, 20–1
  Irish Stew, 112
  Lancashire Hotpot, 111
  Minted Rack of, 108
  Minty Lamb Shanks, 106
  Roast Leg with Mint Sauce, 110
  Roasted Rack of, 108
  Shepherd's Pie, 107
  Steak and Kidney Pudding, 226–7
Lamb's Fry and Bacon, 61
Lamingtons, 260–1
Lancashire Hotpot, 111
lasagne, 46
  Classic, 174
  Vegetable, 164–5
Lattice Berry Pie, 315
Lebanese cucumber, 40
leeks, 40
  Chicken and Leek Cobbler, 220
  Vichyssoise, 78
lemon basil, 42
Lemon Curd, 346
Lemon Delicious, 306
Lemon Meringue Pie, 316
Lemon Syrup Cake, Semolina, 260
Lemon Tarts, Little, 292–3
lemon thyme, 42
lemongrass, 42
Lentil Burgers, 170
lettuce, 40
Lime Butter Filling, 294
Lime Marmalade, 348
Little Lemon Tarts, 292–3
lobster, 30, 31, 33, 36
Lobster Mornay, 157
Lobster Thermidor, 156–7

macaroni, 46
Macaroni Cheese, 182
Macaroni, Coconut, 282
Madeira Cake, 252
marinades, 114
marjoram, 42
marmalade
  Lime, 348
  Three-fruit, 334
Marshmallow Filling, 295
Marshmallows, Toasted, 342–3
Mashed Potato, 192
Matchsticks, 296–7
mayonnaise, 362
measurements, 50–1
meat, 8, 9, 14, 15, 16, 17, 18–23
  see also bacon; beef; chicken; ham; lamb; pork; veal
Meat Loaf, 97
Meat Pie, 230–1
Meatballs, Pasta and, 177
Melting Moments, 279
Meringue Pie, Lemon, 316
Meringues, 263
Mince Pies, Fruit, 287
Minestrone, 68
Mint Jelly, Rich, 352
Mint Sauce, 110
Minted Rack of Lamb, 108
Minty Lamb Shanks, 106
Mixed Berry Jam, 346
Monte Creams, 278
Moules Mariniere, 155
Mousse, Chocolate, 311
Mud Cake, Chocolate, 244
Muesli, 57
Muesli, Swiss, 56
Muesli, Toasted, 56
Muesli Slice, Crunchy, 291
muffins, 270
  Banana, 270
  Chocolate, 271
  Oat and Date, 64
  Wholemeal, 64

Mulligatawny, 85
mushrooms, 40
Cream of Mushroom Soup, 87
Creamy Boscaiola, 181
preparation of, 39
Stuffed Field, 168
mussels, 36
Moules Mariniere, 155
Paella, 186–7
preparation of, 34
Spaghetti Marinara, 151
storage of, 31
Tomato and Wine with, 156
Mustard Cream, 116
Mustard Vinaigrette, 212

nachos
Bean, 173
Beef, 105
noodles
Chicken Chow Mein, 187
Chicken Noodle Soup, 69
Fried, 188–9
Singapore, 188
Nut and Date Rolls, 252
Nut Roast 160

Oat and Date Muffins, 64
octopus, 31, 35, 36
Octopus, Char-grilled Baby, 159
Omelette, 54
Omelette, Herb, 54
onions, 40
Bacon and Onion Rosti, 198
Caramelized Onion Quiche, 219
French Onion Soup, 71
Pickled, 354
storage of, 9
Orange Butter, 322
Orange-glazed Ham, 116–17
oranges
Citrus Summer Salad, 62
Cream Cheese Filling, 295
Custard Orange Cake, 265
Passionfruit and Orange Sorbet, 327
Poppy Seed Cake, 247
oregano, 42
Osso Buco with Gremolata, 120–1
oven temperatures, 50
Oxtail Soup, 73
oysters, 36
Kilpatrick, 152
Mornay, 152
Oysters Kilpatrick, 152
Oysters Mornay, 152

Paella, 186–7
pan-frying
chicken 26
meat, 15
Pancake Stack, 55
Parmigiana, Veal, 120
parsley, 42
Parsley Sauce, 92
Parsnip Mash, Creamy, 192
parsnips, 39, 40
Passionfruit and Orange Sorbet, 327
Passionfruit Frosting, 266
Passionfruit Glace Icing, 295
Passionfruit Soufflé, Hot, 330
pasta, 44, 46–7
Creamy Boscaiola, 181
making, 370
Meatballs and, 177
Salad, 211
see also cannelloni; fettucine; lasagne; macaroni; spaghetti; tagliatelle
Pasta Sauce, Tomato, 179
Pasties, Cornish, 232
pastry
Choux, 298, 358
Danish, 358
Plain Shortcrust, 357
Puff, 359
Rough Puff, 358
Sweet Shortcrust, 357
pâté
Chicken Liver, 133
Smoked Trout, 143
Patties, Salmon, 147
pavlova
Fresh Fruit, 302
Grandma's, 303
Pea and Ham Soup, 75
Peach Melba, 305
Peanut Brittle, 340
Peanut Butter Biscuits, 276–7
Peanut Sauce, 128
Pears, Poached, 312
peas, 39, 40
Pecan Pie, 320–1
peelers, 12
penne, 46
Pepper Steak, 94
Peppercorn Sauce, Veal with, 122
peppermint, 42
Peppermint Filling, 295
Pesto with Tagliatelle, 180
Piccalilli, 352
Pickled Beetroot, 354
Pickled Onions, 354
pickles
Beetroot, Pickled, 354
Dill, 354
Fruit Chutney, Spicy Dried, 350

Onions, Pickled, 354
Piccalilli, 352
Rich Mint Jelly, 352
Tomato Sauce, 350
pies (savoury)
Bacon and Egg, 225
Country Vegetable, 221
Deep-dish Chicken, 222–3
Meat, 230–1
Spinach, 223
pies (sweet)
Apple, 317
Lattice Berry, 315
Farmhouse Rhubarb, 318
Lemon Meringue, 316
Pecan, 320–1
Pine Nut and Cheese Filo Triangles, 233
Pineapple Upside-down Cake, 258
pippis, 31
Pizza Base, 228
Pizza Sauce, 228
Plain Shortcrust Pastry, 357
Plum Cobbler, 329
Plum Sauce Marinade, 114
Poached Eggs, 53
Poached Pears, 312
Poached Salmon with Hollandaise Sauce, 146
polenta, 46
Polenta Bread, Sour Cream, 242
Poppy Seed Cake, Orange, 247
pork
cuts of, 22–3
Normandy Sauce with, 117
Pasta and Meatballs, 177
Roast Pork and Apple Sauce, 112–13
Singapore Noodles, 118
Sweet and Sour, 115
Won Ton Soup, 76
see also bacon; ham
Pork and Veal Terrine, 118
Pork Pie, 224–5
Pork Ribs, 114
Porridge, 63
Pot Roast, Beef, 100–1
potato salad
Cold, 209
Hot, 208–9
potatoes, 40
Bacon and Onion Rosti, 198
Baked Jacket, 194
Cheesy, 192
Chips, 192
Colcannon, 192
Creamy Parsnip Mash, 192
Croquettes, 204
Duchess, 197
Gnocchi with Tomato and Basil Sauce, 172–3
Hash Browns, 60–1
Hasselback, 196
Herbed Mash, 192
Mashed, 192
preparation of, 39
Roast, 200–1
Sauteed Herb, 196
Scalloped, 200–1
storage of, 9
Vichyssoise, 78–9
Wedges, 193
Prawn Cocktail, 154
Prawn Cutlets with Tartare Sauce, 154–5
prawns, 36
buying, 30
Fried Noodles, 188–9
Fried Rice, 185
Garlic, 150
Paella, 186–7
preparation of, 34
Seafood Crepes, 149
Seafood Laksa, 80–1
Singapore Noodles, 188
Spaghetti Marinara, 151
storage of, 31
Won Ton Soup, 76
Profiteroles, 298–9
pumpkin, 40
preparation of, 39
Scones, 269
Soup, 77
Stuffed, 204–5
purple basil, 42

quiche
Caramelized Onion, 219
Quiche Lorraine, 216–7
Salmon and Spring Onion, 218

Rabbit in Red Wine, Country, 136
rainbow trout, 36
Raspberry Jam, 348–9
Ratatouille, 198
ravioli, fresh, 46
refrigeration, 9, 14, 24, 30, 31, 48–9
Rhubarb Crumble, 328
Rhubarb Pie, Farmhouse, 318
rice, 45, 46–7
Creamed, 324
Fried, 185
Paella, 186–7
Risotto Parmesan, 182
Salad, 210
Smoked Fish Kedgeree, 184
Vegetable Pilaf, 183
Rice Custard, Baked, 324
Rich Chocolate Icing, 267

Rich Chocolate Self-saucing Pudding, 308
Rich Mint Jelly, 352
Ricotta Cannelloni, Spinach and, 176–7
risoni, 46
Risotto Parmesan, 182
Rissoles with Gravy, 100
Roast Beef with Yorkshire Puddings, 88
Roast Chicken with Breadcrumb Stuffing, 124–5
Roast Duck with Orange Sauce, 127
Roast Leg of Lamb with Mint Sauce, 110
Roast Pork and Apple Sauce, 112–13
Roast Rack of Lamb, 108
Roast Turkey with Cashew Stuffing, 126–7
Roast Vegetables, 200
roasts
  chicken, 26
  meat, 17
Rock Cakes, 262–3
rocket, 42
Rocket and Eggplant sandwich filling, 214
Rocky Road, 343
rolling pins, 12
Rolls, White Dinner, 240
rosemary, 42
Rosti, Bacon and Onion, 198
Rough Pastry, 358
Rum Balls, 338

sage, 42
salad
  Caesar, 206
  Citrus Summer, 62
  Cold Potato, 209
  Coleslaw, 207
  Greek, 208
  Hot Potato, 208–9
  Hot Tofu, 168
  Niçoise, 213
  Pasta, 211
  Rice, 210
  Tabbouleh, 210–11
  Thai Beef, 104
  Three-bean, 212
  Waldorf, 207
Salad sandwich filling, Tuna, 214
salmon, 36
  Patties, 147
  Poached with Hollandaise Sauce, 146
  Salmon and Spring Onion Quiche, 218
Salsa, Tomato, 162
Sandwich, Steak, 96
Sandwich Fillings, 214
sardines, 36
Satay, Chicken, 128
Satay Sauce, 366
saucepans, 13
sauces (savoury)
  Apple, 112, 113
  Béchamel, 164
  Bernaise, 367
  Bread, 366
  Chilli Plum, 158
  Classic White, 364
  Cocktail, 154
  Cumberland, 365
  Demi Glace, 367
  Dipping, 137
  Green Peppercorn, 365
  Hollandaise, 146
  Hollandaise in a Processor, 365
  Mint, 110
  Mornay, 364
  Parsley, 92
  Peanut, 128
  Pizza, 228
  Satay, 366
  Sweet and Sour, 366
  Tartare, 144–5, 363
  Tomato, 160, 172, 176, 350
  Tomato Pasta, 179
  Veloute, 365
sauces (sweet)
  Berry Coulis, 369
  Butterscotch, 369
  Caramel, 309
  Chocolate Fudge, 369
  Dark Chocolate, 369
  Crème Anglaise, 368
  Easy Vanilla Custard, 368
  Zabaglione, 369
Sausage Rolls, 227
Sauteed Herb Potatoes, 196
Scalloped Potatoes, 200–1
scallops, 36
  Coquilles Saint Jacques, 153
Scaloppini, Veal, 123
Scones, 268
Scones, Pumpkin, 269
Scrambled Eggs, 52
seafood
  buying, 30
  common types of, 36–7
  Fish and Chips, 142–3
  Fisherman's Pie, 140
  freezing, 30, 31
  Paella, 186–7
  preparation of, 31–5
  Salad Niçoise, 213
  Spaghetti Marinara, 151
  storage of, 30–1
  Thai Fish Cakes, 142
  thawing of, 31
  see also calamari; fish; haddock; lobster; mussels; oysters; prawns; snapper; trout; tuna
Seafood Crepes, 149

Seafood Laksa, 80–1
Semolina Lemon Syrup Cake, 260
Shake, Breakfast, 58
shallots, 40
Shepherd's Pie, 107
shopping, 8, 14, 24, 30
Shortbread, 292
shortcrust pastry, 357–8
silverbeet, 40
Singapore Noodles, 188
skate, 36
slices
  Chocolate Caramel, 286
  Coconut Jam, 274
  Crunchy Muesli, 291
  Hedgehog, 296
  Vanilla, 288
Small Toffees, 342
Smoked Fish Kedgeree, 184
Smoked Haddock Chowder, 72
smoked trout, 36
Smoked Trout Pâté, 143
Smoothie, Banana, 58
snapper, 36
Snapper with Garlic and Tomatoes, Baked, 144–5
snow peas, 39, 40
Sorbet, Passionfruit and Orange, 327
sorrell, 42
soufflé
  Cheese, 166
  Hot Passionfruit, 330–1
soup
  Asparagus, Cream of, 86
  Beef Consomme, 84
  Broccoli, Cream of, 79
  Chicken, Cream of, 78
  Chicken Noodle, 69
  Chicken and Corn Chowder, 86
  Chicken and Vegetable, 70
  French Onion, 71
  Hot Beef Borscht, 82
  Minestrone, 68
  Mulligatawny, 85
  Mushroom, Cream of, 87
  Oxtail, 73
  Pea and Ham, 75
  Pumpkin, 77
  Seafood Laksa, 80
  Smoked Haddock Chowder, 72
  Spring Vegetable, 66
  Tom Kha Gai, 83
  Tomato, Cream of, 74
  Vegetable, 80
  Won Ton, 76
Sour Cream Polenta Bread, 242
Southern Fried Chicken, 136–7
spaghetti, 46
Spaghetti Bolognese, 178
Spaghetti Carbonara, 178–9
Spaghetti Marinara, 151
Spaghetti Primavera, 180
spatulas, 12
spearmint, 42
Spicy Dried Fruit Chutney, 350
Spicy Vegetable Couscous, 171
spinach, 40
  Creamed, 202
  Pie, 223
Spinach and Ricotta Cannelloni, 176–7
Sponge Cake, 246
spoons, 12
Spring Onion and Vegetable Quiche, 218
spring onions, 40
Spring Rolls, 230
Spring Vegetable Soup, 66
squash, 40
squid, 31, 35, 36
  see also calamari
Steak and Kidney Pudding, 226–7
Steak Diane, 95
Steak Sandwich, 96
Stew, Irish, 112
stews, 16, 26
Sticky Date Pudding, 308–9
Stir-fried Vegetables, 190
stock, 360–1
  Beef, 360
  bouquet garni, 361
  Chicken, 360
  Fish, 361
  freezing, 361
  Vegetable, 361
storage, 8–9, 14, 24, 30–1
Strawberry Jam, 346
Stroganoff, Beef, 91
strudel
  Apple, 312–13
  Vegetable, 165
Stuffed Capsicums, 201
Stuffed Field Mushrooms, 168
Stuffed Pumpkins, 204–5
sugar snap peas, 40
Summer Berry Flan, 318–19
Summer Pudding, 323
Super Supreme, 228–9
swede, 40
Sweet and Sour Pork, 115
Sweet and Sour Sauce, 366
Sweet Chilli Chicken Wings, 135
sweet potato, 39, 40
Sweet Shortcrust Pastry, 357–8
Swiss Muesli, 56

Swiss Roll, Jam, 258

Tabbouleh, 210–11
Tagliatelle, Pesto with, 180
Tandoori Chicken, 128–9
tarragon, 42
Tartare Sauce, 154–5, 363
Teriyaki Chicken, 139
Terrine, Pork and Veal, 118–19
Thai Beef Salad, 104
Thai Fish Cakes, 142
Thai Green Chicken Curry, 134
Thai-style Dressing, 363
Thai Vegetable Curry, 163
Thousand Island Dressing, 362
Three-bean Salad, 212
Three-fruit Marmalade, 344
thyme, 42
Tiramisu, 321
Toast, French, 60
Toasted Grapefruit, 57
Toasted Marshmallows, 342–3
Toasted Muesli, 56
Toffee Apples, 340–1
Toffees, Small, 342
tofu
  Fried Noodles, 188–9
  Hot Salad, 168
Tom Kha Gai, 83
Tomato and Wine, Mussels with, 156
Tomato Pasta Sauce, 179
Tomato Salsa, 162
Tomato Sauce, 160, 172, 176, 350
Tomato Soup, Cream of, 74–5
tomatoes, 39, 40
tongs, 12
tortellini, fresh, 46
Traditional Corned Beef and Vegetables, 92–3
Trifle, English, 314
trout, 36
  Almonds with, 144
  Smoked Pâté, 143
tuna, 36
  Salad Niçoise, 213
  Salad sandwich filling, 214
Tuna Mornay, 148
Turkey with Cashew Stuffing, Roast, 126–7
turnip, 40

Vanilla biscuit icing, 295
Vanilla Custard, Easy, 368
Vanilla Fudge, 336
Vanilla Slice, 288
veal
  cuts of, 20–1
  Osso Buco with Gremolata, 120–1
  Parmigiana, 120
  Pasta and Meatballs, 177
  Peppercorn Sauce with, 122
  Pork and Veal Terrine, 118–19
  Scaloppini, 123
  Wiener Schnitzel, 119
Veal Parmigiana, 120
Veal Scaloppini, 123
Vegetable Couscous, Spicy, 171
Vegetable Curry, Thai, 163
Vegetable Frittata, 167
Vegetable Frittata, Grated, 167
Vegetable Fritters, 199
Vegetable Lasagne, 164–5
Vegetable Pie, Country, 221
Vegetable Pilaf, 183
Vegetable soup, 80
  Chicken and, 70–1
  Spring, 66
Vegetable Stock, 361
Vegetable Strudel, 165
vegetables
  Asian Greens, 190–1
  Char-grilled, 205
  preparation of, 38–9
  Roast, 200
  Stir-fried, 190
  storage of, 9
  types of, 40–1
  see also under vegetable eg asparagus
Veloute Sauce, 365
Vichyssoise, 78–9
vinaigrette
  Basic, 362–3
  Mustard, 212

Waldorf Salad, 207
whisks, 12
White Christmas, 339
White Dinner Rolls, 240
White Sauce, Classic, 364
whitebait, 36
Wholemeal Bread, 243
Wholemeal Muffins, 64
Wiener Schnitzel, 119
wild rice, 46
Won Ton Soup, 76

Yoghurt, Homemade, 58
Yorkshire Puddings, 88

Zabaglione, 369
zucchini, 39, 40

ACKNOWLEDGEMENTS

STYLISTS:

Mary Harris, Rosemary Mellish, Georgina Dolling, Carolyn Fienberg, Donna Hay, Vicki Liley, Kay Francis, Marie-Hélène Clauzon, Amanda Cooper, Lucy Mortensen, Jane Hann, Amanda Talbot.

PHOTOGRAPHERS:

Tony Lyon, Luis Martin, Chris Jones, Joe Filshie, Reg Morrison, Andrew Furlong, Andre Martin, Jon Bader, Andrew Elton, Andy Payne, Damien Wood, Phil Haley, Craig Cranko, Sue Stubbs.

HOME ECONOMISTS:

Tracey Port, Kerrie Ray,Christine Sheppard, Anna Beaumont, Michelle Lawton, Beth Mitchell, Justine Poole, Alison Turner, Jo Forrest, Myles Beaufort, Wendy Brodhurst, Jo Glynn, Alex Diblasi, Sharon Glover, Angela Nahas, Beverley Sutherland Smith, Anna Paola Boyd, Maria Sampsonis, Tatjana Lakajev, Wendy Goggin, Rachel Mackey, Rosemary Penman, Janelle Bloom, Toiva Longhurst, Margot Smithyman, Nadia Kretchmer, Ann Bollard, Jody Vassallo, Kathy Knudsen.

RECIPE DEVELOPMENT:

Tracy Rutherford, Kerrie Mullins, Jody Vassallo, Dimitra Stais, Roslyn Anderson, Anna Beaumont, Amanda Cooper, Michelle Earl, Lulu Grimes, Kathy Knudsen, Barbara Lowery, Jo Richardson, Melanie McDermott, Voula Mantzouridis, Rebecca Clancy, Alex Grant-Mitchell, Tracey Port, Wendy Berecry, Jacki Passmore, Stephanie Souvlis, Liz Nolan, Amanda Biffin, Sally Parker, Coral Kingston, Jean Miles, Denise Munro, Rachel Mackey, Kerrie Carr, Marie McDonald, Jennene Plummer, Kate Carey, Michelle Lawton.

IMPORTANT

Those who might be at risk from the effects of salmonella food poisoning (the elderly, pregnant women, young children and those suffering from immune deficiency diseases) should consult their GP with any concerns about eating raw eggs.

Published by Murdoch Books® a division of Murdoch Magazines Pty Ltd,
GPO Box 1203, Sydney NSW 1045

Managing Editor: Rachel Carter
Editors: Jane Price, Justine Upex
Designer: Michelle Cutler
Food Director: Jane Lawson
Food Editor: Dimitra Stais
Photographer (cover): Tony Lyon
Stylist (cover): Carolyn Fienberg
Stylist's Assistant (cover): Kerrie Mullins
Picture Librarian: Anne Ferrier

Chief Executive: Mark Smith
Publisher: Kay Scarlett

National Library of Australia
Cataloguing-in-Publication Data
Cooking: a commonsense guide.
Includes index. ISBN 1 74045 171 6

PRINTED IN SINGAPORE
Printed by Tien Wah Press, Singapore
First printed 1998. Reprinted 1999 (twice), 2000 (twice), 2001.
©Text, design, photography and illustrations Murdoch Books® 1998. All rights reserved. No part of this publication may be reproduced, stored in a retrieval system or transmitted in any form or by any means, electronic, mechanical, photocopying, recording or otherwise without the prior written permission of the publisher.
Murdoch Books® is a trademark of Murdoch Magazines Pty Ltd.